EMOTIONS, TECHNOLOGY, AND LEARNING

Emotions and Technology

Communication of Feelings for, with, and through Digital Media

Series Editor

Sharon Y. Tettegah

Emotions, Technology, and Learning

Volume Editors

Sharon Y. Tettegah and Michael P. McCreery

EMOTIONS, TECHNOLOGY, AND LEARNING

Edited by

SHARON Y. TETTEGAH
Professor, University of Nevada, Las Vegas
College of Education, Las Vegas, NV, USA

Beckman Institute for Advanced Science and Technology,
National Center for Supercomputing Applications,
affiliate, University of Illinois, Urbana, IL, USA

MICHAEL P. McCREERY
Department of Teaching and Learning,
University of Nevada,
Las Vegas, NV, USA

AMSTERDAM • BOSTON • HEIDELBERG • LONDON
NEW YORK • OXFORD • PARIS • SAN DIEGO
SAN FRANCISCO • SINGAPORE • SYDNEY • TOKYO
Academic Press is an imprint of Elsevier

Academic Press is an imprint of Elsevier
125 London Wall, London, EC2Y 5AS, UK
525 B Street, Suite 1800, San Diego, CA 92101-4495, USA
225 Wyman Street, Waltham, MA 02451, USA
The Boulevard, Langford Lane, Kidlington, Oxford OX5 1GB, UK

Notices

Knowledge and best practice in this field are constantly changing. As new research and experience broaden our understanding, changes in research methods, professional practices, or medical treatment may become necessary.

Practitioners and researchers must always rely on their own experience and knowledge in evaluating and using any information, methods, compounds, or experiments described herein. In using such information or methods they should be mindful of their own safety and the safety of others, including parties for whom they have a professional responsibility.

To the fullest extent of the law, neither the Publisher nor the authors, contributors, or editors, assume any liability for any injury and/or damage to persons or property as a matter of products liability, negligence or otherwise, or from any use or operation of any methods, products, instructions, or ideas contained in the material herein.

Library of Congress Cataloging-in-Publication Data
A catalog record for this book is available from the Library of Congress

British Library Cataloguing in Publication Data
A catalogue record for this book is available from the British Library

ISBN: 978-0-12-800649-8

For information on all Academic Press publications
visit our website at http://store.elsevier.com/

Publisher: Nikki Levy
Acquisition Editor: Emily Ekle
Editorial Project Manager: Timothy Bennett
Production Project Manager: Caroline Johnson
Designer: Matthew Limbert

Typeset by SPi Global, India

Printed and bound in the United States of America

Working together
to grow libraries in
developing countries

www.elsevier.com • www.bookaid.org

CONTENTS

Contributors   *xi*

Foreword   *xiii*

Preface   *xvii*

Section I   Emotions and Learning in Online Environments   **1**

1. Turning MOOCS Around: Increasing Undergraduate Academic Performance by Reducing Test-Anxiety in a Flipped Classroom Setting   **3**

Gwen C.M. Noteborn, Georgia Earnest García

Introduction   3
Evolving from Video-Based Education to MOOCs, then SPOCs   4
Academic Emotions and Student Performance   7
Research Question   9
Methods   9
Participants   12
Materials   13
Data Collection Procedures and Analyses   14
Results   15
Discussion   17
Limitations and Implications for Further Research   18
References   20

2. Emotional and Social Engagement in a Massive Open Online Course: An Examination of Dino 101   **25**

Lia M. Daniels, Catherine Adams, Adam McCaffrey

A Brief Primer on MOOCs   26
Engagement as a Social Psychological Construct   27
Engaging MOOCs   29
Engagement with the Instructor   30
Dino 101: Dinosaur Paleobiology   31
Data Sources   32
The Learning Climate Shared with Other Students   32
Conclusion   38
References   39

3. Affect in Online Discourse: The Case of the United Nations Millennial Development Goals Topics   **43**

Scott J. Warren, Jenny S. Wakefield

Framework   45
Method   49
Discussion   52
Conclusion   64
Acknowledgment   66
References   66

4. Loving this Dialogue!!!! ◉: Expressing Emotion Through the Strategic Manipulation of Limited Non-Verbal Cues in Online Learning Environments   **69**

Krystle Phirangee, Jim Hewitt

Introduction   69
Our Research   74
Results   74
Discussion   82
References   84

Section II   Technology, Emotions, and Classroom Use   **87**

5. Using Errors to Enhance Learning Feedback in Computer Programming   **89**

Man-Wai Chu, Jacqueline P. Leighton

LEAFF Model   90
Method   94
Materials   98
Results   100
Discussion and Conclusion   107
Acknowledgement   110
Appendix A   110
Appendix B   111
Appendix C   114
Appendix D   115
References   116

6. Emotions in Learning with Video Cases   **119**

Martin Gartmeier, Tina Hascher

Introduction   119
Emotions Conceptualized   121

Emotional Potential of Video Cases   123
Conclusions on Learning with Video Cases   128
Discussion and Outlook   131
References   132

7. Identifying and Tracking Emotional and Cognitive Mathematical Processes of Middle School Students in an Online Discussion Group   135

Amos Lee, Sharon Tettegah

Literature: Online Learning and Math Discussions   136
Methods   138
Results   144
Discussion   146
Appendix A   151
Appendix B   151
Appendix C   152
References   152

8. Online Learning, Multimedia, and Emotions   155

Matthew Swerdloff

Defining Emotions   155
Learning and Emotions   156
The Case for the Use of OLaM to Improve Academic Achievement   159
On Overview of the Cognitive Theory of Multimedia Learning   161
Emotional State and Adoption of New Computer Initiatives   163
The Effect of Computer-aided Instruction on Emotion in the School Setting 165
The New York Grade Three Study on Feelings, Attitude, and Achievement 166
Discussion   172
Some Implications for Education   172
Conclusion   173
References   174

9. New Media, Literacy, and Laughter: LOL in the English Classroom   177

Beth A. Buchholz, Julie Rust

Theoretical Framework   178
Reconsidering Reading & Writing in the English Classroom   180
Methods   181
Implications   194
References   196

10. "I'm White Trying to Play a Black Dude": The Construction
    of Race, Identities, and Emotions in Actual and Virtual Spaces   199

Mary Beth Hines, Michael L. Kersulov, Chuck Holloway, Rebecca Rupert

Introduction   199
Critical Sociocultural Perspectives   202
Twenty-First Century Literacies: Digital Media in Language and Learning   203
Intersections of Identity, Emotions, and Digital Media Performances   204
The Emotional as Political: "Socially Assigned Disposability" in School Systems   205
White Privilege and Blackface   206
Blackface Legacies in the Classroom Construction of Race   206
The Larger Study   207
The Context   208
Shelly's Commitments to Digital Media, the Students, and Social Justice   209
The Monster Unit and Shelly's Class   209
Blackface as Catalyst for Emotional Turmoil   210
Drawing a Line or Crossing a Line? Another Teacher's Perspective   212
Shelly's Social Construction of Emotion in Response to the Blackface Group   214
Conflicting Emotions: Perspectives from a Former Administrator   214
Shelly: Building a "Safe and Inclusive Community" Onsite and Online   216
Students' Perspectives on the Blackface Production   217
The Political and Social Construction of Emotions Mediated by Technology   217
Conclusion   218
References   220

Section III   Exploring Affect With and Through Technology:
    Research and Practice   223

11. Leveraging the Social Presence Model: A Decade of Research
    on Emotion in Online and Blended Learning   225

Aimee L. Whiteside, Amy Garrett Dikkers

Introduction: The Power of Emotions for Learning   225
Social Presence and the SPM   226
Lessons Learned: A Decade of SPM Research   227
Reflections and Moving Forward   238
References   239

12. Technology and Human Cultural Accumulation: The Role
    of Emotion   243

Geoff Woolcott

Introduction—Emotion, Technology, and Education   243

Accumulating Culture   244
Linking Emotion with Learning   246
Taking a Broad View of Technology   249
Surviving Involves Problem Solving   252
Embracing Technology Within a Systems View   254
Conclusion—What this Means for Education   258
References   260

13. Empathy, Emotion, Technology, and Learning   265

Bridget Cooper

Introduction   265
Learning and Technology   267
How Learning Happens and its Relationship to Empathy   269
Understanding the Role and Nature of Empathy in Teaching and Learning   274
Characteristics of Fundamental Empathy   274
Can Technology Support Fundamental Empathy?   275
Profound Empathy   276
Benefits of Profound Empathy   283
Problems with Technology and Emotion   284
Guidelines for the Use and Design of Learning Technology   285
Generic Features Required for Learning with Technology   285
Potential Generic Features to Avoid   286
Creating Future Societies Through High Levels of Learning and Education   286
References   287

Index   289

CONTRIBUTORS

Catherine Adams
University of Alberta, Edmonton, AB, Canada

Beth A. Buchholz
Appalachian State University, Boone, NC, USA

Man-Wai Chu
University of Alberta, Edmonton, AB, Canada

Bridget Cooper
University of Sunderland, Sunderland, UK

Lia M. Daniels
University of Alberta, Edmonton, AB, Canada

Amy Garrett Dikkers
Department of Educational Leadership, University of North Carolina Wilmington, Wilmington, NC, USA

Georgia Earnest García
University of Illinois at Urbana-Champaign, Champaign, IL, USA

Martin Gartmeier
TUM School of Education, München, Germany

Tina Hascher
University of Bern, Bern, Switzerland

Jim Hewitt
Department of Curriculum, Teaching and Learning, Ontario Institute for Studies in Education, University of Toronto, Toronto, ON, Canada

Mary Beth Hines
Indiana University, Bloomington, IN, USA

Chuck Holloway
Indiana University, Bloomington, IN, USA

Michael L. Kersulov
Indiana University, Bloomington, IN, USA

Amos Lee
University of Illinois at Urbana-Champaign, Urbana, IL, USA

Jacqueline P. Leighton
University of Alberta, Edmonton, AB, Canada

Adam McCaffrey
University of Alberta, Edmonton, AB, Canada

Gwen C.M. Noteborn
Maastricht University, Maastricht, The Netherlands

Krystle Phirangee
Department of Curriculum, Teaching and Learning, Ontario Institute for Studies in Education, University of Toronto, Toronto, ON, Canada

Rebecca Rupert
Indiana University, Bloomington, IN, USA

Julie Rust
Millsaps College, Jackson, MS, USA

Mathew Swerdloff
Hendrik Hudson School District, Montrose, NY, USA

Sharon Tettegah
University of Illinois at Urbana-Champaign, Urbana, IL, USA

Jenny S. Wakefield
University of North Texas, Denton, TX, USA

Scott J. Warren
University of North Texas, Denton, TX, USA

Aimee L. Whiteside
Department of English and Writing, University of Tampa, Tampa, FL, USA

Geoff Woolcott
Southern Cross University, Lismore, NSW, Australia

FOREWORD

With respect to technology, it is important to place terms and tools within a historical context, given that in today's society, when speaking to a person who is a Millennial (individuals who are born in the early 1980s to 2000), s(he) may tell you that technology is the Internet and Smart Phones. For the Millennial, then, technology may only mean digital or biotechnologies. If we were to speak broadly to some individuals from The Silent Generation, Boomers, Millennials, and Generation Y, technology may also mean automobiles, airlines, overhead projectors, flashlights, microwaves, ATMs, etc. Hence, technology in the twenty-first century can mean many things. For example, technology could mean software applications, hardware, social media platforms, functional magnetic resonance imaging, mobile technology, learning and content management systems, just to name a few.

Humans and other animals have used tools for centuries; however, the most important aspect of any tool is how we use and interact with it and the emotional responses we experience, while we interact with it either physically or psychologically. The focus of this book series is to provide a variety of conceptual, theoretical, and practical perspectives on the role of emotions and technology. Various psychological and social-emotional aspects of communicating through and with many types of technology are engaged in ways that extend our understanding of technology and its consequences on our lives.

A specific goal and purpose of this book series focuses on emotions and affective interactions with and through technology. In some cases, these interactions are user-to-user, supported by the technology. In other instances, these interactions are between the user and the technology itself. Let us take, for example, researchers who have used animated social simulation technology to measure emotions of educators (Tettegah, 2007) and others, who use biotechnology to measure decision-making and emotional responses of users of technology (Baron-Cohen, 2011; Decety & Ickes, 2009). In a recent article, Solomon (2008) points out, "One of the most critical questions about human nature is the extent to which we can transcend our own biology (p. 13)." I would argue that through our use of technology we, in fact, are attempting to extend and transcend our emotions by way of robots and other intelligent technological agents. As such, we should then ask ourselves: why are discussions of emotions and technology so important?

Inquiry regarding the nature of emotions is not new. In fact, examples of such forms of inquiry have been documented since the dialogues of Socrates and Plato. Researchers and practitioners in psychology, sociology, education, and philosophy understand the complicated nature of emotions, as well as [the importance of] defining emotions and social interactions. The study of emotions is so complicated that we still continue to debate within the fields of philosophy, education, and the psychology, the nature of emotions and the roles of affective and cognitive processes involving human learning and behavior. The volumes in this series, therefore, seek to present important discussions, debates, and perspectives involving the interactions of emotions and various technologies. Specifically, through this book series on Emotions and Technology, we present chapters on emotional interactions with, from, and through technology.

The diversity of emotions, played out by humans with and through technology, run the gamut of emotions, including joy, anger, love, lust, empathy, compassion, jealousy, motivation, frustration, and hatred. These emotional interactions can occur through interactions with very human-looking technologies (e.g., avatars, robots) or through everyday commonplace technologies (e.g. getting angry at an ATM machine when the user fails to follow directions). Hence, understanding the ways in which technology affords the mediation of emotions is extremely important toward enhancing our critical understanding of the ways in which student minds, through technology, are profoundly involved in learning, teaching, communicating, and developing social relationships in the twenty-first century.

The majority of the chapters presented in the books included in the series will no doubt draw on some of the recent, pervasive, and ubiquitous technologies. Readers can expect to encounter chapters that present discussions involving emotions and mobile phones, iPads, digital games, simulations, MOOCs, social media, virtual reality therapies, and Web 2.0/3.0 technologies. However, the primary focus of this book series engages the readers in psychological, information communication, human computer interaction, and educational theories and concepts. In other words, technologies will showcase the interactions, however, the concepts discussed promise to be relevant and consistent constructs, whether engaging current technologies or contemplating future tools.

The whole book series began with a call for a single volume. However, there was such a huge response that one volume turned into eight volumes. It was very exciting to see such an interest in literature that lies at the intersection of emotions and technology. What is very clear here is that human beings are becoming more and more attached to digital technologies, in one form or another. In many ways, we could possibly posit the statement that many individuals in the world are inching their way toward becoming cyborgs. It is apparent that digital technologies are in fact more and more second nature to our everyday life. Actually, digital technologies are changing faster than we are aging.

The life of a new technology can be 6 months to 1 year, while the human lifespan ranges from 0 to 80+ years. With the aforementioned in mind, humans have to consider how their emotions will interact and interface with the many different technologies they will encounter over the course of such a lifetime. It seems as if it were only yesterday when the personal computer was invented and now we have supercomputing on a desktop, billions of data at our fingertips on our smartphone computers, and nanotechnology assisting us with physiological functions of living human animals. Regardless of the technology we use and encounter, emotions will play a major role in personal and social activities.

The major role that technology plays can be observed through the many observations of how humans become excited, frustrated, or relieved, when interacting with new technologies that assist us within our daily activities.

Our hope is that scholars and practitioners from diverse disciplines, such as: Informatics, Psychology, Education, Computer Science, Sociology, Engineering and other Social Science and Science, Technology, Media Studies and Humanities fields of study will find this series significant and informative to their conceptual, research, and educational practices. Each volume provides unique contributions about how we interact emotionally with, through, and from various digital technologies. Chapters in this series range from how intelligent agents evoke emotions, how humans interact emotionally with virtual weapons, how we learn or do not learn with technology, how organizations are using technology to understand health-related events, to how social media helps to display or shape our emotions and desires.

This series on Emotions and Technology includes the following volumes: (1) Emotions, Technology and Games, (2) Emotions, Technology, Design and Learning, (3) Emotions, Technology and Behaviors, (4) Emotions, Technology and Learning, (5) Emotions, Technology and Health, (6) Emotions, Technology and Design, (7) Emotions, Technology and Social Media, and (8) Emotions and Mobile Technology.

Sharon Tettegah
University of Nevada, Las Vegas, USA

ACKNOWLEDGMENTS

I would like to give a special thank you to Martin Gartmeier, Dorothy Espelage, Richard Ferdig, WenHao David Huang, Grant Kien, Angela Benson, Michael McCreery, Safiya Umoja Noble, Y. Evie Garcia, and Antonia Darder, and all of the authors for their reviews and contributions to this work.

REFERENCES

Baron-Cohen, S. (2011). *The science of evil*. New York: Basic Books.

Decety, J., & Ickes, W. (2009). The social neuroscience of empathy. Cambridge: The MIT Press.

Solomon, R. C. (2008). The philosophy of emotions. In M. Lewis, J. M. Haviland-Jones, & L. F. Barrett (Eds.), *The handbook of emotions* (3rd ed., pp. 3–16). London: Guildford Press.

Tettegah, S. (2007). Pre-service teachers, victim empathy, and problem solving using animated narrative vignettes. *Technology, Instruction, Cognition and Learning, 5*, 41–68.

PREFACE

Emotions and learning are increasingly becoming an important topic in the area of technology across multiple fields. Issues including emotional engagement, emotionally safe learning environments, emotional skills development, and connectedness through emotion suggest that learning and technology are intertwined with emotions at every level. *Emotions, learning, and technology* is particularly relevant for today's learner, just as Pekrun (2006) has argued that emotions have a mediating role in the learning process.

Looking back a decade ago, very few book chapters presented discussions on the intersection of emotions, technology, and learning. The index of The International Handbook of Virtual Learning Environments (Weiss, Nolan, Hunsinger, & Trifonas, 2006) includes a few references to emotions or affect. For example, the subject index included words such as anxiety and frustration. Several articles in the handbook volume mention behaviors associated with emotions such as stimulating and enjoyment (Schofield, 2006) or present a discussion on virtual schools and how the reduction of empathy (Russell, 2006) may occur when teaching and learning in online environments.

The study of emotions through a larger lens continues to grow in importance because of the increase in online learning. Large concentrations of students and universities are participating in distance education, eLearning, online learning, and mobile learning. Due to increases in students who engage in learning in electronic environments, instructors are becoming more concerned with student's emotional dispositions. In the past instructors could gauge, although sometimes in limited ways, student's emotional states, but with the decreased frequency of face-to-face contact, it is difficult to know what and how students are feeling emotionally as they interact and learn in technology-mediated environments. Surprisingly, learning research clearly indicates that social and emotional support plays an important role in the retention of information and the acquisition of knowledge (Bransford, Brown, & Cocking, 2000). For this reason, it is very important to understand the role emotions have in the learning process in both face-to-face and virtual learning environments.

When researching the area of emotions and learning in online environments, we find diversity among approaches. Much of the work involving emotions and online learning compare face-to-face and online learning, with a focus on self-regulation and achievement motivation related emotions, such as boredom, frustration, and enjoyment (Artino & Jones, 2012; Butz, Stupnisky, & Pekrun, 2015; Daniels & Stupnisky, 2012; Marchand & Gutierrez, 2012). As demonstrated in prior research, Pekrun and Stephens (2010) state that "emotions are ubiquitous in achievement settings" (p. 38).

A big question remains, how does one have collaboration and social interaction without emotions? The failure to address both positive and negative emotions as core to learning is a serious deficit for the study of learning. Based on prior literature, the discussions presented would lead us to believe that behaviors such as motivation, and anxiety and frustration are the only, or at least primary, emotions attached to learning (Wang, 2014).

Authors in this volume will provide the readers with insights and discussions about the intersection of emotions, technology, and learning. The readers will experience chapters that are empirical, conceptual, and theoretical from multiple disciplines.

EMOTIONS AND LEARNING IN ONLINE ENVIRONMENTS

We should keep in mind that there are a variety of online environments, and depending on the learning, an individual may have a different emotional experience while learning through a MOOC compared to a LMS. This part of the volume addresses various emotions (e.g., social, achievement) related to teaching and learning within and among different environments from Massively Open Online Courses (MOOCs), Learning Management Systems (LMS), and blended/hybrid environments.

This section begins with Noteborn and Garcia's exploration of the idea that small private online classes (SPOCs) could leverage MOOC technology in order to reduce test anxiety within a blended learning (i.e., face-to-face education within online support) scenario. Through harnessing video vignettes, an instructor could provide additional user-controlled learning opportunities to aid students in preparing for a high stakes exam. Results indicated that the use of video vignettes increased overall course passage rates for the course, and the vignettes were an effective tool for decreasing test anxiety.

Daniels and her colleagues go on to examine how social and emotional engagement emerges in an xMOOC; Dino 101. Findings from the study suggest that while MOOCs can be an emotionally pleasant environment that is enjoyable and even inspires students, it appears that design factors, student expectations, and class size may hinder the social experience. Those students, who are looking to experience a bi-directional or constructivist learning experience, may find current iterations of MOOCs less than satisfactory. This last point is particularly relevant for those interested in increasing completion rates.

Driven by a desire to liberate students from the normalization of learning and to engage in deep real-world topics, Warren and Wakefield set out to conduct a study fostered by a course designed to teach technology content, but they also designed a framework that used personal narrative to elicit emotional responses. Within this framework, learners were able to explore how power and perceived reality influenced themselves and American society at-large. Further, the awareness of the complexity of societal problems (i.e., HIV/AIDS) helped to catalyze deeper critical thinking and an intensity of emotions that may not be typically experienced when exposed to traditional media framing of the topic.

Finally, Phirangee and Hewitt's chapter, "Loving this dialogue!!!: Expressing emotion through the strategic manipulation of limited nonverbal cues in online learning environments," maintain that learning is grounded in sociocultural experiences and the process of learning involves cognition and emotion. In their study, findings indicate that learners introduce non-verbal cues, such as emoticons, as forms of compensatory emotions. Student's online notes and semi-structured interviews were analyzed to determine how and why students use non-verbal cues. Overall students, in their study, expressed emotions by using emoticons, punctuation, and affective (like) buttons. With the current research on affective computing, perhaps students will be able to overcome the limits of emoticons, punctuation, and affective buttons to express their emotions when they are not in face-to-face environments.

TECHNOLOGY, EMOTIONS, AND CLASSROOM USE

One of the next best mediums to express emotions is probably through tools that allow verbal and visual cues, and access to human interactions, such as telephones (landline and mobile), voice over Internet protocol (VoIP), and video. Human expressions involving video may come in all forms from video blogging, Face Time, Skype, and also video recordings where individuals can view and then respond to others that are displayed through the video, synchronously and asynchronously.

The first chapter in this section by Chu and Leighton build upon the universally recognized idea that creating emotionally safe learning environments allow students to experiment, make errors, and receive meaningful feedback without fear. Specifically, the authors investigated these constructs within a computer programming instructional intervention that was based on the Learning Errors and Formative Feedback (LEAFF) model. Results illustrated the importance of teaching and learning within a framework and environment that is built on trust. Specifically, students maintained positive feelings of well-being, sought out help from peers, and viewed errors as a core component of learning.

Gartmeier and Hasher analyze the role of emotions and learning through video cases. They argue that it is important to understand sense making and the role of emotions in the study of authentic experiences involving video cases. In addition, they present a discussion on the importance of videos, and reflection, and the induction of perspective taking and empathy. They conclude that the use of videos assist learners in their development of professional competencies and emotional regulation.

Lee and Tettegah examined how online math discussions occur and provide useful tools for enhancing these discussions. More specifically, through identification analysis, within a framework of systemic functional linguistics, the authors were able to track participant discussions of math terms and the overall process of problem solving through Edmodo, which is an online communication tool many teachers use for teaching and learning. This is of particular importance as an increasing number of K12 students are enrolling in online classes. As the study demonstrates, there is still a need for additional scaffolds to help students account for multithreaded discussions and a dictionary of relevant terms that can both help to facilitate discussion and reduce anxiety.

Using Mayer's multimedia theoretical framework, Swerdloff contends that it is important to observe attitudinal and emotional changes that students undergo while engaged in Online and multimedia (OLaM) learning. A discussion of neuroscience, psychological, and educational definitions is presented. Quantitative and qualitative methods are used in this study to examine student's emotional states and responses while engaging in OLaM learning.

"Not so serious business" chapter by Buccholz and Rust provides the reader with a bit of insight from the title. They maintain that technology-mediated humor is just as important, as other emotional constructs, in learning English, in particular. In their study, ethnographic methods reveal three-main functions of humor and what 'being funny' means: affiliation building, critiquing, and unsettling. They provide settling and unsettling aspects of inserting humor as a part of teaching and learning activities.

In closing this section, Hines and colleagues draw upon a 4-year critical qualitative study at an alternative high school. The goal of the study was to examine, in a virtual environment, how students create multimodal texts that include visual, audio, graphics, and/or print to construct meaning out of a young-adult novel that was introduced to them by their teacher. However, in response to the assignment, one student group dawned black-face to portray the main character. The student's actions resulted in the examination of an educator's struggle with race in the classroom, particularly in lieu of the fact that not all persons in the classroom are politically aware or sensitive to matters of race and injustice.

EXPLORING AFFECT WITH AND THROUGH TECHNOLOGY: RESEARCH AND PRACTICE

Finally, we acknowledge that many articles have been written about emotions, and more recently emotions and technology (Butz et al., 2015; Tettegah, 2005). However, the lack of literature for the purposes of integrating theory, research, and practice in the area of emotions, learning, and the use of technology is the driving force in this section.

Whiteside and Dikkers deliver a chapter using the Social Presence Model (SPM) and case study method to explore emotional experiences, and connectedness among students and teachers. Their case study includes 4 years of data involving superintendents, principals, technology coordinators, media specialists, teachers, and other K-12 school leaders. Results from their study conclude that emotional support is important for students who transition to higher education from high school, and that "case studies demonstrate that SPM is significance for teachers, as they reflect on and adjust their instructional practices to create connections with and among their students." (This volume).

Woolcott offers a reconceptualization of learning, emotions, and technology within a biologically based framework of information processing. More specifically, he argues that within industrialized societies, most children and adolescents spend a substantial amount of time engaged in institutionalized education where individuals learn complex educational, emotional, and cultural information that might otherwise not be learned. However, he posits that the accumulation of technology has resulted in a cultural component that results in a broad view of technology as knowledge, skills, and experiences rather than media or tools.

In the final chapter, Cooper describes how empathy and positive emotions may or may not support various technologies. In her discussion, she carefully carves out the benefits, deficits, and human impact of using technologies for teaching and learning. She follows with a description of the characteristics of fundamental empathy and whether various technologies can support the development of empathy and human interaction. A conclusion with guidelines and recommendations on the use and design of technology is provided.

Sharon Tettegah, Michael McCreery
Department of Teaching and Learning,
University of Nevada, Las Vegas, NV, USA

REFERENCES

Artino, A. R., & Jones, K. D. (2012). Exploring complex relations between achievement emotions and self-regulated learning behaviors in online learning. *Internet and Higher Education, 15,* 170–175.

Bransford, J. D., Brown, A. L., & Cocking, R. R. (Eds.). (2000). *How people learn: Brain, mind, experience, and school.* Washington, DC: National Academies Press.

Butz, N. T., Stupnisky, R. L., & Pekrun, R. (2015). Students' emotion for achievement and technology use in synchronous hybrid graduate programmes: A control-value approach. *Research in Learning Technology, 23,* 1–16.

Daniels, L. M., & Stupnisky, R. L. (2012). Not that different in theory: Discussing the control-value theory of emotions in online learning environments. *Internet and Higher Education, 15,* 222–226.

Marchand, G. C., & Gutierrez, A. P. (2012). The role of emotion in the learning process: Comparisons between online and face-toface learning settings. *Internet and Higher Education, 15,* 150–160.

Pekrun, R. (2006). The control-value theory of achievement emotions: Assumptions, corollaries, and implications of educational research and practice. *Educational Psychology Review, 18*(4), 315–341. http://dx.doi.org/10.1007/s10648-006-9029-9.

Pekrun, R., & Stephens, E. J. (2010). Achievement Emotions: A Control-Value Approach. *Social and Personality Psychology Compass, 4,* 238–255.

Russell, G. (2006). Virtual schools: Reflections on key issues. In J. Weiss, J. Nolan, J. Hunsinger, & P. Trifonas (Eds.), *The International handbook of virtual learning environments* (pp. 329–364). The Netherlands: Springer.

Schofield, J. (2006). Realizing the Internet's educational potential. In J. Weiss, J. Nolan, J. Hunsinger, & P. Trifonas (Eds.), *The International handbook of virtual learning environments* (pp. 301–327). The Netherlands: Springer.

Tettegah, S. (2005). Technology, narratives, vignettes, and the Intercultural & Cross Cultural Teaching Portal. *Urban Education, 40*(4), 268–293.

Wang, M.-J. (2014). The current practice of integration of information communication technology to English training and the emotions involved in blended learning. *Turkish Journal of Educational Technology, 13*(3), 188–201.

Weiss, J., Nolan, J., Hunsinger, J., & Trifonas, J. (2006). *The international handbook of virtual learning environments* (vols. I & II). The Netherlands: Springer.

Emotions and Learning in Online Environments

CHAPTER 1

Turning MOOCS Around: Increasing Undergraduate Academic Performance by Reducing Test-Anxiety in a Flipped Classroom Setting

Gwen C.M. Noteborn[a], Georgia Earnest García[b]
[a]Maastricht University, Maastricht, The Netherlands
[b]University of Illinois at Urbana-Champaign, Champaign, IL, USA

INTRODUCTION

The demand for reduction in time-to-competency in today's knowledge-based economy (IBM, 2010) along with escalating tuition fees and a tight labor market have put pressure on universities to graduate better prepared students in a timely and effectively manner. Economic constraints, inflicted by budget-cuts, have meant that universities are seeking instructional approaches that focus on economies of scale, whereas a tight labor market has thwarted application procedures, placing higher demands on skill- and competency-based education. These changes raise basic questions about how to create, preserve, and share knowledge.

In response to the above situation, institutions of higher education have embraced the implementation of online technologies, such as massive open online courses (MOOCs), to offer more efficient and effective education. With the introduction of MOOC technologies, universities can acquire economies of scale by educating large numbers of students in a cost-efficient manner. In essence, MOOC developments are like the fast food industry in the fifties (Richardson, 2012) because they provide a way to supersize education (De Angelis, 2013). However, the need to teach more students with fewer resources is a complex situation. Educational administrators often are unwilling to pay for the instructional staff and resources needed to support the increased number of students in MOOCs.

Emotions, Technology, and Learning
http://dx.doi.org/10.1016/B978-0-12-800649-8.00003-1
3

Evaluations of MOOCs show that they currently fail to effectively teach, assess, and accredit massive numbers of students because many students do not complete the courses (Adams, Yin, Vargas Madriz, & Mullen, 2014; Andersen & Ponti, 2014; Baggaley, 2014; Knox, 2014; Yang, Sinha, Adamson, & Rose, 2013). For example, Jordan (2013) reported that less than 10% of the students who enrolled in MOOCs completed the courses, with Cousera reporting completion rates closer to 5% (Koller, Ng, Do, & Chen, 2013).

A significant difference between online learning environments and the traditional learning environment is the reduced role of the teacher in the online environment (Kirschner, Strijbos, Kreijns, & Beers, 2004). Although educational researchers have shown the importance of teacher and peer engagement in mediating students' affective reactions to instruction (Koehler & Mishra, 2009; Kop & Hill, 2008), such emphases generally are not supported in online courses. For example, Govindasamy (2001) found that lack of learner engagement in online courses resulted in declining participation or poor performance. Despite the growing recognition that emotions are central to how students perform within and experience the learning environment (Goetz, Pekrun, Hall, & Haag, 2006), the role of emotions in the context of online educational videos remains an under researched area (Goetz et al., 2006).

The purpose of this chapter is to explore how implementation of MOOC technologies through a small private online class (SPOC) in a high-stakes, required, on-campus finance course helped to address student emotions and increase academic performance. In particular, we investigated the role of test-anxiety in MOOC-based education in relation to students' performances on the final exam, which constituted the students' course grades. Our findings have implications for other educators who want to effectively address student emotions when incorporating MOOC technologies in large on-campus courses.

EVOLVING FROM VIDEO-BASED EDUCATION TO MOOCs, THEN SPOCs

Video-based learning has rapidly improved due to technical improvements such as resolution, bandwidth (Maniar, Bennett, Hand, & Allan, 2008), and online video streaming. As a result, video-based learning has advanced from passive linear broadcasting to engaging computer-human interaction for learners (Hasler, Kersten, & Sweller, 2007; Merkt, Weigand, Heier, &

Schwan, 2011; Shephard, 2003). In fact, video now is one of the most frequently used media in classroom settings (Merkt et al., 2011); a trend that is unlikely to change in the coming years.

One reason why videos have become so popular is that they provide the opportunity for vicarious or observational learning in which students can observe and model others (Bandura, 1977). Vicarious learning stimulates the acquirement of new responses by learners; in particular, when a social (often human) model explains an ideal didactical execution of a task (Gog & Rummel, 2010). In the context of educational video, the task could be a complex calculation, where the human model is the teacher starring in the video and the acquirement of new responses is the ability of learners to perform the calculations individually over time. Learners encode what they observe and store it in memory for later use. Researchers have found that observational learning, especially for novices, can be highly effective in increasing student performance (Groenendijk, Janssen, Rijlaarsdam, & van den Bergh, 2013). The use of interactive video offers students the possibility of adjusting their learning according to their own preferences in terms of time, pace, and place, resulting in a more learner-centered approach (Baecker, Moore, & Boudreau, 2003; Traphagan, Kucsera, & Kishi, 2009). Online video empowers today's learners to become more self-directed and self-determined in their learning by creating and constructing new knowledge and making choices about their learning paths (McLoughlin & Lee, 2007). Researchers report that students prefer courses that include online lectures compared to traditional courses with offline lectures (Traphagan et al., 2009; Woo et al., 2008). As a result, an increasing number of higher education institutions are moving their content online by offering virtual lectures to support student learning (Gorissen, Van Bruggen, & Jochems, 2012).

MOOCs are one of the most debated applications of video-based education. MOOCs typically are open to any learner with access to the necessary technology. They are considered cost effective due to limited instructor involvement and unlimited potential student enrollment. The term MOOC was first coined to refer to a course developed by Downes and Siemens in 2008, entitled "Connectivism and Connectivity Knowledge." Exploiting the possibility for interaction among a wide variety of participants, they used an online tool to provide a rich learning environment for 25 on-campus students and 2300 off-campus students from around the globe who enrolled in the course. In May 2013, Udacity (a MOOC platform), AT&T, and the Georgia Institute of Technology announced the first entirely MOOC-based Master's degree, with tuition fees reduced by 80% compared to the typical off-campus fees (Onink, 2013). However, the MOOC honeymoon appears to be winding down (Fox, 2014), with prominent universities such as Harvard, the University of California at Berkeley (UC Berkeley), and the University of Massachusetts (Rivard, 2013) withdrawing or reconsidering their investments in MOOCs saying: We are already "post-MOOC." The lack of effectiveness of MOOCs should not be all that surprising, given that educational researchers have shown that substituting face-to-face learning with online technologies can lead to lack of interaction between teacher and students and among students (Laurillard, 2002), lower student motivation (Merisotis & Phipps, 1999), promote procrastination in asynchronous learning (Lim, 2002), and student feelings of isolation, danger, and arbitrariness (Hara & Kling, 1999).

Combining MOOCs with face-to-face education appears to reduce some of the adverse emotional effects that result from exclusive technology-based learning due to a lack of personal interaction (Hara & Kling, 1999; Laurillard, 2002; Petrides, 2002). For example, researchers have reported that complementing traditional education with online materials, compared to online education by itself, can have a positive effect on student performance (Boyle, Bradley, Chalk, Jones, & Pickard, 2003; Lim & Morris, 2009; O'Toole & Absalom, 2003), student flexibility and autonomy (Lebow, 1993; Radford, 1997; Tam, 2000), and student control over their learning (Osguthorpe & Graham, 2003). As a result, several universities are experimenting with hybrid or blended learning that includes aspects of MOOC technology with face-to-face interactions.

One of these experiments is the use of SPOCs, first defined by UC Berkeley professor Armando Fox (Fox, 2013). SPOCS are based on MOOC technology but capitalize on the flipped-classroom concept by incorporating online interactive videos into the traditional curricula. Students can follow the SPOC at their own pace, but still take advantage of the teacher-student interactions and peer collaborations that occur in the traditional format. In addition, SPOCS theoretically can be designed to reduce cognitive load and optimize students' working memory. For example, SPOCs that utilize multimedia can include picture in picture educational video that simultaneously presents video, audio, and text, in which a talking head (such as a lecturer) is synchronous with the audio and a screen that includes PowerPoint slides or other sources. According to Chen and Wang (2011), the use of picture in picture video decreases cognitive load. Mayer and Chandler

(2001) assert that the use of multimedia helps students to produce new knowledge because it facilitates their integration of existing knowledge with the presented knowledge. Inclusion of SPOCS, which present short lecture-lets and the possibility for self-testing, allows novices to slice learning materials into digestible pieces. The chunking of material for novices, who have limited background knowledge about the topic, reduces their cognitive load by keeping the new material within the constraints of their working memory, or about seven (plus or minus two) chunks of information (Miller, 1994).

Early results of blended learning with SPOCs are promising. For example, at San Jose State passing rates and student grades for students enrolled in blended learning with SPOCs significantly increased compared to passing rates and student grades for students in the traditional curricula or in the Udacity course, which was taught entirely online. Now, UC Berkeley, Harvard, and MIT are experimenting with SPOCs (Rivard, 2013). Initial results from pilot studies at UC Berkeley indicate that the SPOC model has increased enrollment fourfold while yielding higher instructor and course ratings. Some describe SPOCs as an almost inevitable evolution of the MOOC, replacing the massive with the community (Shukie, 2013), while others speculate that SPOCS will become the twenty-first century textbook.

ACADEMIC EMOTIONS AND STUDENT PERFORMANCE

Emotions are omnipresent in an academic setting, affecting how students engage and perform (Pekrun & Linnenbrink-garcia, 2012). Emotions are subjective experiences during which the context plays a role (Linnenbrink, 2006), creating a context-dependency (Goetz, Cronjaeger, Frenzel, Lüdtke, & Hall, 2010). The range of emotions reported for university students include anger, anxiety, boredom, enjoyment, frustration, hope, interest, and pride (Pekrun, Goetz, Titz, & Perry, 2002). Researchers have shown that positive emotions, such as enjoyment, facilitate the recovery of positive material (Isen, 1990), whereas negative emotions, such as anxiety, reduce performance (Beier & Kanfer, 2010).

Whereas emotions in general are cross-situational, academic emotions refer to those emotions that students feel while participating in academic activities. They are the feelings that students experience while sitting in class, listening to lectures, interacting with instructors and peers, doing homework, collaborating online, completing assignments, or taking a test, etc.

The positive or negative emotions students experience while engaged in academic tasks influence their goals and, thereby, their learning processes (Bruinsma, 2004; Kay, 2008). Positive-activating emotions, such as enjoyment, are positively related to the use of deep-level cognitive learning strategies, whereas negative-activating emotions, such as anxiety, function as motivational barriers, interfering with students' ability to learn in academic settings (Beier & Kanfer, 2010; Isen, 1990). Achievement emotions are academic emotions directly tied to the achievement activity itself or to the outcome associated with the activity, such as taking an examination or the actual examination grade (Pekrun, 2006). According to Pekrun, Goetz, Frenzel, Barchfeld, and Perry (2011), achievement emotions are induced by the amount of control that students perceive having over activities to which they assign task value.

An important emotion in relation to learning is test anxiety. Although there are multiple conceptualizations of test anxiety, most recent conceptualizations of this construct focus on fear of failure (Meijer, 2001). Several researchers have reported that test anxiety can negatively influence academic performance or outcomes (Valiente, Swanson, & Eisenberg, 2012). Others have shown that students' academic self-concept, or views of their competence, affected their test anxiety, with lower views of their competence leading to higher test anxiety (Goetz, Preckel, Zeidner, & Schleyer, 2008; Schwarzer, Mueller, & Greenglass, 1999; Zeidner & Schleyer, 1999). In addition, intrusive thoughts, which can hamper academic performance, were reported in low perceived competence situations (Elliott & Dweck, 1988). Researchers also found that interventions to improve students' perception of competence were effective in increasing their performance (Marsh & Craven, 2006; Marsh & Yeung, 1997; O'Mara, Marsh, Craven, & Debus, 2006).

Although researchers have shown the importance of academic emotions in student learning (Pekrun, 2006; Pekrun et al., 2011), few have investigated academic emotions in online learning environments. One of the few is a study by Artino (2009), in which the impact of academic emotions on academic success was investigated with 481 undergraduates at the US Naval Academy who were enrolled in a compulsory, self-paced, online course in aviation psychology. However, the results did not show a significant relationship between academic emotions and academic success. Artino gave two possible reasons for these findings: the low control that students had over the learning activities in the course and the technical frustration that many of them felt during the course.

RESEARCH QUESTION

Learning environments that have the potential to facilitate high student control over student learning, such as SPOCs, provide us with the unique opportunity to investigate the relationship between achievement emotions and learning. We predict that SPOC usage in a required finance course will increase undergraduates' perceptions of competence and reduce their test anxiety by lowering the negative effects of an evaluation situation (Van Yperen, 2007). Therefore, we formulate the following research question: To what extent does test anxiety predict academic performance in a high stakes hybrid course that includes a SPOC?

METHODS

University and Course Setting

The course Finance 1.5 was taught within the regular setting of a mid-sized European University. The university's pedagogical approach is student-centered, based on the concept of problem-based learning (PBL), in which students learn through the experience of problem solving (Sevilla, 2012). Within PBL, learning is considered an interactive and social process, where knowledge is created by means of collective problem solving. Students deal with ill-defined problems (referred to as "wicked") that consist of phenomena that require explanation and group discussion. The application of theory revolves around cases consisting of real-life wicked problems. Problems are discussed within small group meetings, consisting of about 10-15 students, facilitated by a tutor, who should be an expert in the field. The role of the tutor is limited and focuses on guiding the discussion and process of collective problem solving rather than transmitting knowledge to the students. Prior to the tutorial meetings, students are required to clarify problems and gain insights through individual self-study and papers, which they share with their peers in small group-discussions. In PBL, lectures play a minor role in the curriculum.

Finance 1.5 is a required 8-week course that all undergraduates in business and economics must pass to proceed to their second year of studies. Students who fail the course may take it and/or the final examination a second time. If they do not pass the second time, they receive "negative binding study advice" (negative BSA), indicating that they must leave the university. Students take the course for the first time in the last 2 months of their first year of study in their specific curricula: economics or business economics; econometrics or operations research; fiscal economics; and international business.

Prior to the introduction of the SPOC, students in Finance 1.5 met bi-weekly in small groups with their tutors for 2 h each session, for a total of nine sessions. Attendance at the small group meetings was mandatory, with sufficient participation needed to pass the overall course. During the 8 weeks, six (2-h) lectures are given by a professor of finance or business expert. Attendance at the lectures was mandatory. The required readings consisted of a course book. Students also were given a syllabus that described the weekly workload. At the end of the course, students had to pass (5.5 on a 10-point scale) a final examination consisting of 66 true-false questions. Average passing rate for the course was about 50% for the last 5 years.

There were several challenges with the course. First, as an obligatory entrance course, there was a large range in student's entry levels of knowledge. Second, depending on their majors, many of the students did not see the relevance of the course for their programs of study. Third, initial enrollment in the course was large (almost 900 students) and increasing, creating organizational constraints. The size of the permanent instructional staff was insufficient to meet the teaching demands of PBL given the increased enrollments in the course. This staff-shortage meant that part-time tutors from different domains inside and outside the university were hired on a temporary basis, creating a range of knowledge among the tutors.

Revision of Finance 1.5 as a Blended Course with a SPOC

Much of the structure of the face-to-face component of Finance 1.5 stayed the same, consistent with the university's focus on PBL. For example, within the course framework of 8 weeks, nine mandatory 2-h tutorial sessions (10-15 students) took place. However, in contrast to previous years, the six lectures given by a professor in finance or a business expert were non-mandatory, and the length of the lectures was reduced from 120 to 90 min each, and made available afterwards on demand. To pass the course, students still had to take a final examination of 66 true-false statements and obtain a passing score of 5.5 on a 10-point scale.

However, now within an electronic learning environment (Blackboard), students could access the syllabus for their face-to-face instruction and the non-mandatory SPOC. The SPOC could be accessed through a browser after signing in with a username and password.

Design of the SPOC for Finance 1.5

The SPOC offered course material in a different manner than the face-to-face components, with unfolding modules per week/topic. Each module consisted of a theoretical video, an expert video, and the opportunity for self-testing. In the theoretical video-clip, a professor explained the theoretical material relevant for that week. Students were also offered a short video in which a professor or business expert described or modeled the business application of the theoretical topic. Lastly, students could track their understanding and performance by participating in an online self-test or formative assessment, which included automated and detailed feedback. The formative assessment could be done indefinitely with rotating questions. At the end of the course, an online practice exam consisting of 66 questions was placed online, again offering substantial feedback on the answers. A graphical representation of the Finance 1.5 SPOC is depicted in Figure 1.1.

Within the SPOC, the studio-recorded theoretical and practical videos (termed lecture-lets) varied in length between 4 and 20 min. Each lecture-let combined video and audio with a synchronized view of the lecturer and the learning material (often a PowerPoint presentation). Because the videos were pre-recorded, the quality of the presentation and material presented

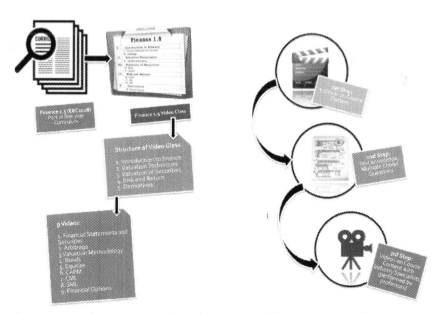

Figure 1.1 Graphical representation of the set-up of the Finance 1.5 SPOC.

Figure 1.2 Graphical representation of the user-interface of a lecture-let in the Finance 1.5 SPOC.

could be controlled. The content of the lecture-lets was scripted in advance, and multiple recordings sometimes were made before releasing the final versions to students online.

The recordings were produced using the lecture capturing system Mediasite by Sonicfoundry, which allowed for the streaming of online video material instead of having to upload and download material, which compromises both speed of access and ease of use. Mediasite captures a number of different media-streams at once. First, an external video camera captures the video of the lecturer. Second, the lecturer's audio is captured through a wireless microphone. And finally, the video graphics array (VGA) signal is rerouted through the system capturing the lecturer's screen (often a PowerPoint). The user interface consists of a three-window display: one window displays the video of the instructor, one displays the captured VGA signal (PowerPoint in this case), and one displays the navigational options. Students are able to navigate through the clips using a time slider or the slides display, offering flexibility and tailoring to individual needs. A graphical representation of the user-interface is depicted in Figure 1.2.

PARTICIPANTS

In total, 888 students initially enrolled in the course. Only, 875 students took the final exam. Of these, 669 completed the paper questionnaire. All of the participants were first year bachelor students, but with different majors.

The students were divided into cohorts based on their majors: 540 students had a background in International Business, 260 students in Economics or Business Economics, 44 students in Fiscal Economics, and 44 students in Econometrics or Operations Research.

MATERIALS
Test Anxiety Measure
To collect data on test-anxiety, the following three items were adapted from the Motivated Strategies for Learning Questionnaire (Pintrich & de Groot, 1990): (8) "When I take a test, I think about items on other parts of the test I can't answer." (14) "When I take a test I think of the consequences of failing." (19) "I have an easy, upset feeling when I take an exam." The introduction to the questionnaire clearly stated that all data would be treated confidentially. The instructions asked the students to answer the questions according to their feelings for the Finance 1.5 course. Participants responded on a 1 (not at all true of me) to 7 (very true of me) scale. The reliability of the construct was above the cut-off point ($\alpha = 0.70$). Scores were averaged to form the test anxiety index. Paper questionnaires were used to ensure a high response rate.

Academic Performance Measure
The academic performance measure was the grade on the Finance 1.5 final examination. The examination evaluated how much conceptual and procedural knowledge the students had learned, and included both theoretical and procedural questions, with the latter involving calculations. The exam was in a true–false format. To avoid guessing, points were deducted for incorrect answers. Students could leave questions blank or indicate a question mark, resulting in no points added or deducted. The examination scores were converted to a 1–10 scale, with 10 being the highest possible grade a student could obtain.

Course Evaluation
At the end of the course, but before the final examination took place, a non-mandatory course evaluation was sent via e-mail to all students enrolled in the course. The course evaluation was developed by the university and included closed-questions on instructor (professor and/or tutor) competence, quality of learning material and resources, performance of the tutorial

group, overall course evaluation, and time-investment. Students answered the questions on a 5-point Likert scale, except for the overall course evaluation, which was measured on a 10-point scale. Two open-ended questions also were included on the university evaluation, one asking students to list positive aspects of the course and the other asking students to list areas that needed improvement. In addition, for the Finance 1.5 blended course, four open-ended questions were included, namely: "What positive aspects do you see referring to the 'Finance Video Class module'?" "Which aspects of the 'Finance Video Class module' could be improved?" "Do you see any possible applications of similar video modules in other courses? If any, in which courses?" and " In what way did the 'Finance Video Class module' help you prepare for your exam?"

DATA COLLECTION PROCEDURES AND ANALYSES

As students participated in the SPOC, the number of times they accessed the lecture-lets were documented through the statistics logged and made available by Blackboard, the electronic learning environment hosting the SPOC. The statistics gave detailed information on SPOC usage by logging the time of access combined with student-ID per lecture-let.

Each of the tutors distributed paper questionnaires from the MSLQ (Pintrich & de Groot, 1990), which included the three adapted test anxiety questions, to the students in attendance during the last tutorial session, before the final examination. A total of 669 students completed the questionnaires, resulting in a response rate of 76%. The questionnaire results were automatically processed though computer software that read the data. The data then were imported into Excel and converted to SPSS. Cronbach's alpha for the text anxiety measure was above 0.70, indicating high reliability for this measure.

The course evaluation form was sent to the students through e-mail before the final examination. Only 232 students, or 26%, submitted the course evaluation. As the course evaluation was collected per major, all results were added and averaged to constitute the average course evaluation. In addition, students' comments from two cohorts (International Business Economics and Business Economics) were selected to illustrate their evaluation responses.

Final examination scores were collected for the 875 students who took the examination for the first time. Students were given 3 h to complete the final exam, and completed it in a large lecture hall. The exam results were automatically processed through computer software that read the data. The scores were imported into Excel and converted to SPSS.

Correlations between the number of times the students accessed the lecture-lets, their test anxiety scores, and the final examination scores were computed. In addition, the number of times that students viewed/accessed the lecture-lets and their text anxiety scores were regressed on the final examination scores.

RESULTS

The results in Table 1.1 show the means, standard deviations, and correlations for students' test anxiety, the number of views of the lecture-lets, and students' academic performance. The mean for test anxiety was 4.07 (SD = 1.37), ranging from 1 to 7. The mean number of views was 167.38 (SD = 140.88), ranging between 1 and 907 views per student, with 92% of the students enrolled in the course watching the SPOC at least once. Seventy-three students who participated in the examination never watched the Finance 1.5 SPOC. The average examination grade was 6.18 (SD = 1.38) with grades ranging from 2.5 to 10. The correlation between the number of views was positively related to students' academic performance (β 0.114, p 0.001) and negatively related to test anxiety (β −0.129, p 0.001). Test anxiety was negatively correlated with students' academic performance (β −0.075, p 0.005).

Tables 1.2-1.4 present the results of the ordinary least squares (OLS) regression. The results show that the number of views significantly predicted

Table 1.1 Mean, SD, Cronbach alpha and correlation analysis

Variable	Mean	SD	Alpha	Test-anxiety	Number of views	Academic performance
Test-anxiety	4.065	1.365	0.703		−0.129**	−0.075*
Number of views	167.38	140.88				0.114**
Academic performance	6.176	1.382				

Notes: N = 875 students. *p-value < 0.05 (two-tailed). **p-value < 0.01 (two-tailed).

Table 1.2 OLS regression results: test anxiety explaining academic performance

Dependent variable	β	p
Test anxiety	−0.075	0.05*
R^2	0.006	

Note: N = 875 students, *p < 0.05.

Table 1.3 OLS regression results: number of views explaining test anxiety

Dependent variable	β	p
Number of views	−0.129	0.001**
R^2	0.017	

*Note: N=875 students, **p-value <0.01.*

Table 1.4 OLS regression results: number of views explaining academic performance

Dependent variable	β	p
Number of views	0.114	0.001**
R^2	0.013	

*Note: N=875 students, **p-value <0.01.*

academic performance. In addition, the number of views was inversely related to test anxiety, and test anxiety was inversely related to academic performance.

The model as represented in Figure 1.3 was confirmed, that is, the number of times that the students viewed the lecture-lets influenced academic performance directly, and indirectly, through test anxiety.

The increased student-passing rate for the course and the course evaluations indicated that the blended version of Finance 1.5 with the SPOC was effective. Compared to the previous passing rate of 50% for Finance 1.5, the passing rate for students who took the examination for the first time after completing the blended version of Finance 1.5 with the SPOC was 64.5%, or an increase of almost 15%. Course evaluation results also were positive. The overall course evaluation average of 7.46 ($n=232$) for the blended version of the course was higher than the previous year, 7.36 ($n=269$). The students' answers to the open-ended questions about the positive aspects of the course regularly mentioned the implementation of the SPOC with the video-classes, and the students' answers about the negative aspects of the course often mentioned the need for even more lecture-lets in

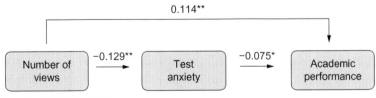

Note: * p<0.05, ** p<0.01

Figure 1.3 Conceptual model on the relation between number of views, test anxiety, and academic performance.

Table 1.5 Students' reactions to the Finance 1.5 SPOC

Q: What did you find positive about the Finance 1.5 video class?
- *"I thought of them as very helpful, giving a short summary and explanation of the topic and the possibility to do a test."* (Anonymous, International Business Student)
- *"I really like the fact the videos elaborated on certain topics that were not entirely explain in the tutorial meetings."* (Anonymous, International Business Student)
- *"I could always stop and listen as often as I wanted it to, in order to fully understand the topic. That helped me a lot."* (Anonymous, International Business Student)

Q: What could be improved about the Finance 1.5 video class?
- *"It could go a little bit more into depth. And it is not necessary to see the face to the voice that is speaking! Rather make the window with the graphical illustrations bigger! And add more graphical stuff!"* (Anonymous, International Business Student)

Q: In what other courses do you see the possibility to implement video classes?
- *"Personally I think there should be such material for every course!"* (Anonymous, Economics or Business Economics Student)
- *"In every quantitative course and even only for models which can be visualized, it would be great to have a short introduction of the model next to the book, for revising"* (Anonymous, Economics or Business Economics Student)
- *"I would be glad to see these video modules applied to every course!"* (Anonymous, Economics or Business Economics Student)
- *"I think that the content can be visualized in all courses, since you can learn better, if somebody presents it to you."* (Anonymous, Economics or Business Economics Student)
- *"Certainly for accounting! Those courses are both very similar and those video classes help to understand the material."* (Anonymous, Economics or Business Economics Student)

Q: In what way did the finance 1.5 video class help you study?
- *"Revision of old knowledge, visual support leads me to higher knowledge retention rate."* (Anonymous, Economics or Business Economics Student)
- *"Understanding the relationship between theory and reality"* (Anonymous, Economics or Business Economics Student)

the SPOC. Table 1.5 presents representative answers from the two cohorts of students about what they found positive in the use of the SPOC in Finance 1.5, how/if the SPOC helped students prepare for the examination, what could be improved and in what other domains SPOCs should be applied, if any.

DISCUSSION

This study analyzed the impact of SPOC usage on test anxiety and its subsequent influence on the academic performance of students. Prior research showed that test anxiety significantly predicts academic performance (Pekrun et al., 2002). Our research confirmed these findings. We showed that there was a direct relationship between the number of views of lecture-lets in the SPOC and students' academic performance, indicating that SPOC usage increased academic performance directly. In addition, we found that SPOC usage (expressed by number of views) could decrease test anxiety and subsequently enhance academic performance.

Our findings also indicated that implementing MOOC technology through a SPOC in a blended learning environment was an effective way of reducing test anxiety. We suspect that the use of online interactive video and formative assessments increased students' self-concept or sense of self-control (Marsh & Craven, 2006; Marsh & Yeung, 1997; O'Mara et al., 2006), reducing their anxiety about the course, and the final examination. Further, the instructional design of the SPOC, with its emphases on cognitive load reduction, chunking of new information, and vicarious learning probably helped students to better learn the course material. On the course evaluations, several students mentioned that the provision of theoretical and applied lecture-lets throughout the course facilitated their linking of theory to application. The increased passing rate for the course (64.5%), compared to the past (50%), indicated that the addition of the SPOC was an effective way to enhance students' learning.

Lastly, our results suggest that MOOC technology can be effective (i.e., enhance academic performance) when implemented correctly. By using MOOC technology through a SPOC in combination with face-to-face education, the positive features associated with MOOCs, such as cost-efficiency and high enrollments, can be capitalized on, without diminishing the emotional benefits characteristic of face-to-face education (Hara & Kling, 1999). Effective use of MOOC technology especially is important for curricula with massive numbers of students, such as first-year required courses (Huon, Spehar, Adam, & Rifkin, 2007).

LIMITATIONS AND IMPLICATIONS FOR FURTHER RESEARCH

There are important limitations that should be considered when interpreting the results. First, the reader should consider that the construct of anxiety measured in this study could have a pre-disposition in itself; that is, some students may have a minimum level of test-anxiety embedded in their personality, creating a possible bias in the results. Further research should investigate the role of personality when looking into emotions such as anxiety in relation to SPOCs. Second, by treating all students in the sample as a group, we leveled the differences in educational background. It would be interesting to see if there is any difference in findings between the effects of SPOC on test anxiety and academic performance among students according to their educational majors, gender, or nationalities. For example, there only were 10 students with a background in econometrics that participated in the Finance 1.5 test-anxiety questionnaire and course evaluation. The average number of SPOC views for this group was 144, whereas the mean number of views for all students in the sample was significantly higher (167). We suspect that the students in the econometrics major might not have accessed the SPOC as often as the other students because they had a stronger background in the course topic. A bigger and more diverse sample would be needed to conduct such analyses.

Our results also indicate that there might be alternative emotional factors that influence students' academic performance when SPOCs are included in a blended course. Among others, these include self-efficacy and intrinsic or extrinsic motivation, along with non-emotional factors, such as learning strategies and grade point average. Further research is needed to investigate which students benefit the most from the use of SPOCs in education and how to further differentiate SPOC implementation in order to address the individual needs of students and avoid the negative emotional effects of MOOCs.

Lastly, this research took place in an obligatory first year course in finance. Implementing a blended learning approach might be especially effective with abstract courses (Bassili & Joordens, 2008) such as finance, which students typically view as difficult. For example, in Finance 1.5, students had to keep up with material as the work built incrementally (Le, Joordens, Chrysostomou, & Grinnell, 2010) and assignments progressively increased in difficulty. There was an emphasis on the deep-learning of specific cognitive skills (Biggs, Kember, & Leung, 2001) relevant to multifaceted calculation assignments. Our results might be different for less abstract courses (e.g., courses with less calculations) or in different stages of the curricula, where students' motivation and aptitude for the material are likely to differ.

In conclusion, when considering implementing MOOC technologies in education, educators should consider combining SPOCs with face-to-face education. By doing so, they can reduce in-class time and capitalize on the efficiency of MOOC technology to teach massive numbers of students, while still addressing student emotions and increasing academic effectiveness. Although our experience shows that developing an effective SPOC requires an additional time investment, the outcomes are promising. Moreover, when designed with care, the SPOC can be used for several years in combination with face-to-face education.

REFERENCES

Adams, C., Yin, Y., Vargas Madriz, L. F., & Mullen, C. S. (2014). A phenomenology of learning large: The tutorial sphere of xMOOC video lectures. *Distance Education*, *35*(2), 202–216. http://dx.doi.org/10.1080/01587919.2014.917701.

Andersen, R., & Ponti, M. (2014). Participatory pedagogy in an open educational course: Challenges and opportunities. *Distance Education*, *35*(2), 234–249. http://dx.doi.org/10.1080/01587919.2014.917703.

Artino, A. R. (2009). Online learning: Are subjective perceptions of instructional context related to academic success? *The Internet and Higher Education*, *12*(3–4), 117–125. http://dx.doi.org/10.1016/j.iheduc.2009.07.003.

Baecker, R., Moore, G., & Boudreau, A. Z. (2003). Reinventing the lecture: Web casting made interactive. In *Proceedings of the tenth international conference on human-computer interaction 2003*. Retrieved from, http://commons.pacificu.edu/edufac/20.

Baggaley, J. (2014). MOOCS: Digesting the facts. *Distance Education*, *35*(2), 159–163. http://dx.doi.org/10.1080/01587919.2014.919710.

Bandura, A. (1977). Self-efficacy: Toward a unifying theory of behavioral change. *Psychological Review*, *2*(84), 191–215.

Bassili, J., & Joordens, S. (2008). Media player tool use, satisfaction with online lectures and examination performance. *Journal of Distance Education*, *22*, 93–108.

Beier, M. E., & Kanfer, R. (2010). Motivation in training and development: A phase perspective. In S. W. J. Kozlowski & E. Salas (Eds.), *Learning, training, and development in organizations* (pp. 65–97). Mahwah, NJ: Erlbaum.

Biggs, J., Kember, D., & Leung, D. Y. (2001). The revised two-factor study process questionnaire: R-SPQ-2 F. *The British Journal of Educational Psychology*, *71*, 133–149. http://dx.doi.org/10.1348/000709901158433.

Boyle, T., Bradley, C., Chalk, P., Jones, R., & Pickard, P. (2003). Using blended learning to improve student success rates in learning to program. *Journal of Educational Media*, *28*, 165–178.

Bruinsma, M. (2004). Motivation, cognitive processing and achievement in higher education. *Learning and Instruction*, *14*(6), 549–568. http://dx.doi.org/10.1016/j.learninstruc.2004.09.001.

Chen, C. M., & Wang, H. P. (2011). Using emotion recognition in technology to assess the effects of different multimedia materials on learning emotion and performance. *Library & Information Science Research*, *33*(3), 244–255.

De Angelis, A. (2013). Global fast food restaurant industry to increase by 4.2% per year through 2018. Yahoo! Finance.

Elliott, E. S., & Dweck, C. S. (1988). Goals: An approach to motivation and achievement. *Journal of Personality and Social Psychology*, *54*, 5–12. http://dx.doi.org/10.1037/0022-3514.54.1.5.

Fox, A. (2013). From MOOCs to SPOCs. *Communications of the ACM*, *56*(12), 38–40. http://dx.doi.org/10.1145/2535918.

Fox, A. (2014). Ubiquity symposium: MOOCs and technology to advance learning and learning research: From MOOCs to SPOCs: curricular technology transfer for the 21st century. *Ubiquity*, *2014*(June), 3.

Goetz, T., Cronjaeger, H., Frenzel, A. C., Lüdtke, O., & Hall, N. C. (2010). Academic self-concept and emotion relations: Domain specificity and age effects. *Contemporary Educational Psychology*, *35*(1), 44–58. http://dx.doi.org/10.1016/j.cedpsych.2009.10.001.

Goetz, T., Pekrun, R., Hall, N., & Haag, L. (2006). Academic emotions from a social-cognitive perspective: Antecedents and domain specificity of students' affect in the context of Latin instruction. *The British Journal of Educational Psychology*, *76*(Pt 2), 289–308. http://dx.doi.org/10.1348/000709905X42860.

Goetz, T., Preckel, F., Zeidner, M., & Schleyer, E. (2008). Big fish in big ponds: A multilevel analysis of test anxiety and achievement in special gifted classes. *Anxiety, Stress, and Coping*, *21*, 185–198. http://dx.doi.org/10.1080/10615800701628827.

Gog, T., & Rummel, N. (2010). Example-based learning: Integrating cognitive and social-cognitive research perspectives. *Educational Psychology Review*, *22*(2), 155–174. http://dx.doi.org/10.1007/s10648-010-9134-7.

Gorissen, P., Van Bruggen, J., & Jochems, W. (2012). Students and recorded lectures: Survey on current use and demands for higher education. *Research in Learning Technology*, *20*(3), 297–311, http://dx.doi.org/10.3402/rlt.v20i0.17299.

Govindasamy, T. (2001). Successful implementation of e-learning: Pedagogical considerations. *The Internet and Higher Education*, *4*, 287–299. http://dx.doi.org/10.1016/S1096-7516(01)00071-9.

Groenendijk, T., Janssen, T., Rijlaarsdam, G., & van den Bergh, H. (2013). The effect of observational learning on students' performance, processes, and motivation in two creative domains. *British Journal of Educational Psychology*, *83*, 3–28. http://dx.doi.org/10.1111/j.2044-8279.2011.02052.x.

Hara, N., & Kling, R. (1999). A case study of Students' frustrations with a web-based distance education course. *First Monday*, *4*(12). Retrieved September 30, http://www.firstmonday.org/issues/issue4_12/hara/index.html.

Hasler, B. S., Kersten, B., & Sweller, J. (2007). Learner control, cognitive load and instructional animation. *Applied Cognitive Psychology*, *21*, 713–729. http://dx.doi.org/10.1002/acp.1345.

Huon, G., Spehar, B., Adam, P., & Rifkin, W. (2007). Resource use and academic performance among first year psychology students. *Higher Education*, *53*, 1–27. http://dx.doi.org/10.1007/s10734-005-1727-6.

IBM. (2010). Capitalizing on complexity: Insights from the Global Chief Executive Officer study.

Isen, A. M. (1990). The influence of positive and negative affect on cognitive organization: Some implications for development. In N. L. Stein, B. Leventhal, & T. Trabasso (Eds.), *Psychological and biological approaches to emotion* (pp. 75–94). Hillsdale, NJ: Erlbaum.

Jordan, K. (2013, February 13). MoocMoocher: Synthesising MOOC completion rates Retrieved from http://moocmoocher.wordpress.com/2013/02/13/synthesising-mooc-completion-rates.

Kay, R. (2008). Exploring the relationship between emotions and the acquisition of computer knowledge. *Computers & Education*, *50*(4), 1269–1283. http://dx.doi.org/10.1016/j.compedu.2006.12.002.

Kirschner, P. A., Strijbos, J.-W., Kreijns, K., & Beers, P. (2004). Designing electronic collaborative learning environments. *Educational Technology Research and Development*, *52*(3), 47–66. http://dx.doi.org/10.1007/BF02504675%.

Knox, J. (2014). Digital culture clash: "Massive" education in the e-learning and digital cultures MOOC. *Distance Education*, *35*(2), 164–177. http://dx.doi.org/10.1080/01587919.2014.917704.

Koehler, M. J., & Mishra, P. (2009). What is technological pedagogical content knowledge (TPACK)? *Contemporary Issues in Technology and Teacher Education*, *9*, 60–70. http://dx.doi.org/10.1016/j.compedu.2010.07.009.

Koller, D., Ng, A., Do, C., & Chen, Z. (2013). Retention and intention in massive open online courses: In depth. *Educause Review*, 1–8. Retrieved from, http://www.educause.edu/ero/article/retention-and-intention-massive-open-online-courses-depth-0.

Kop, R., & Hill, A. (2008). Connectivism: Learning theory of the future or vestige of the past? *International Review of Research in Open and Distance Learning*, *9*(3). Retrieved on September 15, 2014, from, http://www.irrodl.org/index.php/irrodl/article/view/523/.

Laurillard, D. (2002). p. 256, *Rethinking university teaching: A conversational framework for the effective use of learning technologies*. Oxford, UK: Routledge Falmer.

Le, A., Joordens, S., Chrysostomou, S., & Grinnell, R. (2010). Online lecture accessibility and its influence on performance in skills-based courses. *Computers & Education*, *55*(1), 313–319. http://dx.doi.org/10.1016/j.compedu.2010.01.017.

Lebow, D. (1993). Constructivist values for instructional systems design: Five principles toward a new mindset. *Educational Technology Research and Development*, *41*, 4–16. http://dx.doi.org/10.1007/BF02297354.

Lim, D. H. (2002). Perceived differences between classroom and distance education: Seeking instructional strategies for learning applications. *International Journal of Educational Technology*, *3*(1). Retrieved from, http://www.editlib.org/p/95353/.

Lim, D. H., & Morris, M. L. (2009). Learner and instructional factors influencing learning outcomes within a blended learning environment. *Educational Technology and Society*, *12*, 282–293.

Linnenbrink, E. A. (2006). Emotion research in education: Theoretical and methodological perspectives on the integration of affect, motivation, and cognition. *Educational Psychology Review*, *18*(4), 307–314. http://dx.doi.org/10.1007/s10648-006-9028-x.

Maniar, N., Bennett, E., Hand, S., & Allan, G. (2008). The effect of mobile phone screen size on video based learning. *Journal of Software*, *3*, 51–61. http://dx.doi.org/10.4304/jsw.3.4.51-61.

Marsh, H. W., & Craven, R. G. (2006). Reciprocal effects of self-concept and performance from a multidimensional. *Perspectives on Psychological Science*, *1*, 133–163. http://dx.doi.org/10.1111/j.1745-6916.2006.00010.x.

Marsh, H. W., & Yeung, A. S. (1997). Causal effects of academic self-concept on academic achievement: Structural equation models of longitudinal data. *Journal of Educational Psychology*, *89*(1), 41–54. http://dx.doi.org/10.1037/0022-0663.89.1.41.

Mayer, R. E., & Chandler, P. (2001). When learning is just a click away: Does simple user interaction foster deeper understanding of multimedia messages? *Journal of Educational Psychology*, *93*(2), 390–397. http://dx.doi.org/10.1037//0022-0663.93.2.390.

McLoughlin, C., & Lee, M. J. W. (2007, December). Social software and participatory learning: Extending pedagogical choices with technology affordances in the Web 2.0 era. In R. Atkinson & C. McBeath (Eds.), *ICT: Providing choices for learners and learning. Proceedings ASCILITE. Singapore* (pp. 664–675). http://dx.doi.org/10.1111/j.1083-6101.2007.00367.x.

Meijer, J. (2001). Learning potential and anxious tendency: Test anxiety as a bias factor in educational testing. *Anxiety, Stress & Coping*, *14*, 337–362. http://dx.doi.org/10.1080/10615800108248361.

Merisotis, J. P., & Phipps, R. A. (1999). What's the difference? Outcomes of distance vs. traditional classroom-based learning. *Change: The Magazine of Higher Learning*, *31*, 12–17. http://dx.doi.org/10.1080/00091389909602685.

Merkt, M., Weigand, S., Heier, A., & Schwan, S. (2011). Learning with videos vs. learning with print: The role of interactive features. *Learning and Instruction*, *21*(6), 687–704. http://dx.doi.org/10.1016/j.learninstruc.2011.03.004.

Miller, G. A. (1994). The magical number seven, plus or minus two: some limits on our capacity for processing information. 1956. *Psychological Review*, *101*, 343–352. http://dx.doi.org/10.1037/h0043158.

O'Mara, A. J., Marsh, H. W., Craven, R. G., & Debus, R. L. (2006). Do self-concept interventions make a difference? A synergistic blend of construct validation and meta-analysis. *Educational Psychologist*, *41*, 181–206. http://dx.doi.org/10.1207/s15326985ep4103_4.

O'Toole, J. M., & Absalom, D. J. (2003). The impact of blended learning on student outcomes: Is there room on the horse for two? *Journal of Educational Media*, *28*(2–3), 179–190. http://dx.doi.org/10.1080/1358165032000165680.

Onink, T. (2013). Georgia Tech, Udacity Shock Higher Ed With $7,000 Degree. Retrieved October 01, 2014, from http://www.forbes.com/sites/troyonink/2013/05/15/georgia-tech-udacity-shock-higher-ed-with-7000-degree/.

Osguthorpe, R., & Graham, C. (2003). Blended learning environments: Definitions and directions. *Quarterly Review of Distance Education*, *4*, 227–233. Retrieved from, http://www.eric.ed.gov/ERICWebPortal/recordDetail?accno=EJ678078.

Pekrun, R. (2006). The control-value theory of achievement emotions: Assumptions, corollaries, and implications for educational research and practice. *Educational Psychology Review*, *18*(4), 315–341. http://dx.doi.org/10.1007/s10648-006-9029-9.

Pekrun, R., Goetz, T., Frenzel, A. C., Barchfeld, P., & Perry, R. P. (2011). Measuring emotions in students' learning and performance: The Achievement Emotions Questionnaire (AEQ). *Contemporary Educational Psychology*, *36*, 36–48. http://dx.doi.org/10.1016/j.cedpsych.2010.10.002.

Pekrun, R., Goetz, T., Titz, W., & Perry, R. P. (2002). Academic emotions in students' self-regulated learning and achievement: A program of qualitative and quantitative research. *Educational Psychologist*, *37*, 91–105. http://dx.doi.org/10.1207/S15326985EP3702_4.

Pekrun, R., & Linnenbrink-garcia, L. (2012). Academic emotions and student engagement. In S. L. Christenson, A. L. Reschly, & C. Wylie (Eds.), *Handbook of research on student engagement* (pp. 259–282). New York: Springer. http://dx.doi.org/10.1007/978-1-4614-2018-7.

Petrides, L. A. (2002). Web-based technologies for distributed (or distance) learning: Creating learning-centered educational experiences in the higher education classroom. *International Journal of Instructional Media*, *29*, 69–77.

Pintrich, P. R., & de Groot, E. V. (1990). Motivational and self-regulated learning components of classroom academic performance. *Journal of Educational Psychology*, *82*, 33–40. http://dx.doi.org/10.1037/0022-0663.82.1.33.

Radford, L. (1997). On psychology, historical epistemology, and the teaching of mathematics: Towards a socio-cultural history of mathematics. *For the Learning of Mathematics*, *17*, 26–33.

Richardson, J. (2012). The history of supersizing: How we've become a nation hooked on bigger is better. *Alternet*.

Rivard, R. (2013). Measuring the MOOC dropout rate. *Inside Higher Ed*. Retrieved from, http://www.immagic.com/eLibrary/ARCHIVES/GENERAL/GENPRESS/I130308R.pdf.

Schwarzer, R., Mueller, J., & Greenglass, E. (1999). Assessment of perceived general self-efficacy on the internet: Data collection in cyberspace. *Anxiety, Stress & Coping*, *12*(2), 145–161. http://dx.doi.org/10.1080/10615809908248327.

Sevilla, M. (2012). *Problem based learning in the 21st century*. Charleston: CreateSpace Independent Publishing Platform.

Shephard, K. (2003). Questioning, promoting and evaluating the use of streaming video to support student learning. *British Journal of Educational Technology*, *34*(3), 295–308. http://dx.doi.org/10.1111/1467-8535.00328.

Shukie, P. (2013). Why COOCs offer real hope in the MOOC universe. Retrieved October 01, 2014, from http://shukiesweb.blogspot.co.uk/2013/10/why-coocs-offer-real-hope-in-mooc.html.

Tam, M. (2000). Constructivism, instructional design, and technology: Implications for transforming distance learning. *Educational Technology & Society, 3,* 50–60.

Traphagan, T., Kucsera, J. V., & Kishi, K. (2009). Impact of class lecture webcasting on attendance and learning. *Educational Technology Research and Development, 58*(1), 19–37. http://dx.doi.org/10.1007/s11423-009-9128-7.

Valiente, C., Swanson, J., & Eisenberg, N. (2012). Linking students' emotions and academic achievement: When and why emotions matter. *Child Development Perspectives, 6*(2), 129–135. http://dx.doi.org/10.1111/j.1750-8606.2011.00192.x.

Van Yperen, N. W. (2007). Performing well in an evaluative situation: The roles of perceived competence and task-irrelevant interfering thoughts. *Anxiety, Stress, and Coping, 20*(4), 409–419. http://dx.doi.org/10.1080/10615800701628876.

Woo, K., Gosper, M., McNeill, M., Preston, G., Green, D., & Phillips, R. (2008). Web-based lecture technologies: Blurring the boundaries between face-to-face and distance learning. *Research in Learning Technology, 16*(2), 81–93. http://dx.doi.org/10.3402/rlt.v16i2.10887.

Yang, D., Sinha, T., Adamson, D., & Rose, C. P. (2013). "Turn on, tune in, drop out": Anticipating student dropouts in massive open online courses. In *Proceedings of the 2013 NIPS data-driven education workshop,* (pp. 1–8).

Zeidner, M., & Schleyer, E. (1999). The big-fish-little-pond effect for academic self-concept, test anxiety, and school grades in gifted children. *Contemporary Educational Psychology, 24*(4), 305–329. http://dx.doi.org/10.1006/ceps.1998.0985.

CHAPTER 2

Emotional and Social Engagement in a Massive Open Online Course: An Examination of Dino 101

Lia M. Daniels, Catherine Adams, Adam McCaffrey
University of Alberta, Edmonton, AB, Canada

Massive open online courses (MOOCs) are a relatively new phenomenon that have left an unprecedented mark on the ideology of online learning (Liyanagunawardena, Adams, & Williams, 2013). In their short 5-year history, MOOCs have attracted learners from around the world and gained notoriety at world-class educational institutions (Clarke, 2013). Some have argued that the MOOC movement represents a revolution in teaching that frees information from the barriers of paying for expensive courses to now providing classes from the most prominent professors at no cost (Cusumano, 2013). In contrast, others see the MOOC movement as a reinvention of old classroom-learning theories being enacted in new ways involving students networking across the world and engaging in new forms of acquiring knowledge (Siemens, 2004). To date, it seems that MOOC designers, instructors, and researchers are undecided on the extent to which MOOC learners can be considered "students" like those found in face-to-face, blended, or other less massive or open online learning environments (Kolowich, 2014). Like Kolowich, we argue that indeed, today's MOOC learners are not traditional students; for the most part, they appear unconcerned with grades, credits, or even completion. MOOC learners engage in learning to be exposed to material they always wanted to learn with the bonus of accessing world-renowned experts (Hew & Cheung, 2014). By extension, they may have very different expectations of how they will engage in their learning. If this is indeed the case, one psychological principle that needs to be considered is engagement. It is our intention to examine students' perceptions and experiences of engagement, focusing specifically on social and emotional engagement, in one edX and Coursera-type massive open online course (xMOOC): Dino 101.

Emotions, Technology, and Learning
http://dx.doi.org/10.1016/B978-0-12-800649-8.00004-3

A BRIEF PRIMER ON MOOCs

Siemens (2012) differentiated between connectivist massive open online courses (cMOOCs) and later xMOOCs. cMOOCs were originally developed based upon connectivist pedagogies that take advantage of the online environment for connecting students (Siemens, 2012). With this theory in mind, the first MOOC was designed to provide students with an array of resources and without any particular structure to what they should learn. Students were asked to learn based upon their own interests and to build upon their knowledge from others within the class. Siemens and Downes, the pioneers of the cMOOC, argued that learning online could not be fully explained by the previous behaviorist, cognitivist, or constructivist ideas, and that there were different theories of learning that can be harnessed within the online environment (Liyanagunawardena et al., 2013).

Historically, the design of MOOCs emerged from a variety of these learning perspectives, including objectivism, pragmatism, interpretivism, and connectivism (Kop & Hill, 2008). Objectivism sees reality as being external and knowledge is experientially acquired, whereas pragmatism sees knowledge as an experience of inquiry, reflection, and action. Interpretivism sees knowledge as the internal construction of ideas that are tested through socialization. Connectivism postulates that students learn best when they are able to engage socially with the material to build and share their ideas with others. It is the connections and networks that students create with others that broaden knowledge. This sharing of ideas from one person to another has the potential for ideas to be critically thought about many times over and for ideas to be redeveloped through socializing in online learning environments. The construction of ideas is similar to Vygotsky's theory of scaffolding and proximal learning (Nassaji & Swain, 2000). Vygotsky's theory states that people learn best when they are exposed to those who know slightly more and are able to help them reach a greater level of understanding. This sort of connectivist, spontaneous, and practical sharing of ideas was the foundational philosophy guiding the initial cMOOCs.

The problem with the original ideas for cMOOCs was they expected knowledge to be created, shared, and collected—a tall order in any learning environment, never mind one with thousands of learners who may never share the same physical space. Thus, with the increase in popularity of MOOCs in general, a shift occurred toward xMOOCs, or MOOCs that follow a more conventional and structured method, similar to traditional university courses. Although both are massive, open, and online, xMOOCs are philosophically different than cMOOCs. xMOOCs focus less on sharing ideas and building information and more on traditional models of providing materials for students to learn, encouraging discussion, and even assessing learning through quizzes or tests (Clarke, 2013). In this sense, learners do not necessarily go into these courses to share ideas and develop material together, but instead they are more interested in learning from a leading professor online, for free, and usually through the segments of prerecorded videos. xMOOCs still involve discussion forums and show evidence of a spontaneous creation of groups or artifacts, but ultimately the xMOOC platform is not driven by the underlying philosophy of connectivism.

From our perspective, this type of design raises a question related to engagement, because tens of thousands of people may simply be exposed to "good" or "bad" xMOOCs the same way traditional students have slogged through "good" and "bad" lectures, seminars, and labs. Thus, the question becomes to what extent can engagement be leveraged in an xMOOC, particularly given the unique motivations of its learners.

ENGAGEMENT AS A SOCIAL PSYCHOLOGICAL CONSTRUCT

When MOOC developers talk about engagement, they are talking about completion and participation rates: how many people registered, logged on, want a certificate, *etc*. This is a very different definition than a social psychological approach to engagement in learning. Although many working definitions exist (Appleton, Christenson, & Furlong, 2008; Furlong et al., 2003), most researchers agree engagement is a multidimensional construct most commonly broken down into three components:
- Cognitive engagement (regulation)
- Behavioral engagement (effort, participation, rule following)
- Emotional or affective engagement (positive attitude, interest)

Recently, Klassen, Yerdelen, and Durken (2013) proposed that social engagement is critical in learning environments, because learning is a social task. This may be particularly true in MOOCs, because their massiveness provides an unprecedented opportunity for social connections. Thus, for the purposes of this chapter, we adhere to a modified four-component operationalization of engagement (Fredricks, Blumenfeld, & Paris, 2004; Klassen et al., 2013) that includes the following additional construct:
- Social engagement (connections, belonging)

Cognitive engagement looks at the level of investment learners put into thinking about their tasks. It incorporates the investment of intentional thought required to comprehend complicated ideas and to master the content presented (Fredricks et al., 2004). Some definitions emphasize the importance of psychological investment in learning, while others emphasize a variety of cognitive processes, such as problem solving, positive coping, and desire for learning (Connell & Wellborn, 1991; Newmann, Wehlage, & Lamborn, 1992; Wehlage, Rutter, Smith, Lesko, & Fernandez, 1989). Cognitive engagement is quite similar to intrinsic motivation and positively predicts outcomes, including goal setting and self-regulation (Boekarts, Pintrich, & Zeidner, 2000; Harter, 1981; Zimmerman, 1990). High cognitive engagement in a MOOC may involve seeking out additional information on the material, or preparing for and completing quizzes. Behavioral engagement is often defined in three ways. The first is associated with positive demeanor (e.g., following rules or school attendance; Finn, 1993; Finn & Rock, 1997). The second is the effort associated with paying attention and concentrating on the learning experience (Birch & Ladd, 1997; Skinner & Belmont, 1993). The third is participation in school-related events (Finn, 1993). Empirically, behavioral engagement has also been positively associated with students' on-task behaviors and following rules (Karweit, 1989; Peterson, Swing, Stark, & Wass, 1984). This is the psychological element of engagement that is most similar to the notion of engagement discussed currently in the MOOC literature. Although the expectations for behavior in a MOOC may look different from a traditional classroom, they still exist. For example, a student may be able to stay focused on the video or become distracted and surf the web; each represents a qualitatively different level of behavioral engagement.

Emotional engagement relates to the student's feelings of interest, pleasure, sadness, boredom, and anxiety in the classroom (Fredricks et al., 2004). In other words, emotional engagement looks at the positive and negative reactions that extend from the social and learning environments. Emotional engagement has been positively related to student outcomes including attitudes, emotional experiences, values, and interest (Epstein & McPartland, 1976; Yamamoto, Thomas, & Karns, 1969). An example of emotional engagement is the feeling of excitement a student may experience when watching the lectures or participating in the forums.

Social engagement refers to the willingness to socialize with others and the feeling of belonging. Although social engagement is an emerging construct in the student engagement literature, it has been discussed in the eLearning literature pertaining to social media and Web 2.0 technologies for quite some time (see Rennie & Morrison, 2013, for a more thorough review). From a theoretical perspective, several achievement motivation theories stress some component of social connectedness. For example, self-determination theory (Deci & Ryan, 2000) argues that relatedness is one of three basic psychological needs that, when met, leads to optimal motivation. Similarly, Butler (2012) has recently incorporated relational goals into her achievement goal framework. While specific to online learning, Siemens (2004) argues that the future of online learning lies with the connections students make and the process of social information creation, in order for students to think critically and contribute to knowledge on a global level. Although xMOOCs do not emanate from the connectivist paradigm described above, psychological theory and eLearning pedagogy reinforce that engaging learning of any type should indeed be social (Rennie & Morrison, 2013).

Let's consider an example. In a traditional classroom, we may determine evidence of engagement when a student asks questions in class (cognitive), completes assignments (behavioral), appears excited about the content (emotional), and shares information with her peers (social). In an xMOOC, we may infer engagement when a student starts a debate on the forums (cognitive), logs on regularly to watch full video segments (behavioral), expresses that the content is relevant (emotional), and joins a related Facebook group (social). From a psychological perspective, this four-pronged operationalization of engagement can be applied to face-to-face and online learning environments without much difficulty. A similar argument was made for transitioning other social psychological theories to help explain and design online learning environments (see Daniels & Stupnisky, 2012).

ENGAGING MOOCs

Hew and Cheung (2014) suggest that instructors attempt to engage students in xMOOCs by relying upon a familiar structure much like traditional higher education courses and participating to some extent in online interactions. Neither of these strategies aligns with a social psychological approach to student engagement—which is well established in face-to-face research and we hypothesize can be translated into xMOOCs. In particular, we focus on emotional and social engagement, because these two components stand to make a particularly meaningful contribution to MOOC design as the "massiveness" of the MOOC offers countless opportunities for connection as well as unique opportunities to feel isolated. According to Jacobs (2013), student-to-student interactions across 11 MOOCs warrant an overall grade of B– and are described as "merely decent to unsatisfying." Jacobs is even harder on teacher-to-student interactions, giving a final grade of D. Summing across the current literature, Hew and Cheung (2014) suggest that one of students' major frustrations stemmed from poor quality of discussions and slow responses. It seems that despite the range of opportunities to interact, no platform has, as of yet, successfully brought about the same sense of interaction or conversation that is part of high-quality face-to-face delivery. With MOOCs understood to be in the early stages of development, research on engagement may play a pivotal role in shaping the successful improvement of MOOCs for a different type of learner. This is an important caveat: MOOC learners are a different type of student and thus may enter their MOOC with uncommon expectations for learning (Kolowich, 2014). Just as we expect the social psychological perspective on engagement to function in a MOOC, so too should we remember countless pieces of educational evidence that students' expectations influence their effort and learning (e.g., Eccles & Wigfield, 2002). Thus, learners who go into the MOOC for social engagement reasons may engage in their learning differently than those who expect their learning to come from the experts they are able to access through videos.

ENGAGEMENT WITH THE INSTRUCTOR

Jacobs (2013) has suggested there is a very low level of interaction between students and the instructor in MOOCs: "When it comes to Massive Open Online Courses…you can forget about the Socratic method. The professor is, in most cases, out of students' reach, only slightly more accessible than the pope or Thomas Pynchon" (paragraph 2). The high student–instructor ratio is perceived as especially problematic in xMOOCs. In cMOOCs, students are intended to be learning primarily *via* making multiple and varied connections with their peers, so this ratio is not considered a significant issue in connectivist environments. Ebben and Murphy (2014) contend that "most MOOCs are constructed in a unidirectional manner … epitomizing a narrow view of teaching and learning" and thereby severely limit the potential for student engagement with the instructor (p. 14).

Anderson (2013) compared cMOOCs to xMOOCs using his three distance education interaction modes (student-student, student-content, student-teacher). *Via* their extensive use of digitized lectures and machine-scored quizzes, xMOOCs' achieve scalability by "morphing … student-teacher interaction into student-content interaction" (p. 4). He noted that this cognitive-behaviorist approach has been successfully employed by higher education as well as by distance education for decades. In cMOOCs, student-teacher interaction is substituted for student-student interactions. While claiming a course may succeed by relying solely on one mode of interaction, Anderson recommends a balance of all three to achieve high levels of learning. Finally, Kolowich (2014) indicated that MOOC instructors hold a type of superstar status. Such an elevated and inaccessible position may create a very different type of emotional or social engagement than the one convened with a traditional instructor.

DINO 101: DINOSAUR PALEOBIOLOGY

Dino 101, Dinosaur Paleobiology, was developed on the Coursera platform in 2013 by the University of Alberta to provide students from around the world an opportunity to learn from Canadian paleontologist and renowned dinosaur museum curator, Dr. Philip J. Currie. Within the MOOC, there were four distinct groups of students: (1) University of Alberta students enrolled in PALEO 200, who completed the MOOC for credit at the university; (2) University of Alberta students enrolled in PALEO 201, who completed the MOOC plus a weekly face-to-face seminar and laboratory with Dr. Currie; (3) students on the Coursera "signature track" who earned a certificate by completing the 12 quizzes, a midterm, and a final exam; and (4) those on a noncredit track. The course itself consisted of 12 weekly lessons with an estimated workload of 3-5 hours/week for noncredit participants, and 7-10 hours/week for credit. In September 2013, all 12 lessons were released at the start of the course, and although students were encouraged to follow the prescribed timeline, they were free to complete the course at their own pace. The online format consisted of a variety of learning tools, including video lectures that were 3-16 min long with formative quizzes integrated into the videos, as well as other means of learning, such as discussion boards and online student wikis. The topics for the course included dinosaur appearances, anatomy, death, fossilization, eating, movement, birth, growth, reproduction, attacking and defending, evolution, extinction, and geologic time (Chesney, 2013a, 2013b). In its initial offering, Dino 101 attracted more than 23,000 participants from around the world, representing a wide range of ages, educational backgrounds, social economic standards, and so on (Chesney, 2013a, 2013b). Unlike many other MOOCs (Ho et al., 2014), Dino 101 was equally attractive to male and female learners (Chesney, 2013a, 2013b).

DATA SOURCES

The results described herein pertaining to social and emotional engagement in Dino 101 come from two very different sources. First, we obtained quantitative data from 1005 Dino 101 participants who were willing to complete an online survey distributed *via* email. Anyone who registered for Dino 101 could complete the survey regardless of whether they completed the entire course. The sample of 1005 appeared to represent the group well in terms of demographic information. For example, in line with a "getting to know you survey" administered by the course designers (Chesney, 2013a, 2013b), our sample was 50% male, 49% female, 1% undisclosed, the modal age was 25-34, 57% had participated in a MOOC before. In terms of education, 34% of the sample reported having completed an undergraduate degree, 25% a Master's degree, 9% a college diploma, 8% having some undergraduate or college training, 9% having completed high school, and 4% having less than a high school diploma.

Second, we obtained qualitative data *via* phenomenological interviews with 32 Dino 101 "completers." Completers were defined as Dino 101 registrants who either successfully completed the 12 quizzes (noncredit track), or the 12 quizzes, a midterm, and a final exam (credit track). Ten of the completers were campus-based (credit track) University of Alberta students, 10 were Coursera "signature track," and the remaining 12 participated for free. Of the 10 University of Alberta students, 5 took part in PALEO 200; the other 5 were enrolled in PALEO 201. The interviews were 1-1.5 h in length and were held in-person (for University of Alberta students) or *via* an online communications facility (e.g., Skype) since most Dino 101 participants hailed from across the world.

Together the quantitative and qualitative data reveal interesting dynamics of learners' social and emotional engagement in Dino 101. We consider the results from the two data sources together as they pertain to peer-to-peer feelings of engagement; however, each type of data also provides unique information in regard to student outcomes and perspectives on the instructors.

THE LEARNING CLIMATE SHARED WITH OTHER STUDENTS

Hew and Cheung (2014) conclude that student satisfaction in MOOCs is mixed. In our sample, 51% of respondents indicated that they strongly agreed with the statement "I was satisfied with how much I learned in Dino 101"; however, what contributes to students' satisfaction remains a question.

Thus, we aimed to get a sense of students' emotional and social engagement and their expectations as psychological indicators that may contribute to satisfaction. Overall, pleasant emotions dominated unpleasant. For example, 92.5% of participants said that they were not at all upset, 76% were not at all nervous, almost no one reported feeling ashamed (93% not at all), and 71% were not at all bored. In comparison, 72% said they felt quite a bit or extremely inspired, 65% alert, 82% attentive, and 61% enjoyed their time online. Overall, the mean emotional engagement score was 6.23, SD = 0.95 (min score = 1; maximum possible score = 7). From these responses, it seems that Dino 101 represented a largely emotionally pleasant learning environment (Figure 2.1).

In contrast to the emotional climate of Dino 101, respondents were less positive about the social environment. In fact, the most common response to all the items we asked regarding a sense of belonging or collegiality in Dino 101 was "neutral" (or the midpoint of the scale). Most respondents indicated they were neutral to feeling friendship (60%), feeling like part of a team (47%), and remembering their classmates affectionately (59%). This overall trend may also be reflected in the fact that only 16% of respondents expected interacting with other students to contribute to their learning, in comparison to the 77% who expected the videos to be the main source of their learning (i.e., scored above the neutral midpoint). Overall, the mean social engagement score was 3.61, SD = 1.25 (min score = 1; maximum possible score = 7). This was nearly half the rating level of emotional engagement and thus shows us that social engagement was lacking in comparison. One place we would expect to see social engagement in an xMOOC is in the discussion forums offered.

Forum participation: Successful xMOOC students are reported to participate in discussion forums at much higher rates than their noncompleting

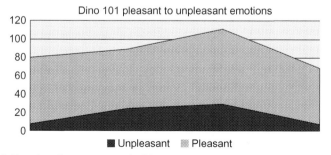

Figure 2.1 Emotional engagement in Dino 101.

counterparts (Breslow et al., 2013; Gillani & Eynon, 2014; Kizilcec, Piech, & Schneider, 2013); however, the overall participation rate on these forums tends to be low. Examining the communication patterns in one xMOOC, Gillani and Eynon (2014) concluded that MOOC learners tend to form crowds, not communities, in discussion forums. Such an analysis suggests that, even among those who contribute to the forums, students may be experiencing qualitatively different forms of social engagement in this context. Only a few of the Dino 101 completers that we interviewed reported that they had contributed to the discussion forums. Some said that they had paid little or no attention to them. One student told us that she was amazed at the depth of the forum discussions, and that she once found herself "spellbound" by a heated argument that had ensued in one of the threads; however, she never ventured a post herself. Another student described feeling overwhelmed by the sheer volume of forum threads, and being deluged daily by email notices of new forum posts.

Lars, a "free Dino 101 student" and grade school teacher who had previously completed five other MOOCs, described spending considerable time trying to locate his own post in a busy forum thread hoping to see if anyone had responded, only to discover that no one had. Over the following week or two, he continued to navigate to his post. Lars also recalled another moment when, while perusing a forum thread about others being inspired to visit local museums, he realized that "this is what MOOCs are really about." While he received no direct response to his own post, Lars nonetheless felt moved by the excitement generated in one of the forum threads.

The quantitative results suggest that overall, the discussion forums did not provide significant opportunities for social engagement, and the qualitative data appears to align with this result; however, the qualitative data showed the discussion forums were a significant source of emotional engagement for some students.

Social engagement at home, together and apart: One unexpected finding from our qualitative interviews was the occurrence of students taking Dino 101 with members of their household, specifically, with a spouse, roommate, or even one's child. Cameron and her partner, both university students, decided to sign up for PALEO 200. She described a moment early on in the course:

I am sitting with my partner in our living room. We decide to login to my account and watch the videos together on the TV. As soon as the first video starts we find the first problem. I want to pause the video, recap what I've just seen, and scribble down a few notes. He doesn't and seems annoyed! We tried to mesh our learning styles together and it just didn't work.

(Cameron, "PALEO 200 student")

On the one hand, taking a MOOC "together" seemed to offer new possibilities for learning: sharing the comfort of one's living room while watching the videos, pausing to discuss key understandings or confusions with one another, keeping one another on task. On the other hand, the couple quickly discovered that each had different ideas and preferences about how best to proceed through the course. So while a MOOC affords new opportunities to learn together locally and globally, it may also present unexpected relational challenges and learning compromises that may sway learners' overall satisfaction.

Effort and satisfaction: In addition to relational challenges and learning compromises, satisfaction and effort may be adjusted in a MOOC environment. Thus we correlated emotional and social engagement with learners' expectations, effort, and satisfaction. Expectations can be considered a precursor to engagement, whereas effort and satisfaction are common outcomes. We highlight five particularly interesting correlations (see Table 2.1). For example, only expectations of interactions with students would contribute to learning was positively related to both emotional and social engagement. In fact, an expectation that videos contribute to learning was negatively related to social engagement. In other words, learners' expectations were linked to the quality of their social and emotional engagement in the course. Learners who expected to learn from videos were uninterested in social engagement, whereas those who approached the course with social expectations benefited in terms of both type of engagement. This is important because both emotional and social engagement were positively correlated with satisfaction and effort. From a practical perspective, this means that as MOOC developers look to create courses that are satisfying and

Table 2.1 Correlation analyses $n = 862$

	1	2	3	4	5
1. Expectation: interacting	–				
2. Expectation: videos	−0.12**	–			
3. Emotional engagement	0.09**	0.14**	–		
4. Social engagement	0.57**	−0.10**	0.22**[l]	–	
5. Satisfaction	0.02	0.17**	0.64**	0.37**	–
6. Effort	0.24**	−0.01	0.19**	0.30**	0.41**

Note: $^*p<0.05$; $^{**}p<0.01$; $^{***}p<0.001$; $^{l}n=924$.

motivate learners to work hard, they need to provide opportunities for social and emotional engagement and attract students with matching expectations.

Expanding upon the correlations, we conducted two regression analyses, one for each of the outcomes: satisfaction and effort. In step 1, we controlled for age and biological sex. In step 2, we entered expectations, and in step 3, we entered emotional and social engagement (Table 2.2). The final model explained 44% of the variance in satisfaction ratings, $F(6, 861) = 115.295$, $p < 0.001$ and 23% of the variance in effort $F(6, 861) = 43.38$, $p < 0.001$. Both age and sex emerged as important predictors, with older students reporting higher levels of satisfaction and effort than younger, and males reporting less satisfaction and effort than females. As foreshadowed by the correlations, expectations that interactions would contribute to learning positively predicted effort and negatively predicted satisfaction—perhaps suggesting that those who expected this did not find it and thus were less satisfied. In contrast, expectations related to the videos positively predicted satisfaction, but not effort—perhaps suggesting the videos were of high quality, but not requiring much effort. Both emotional and social engagement contributed positively to students' satisfaction and effort, although arguably emotional engagement was a more influential predictor.

Together these results support the overarching picture that suggests Dino 101 was a pleasant learning environment, but not necessarily an overly social one, at least among students. It is important to note that the one perspective

Table 2.2 Regression analyses for satisfaction and effort

Predictor variable	Satisfaction			Effort		
	Step 1	Step 2	Step 3	Step 1	Step 2	Step 3
Age	0.05	0.13**	0.13**	0.14**	0.13**	0.17**
Sex (1 = female; 2 = male)	−0.13**	−0.09*	−0.09*	−0.13**	−0.14**	−0.12**
Expectations						
Interactions		0.04	−0.09*		0.25**	0.14*
Videos		0.18**	0.09*		0.04	−0.01
Engagement						
Emotional			0.62**			0.33**
Social			0.10*			0.16**
Adjusted R^2	0.02**	0.05**	0.44**	0.03**	0.09**	0.23**

*$p < 0.01$.
**$p < 0.001$.

lacking from the quantitative results is the relationship between the students and the instructor; however, we were able to some extent capture this perspective in our qualitative data.

A warm, pedagogical sphere or a predetermined script? A previous phenomenological study revealed that some xMOOC students developed an ongoing sense of an intimate, tutorial relationship with their instructor in the context of the teaching videos, even though they were participating in a course with thousands of others (Adams, Yin, Vargas Madriz, & Mullen, 2014). Andy, a "free student" from Europe, described his perceptions of the two main Dino 101 instructors, Philip Currie and Betsy Kruk:

> *In the early days of Dino 101, Dr. Currie, but Betsy especially, talked very quickly— often too quickly—in the videos. Over time though, she started talking at a more natural pace. It helped me to have a sense of relationship with her. They became very human to me, and very warm. I remember thinking, "Oh yeah, she's really getting the hang of this."*

(Andy, "Dino 101 free student")

Over the course of the MOOC, Andy recalled developing a surprisingly warm and "human" connection with both Kruk and Currie. Though initially he was worried about the pace and tempo of the instructors' lectures, he soon acclimatized to their teaching styles; he came to perceive that they, too, were learning, becoming more experienced, relaxed, and able to find "a more natural pace" in their videos. So while xMOOCs may be characterized in the literature as "unidirectional" and lacking significantly in student-instructor interactions, it is possible for students in these massive learning spaces to experience a warm and ongoing connection with their instructor(s).

Other completing students struggled to establish and maintain a connection with the Dino 101 instructors. Anky, a lawyer, found herself initially and occasionally distracted by "Betsy and Dr. Currie, reading a script." She remembered having to push herself past the sense of scriptedness in order to attend to the video. Once she had succeeded, she immediately began the video over to catch what she had missed. Here, the student found it difficult to establish a sense of rapport with an instructor who appeared not to be speaking to her extemporaneously. One might imagine a similar scenario in a film where an actor appears to be reading his or her lines; the viewer is similarly distracted from experiencing the movie itself. Lars recalled a different MOOC where, during one of the video lectures, the instructor made reference to a forum discussion: "From that moment on, I knew he was paying attention to the course, and to us." For him, the Dino 101 videos were missing this palpable sense of "immediacy and instructor engagement" with the goings-on in the MOOC.

A sense of relationship with the instructor also inhered beyond the video lectures. For example, George was impressed by and looked forward to receiving Dr. Currie's weekly emails in his inbox. But another student wondered if the weekly emails were "automated" and written by someone else. In both cases, Dr. Currie has attained a kind of superstar status. For the first student, he appears unexpectedly open and considerate; for the second, the student suspects that like other celebrities, someone else is writing his fan mail.

CONCLUSION

The purpose of this chapter was to bring psychological theory to bear on the notion of engagement in the case of one xMOOC, Dino 101. We focused on emotional and social engagement because of the unique opportunities for MOOCs to support or neglect these specific types of engagement. Overall, it seems that completers had an emotionally pleasant experience in Dino 101. They strongly agree with experiencing a range of pleasant emotions and find following forum posts a source of excitement. It is possible that the pleasant emotional environment is one thing that kept these learners coming back to Dino 101. Or, it may simply be that the content itself provided its own pleasant feelings, bringing students to return out of continued interest. Although these assertions are speculative and neither our quantitative nor qualitative data allow us to make either conclusion with confidence, it intuitively makes sense that students are more likely to return to a pleasant, interesting, or even exciting learning environment than one they perceive as unpleasant. What we can say is that these pleasant emotional experiences were not necessarily associated with similarly high levels of social engagement. We have to wonder if higher levels of social engagement would help improve retention of some learners who are looking for more than a unidirectional learning experience. Both are questions for future research, looking at students who did not complete the course. It is our assertion that improvements within the MOOC environment should look at how they relate to strengthening the four components of engagement (cognitive, behavioral, emotional, and social) either separately or together. Our research suggests that while levels of emotional engagement seem to be rated highly, at least for Dino 101, this same environment does not currently foster a strong sense of social engagement. Whether our intention is to increase the retention rates or improve the learning experience of completers, Dino 101 appears to have room for improvement in terms of social engagement. We recommend focusing on ways to make the discussion forums more interactive and a place for social interactions to support learning. Additionally, it may be useful to consider course assignments or projects that explicitly require social interactions. Finally, improvements in social engagement should not be limited to students, but should also consider ways students can access the instructor. These recommendations may also be applied to other MOOCs being develop and one option for future research is to directly compare MOOCs that intentionally build in opportunities for social engagement to those that are less intention in this area.

REFERENCES

Adams, C., Yin, Y., Vargas Madriz, F. L., & Mullen, C. S. (2014). A phenomenology of learning large: The tutorial sphere of xMOOC video lectures. *Distance Education*, *35*(2), 202–216. http://dx.doi.org/10.1080/01587919.2014.917701.

Anderson, T. (2013). *Promise and/or peril: MOOCs and open and distance education*. Vancouver, British Columbia: Commonwealth of Learning. Retrieved from, http://www.col.org/SiteCollectionDocuments/MOOCsPromisePeril_Anderson.pdf.

Appleton, J. J., Christenson, S. L., & Furlong, M. J. (2008). Student engagement with school: Critical conceptual and methodological issues of the construct. *Psychology in the Schools*, *45*(5), 369–386.

Birch, S., & Ladd, G. (1997). The teacher-child relationship and children's early school adjustment. *Journal of School Psychology*, *35*, 61–79.

Boekarts, M., Pintrich, P. R., & Zeidner, M. (Eds.), (2000). *Handbook of self-regulation: Theory, research and applications*. San Diego, CA: Academic Press.

Breslow, L., Pritchard, D., DeBoer, J., Stump, G., Ho, A., & Seaton, D. (2013). Studying learning in the worldwide classroom: Research into edX's first MOOC. *Research & Practice in Assessment*, *8*, 13–25.

Butler, R. (2012). Striving to connect: Extending an achievement goal approach to teacher motivation to include relational goals for teaching. *Journal of Educational Psychology*, *104*, 726–742. http://dx.doi.org/10.1037/a0028613.

Chesney, J. (2013a). *A look at observation of the implementation of DINO101*. Retrieved from, http://digitallearning.ualberta.ca/digital-learning-at-ualberta/news-and-events/2013/december/mooc-v2-how-dino-101-is-different-and-what-weve-observed-so-far-part2.

Chesney, J. (2013b). *A look at what differentiates Dino 101 from other MOOCs*. Retrieved from, http://digitallearning.ualberta.ca/digital-learning-at-ualberta/news-and-events/2013/december/mooc-v2-how-dino-101-is-different-and-what-weve-observed-so-far-part1.

Clarke, T. (2013). The advance of the MOOCs (massive open online courses): The impending globalization of business education? *Education and Training*, *55*(4/5), 403–413.

Connell, J. P., & Wellborn, J. G. (1991). Competence, autonomy, and relatedness: A motivational analysis of self-system processes. In M. Gunnar & L. A. Sroufe (Eds.), *Minnesota symposium on child psychology:23*. Chicago: University of Chicago Press.

Cusumano, M. A. (2013). Technology strategy and management: Are the costs of 'free' too high in online education. *Communication of the ACM*, *56*(4), 26–29.

Daniels, L. M., & Stupnisky, R. H. (2012). Not that different in theory: A discussion of the control-value theory of emotions in online and face-to-face learning environments. *Internet in Higher Education*, *15*, 222–226.

Deci, E. L., & Ryan, R. M. (2000). The "what" and "why" of goal pursuits: Human needs and the self-determination of behavior. *Psychological Inquiry, 11*(4), 227–268.

Ebben, M., & Murphy, J. S. (2014). Unpacking MOOC scholarly discourse: A review of nascent MOOC scholarship. *Learning, Media and Technology, 39*(3), 328–345.

Eccles, J. S., & Wigfield, A. (2002). Motivational beliefs, values, and goals. *Annual Review Psychology, 53,* 109–132.

Epstein, J. L., & McPartland, J. M. (1976). The concept and measurement of the quality of school life. *American Educational Research Journal, 13,* 15–30.

Finn, J. D. (1993). *School engagement and students at risk.* Washington, DC: National Center for Education Statistics.

Finn, J. D., & Rock, D. A. (1997). Academic success among students at risk for school failure. *Journal of Applied Psychology, 82,* 221–234.

Fredricks, J. A., Blumenfeld, P. C., & Paris, A. H. (2004). School engagement: Potential of the concept, state of the evidence. *Review of Education Research, 74*(1), 59–109.

Furlong, M. J., Whipple, A. D., St. Jean, G., Simental, J., Soliz, A., & Punthuna, S. (2003). Multiple contexts of school engagement: Moving toward a unifying framework for educational research and practice. *California School Psychologist, 8,* 99–114.

Gillani, N., & Eynon, R. (2014). Communication patterns in massively open online courses. *The Internet and Higher Education, 23,* 18–26. http://dx.doi.org/10.1016/j.iheduc.2014.05.004.

Harter, S. (1981). A new self-report scale of intrinsic versus extrinsic motivation in the classroom: Motivational and informational components. *Developmental Psychology, 17,* 300–312.

Hew, K. F., & Cheung, W. S. (2014). Students' and instructors' use of massive open online courses (MOOCs): Motivation and challenges. *Educational Research Review, 12,* 45–58.

Ho, A.D., Reich, J., Nesterko, S., Seaton, D.T., Mullaney, T., Waldo, J., & Chuang, I. (2014). HarvardX and MITx: The first year of open online courses (HarvardX and MITx Working Paper No. 1).

Jacobs, A. J. (2013). Two cheers for Web U! *New York Times, 162*(56113), 1–7.

Karweit, N. (1989). Time and learning: A review. In R. E. Slavin (Ed.), *School and classroom organization* (pp. 69–95). Hillsdale, NJ: Lawrence Erlbaum.

Kizilcec, R. F., Piech, C., & Schneider, E. (2013). Deconstructing disengagement: Analyzing learner subpopulations in massive open online courses. In: D. Suthers, K. Verbert, E. Duval, & X. Ochoa (Eds.), *Proceedings of the third international conference on learning analytics and knowledge* (pp. 170–179). New York, NY: Association for Computing Machinery. http://dx.doi.org/10.1145/2460296.2460330.

Klassen, R. M., Yerdelen, S., & Durken, T. L. (2013). Measuring teacher engagement: Development of the engaged teachers scale (ETS). *Front Learning Research, 1*(2), 33–52.

Kolowich, S. (2014). *Completion rates aren't the best way to judge MOOCs, researchers say.* Northwest, Washington, DC: The Chronicle of Higher Education.

Kop, R., & Hill, A. (2008). Connectivism: Learning theory of the future or vestige of the past? *International Review of Research in Open and Distance Learning, 9*(3). Retrieved from, http://www.irrodl.org/index.php/irrodl/article/view/523/1103.

Liyanagunawardena, T. R., Adams, A. A., & Williams, S. A. (2013). MOOCs: A systematic study of the published literature 2008–2012. *The International. Review of Research in Open and Distance Learning, 14*(3), 202–227.

Nassaji, H., & Swain, M. (2000). A Vygotskian perspective on corrective feedback: The effect of random versus negotiated help on the learning of English articles. *Language Awareness, 9,* 34–51.

Newmann, F., Wehlage, G. G., & Lamborn, S. D. (1992). The significance and sources of student engagement. In F. Newmann (Ed.), *Student engagement and achievement in American secondary schools* (pp. 11–39). New York: Teachers College Press.

Peterson, P., Swing, S., Stark, K., & Wass, G. (1984). Students' cognitions and time on task during mathematics instruction. *American Educational Research Journal, 21*, 487–515.

Rennie, F., & Morrison, T. (2013). *E-learning and social networking handbook: Resources for higher education*. New York: Ruotledge.

Siemens, G. (2004). *Connectivism: A learning theory for the digital age. elearnspace*. http://www.elearnspace.org/Articles/connectivism.htm.

Siemens, G. (2012). *What is the theory that underpins our MOOCs? Blog elearnspace*. Retrieved from, http://www.elearnspace.org/blog/2012/06/03/what-is-the-theory-that-underpinsour-moocs/.

Skinner, E. A., & Belmont, M. J. (1993). Motivation in the classroom: Reciprocal effect of teacher behavior and student engagement across the school year. *Journal of Educational Psychology, 85*, 571–581.

Wehlage, G. G., Rutter, R. A., Smith, G. A., Lesko, N. L., & Fernandez, R. R. (1989). *Reducing the risk: Schools as communities of support*. Philadelphia: Farmer Press.

Yamamoto, K., Thomas, E. C., & Karns, E. A. (1969). School-related attitudes in middle-school-age students. *American Educational Research Journal, 6*, 191–206.

Zimmerman, B. J. (1990). Self-regulated learning and academic achievement: An overview. *Educational Psychologist, 21*, 3–17.

CHAPTER 3

Affect in Online Discourse: The Case of the United Nations Millennial Development Goals Topics

Scott J. Warren, Jenny S. Wakefield
University of North Texas, Denton, TX, USA

We are so spoiled in the U.S., we take clean and healthy water for granted so much—clean water to reduce sickness and disease and clean water in our daily lives. The 2015 Project really opened my eyes and made me aware of how I can help, and also encouraged me to make some small goals for myself to aid in making this world a better place.

Olivia

Critical theorist Michel Foucault (1984) noted in his general evaluation of educational systems that training has been perceived as requiring strict discipline of those subjected to the training by those with administrative power. He posited that this form of power has been used for centuries to mold learners into the types of soldiers and workers the state believes are in its best interest. The central means for state enforcement of preferred norms is testing or examination, and in the United States today, the primary means for enforcing valued knowledge continues to be standardized assessment. As Foucault (1984) concluded, it is this culture of testing that examines the individual so that "he may be described, judged, measured, [and] compared with others, in his very individuality; and it is also the individual who has to be trained or corrected, classified, normalized, excluded, etc. … it functions as a procedure of objectification and subjection" (p. 203).

In much the same fashion, the U.S. educational model is one of transmitting acceptable knowledge; each person emerges with the programming and information necessary to do what is wished by the state, often at the behest of corporations and those with governmental or monetarily

Emotions, Technology, and Learning
http://dx.doi.org/10.1016/B978-0-12-800649-8.00001-8

designated authority. In this way, our educational system produces docile consumers. Here, as in France, Foucault (1984) claimed, "school [is] a sort of apparatus of uninterrupted examination that duplicated along its entire length the operation of teaching … it was woven into it through a constantly repeated ritual of power" (p. 198). These systems of normalizing surveillance, such as the state examination, exercise a form of disciplinary power used to enforce social norms and define what is acceptable knowledge.

Although we encourage our students as instructors to enter into identity formation, to think and discover nature and meaning, and to arrive at knowledge, the central message the system influences—framed by political and economic powers—is one that views students not as individual humans, but as Foucault (1976/1981) called them, individual objects or cases. This generates quiet and attentive students. Viewed from this perspective, the way we determine future success is by testing, because it "is the technique by which power … holds [learners] in a mechanism of objectification … the examination is, as it were, the ceremony of this objectification" (p. 199). It is this objective that, as Freire (1970) correspondingly stated, "attempts to control thinking and action, leads men and women to adjust to the world, and inhibits their creative power" (p. 77).

Educational systems such as those described above become problematic when students move from secondary schools into a university intended to be somewhat emancipatory and freeing. A postsecondary setting transfers control to students: their personal behavior, learning choices, when and where to be, and at what time. More importantly, the university experience teaches that knowledge is changeable and constructed socially or individually; however, because students are trained by the public school system within a power experience to view all knowledge as fixed and testable, when asked to contribute to knowledge construction and confronted with the idea that it is not, they may become rebellious and angry. If our experience is indicative, there may be a visceral emotional response on the part of some learners when this occurs. It is a natural consequence of the system that if students are trained to be passive and comfortable with a teacher's transmission of knowledge, locus of control and related affective problems emerge when that font runs dry. Why should they be discomfited by abstraction and uncertainty?

Learning, however, is not passive receiving; instead, learning is a product of thinking—a messy and complex process coupled with content (Ritchhart, Church, & Morrison, 2011). Learning involves solving problems, making connections, taking action, engaging in interaction, making decisions, and expressing emotions and thoughts—not just restating existing information deemed to be true by those in control of the state. In the process of reaching truth and personal knowledge, learners go through a process of self-discovery, exploring their identity in order to understand what power is and how it situates itself in their consciousness (Moustakas, 1994).

We sought to engage students in communicative acts in an effort to combat the problem of deference to systemic, reified knowledge, and move toward a goal of liberation and engagement of learners through questioning the reality presented to them in the media. As a team of instructors, we wanted to redesign a computer-applications course to challenge the dominating paradigm of acquisition learning. Our redesign focused on a hybrid/online course in computer applications that was intended to foster or deepen student discourses and encourage or promote critical thinking. In this redesigned course, it was necessary for students to learn not only the computer tools, such as word processors, spreadsheets, and databases, but also to apply these tools in both familiar and novel contexts to show transfer. The redesign sought to leverage emancipatory power and teach students by bringing out their subjectivity and individual discovery of the essence of a real-world problematic experience through reflections and peer discussions. As such, the tools were not only for cognition and the challenge of the paradigm, but they were also employed as an expansion of Jonassen's (1996) mindtools—moving students away from learning solely by acquisition or construction to critique established knowledge and the underlying philosophies that lead to them. Further, we felt that understanding the emotional responses of undergraduate students to novel situations that require high levels of self-regulation and reflective learning activities may help us better understand the challenges that accompany innovative learning methods and content.

FRAMEWORK

Edmund Husserl developed what we know as transcendental phenomenology. This is "a scientific study of the appearance of things, of phenomena just as we see them and as they appear to us in consciousness" (Moustakas, 1994, p. 49). Husserl promoted, as Moustakas wrote, a "returning to the self to discover the nature and meaning of things as they appear and in their essence" (1994, p. 26). We do this through acts of reflective attention, looking at a moment that is already past—and in doing so, it allows us to attend to lived experiences and arrive at meaning (Schutz, 1967). According to Solomon (2006), Husserl showed little interest in emotions. Instead, his interest was toward intentionality and meaning; however, one of his students, Max Scheler, picked up on emotions and focused on such emotions as sympathy, love, hate, pity, kindness, generosity, and resentment. Scheler held that our "primary awareness of the world consists of our emotional responses" (Solomon, 2006, p. 416). But emotions are more than simply responses to the world. They are results of special experiences or situations in our lives that have meaning to us.

Plutchik (2001) explained that "emotion is a complex chain of loosely connected events that begins with a stimulus and includes feelings, psychological changes, impulses to action, and specific, goal-oriented behavior" (pp. 345-346) and that this emotional state was set into effect to develop "interaction between the individual and the event or stimulus" (p. 346) that caused the emotion, such as protecting offspring in various ways from imminent danger. As an example, Plutchik wrote that Darwin suggested emotions evolved basically to increase the likelihood of survival. In conjunction with the idea that knowledge comes from communicative acts and individual intentional meaning-making—such as when we experience the world around us and think critically—it is likely that we respond to the world and to lived experiences with emotional states (Wakefield, Warren, & Alsobrook, 2011). The course design of *The 2015 Project* was thus developed not only to teach technology tools, theory, and technology history, but also to elicit emotional student responses that stem from interaction with local, personal narratives tied to the United Nations Millennial Development (UNMD) goals.[1]

Course Design

When there is something important and worthwhile to think about and a reason to think deeply, our students experience the kind of learning that has a lasting impact and powerful influence not only in the short term but also in the long haul. They not only learn, they learn how to learn.

Ritchhart et al. (2011, p. 26).

---

[1] The eight United Nations Millennial Development goals are: (1) eradicate extreme poverty and hunger; (2) achieve universal primary education; (3) promote gender equality and empower women; (4) reduce child mortality; (5) improve maternal health; (6) combat HIV/AIDS, malaria, and other diseases; (7) ensure environmental sustainability; and (8) develop global partnerships (http://www.un.org/millenniumgoals/).

Our course centered upon the use of technology tools as supports for communicating and understanding global problems in the form of two UNMD goals: combating HIV/AIDS and environmental sustainability. The learning took place over five main platforms: (1) the Schoology and (2) Blackboard learning management systems (LMS); (3) an open-source content management system (CMS) that held *The 2015 Project* activities and transmedia navigation experiences; WordPress blogs; and the MyITLab LMS that students used for simulation exercises when learning about the technology applications Microsoft Word, Excel, Access, and PowerPoint.

The Schoology LMS held the weekly instructional course materials. Blackboard held multiple-choice exams and grades. The CMS was set up on an Apache Internet server, chosen because it allowed for posting of links, images, discussions, and searches using a forum format that Blackboard was unable to mirror. On the CMS homepage, students were greeted by messages about current events and article links related to the two topics, HIV/AIDS and environmental sustainability. When logged in using a password they had selected in the CMS website sign-up process, students were able to access the discussion forums, read, and contribute posts containing links, video, and audio. Two different forum channels were represented by the two topics that were discussed, and activities required students to crisscross various technology platforms, including YouTube, email, Twitter, blogs, and other common online means of communication. To seek supporting narratives, students engaged in transmedia navigation—a form of distributed travel across the Internet—rather than a single system. For the CMS activities, students were asked to seek evidence not only for the individual claims presented in the shared news articles, but also to find counterarguments or support for their peers' statements relating to the UN goals while further attempting to construct possible solutions to these global problems. One assignment looked like this:

> Visit The 2015 Project *site http://2015.thinktanktwo.info/ and read what is posted on the home page. The articles relate to current real world issues. Share at least one new thing you have learned about the goal you have chosen to focus on by posting an individual post in the CMS. Find two peer posts of your interest and respond to the posts.*

By situating students in real-world troubles, actively engaging them in technology tools, and taking the focus away from learning decontextualized technology skills, it was believed that students would be given reasons to learn the technology skills, which should result in improved transfer to future work by situating the experience (Cobb, Confrey, diSessa, Lehrer, & Schauble, 2003).

The instructors through scaffolding, learning discourses, and accompanying reflection activities supported this embodied experience.

Students in *The 2015 Project* were guided to discuss with peers topics with global implications from their own perspectives and find possible solutions to these problems, a form of knowledge construction. Instructors acted as facilitators in the thinking process by participating in the ongoing dialog, modeling what is meant with connection making. In the past, it was common that students reflected upon the topic and then ended their post with a question without trying to search for an answer, or simply completed the assignment without interest to return and further respond to peer posts. The instructors tried to bring students back to the forum by pointing to research studies, which held answers to the question or extended on the topic. Such modeling, it was hoped, would spur a dialog where the topic was extended past the surface level. It was set into place so that students would see beyond obvious, superficial responses, and engage more deeply in problem solving (Ritchhart et al., 2011).

We asked students to critique the approaches that different societies were taking to reach the UNMD goals by the target year 2015. Answers to these bigger questions were expected to emerge from discourses among peers as they argued local, national, and global relations among cultures, governments, and economies that contribute to the identified, complex, and worldwide problems. McGonigal and Eklund took a similar approach with the transmedia experience *World Without Oil* (as explained in Warren, Dondlinger, McLeod, & Bigenho, 2011).

During the first weeks of the course, student coursework focused upon rudimentary self-regulation skills while reading several chapters from their course book. The chapters exposed students to computer-literacy concepts including hardware, software, multimedia, ethics, and communication concepts; however, beginning in week four, *The 2015 Project* started, requiring students to develop solutions to weekly real-world challenges. The thought was to establish social and political norms that students were expected to critique and question through constative communicative acts. This included stories related to global problems that had affected communities in the United States in the same way they do in other countries but without the resources the United States has to tackle such problems.

WordPress blogs used for open reflection allowed students to focus upon the world of technology in general, as well as personal growth and understanding of the various technology tools and applications. We foresaw that the design would foster liberating student reflections and encourage public speech acts. We were hopeful that this would guide students away from system-entrenched thinking and provide them practice using the computer software and tools they were learning about in the course.

Course Goals:

- Communicate effectively using standard business technology tools
- Communicate effectively to create a product using the computer literacy tools Word, Excel, Access, and PowerPoint
- Understand how the tools relate to current and future work
- Learn to reflect on problem solving and come to understand how deep thinking works to solve problems
- Generate an effective solution to a global problem
- Show knowledge of, and skills with, technology applications, and work independently and collaboratively in order to solve a particular global problem

METHOD

Participants

Fifty-six undergraduate students from four course sections participated in the CMS forum discussions. They self-selected to include 28 students engaged in discussing the millennial topic HIV/AIDS and 28 discussing the topic environmental sustainability. Students were undergraduates at a southwestern university ranging from freshmen to seniors. Each studied basic computer applications and Internet tools. A gender balance was sought for the groups, but was not possible, due to self-selection. Prior to analysis, students were given pseudonyms to protect their identity.

The 2015 Assignment

The discussion component in *The 2015 Project* required students to visit its associated CMS website every week for 6 weeks (weeks 4-10 of a 16-week course) and read weekly, real-life, emergent stories related to either environmental sustainability or HIV/AIDS. After reading the news stories, students were asked to post to the CMS a critique (providing an argument for, against, or both). They were also asked to find two peer posts of interest and argue these posts.

To aid them in understanding what an argument is, the following definition was given.

Arguments are not fights or debates. They do not contain anger. The definition for "argument" according to Ramage, Bean, and Johnson (2010) was used and explained as follows: An argument: (1) requires the writer or speaker to justify their claims; (2) is both a product and a process; and (3) contains elements of truth-seeking and persuasion. Since the assignment was about student discovery and knowledge creation, the four-course section instructors participated only to spur additional thinking (i.e., encouraged students to think deeply about the topics by further posting story-related and relevant materials to the CMS).

An example of a discussion thread where the instructor interjected included the instructor posting the video *The Story of Bottled Water*[2] within the environmental sustainability goal thread in order to challenge thinking by exposing students to alternative information on concepts about which they had already formed opinions. In this case, students were first asked to watch a short video about bottled water, plastic water bottle waste, and bottle waste maintenance. They then reflected upon the video, which sparked an in-depth discussion. Their emotional responses resulted in discussion of proposing a campus-wide awareness campaign to battle water bottle waste.

In other instances, students were asked to respond to truth claims made in media postings (the posted newspaper stories) and engage in critique using the social media and productivity tools to support their efforts. For example, after reading and discussing progress toward safe drinking water around the world, given the UNMD goals target year 2015, students were asked to use UN reports to learn about progress in three countries of their choice, extract data from the reports, and manipulate the data in Excel to generate visual progress (i.e., tables and graphs). The focus of the tool usage was on cognitive support instead of skills development; we sought to help students understand how they could use the technology to support a learning process involving analysis and synthesis of concepts, rather than as a means of simple delivery of content for memorization and later assessment.

Data Analysis
In reviewing and analyzing the discussion postings, we turned to Herring (2004) and her method of using computer-mediated discourse analysis (CMDA). Herring noted that text-based communication can take many forms, and proposed discussion groups are one such form. CMDA may

[2] http://youtu.be/Se12y9hSOM0.

be used as a methodology for analysis of either qualitative or quantitative analysis of text-based language.

In our study, we used quantitative means to analyze the discussions that students had on the CMS forum, but also included a qualitative component where we analyzed the posts for expressed emotions. With such a high number of posts, we chose to analyze only discussion threads that held a minimum of four interactions to call it a meaningful discussion. The final number of discussion threads included in the analysis was 14 HIV/AIDS threads (84 discussion posts) and 18 environmental sustainability threads (114 discussion posts).

In CMDA, initially, text instances are coded and counted; thereafter, frequency summaries are calculated (Herring, 2004). Meaning is then extracted from frequency counts and correspondence with student utterances in the corpus. Our threads were sorted and organized into two Excel spreadsheets with one for each of the UN goals discussed. The researchers developed a system for analyzing the posts using codes and tally marks. Working through a number of posts generated the initial codes. The two researchers then reviewed students' reflective posts individually and marked them with tally marks in the spreadsheets. New codes were discussed and added as deemed appropriate throughout the coding process. The researchers later sat together to review and discuss the completed coding to reach unanimous agreement, and identify categories and shared emotional meaning from the data.

Posts could be sorted into more than one code, depending upon content. From the codes, the researchers discarded those with codes that held five or fewer tally marks. Final tallied codes from the two UN goal discussions were then counted and placed into 14 broad categories (number of tally marks in parentheses): article support (45), broad claim (42), affective expression (93), initiator call for action (19), acceptance of claims with added call for action (34), acceptance of claim with weak call for action (82), acceptance of claim without call for action (38), reply–agreement with support (75), reply–agreement surface level (64), questions (34), fills assignment only (6), instructor-facilitated discourse (24), expressed awareness (43), and initiator returns to discourse (6).

Analytical Focus

This study had two purposes. First, it was to capture students' informed critiques of culpable social systems involved in the presented UN problems. These were expected to result from their reading of news articles, researching the topics, and thinking about how different societies approach and try reach the UN goals by 2015. The second purpose was to capture the emotions that may have been expressed in the posts when they learned about these real-world issues and became conscious of the world as it stands before them. The following themes emerged from their underlying categories:

- Theme 1: Affect, emotions, and awareness expressions
    - Three categories: affective (including emotions); expressed awareness; and initiator call for action
- Theme 2: Acceptance
    - Three categories: acceptance of claim with call for action; acceptance of claim with weak call for action; acceptance of claim without call for action
- Theme 3: Agreement and questioning
    - Five categories: article support; agreement with support; agreement surface-level; questions statements/asks; initiator returns to discourse

DISCUSSION

Our analysis resulted in categories that were then merged to three themes. The themes included affect, emotions, and awareness expressions; acceptance; and agreement and questioning. The following sections provide a discussion of these themes and examples from student posts.

Theme 1: Affect, Emotions, and Awareness Expressions

The first theme includes the categories we identified as:

- Affective (including emotions)
- Expressed awareness
- Initiator call for action

Tomkins (1980) stated that "the affect system provides the primary blueprint for cognition, decision, and action" and that "humans are responsive to whatever circumstances activate positive or negative affect" (p. 142). Within these discussion topics of HIV/AIDS and environmental sustainability, our learners responded with positive and negative statements of concern and care. They were both eager to help solve larger problems presented, but also were frustrated about their inability to do so—at least not by the UNMD goal deadline of 2015.

In one example of this type of affective expression related to reversing the spread of HIV/AIDS, Audrey shared on a positive note: "This goal is very realistic if people can take it seriously. I do feel by 2015 the reverse of

HIV/AIDS can happen and there will be fewer people who die from this disease compared to how many are now." However, Sheila shared a more pessimistic and apprehensive note:

> I don't think that the reversal of AIDs is possible; the virus is already out there. All we can do now is educate to prevent new cases of HIV/AIDS. If no one else gets the virus, then after people who have had it pass on then the issue of HIV/AIDS will be gone. This will not be by 2015.

Both students shared their awareness and a deeper understanding of the larger problem, but from different perspectives. Plutchik (2001) noted that emotions have opposite poles. The two posts above illustrate how through online constative communicative acts, those in which there is disagreement—both the positive and negative affect—often emerge in student utterances.

Another example is a post by Princess, an African-American, who was engaged in the topic on how HIV racial disparity grows. For her, the awareness was heightened to the extent that she became uneasy by the reality that she was reading about. She shared:

> … being African American, this really interested me. The article states that Blacks are being affected more than any other racial/ethnic group and the statistics are disturbing. I think HIV/AIDS awareness and prevention should really be pursued and pushed more than ever, especially in the Black community, which it affects the most. I think some things that might help in the awareness and prevention process are knowing if their partners are infected and better and more frequent health care.

Evident here is a point unnoticed by other students. She recognized the challenge of race in the context of seeking solutions and increasing visibility of the multifaceted nature of the problem, which was presented in the transmedia experience—not at a microlevel, but from a more global perspective. An instructor asked Princess how she would address this problem in the context of a friend who shared that she was having unprotected sex. When answering, Princess expressed trepidation and care for her friend. She responded:

> I would STRONGLY (sic) discourage it! I would stress the harms (and there are so many) of having unprotected sex: the possibility of contracting an STD or HIV/AIDS, and the possibility of becoming impregnated, etc. Unless my friend is married and in a committed relationship with her partner (knowing her partner's health status), I wouldn't condone it at all.

Her response was in keeping with much of the literature provided by the course, giving additional perspective on her personal view of premarital sex and safe behaviors.

Sara, another student, in her summary of *The 2015 Project* experience toward the end of the semester, wrote:

> Until doing research for this project, I had not thought about how our own economic crisis might have fallen back on others' in our world, and honestly, I was pretty self-centered and unconcerned with what was going on in the world around me.

Evinced in this passage is a reflection on her standing in relation to the 2015 UNMD goals. Sara's newfound awareness of her self-centered worldview was typical of coded utterances made by many students as they concluded their coursework. While emotions of surprise and disappointment were common, like Sara, they were generally followed by utterances commonly associated with newfound sympathy for people in similar situations—not only in local settings, but also in larger, global contexts, initiated through their recent awareness. Their sympathy became more evident in the solutions that students offered to deal with large, ill-structured problems to combat HIV/AIDS and improve environmental sustainability. In doing so, the cognitive and emotional distance was reduced between the learner and those they were asked to help in the context of the transmedia experience.

These shared emotions were matched with discussions in the CMS forum to determine if they were influential in helping to promote emancipatory discourses. In particular, the designers hoped—but did not expect—that the exposure to global problems that were moved to local settings would connect a sense of realism. The emotions that would then emerge, while we did not know how, would help students engage in some form of metacognitive reflection that could shift their epistemic view of power and relationships, and highlight how such views might affect some change in view, if not behavior.

Several students reported that their discursive interactions in the class forums helped them to better understand how emotion and systems of power affected their current and future learning and gave them an awareness of the larger issues. Combined with their reflections on the topical prompts the curriculum presented, the peer interactions and readings allowed students to develop a representation of the learning phenomena they experienced during the project. This allowed them to change their personal views. In their reflections, students noted how they projected that the learning and research they had conducted on the UNMD goals would impact their lifeworld outside of school and how it may influence their future learning experiences. The data revealed a substantial number of findings (142 codes) related to student affect and expressions of awareness, our first theme. Words such as "help," "cure," "treatment," "education," and "needs" illustrate this first theme (see Figure 3.1).

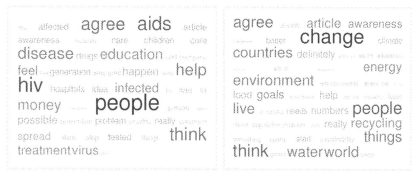

Figure 3.1 Tag clouds for HIV/AID (left) and environmental sustainability (right).

Theme 2: Acceptance

The second theme of acceptance included several broader categories:

- Acceptance of claim with call for action
- Acceptance of claim with weak call for action
- Acceptance of claim without call for action

For many students, UNMD's HIV/AIDS and environmental sustainability goals were new territories to explore. As Plutchik (1980) noted, such in-depth exploration of new territories generates feelings of anticipation. As an example, this became evident when students discussed the topic of wildfires[3] in a thread where Josh initially summarized the contents of the article:

More data on how mankind is affecting the environment. In the article about more catastrophic fires, scientists point to fire suppression as one of the causes for catastrophic wildfires. Naturally-occurring wildfires actually work toward depleting the environment of combustible material. When these fires are suppressed, the environment has an abundance of combustible material. Coupled with the drought many states have experienced, this has resulted in huge fires that have burned hundreds of thousands of acres. Scientists believe that new policies need to be considered to allow normal wildfires to happen by studying existing records on charcoal deposits in lakebed sediments, which established a baseline of fire activity.

However, while the summary was accurate, it lacked analysis leading to any call for action. Jennifer then picked up on Josh's synopsis and responded with hope and further offered a weak call for action:

I can see how letting these fires occur naturally could clear out material that is prone to catching fire, but I also understand the damage and devastation that wildfires have caused families and their homes. The concern for people's (sic) lives being at risk is definitely high when considering just letting these fires occur, but if

[3] http://www.pnas.org/content/109/9/E535.full.

there is a way to control them in a way that would eliminate the dangers for people and frequency of the fires, then I think it is absolutely worth considering.

The weakness in her statement stemmed from her doubt that there was a way to control the fires. She did not attempt to explore ways that this could take place. James responded to her post and explained the situation through a mere acceptance statement by sharing the reality as he saw it:

Part of the problem is that humans are building homesteads in areas that are naturally prone to wildfires, much like people who move into marshy areas and then drain the water, which causes an environmental imbalance for the plants and animals that reside in the marshes.

He then shared from his experience, which led to an implied call for action, one tinged with expectancy (i.e., acceptance of the situation if nothing was done):

When I first moved into my neighborhood, it was not uncommon to see a herd of deer in my front yard. After a heavy rain, I had to be on the lookout for rattlesnakes in the trees! Luckily, my neighborhood is built on a bluff and not over the aquifer, which some of the neighborhoods are starting to build on. [My city] may have more water problems in the future if we pave over the aquifer.

Beyond summarizing his concrete and illuminative experience, James transferred the academic content and problem to a real-world, local challenge. His doing so provided peers not only with his apprehensive emotional response, but also served as an example for others to follow as they struggled to synthesize the problem to their own micro- and meso-level contexts.

Intersubjective Acceptance

Another thread related to affective agreements was taken from the beginning of the discussion weeks when students showed signs of developing deep and holistic acceptance in a discussion of environmental sustainability. They saw the problems, accepted that there were ways to alleviate them, and that joining forces would be necessary. For example, John noted:

I have been reading over a lot of people's posts and I have to say I agree with most of them. We have the same outlook on a lot of the issues (sic). A few people state if more people could get involved and help out, we probably could meet this 2015 goal and few think it's (sic) not possible. I understand both views but I have to say I'm more for the ones that say if more get involved, we could reach it.

Up to this point, the majority of the discussion had focused on the negative aspects of the size and scope of the problem. Each response was nonresponsive to the others who had posted. Here, John summarized the discussion as it stood then. Effectively, the group was broken into two camps of acceptance over the situation: the hopeful and those who despaired that the goal was out of reach. Again, we saw Plutchik's (2001) two emotional poles emerge. Based upon these poles, the hopeful group noted that the common outlook was a wish for more people to get involved to work toward the greater goal. That is, the larger the group who could be assembled toward solving the UNMD goal challenge, the more interest and motivation there would be toward solving problems, and the effort would facilitate a sense of general empowerment and action toward this greater good.

Further, the latter group's negative outlook led to apathy—an acceptance of the current state of the world and their role within it. Judy studied information she had gleaned from the course resources, including then current news articles, and concurred with John's positive outlook. She said:

I agree with your outlook. The more exposure to this issue of people living in slum dwellings and throughout the world, the more people are likely to be involved. Not only are countries becoming involved, but (also) private companies are starting to have their own separate goals on how to decrease poverty around the world. I am hopeful that the 2015 goal is obtainable and is just the beginning in decreasing global poverty.

Judy specifically mentioned that she is hopeful as a result of her acquisition of this new knowledge taken from primary sources she sought, spurred by course requirements. As with John, she concurred with the idea that broad alliances are more effective at solving problems. She identified different groups currently involved in seeking solutions to poverty. These ranged from governmental to private interests. While still only presenting an acceptance with a weak call for action, she added to her own positive outlook.

The aforementioned assertion spurred both positive and negative emotions in Robert. He accepted Judy's claim and her call for action and penned his own acceptance and another weak call for action. He noted:

Agreed. For a global issue to truly be solved, it has to be done 'globally'. Not just one company or one country making a push for it, but many joining together in order to accomplish this goal. Is it attainable? Yes. But, in order to do so drastic changes and efforts must come about and they must do it soon.

Here, Robert notes both a concurrent hopefulness in line with John and Judy, but also apprehension that could lead to later despair. Eric continued the discussion and shared the assertion that large groups working in concert are necessary to overcome the huge challenge, but he had no overarching idea of how this will come about. Regardless, in his post, he is hopeful, but also somewhat frustrated.

> Definitely agree here. As cliché (sic) as it sounds, it will take everyone working together and making drastic changes and sacrifices, but it is certainly an attainable goal. Most of the reason things are the way they are right now is [such as the economy resulted from a] collaborative effort on everyone's part. Several divided factions have attempted to tackle this goal individually with moderate success. But in order to truly reach the goal, it will take effort on most everyone's part. It can certainly be done.

Abby appears influenced by the above discourse and noted the need for group action as a centerpiece for addressing the global problem. Her enthusiasm, however, was tempered by a worry that a solution was unattainable without group action. Her post was one of acceptance and a weak call for action.

> I agree with all of you. It takes one person to think or come up with a plan to do better, but it takes people coming together to turn the plan into an action that may have a positive impact!

Finally, Ashley was interested in a global, governmental approach to address poverty.

> I definitely agree that if we could all pitch in, we could make a difference. I wonder if the economies around the world would improve if governments spent money and time creating programs to help impoverished countries. If enough people are interested, there could be tons of new jobs working to help people who need it, while putting more jobs out there and money into people's pockets.

Her use of the word "if" in this set of utterances is an important one. Throughout this discussion, students were worried that without a joint effort of large organizations ranging from governmental to corporate, that the problem was too large to be affected by individuals. The refrain from our hopeful students was that large problems could be addressed if people were willing to work together to do so. Without this alignment, an underlying note of despair was present.

Accepting the Lesson

Like many other students, Mason submitted to acceptance of what he had learned. In his end–of–project summary, he wrote:

> I learned through research for this project that there is some effort on everyone's part in awareness of the issue that a great change can be made in lives of the less

fortunate…. I was educated on the fact that many people are actually leading toward their own demise just because they are not properly educated about the detriment of their practice of open defecation upon their environment and the people within it.

Although Mason did not share a call for action, he, like several others, did not stop his reflection with himself. Instead, he stepped outside the box to see his thinking as a means of service to others, a habit we hope to foster in future designs.

Theme 3: Agreement and Questioning

The third theme included the categories:

○ Article support
○ Agreement with support
○ Agreement surface-level
○ Questions statements/asks
○ Initiator returns to discourse

Throughout this project, we sought to increase student exposure to content, questions, and discussions that would drive them to be freer thinkers; however, our analysis revealed that missing from the conversations was the students' broader calls to action for what they should do. Students often expressed that "something" should be done, or "the *government* [emphasis added] should…." We interpreted this as a feeling that all action must be taken within the existing power structure system; however, students believed that they had no real power to do so. They may have expressed sadness at the state of things and for those affected by a situation, but had little to no ability to move beyond a statement of emotion toward a plan of action.

Learning, however, comes from engaging with the material, asking questions, and discoursing with peers and instructors. Reading about sustainable development,[4] two students asked questions. Louise postured:

How the hell do we get there? In one article assigned this week, 'Seizing Sustainable Development,' I found this information both surprising and startling. 'By 2030, as the human population swells and appetites increase, the world will need at least 50% more food, 45% more energy, and 30% more water. Our planet is approaching, and even exceeding, scientific tipping points.' I understand it's hard to change and that change takes time but it's even harder to reverse something once it has

---

[4] https://www.project-syndicate.org/commentary/seizing-sustainable-development.

already come to pass. How do we make the changes and will we do it before it's too late? Impertinent (sic) questions that need to be answered. Also, and maybe most importantly, what can we do to stop the fighting and start the embracing of sustainability?

Later in the discussion, Louise returned to provide affective expressions of hope, a call for action, and to ask and answer additional questions:

There are, of course, many small steps that we could take. We can recycle, we can buy less stuff, reuse the stuff we have; we can grow our own vegetables, we can find jobs in town or move to where we work, etc. It will take even more than all of these things combined though. This is not some hippie revolution, or political debate, UNMDG goal 7 is just one in 8 different goals that seem to be far from accomplished.

Louise provided some solutions while identifying the core challenge stemming from the complexity, size, and scope of the UNMD goals. She arrived at some important conclusions and proposals to overcome through educational experiences, but also recognized the limits of her understanding. She went on to say:

How can we strengthen the cause? Education. Education and a shift in worldviews. How do we get children out of slums and clean water to the world? I don't really know the answer to that. Hope, maybe, definitely hard work, and a back-to-the-basics-approach.

To educate people about the issues was a common agreement by students toward solving the problems. Education, it was believed, would lead to knowledge, and through knowledge, solutions would emerge. For example, in the area of HIV/AIDS, Leena noted:

I'm pretty much in the same boat as you with knowledge about HIV/AIDS. I have, however, heard that the death is not always painful depending on how the virus was dealt with through the duration of it. I am also very much interested in it because there's no cure. It really saddens me that the virus continues to be passed down from generation to generation.

As a result of the transmedia experience, Leena indicated she thought more deeply about the issue than previously, but failed to go further and learn or suggest more. Instead, she was content to lean on anecdote and poor memory rather than research and evidence. A fleeting interest without effort is insufficient to move students toward emancipation, spurred by an emotional response to the huge problem placed before them.

It was clear through students' agreements that our learners believed that someone other than they themselves should take action, indicating that they felt a lack of power to take action or even to suggest action. Emma wrote:

> *…there is evidence that improvements have been made, although they are minute compared to the changes that must be made to make a great impact…. I think we could raise awareness on campus of this issue by starting an organization with the goal of boycotting the sale of bottled water in exchange for using the filtered water fountains on campus, less people would buy water bottles, and we could donate the money toward the cause of helping other countries realize their goals of obtaining clean and safe drinking water …*

This post was typical of student responses in this vein. They were often at a loss to suggest complete solutions or share ideas; however, they expressed (and agreed with each other on this) that they hoped something would be done, especially locally, rather than expressing real interest to engage in acts as individuals. Instead, they noted the lack of collaboration by others, such as governments and global political organizations, but failed to see their own role to encourage or mitigate the problem. In this case, the emotion tied to the activities never reached a level sufficient for our learners to feel empowered to act upon the problem. They sought easy solutions implemented by others in which they could participate without having to take executive actions of their own. The example below is from the second largest category we identified, Acceptance of claim with weak call for action, but she agrees with the other students. Mary believed:

> *I think to have an idea and want to stop HIV/AIDS by 2015 is amazing. But like many people have already said, there needs to be an actual plan and steps to achieving this goal. Then after they have come up with those, it needs to be carried out. I also would like to see more on this and to see what the plan for the next steps will be. I hope that someday we will be able to reach this [goal of eliminating HIV/ AIDS by 2015].*

Again, this student acknowledged a need for both a plan of action and an action to take place; however, rather than the offer of a solution, the student's proposal was not to take personal action, but rather a wish to "see more on this" by some amorphous, nonspecific person, who should develop a plan of action.

When students proposed solutions, they were expressed as vague notions that "something" should be done, or "the government should…." Despite acknowledgment of a problem that needs action, students placed the agency for change outside themselves, agreed with each other, and failed to understand any need for personal action outside the existing systems (e.g., school, federal government). Yet, in other cases, students began to understand the complexity and intractability of the global problem they encountered and realized that there was no simple solution. Marcy wrote:

> I think it is just a lot of different things that cause our generation to be where they are. There is also not an easy solution to this problem. We just have to try to edu-cate people and help them with resources and whatnot. I am sure there are many other things that we can do to help; it just depends on the place we are trying to help (italics added).

While students acknowledged a lack of simple solutions, they suggested the obvious—improvement through education. Further, they indirectly acknowledged that they neither understood the problem well nor sought other possible solutions. It was apparent that it was sufficient to simply acquire knowledge that the problem exists and needs to be addressed. This is perhaps a nod to American educational standards that are focused on knowledge acquisition without adequate ability to understand or synthesize it into something upon which they can act.

In another case, one student acknowledged that while the problem was large and difficult, and perhaps impossible to truly tackle completely, there was a need to improve knowledge among the larger populace. Tanya shared:

> I totally agree with you, Anna! We can't control Mother Nature at all; she does what she wants, obviously. But we can definitely still educate and create awareness of this ever-growing issue. It will be a challenge to correct, but every little change towards the better can eventually lead to a more sustainable environment.

Positive, though passive, awareness–agreement on the part of this student was unlikely to lead to personal action by Tanya or any others who responded likewise. Other learners similarly put forward their agreement with peers about the need to do something, but more support was offered for their claims in terms of how the world (not them) can or should address these problems, without any personal action described.

Within the third theme, we found posts of agreement and surface-level engagement. Significant words (Figure 3.1) included "something," "some-one," and "possible," which indicated optimism, possibilities, and hope that someone should do something; however, that someone was not them.

General Remarks on the Analysis

We found that this type of seeking and sharing of evidence in support of posts on the CMS helped to promote emancipatory discourse in the sense that students expressed their awareness of important worldwide issues. Students reported that the discursive interactions they had in the discussion forums helped them to better understand how emotions and systems of power affected their current and future learning. Then, combined with their own reflections on the topical prompts the curriculum presented, students were able to develop a representation of the learning phenomena they experienced during the project.

The representation of *The 2015 Project* helped learners frame feelings about their perceived reality in the context of how power was experienced not only by themselves, but also by those they more closely identify with as fellow Americans with common experiences. The context for global problems was shifted to simulate fictional experiences of Americans more like themselves (e.g., common language, cities they lived in or have visited). Through this experience, students were exposed to global problems facing people in impoverished environments and asked to work toward a goal of helping illuminate the distortions present in regular human communication. Often, a result of the use of technologies, as extended from Habermas (1970) critique, is that systems, which include computer-mediated communications, tend to distort human communication (Feenberg, 1996). This commonly occurs due to linguistic imperfections inherent in inadequate tools, such as asynchronous forums meant to recreate in-person discourses. The challenge to be understood, tell the truth, and other language goals upon which we contend that online teaching and learning rely emerge (Warren, Wakefield, & Mills, 2013). The idea of enframing and revealing, especially as we sought to do here with the emotional utterances of student discussants, was put forth by Martin Heidegger (1977) and is defined as:

> Enframing is the gathering together that belongs to that setting-upon which sets upon man and puts him in position to reveal the real, in the mode of ordering, as standing-reserve… The essence of modern technology lies in enframing. Enframing belongs within the destining of revealing (pp. 12-13).

Although Heidegger was more concerned with moods than emotions, his concept of technology as a tool to help us further analyze *The 2015 Project* as a technological system and its impact on the emotional states of learners is, as we see it, an important one. In the context of this study, we leveraged the transmedia experience as a form of technology to enframe learning. We understand that technology has an impact on what is revealed or hidden in our analysis of outcomes. As such, there is the caveat that we only know what has been told to us and that the technology is likely deforming the meaning and possibly the intent of the discussant as they put fingers to keys. Our ability to comprehend from computer-mediated discourse is proportional to the skills of the communicator.

A Role for Technology to Support Discussions Tied to Emotion

Technology can support multiple forms of emancipation for learners through its ability to connect those over long distances and an associated, free sharing of knowledge in online settings. In the context of *The 2015 Project*, discourses were encouraged to help learners understand the world as it is—that is, in the context of the evidence, simulated or not, that students encountered. These discourses allowed students to break down the distortions surrounding an understanding of how our educational system restricts their freedom to see and discuss large, intractable problems of the world as depicted in the UNMD goals. These are difficult challenges that students are usually shielded from because they live in the United States.

Such discourse is expected to help free people from institutional forces that limit their personal control by "framing" a vision of the world as it is now, with some of the cultural and political blinders removed (Habermas, 1974); however, the limits and possibilities have long been perceived as beyond our control to change, which leads to feelings of despair and disempowerment.

As we do today, Habermas and McCarthy (1987) recognized the increasing dominance of economic and political institutions in the lived experiences of individuals. They therefore called for increased emancipatory discourses intended to help restore some sense of the individual. These discourses could restore freedom to act or to understand the ways in which we are not free; and this liberation could lead to a reduction of despair in the face of large, global problems and increased hopefulness in individuals who feel empowered to act.

CONCLUSION

Our chapter informed students' reflections and emotions around real-world topics presented for weekly discussions in an undergraduate course. Students discussed environmental sustainability and HIV/AIDS and created individual assignments using the applications they were learning, including Word, Excel, Access, and PowerPoint. The real world-topics contributed to increased critical thinking among students and stirred deep emotions about issues that many of them had not considered.

In general, we found that initially students met the basic requirements of the assignment through surface-level reflections and minimal responses on required topics. Their demands for general action included little planning and no personal agency on their part; however, some topics elicited deeper thinking. As students progressed through the activities, their responses gained additional depth, although they still displayed a lack of empowerment to solve problems collaboratively or on their own. They expressed emotions related to feelings of awareness, unease, acceptance, agreement, and in some cases, hopelessness and despair. In many instances, students did not know what they could do to contribute to solutions of large problems, such as those the UNMD goals provided. Some students did try to find solutions, such as when Erica wrote: "If we could come up with a way to educate those we are trying to help… this practice is detrimental to their health and causes many other problems they are facing…".

Freshwater and Robertson (2002) noted that in psychotherapy, the growth of social self includes imminent development of emotions—such as when people who come in contact with distress feel uncomfortable but also "feel better" about themselves as they recognize the emotion. Similarly, through learning about the UNMD goals and related world problems, our students' social awareness of themselves in a world with multifaceted, often stressful societal needs, issues, and power relationships, increased and resulted in expressions of emotions that contributed to their personal growth. This awareness came about through their weekly article and website readings, assignments (calculations and writing about the issues), and peer communication. Sharing personal views and stories on the forum was not just a discussion in a computer applications course. This communication evolved into a venue to vent emerging emotions when faced with real-world problems such as initial surprise, followed by fear, hopelessness, sadness, and very much the shared emotion of acceptance, our second theme.

Our study was limited by the sample size of both the groups as well as the number of utterances students made in the CMS. Since the main focus of the course was to learn computer applications, it is possible that another subject area more directly relevant to the kinds of thinking we sought to engender by this design would result in improved or different outcomes.

One of our goals with this research was to better understand the challenges that accompany innovative learning methods and content. We feel we achieved this goal, and despite the limitations mentioned above, we believe this research can guide future transmedia developments, as well as those who conduct curriculum design for undergraduate learners. We hope that our experiences and those of our students can aid professionals to develop improved, liberating curricula to reach emancipatory and deeper student thinking through engaging discourses. By sharing our experience, we hope to enable instructors to support the development of learners who can function effectively in a globalized community.

ACKNOWLEDGMENT

The authors want to acknowledge Jonathan S. Gratch, who assisted with the course design. A brief version of this research was presented as a concurrent session at the annual conference of the American Educational Research Association, AERA 2014.

REFERENCES

Cobb, P., Confrey, J., diSessa, A., Lehrer, R., & Schauble, L. (2003). Design experiments in educational research. *Educational Researcher, 32*(1), 9–13. http://dx.doi.org/10.3102/0013189X032001009.

Feenberg, A. (1996). Marcuse or Habermas: Two critiques of technology. *Inquiry, 39,* 45–70. Retrieved from, http://www-rohan.sdsu.edu/faculty/feenberg/marhab.html.

Foucault, M. (1976/1981). Two lectures—Lecture two: 14 January 1976. In C. Gordon (Ed.), *Power/Knowledge: Selected interviews & other writings 1972–1977* (pp. 92–108). New York: Random House/Pantheon.

Foucault, M. (1984). *Foucault reader.* New York: Pantheon.

Freire, P. (1970). *Pedagogy of the oppressed.* New York: Continuum International Publishing Group.

Freshwater, D., & Robertson, C. (2002). *Emotions and needs.* Philadelphia, PA: Open University Press.

Habermas, J. (1970). On systematically distorted communication. *Inquiry, 13*(1–4), 205–218.

Habermas, J. (1974). *Theory and practice.* London: Heinemann.

Habermas, J., & McCarthy, T. (1987). *The theory of communicative action: Volume 2. Lifeworld and system (English tr., Vol. 2).* Boston, MA: Beacon Press.

Heidegger, M. (1977). *The question concerning technology* (pp. 3–35). New York, NY: Harper & Row, Publishers.

Herring, S. C. (2004). Computer-mediated discourse analysis: An approach to researching online behavior. In S. A. Barab, R. Kling, & J. H. Gray (Eds.), *Designing virtual communities in the service of learning* (pp. 338–376). Cambridge, UK: Cambridge University Press.

Jonassen, D. H. (1996). *Computers in the classroom: Mindtools for critical thinking* (pp. 1–291). Englewood Cliffs, NJ: Prentice Hall.

Moustakas, C. (1994). *Phenomenological research methods.* Thousand Oaks, CA: Sage Publications.

Plutchik, R. (1980). A general psychoevolutionary theory of emotion. In R. Plutchik & H. Kellerman (Eds.), *Emotion: Theory research and experience* (pp. 3–33). New York, NY: Academic Press, Inc.

Plutchik, R. (2001). The nature of emotions. *American Scientist, 89*(4), 344–350.

Ramage, J. D., Bean, J. C., & Johnson, J. (2010). *Writing arguments. A rhetoric with readings.* New York: Longman.

Ritchhart, R., Church, M., & Morrison, K. (2011). *Making thinking visible: How to promote engagement, understanding, and independence for all learners.* San Francisco, CA: Jossey-Bass.

Schutz, A. (1967). *The phenomenology of the social world*. Evanston, IL: Northwestern University Press.

Solomon, R. C. (2006). Emotions in continental philosophy. *Philosophy Compass, 1*(5), 413–431.

Tomkins, S. S. (1980). The function of emotions in behavioral systems: A systems theory analysis. In R. Plutchik & H. Kellerman (Eds.), *Emotion: Theory research and experience* (pp. 141–164). New York, NY: Academic Press, Inc.

Wakefield, J. S., Warren, S. J., & Alsobrook, M. (2011). Learning and teaching as communicative actions: A mixed-methods twitter study. *Knowledge Management & E-Learning, 3*(4), 563–584. Retrieved from, http://www.kmel-journal.org/ojs/index.php/online-publication/article/viewFile/145/115.

Warren, S. J., Dondlinger, M. J., McLeod, J. J., & Bigenho, C. (2011). Opening the door: An evaluation of the efficacy of a problem-based learning game. *Computers & Education, 58*, 1–15. http://dx.doi.org/10.1016/j.compedu.2011.08.012.

Warren, S. J., Wakefield, J. S., & Mills, L. A. (2013). Learning and teaching as communicative actions: Transmedia storytelling. In L. Wankel & P. Blessinger (Eds.), *Increasing student engagement and retention using multimedia technologies Part F: Video annotation, multimedia applications, videoconferencing, and transmedia storytelling cutting edge technologies in education* (pp. 67–95). Bingely, UK: Emerald Group Publishing. http://dx.doi.org/10.1108/S2044-9968(2013)000006F006.

CHAPTER 4

Loving this Dialogue!!!! 😊: Expressing Emotion Through the Strategic Manipulation of Limited Non-Verbal Cues in Online Learning Environments

Krystle Phirangee, Jim Hewitt
Department of Curriculum, Teaching and Learning, Ontario Institute for Studies in Education, University of Toronto, Toronto, ON, Canada

INTRODUCTION

Since the early days of computer-mediated conferencing (CMC), emotion has been a topic of interest in educational research (Hiltz, 1986; Kiesler, Siegel, & McGuire, 1984; Feenberg, 1989). In those early days, students used telephone-based modems to dial up university-based servers, where they could read messages left by their instructor and classmates and contribute messages of their own. It was a crude and slow process, and text had to be edited one line at a time, but it allowed students to have rudimentary discussions with one another. These courses generally worked quite well, but researchers discovered that their efforts to nurture academic discussions were occasionally interrupted by outbreaks of angry student messages (Feenberg, 1989; Hiltz, 1986). They developed a name for this phenomenon: "flaming" (O'Sullivan & Flanagin, 2003). Many researchers attributed the "flaming" phenomenon to a lack of non-verbal cues in online spaces, such as smiling, nodding, and other gestures and expressions (Alonzo & Aiken, 2004; Derks, Fischer, & Bos, 2008; O'Sullivan & Flanagin, 2003). It was hypothesized that this lack of cues produced misunderstandings (Kiesler et al., 1984), or led to the depersonalization of others in the discourse (Feenberg, 1989). Statements of disagreement, criticism, or sarcasm, which might be tempered with a smile in a regular classroom setting, could be viewed as threatening or hostile when read as naked text, leading to an escalation in angry remarks. Instructors began

Emotions, Technology, and Learning
http://dx.doi.org/10.1016/B978-0-12-800649-8.00010-9
69

developing countermeasures for flaming; they instructed their students to take care when disagreeing with another person's point of view and to limit their use of sarcasm. Through these and other measures, instructors hoped to nurture a more emotionally reserved, academic form of discourse that was largely lacking in passion and inflammatory language.

Much has changed over the past few decades. Today, "flaming" is less common in online courses and the phenomenon is less frequently discussed in the online learning literature (Derks et al., 2008). Modern-day students have grown up with the web and many are highly accustomed to text-based interaction thanks to their experiences with web discussion boards, text messaging apps, and social media. Today's learners are savvier about expressing themselves online, and this presumably helps them in their online courses (Derks et al., 2008; Sherblom, 2010). What are today's students doing to convey emotion in online courses? How does the expression of emotion, positive, and negative affect their experience in the course? How do they make use of various cues to express emotion? Over the past year, we have conducted a series of studies (Makos, Oztok, Zingaro, & Hewitt, 2013; Oztok, 2013; Oztok & Brett, 2011; Oztok, Lee, & Brett, 2012) to explore these questions. Our research is grounded in a social constructivist philosophy, which proposes that individual learning has a social and cultural foundation, often taking place through interaction and collaboration with others. In the case of online learning, students lack many of the traditional visual and verbal cues that are available in face-to-face settings (Switzer, 2009). What compensatory strategies have students developed and how do these strategies affect peer interaction and the culture of online courses?

Traditional View of Emotion

For the purpose of this chapter, emotion is defined as "the recognition, expression and sharing of emotions or moods between two or more individuals" (Derks et al., 2008, p. 3). Emotion is a complex phenomenon. Because there is a lack of consensus in defining emotion, and disagreement regarding its role, it has been slow to capture the interests of many scholars. Historically, scholars have tended to view emotion as potentially disruptive to the attainment of cognitive objectives (Cleveland-Innes & Campbell, 2012). The notion of a "cognition versus emotion" divide can be traced back to Plato, who argued that emotions were "irrational urges" that needed to be controlled (O'Regan, 2003). In a similar fashion, Emmanuel Kant argued that emotion was an "illness of the mind" (O'Regan, 2003), erratic and untrustworthy, and at odds with rational thought. These views continue to resonate with modern-day instructors, perhaps resulting in the devaluing of emotion and its role within the realm of education. Early psychological research viewed emotion and cognition separately, as if they had little relationship with one another in education (O'Regan, 2003). Today, emotion and cognition are coming to be seen as important and interconnected elements of learning. Emotion is no longer viewed as separate or disconnected from cognition; in fact, it is now recognized as being an integral part of learning (O'Regan, 2003; Shuck, Albornoz, & Winberg, 2013; Zembylas, 2008). However, in online learning environments (OLE), where emotional expression is trickier and fraught with uncertainty, there is arguably still a tendency to discount the value of emotion, in favor of an emotionally dispassionate style of writing, similar to that of academic texts.

Online Learning and Emotion

Often characterized as boring, with cold and impersonal communication (MacFadden, 2005; Vrasidas & Zembylas, 2003; Walther, Anderson, & Park, 1994), online learning is frequently viewed as less emotional compared with face-to-face classes. However, research (Cleveland-Innes & Campbell, 2012; Derks et al., 2008; Zembylas, 2008) suggests that students commonly experience emotions in distance education courses. Zembylas (2008) shows that students often report both positive emotions (which include: joy, enthusiasm, excitement, pride, contentment, and surprise) and negative emotions (which include: fear, anxiety, alienation, stress, and guilt) in online courses. According to Zembylas (2008), students can experience positive emotions when they post an idea that others value, or when they ask a question and obtain a response. Such events impact positively on their self-confidence and make them feel more comfortable interacting with their peers. On the other hand, students can experience negative emotions when they are unfamiliar with online learning, or do not know how to navigate the online environment (Zembylas, 2008). Feelings of alienation and isolation can develop when they cannot find satisfying ways to communicate with others (Zembylas, 2008). They might post a message, for example, and not receive a response—leading them to worry that they are being ignored, or that they have said something objectionable. This sense of alienation is understood to be a contributing factor to the high attrition rates in distance education (Rovai & Wighting, 2005). When students feel emotionally disconnected from their peers and their instructor, they may choose to leave the course altogether. Rovai and Wighting (2005) discovered that alienation is inversely related to a sense of community and can occur in two different ways. First, if students do not feel that they belong, or if they do not feel part of a collaborative endeavor, it will weaken the sense of community and cause people to feel alienated. Students need to feel connected to each other on an emotional level. Second, when learners' personal and cultural beliefs clash with societal beliefs, they are also likely to experience a weaker sense of community because they do not feel normal. They assume that others would reject and devalue their beliefs, if those beliefs were shared, thus leading them to feel alienated and isolated. Such students are less likely to interact openly with their peers in an OLE, or view themselves as part of a community.

While Zembylas (2008) and Rovai and Wighting (2005) describe the phenomenon of alienation and its negative effect on the online community, they differ fundamentally in their explanations of how these negative emotions arise. Zembylas (2008) suggests that alienation is partially a product of the medium and students' struggle to find ways to communicate with their peers in an OLE, which lacks the visual and aural cues of face-to-face discourse. Rovai and Wighting (2005), in contrast, suggest that feelings of alienation have a cultural basis, occurring when students' personal beliefs clash with the perceived beliefs of their classmates and instructor. Both explanations may have merit and both may be contributing factors. When students feel they cannot properly and appropriately communicate with other peers online, whether it is due to a lack of cues or because they believe their beliefs would be devalued, it becomes more difficult for students to bond and enjoy an open exchange of ideas.

Limited Cues, Limited Emotions?

In an attempt to delve more deeply into the notion that CMC is a more emotionally constrained medium, Derks et al. (2008) compared the different ways that emotion was expressed in computer-mediated communication (CMC) and face-to-face environments. Was there evidence that text-based discussions constrained emotional expression, as Zembylas (2008) proposed? Surprisingly, Derks et al. (2008) discovered a similar range of emotional expression across both conditions. While online environments lack the visual and verbal cues of face-to-face discourse, the authors discovered that many people were employing compensatory mechanisms, such as emoticons, to reduce the ambiguity of a text passage or convey emotional intent (Derks et al., 2008). The asynchronous nature of CMC may also be an important factor; people who are cognizant of the limited online cues in CMC can invest more time crafting a passage of text to ensure that misunderstandings are minimized. Thus, Derks et al. (2008) suggest that learners have invented strategies and developed conventions that allow online discourse to be as emotionally rich as face-to-face discourse.

Both Derks et al. (2008) and Sherblom (2010) suggest that the lack of traditional visual and verbal cues in OLEs has led to the development of new ways of expressing emotion in online environments. Sherblom (2010) argues that humans are social information processors who adapt their communication and information-gathering strategies in response to the medium. Emotion is such a vital part of communication that people manipulate available cues, or invent new ones, to gather information about others' emotions and attitudes. Acquiring this information may require more time and effort on the part of online learners, in addition to understanding the different emotional cues that people use. However, it is a vital part of our communication.

The Importance of Recognizing Cues

In a face-to-face classroom, instructors have an opportunity to notice and interpret non-verbal cues, modify instruction where necessary, and provide timely feedback to students (Berenson, Boyles, & Weaver, 2008). This practice is trickier in an OLE, simply because there are fewer cues. Unless instructors know the specific cues that students use, and how they use them, it is difficult to modify instruction and provide feedback to students (Rovai & Wighting, 2005). MacFadden, Maiter, and Dumbrill (2002) conducted a study in which they looked at the experiences of 19 learners in a 6-week online course on cultural competency. The researchers concluded that a lack of social cues reduced the effectiveness of feedback that students provided to their peers. This lack of cues also produced anxiety and confusion among students. Interviews with instructors revealed difficulties determining the level of emotional engagement in the online class. As a result, the instructors ultimately opted to end the online discussion to avoid alienating students. However, they also observed that if it had been a face-to-face class, they probably would have been able to continue the discussion by relying on social cues. As Palloff and Pratt (2007, p. 7) suggest, "Professors, just like their students, need the ability to deal with a virtual world in which, for the most part, they cannot see, hear, or touch the people with whom they are communicating." Therefore, it is important to understand how students express emotion in an OLE using these limited social cues because they can help educators better understand "how emotions shape student engagement and learning" (Linnenbrink-Garcia & Perrun, 2011, p. 1).

OUR RESEARCH

Our study focused on the types of non-verbal cues that students used to express emotion in an online graduate course taught at a major North American university. Data was collected from two sources: students' online notes and the transcripts of semi-structured interviews. In total, 45 students signed up for the course, which took place over a 12-week period in an OLE called "Pepper." More specifically, Pepper offers a variety of specialized knowledge building features and social networking tools to support learners in collaborating and sharing information. The analysis of the note content allowed researchers to identify the specific non-verbal cues that students used to help express their emotions online. Four students from the course: Cole, Maggie, Aliyah, and Kathy (pseudonyms) participated in the interviews, which provided insights into how students expressed their emotions online and how they interpreted different types of cues in other people's writing.

To analyze students' online notes, a content analysis was employed to make inferences (Bryman, 2004) about the types of non-verbal cues students were using. Once all students' online notes were coded, the categories were compared. However, the analysis of online notes only revealed *how* students were using cues. To better understand *why* students were using these cues, a series of semi-structured interviews were conducted. Although the interviews were guided by specific questions, participants were encouraged to describe their rationale for employing a particular cue in a particular situation, and how they interpreted cues used by others.

RESULTS

The content analysis of students' online notes identified three broad categories of non-verbal cues: emoticons, excessive punctuation, and the 'Like' button. Each of these is discussed in turn:

Emoticons

The content analysis revealed that students used emoticons to accompany a statement with an emotion, much in the same way that a person speaking in a class might use certain facial expressions or vocal intonations while discussing an idea. Four emoticons were used consistently throughout the OLE: the smiley emoticon, the sad emoticon, the wink emoticon, and the tongue emoticon. The smiley emoticon was sometimes used when students expressed support for someone with a similar view. As one student wrote when replying to a peer: "We are on the same page ☺." Some used the smiley emoticon when sharing resources. For instance a student wrote: "Sure—you might want to check out Siemens ideas on connectivism, that is where mine stems from ☺." More often, the smiley emoticon was used when thanking another peer for providing clarification: "Thanks Rachel and thanks for connecting me to Julia's story—its difficult trying to 'join up the dots' on here sometimes and that connection and your comment helped ☺." Lastly, students would use a smiley emoticon when providing a new perspective to consider. For example one student wrote: "Some of it may come down to how engaging the approach is for the variety of students and their learning preferences. Constructivist approaches can be very engaging and some people need to 'de-programmed' from their traditionalist upbringing ☺." In general, the smiley face was regularly used when students provided or received feedback from peers. If the feedback contained a suggestion, or an alternative interpretation of an idea, the smiley face helped prevent the reader from interpreting the comment in a negative or critical fashion.

The sad emoticon was used when students were facing a challenging task, or struggling to understand a specific concept or weekly reading. For instance, when a student struggled to post a video, he wrote: "Hi Coby, Kylie and Ashley, Thank you so much for your insights into question one and your amazing video posts! I wanted to post one myself but have somehow managed to psych myself out ☹." Similarly, when students encountered a difficult concept or reading they used the sad emoticon: "Like Kylie, I agree that was a challenging read, one that might need another reading in a few days from now so it can sink a little better. Right now, I actually feel a bit more unclear about constructivism than I did yesterday; it is more complex than I realized. But that's what I like in a reading, and it has presented a good challenge ☹." Students used the sad emoticon throughout the online course when they encountered a difficult activity. The icon had the effect of humanizing the author by acknowledging a struggle or a weakness that the author was working to overcome.

Compared with the sad and smiley emoticons, the wink and tongue emoticons were used the least within the online discussion. Typically, the wink and tongue emoticons were used to help convey the intention of humor or sarcasm in a note. For example, one student wrote: "However, I am sure we have all met fully formed adults with an inability to consider another point of view ☺." In one case, after a student challenged a classmate's idea, an attempt was made to offer a humorous concession by writing, "So it does seem like they [the authors] are arguing over semantics (i.e. whether egocentric speech is cognitive or social) and it's driving me bonkers ☺." The wink and tongue emoticons were intended to let others know that the author's statements were intended in a friendly and collegial fashion.

Overall, interview participants indicated that they used emoticons to soften the tone of their messages. Many emphasized that they used emoticons to control the tone they were presenting to their peers. For instance, Cole stated:

> If you're trying to be critical, or if you're not agreeing with somebody, or trying to repair communication in some way, and trying to soften that communication then often you will use an emoticon to signal that … you're also helping the other person maintain face and in order to do that you're going to use emoticons.

Similarly, Maggie emphasized that emoticons helped her convey a note's tone, such as if it was going to be friendly or sad. She states:

> I think emoticons help a lot when projecting certain tones because I'm a very visual person. So, seeing a little smiley face, I'm like 'oh look they're happy.' So, I think those types of things helps, at least me, tell if someone was being more friendly. I also think if I used those [emoticons] other people might have felt, okay she's friendly or whatever.

Aliyah emphasized that she did not use emoticons often, but if she did, it was to communicate a friendly tone. She states:

> I don't remember using them a lot but maybe I'm wrong but I probably did a smile or something. If I did use them it was probably to clarify that my tone is happy in nature. I don't think I would ever use an angry face but I would probably use a smile or wink to show that it's a friendly tone.

Therefore, students found emoticons to be very helpful in text-based communication when trying to project specific tones to others. These learners seemed to be aware that the lack of traditional cues in text-based communication could unintentionally produce misunderstandings—the same types of misunderstandings that sometimes led to flaming in the early days of CMC. Their proficiency with emoticons reflected a sensitivity to this concern, which they likely developed through experiences in other web-based communication environments.

While students demonstrated proficiency with smiley, sad faces, and other emoticons, they also questioned whether it was appropriate to use them. All participants reported they were initially hesitant to use emoticons in their online notes because they were not sure they were appropriate in an academic course, even if they added clarity to their emotions and tone. They worried that the instructor might disapprove of them. For instance, Maggie stated:

> So, emoticons I didn't want to use them too much because I found or thought people didn't really use them. When I first got into the OLE, I wondered if this was non-academic to use and I was kind of afraid to use them … I also think emoticons, it stems from who your professor is. Some professors are more open and comfortable with you being a little bit more … I don't want to say unprofessional because it's not unprofessional to use emoticons, maybe informal.

Some participants opted not to use emoticons because they were uncertain how to use them in an academic setting and struggled with whether it was appropriate for formal learning. Kathy stated:

> I don't think I really used emoticons because I wasn't sure how to in an OLE, or if we were allowed to use them. I used them in Facebook and e-mails all the time but in this forum I don't know if I knew how to do it in an academic setting, so I didn't. If I knew how to use it I would have done so all the time because … if you're saying something and you're hoping someone knows or gets you're smiling as you type you could just put a little happy face, in hopes they get what you're saying and how you feel I guess.

Similarly, Aliyah made an intentional effort not to use emoticons. She felt emoticons were informal and should be used in more social platforms, such as Facebook. She stated:

> I don't tend to use them a lot. I tend to use them with certain people. I guess I've always thought of emoticons as being more of a social thing or kind of informal. So, it's more for a social situation on FB or texting I think there I used them a little bit. But in an academic environment I don't remember using them a lot.

Earlier research suggests that the absence of traditional face-to-face cues in online environments can be compensated to a certain extent using emoticons (Rojas, Kirschenmann, & Wolpers, 2012; Weiss, 2000). Our research supports these findings; the students in our study regularly used emoticons to convey a particular tone or expression (Aragon, 2003). According to Tu and McIsaac (2002), the ability to express feelings is a prerequisite for the development of strong social connections. Emoticons appear to be helpful in this regard. In addition to providing emotional information about the author, they also add context to the text, which is important for learners (Gunawardena & Zittle, 1997). Although participants value discussions with emoticons, many worried about using emoticons in an academic setting. In some sense, this seems odd, since one would not criticize a student for smiling or nodding while talking in a face-to-face class. Discussions in traditional seminar-style courses have always contained emotional cues, yet students feel reluctant to embrace emotional cues in online courses. This reluctance likely has its historical and cultural roots in the cognition versus emotion divide discussed earlier in this chapter. Students know that formal academic writing is sometimes criticized if it is not "objective," and so they are understandably hesitant to adopt tools that might lower their instructor's opinion of them. Learners feel caught between two competing pressures: the pressure to build a collaborative learning community (which requires the expression of emotion and the engendering of trust) and the pressure to produce objective, non-emotional, academic writing.

Unconventional Punctuation

The content analysis revealed that students often used punctuation (specifically exclamation marks and ellipses) in unconventional ways to express emotions. Participants reported that punctuation helped them show enthusiasm, frustration, or to signal to others that more time was needed to explore an idea. It also allowed them to draw attention to specific ideas within a note. Repeated exclamation marks helped them express excitement for certain ideas, or for the discourse as whole. For instance, one student wrote: "Loving this dialogue!!!!" Another student expressed excitement for a question posed by her peers, by writing: "Thanks for providing such a wonderful and open-ended question Lisa and Dan. It is going to spark some great conversation!!!" Sometimes the exclamation mark was used to express frustration when students encountered a difficult task. For example, when a student struggled with a weekly reading, he wrote: "it sure would be helpful if these types of papers were written in a more accessible ways!!" One student felt nervous about implementing a new learning model, saying: "Am now going to try model this … gosh I hope it works!!!!!!" In general, students used the exclamation mark to express excitement for an idea or to express frustration with a task.

Participants acknowledged that they used the exclamation mark to show excitement. Aliyah observed, "So, I did use the exclamation mark, but I did it when I was excited about someone's comment, or if I really related to something I would use it." Cole agreed that his peers used the exclamation mark to express excitement for ideas, but he also felt there was no need for it. He remarked:

Personally, I didn't really use the exclamation mark, and when I saw it I would think yeah okay no need for so many exclamation marks, but I think it's an area everybody is learning and that there are no hard and fast rules. And different types of interaction require formal and informal approaches and modes of acceptable behavior.

Other participants stated that they used the exclamation mark excessively to emphasize an idea or to let their peers know that it was an important point. Kathy wrote: "I used the exclamation marks a bit, not to show excitement because I don't really get excited, but to emphasize something, or that I had a strong feeling about a point I guess." Similarly, Maggie also believed that excessive use of the exclamation mark meant that students were trying to emphasize an important point. She states:

Sometimes I would see a couple of exclamation marks and then I would think okay that point they really want to emphasize, or it's something really important, so I have to keep it in mind because it's very important to them.

Thus, some people used the exclamation mark to call peoples' attention to particular points, as well as expressing excitement or frustration for a specific idea. However, again, as in the case of the emoticons, people raised concerns about what was considered "acceptable behavior."

Ellipses were another form of punctuation used by students to convey emotion. They reportedly used the characters "…" to indicate reflective thinking, or perhaps suggest that an idea was still under consideration. For example, a student wrote: "Loved reading everyone's earlier school experiences! Cole's comment regarding the need to question or reflect upon the definition of success resonated deeply for me … what does success really mean? Hmmmmm …" These types of comments, with excessive ellipses, popped up regularly in the online discussions we examined. Another student wrote:

Thank you Megan for your thoughts on intellectualist theories and situated learn-ing. I too agree there is a time and place for both ⋯ however, I do believe that without the application of information processing, authentic learning does not occur. So as I see it within the frame of this question, it's not so much a matter of standing between ⋯ rather, in this type of learning situation, a matter of ensur-ing the process of learning evolves or flows naturally from concepts to real-world practice.

In this example, it is suggested that the author wanted to suggest that he was still thinking about the subject matter and did not want his comments to be judged too quickly or harshly.

In the interviews, participants acknowledged that ellipses were used to indicate to their peers that they needed more time to think about a point or that they were confused. Kathy states: "I do use the dots to express to people that I'm making a judgment call here, or that I'm still thinking about something." Similarly, Maggie explained that excessive ellipses were a great indicator of knowing that the author needed more time to think. She states:

> Also, sometimes people would end their notes with a dot, dot, dot, you know a few dots and that told me they were still thinking. These things were sometimes nice too because it indicated to me okay they're dwelling on that thought, they just need to give it some time, maybe they will come back tomorrow and post something different, and add onto what they've said.

Aliyah said that she personally tried not to use ellipses, but admitted that she had done so on occasion to indicate to others that she was still thinking. She states:

> With the ellipsis I never used more than three but I think I may have a couple of times. I think I remember someone posting when it was their week to do the question. They posted a really, really good question, and I was just so perplexed. I remember putting a statement saying: I'm going to have to get back to you on this one I'm still thinking. I then put the ellipsis just to say I'm going to come back to this, I'm still thinking and reflecting on it. I think using ten dots probably means they're really confused or still grappling with the topic or concept.

Cole felt that ellipses were helpful for building and negotiating meaning, when people have only partial understandings. He states:

> Thinking about my observations of it I think people when they were delivering their post [in the beginning of a discussion] it tended to be a bit more formal. When they got into the thread about what they thought then the exchanges became a bit more informal. And I think that's because when you get into those exchanges then you're negotiating meaning, but you're also helping the other person maintain face, and in order to do that you're going to use emoticons, and you're going to use language when your using more pronouns like "we" and "our" and all those kinds of things.

In general, students used ellipses to indicate to their peers that they were still thinking about a point. For some participants, the ellipses allowed others to know that they were still pondering and grappling with a point or topic. This allowed them to signal to the instructor, and their peers, that their ideas are still in development. This provides a means by which students can begin talking about notions that are difficult to grasp, while at the same time reducing the risk that one will be criticized or judged harshly for doing so.

The "Like" Button

Facebook created and popularized the "Like" button. Usually used in social media to indicate whether a person likes, enjoys, or supports certain content, it is a simple and quick way to communicate approval. In Pepper the Like button was added so students can "Like" each other's notes. The content analysis suggests that students used the button for a wide variety of communicative purposes. For instance, students "Liked" notes to:

- acknowledge peers who shared personal experiences with the class;
- indicate appreciation for notes that reflect their own perspectives;
- thank students who shared or produced particularly valuable resources;
- show support for students who discuss a personal struggle;
- recognize efforts to refer to/synthesize other people's ideas, or class readings;
- show appreciation for someone who responds to his or her note.

All participants indicated that the Like button was used to express support for their peers, as well as to indicate that they "Liked" and enjoyed certain content. Students revealed that using the Like button was a quick way to show approval for a peer's idea. For example, Aliyah emphasized that she used the Like button often to give quick support. She stated: "I used the 'Like' button to say 'good job' or you know a high five kind of thing." Similarly, Kathy indicated that she used the Like button to show her peers that she valued their thoughts. "With the 'Like' button I felt like I could value what people were saying. So, when I got people liking something, it felt like a sense of approval and understanding with one another." Cole believed the Like button was a good way to acknowledge a peer's post but also remarked that sometimes there was a degree of reciprocity involved. He stated:

> I liked posts other people liked. Especially, if somebody liked me, my posts, then I would generally like them. I went through a small stage of trying to be a bit more selective with it and then I just gave up just because there was no point really. I don't think it's suppose to be something that you should heavily police yourself with, do you know what I mean? It's an acknowledgement; it's kind of like nodding your head or something like that … And that's how I see the like button it's just about nodding your head, somebody's paying attention, but they haven't actually participated.

Maggie reported that she used the Like button in the same ways as her classmates. However, she also emphasized that the Like button did not help her communicate better. Rather, it helped her more smoothly express a friendly tone to others. She states:

> I think the 'Like' button was one because I would go through it and if I really thought a note was really well-written or if it was very clear to me or if it was a good length because I know sometimes people would write a lot and some people would write just the right amount I would like it to show them I appreciate what you put out there … I don't really think the like button helped me to

communicate better, but the link feature definitely helped me to communicate bet-
ter ... I think the like button definitely helps you to do this because it's like you click
it, and it means I like it, good job.

According to participants, the Like button allowed online learners to support their peers in a quick and easy manner. All participants admitted to using the Like button often, perhaps because it held strong and similar meanings for all online learners. Many participants also expressed that they enjoyed receiving "Likes" because it made them feel good about their contributions. In this sense, it is a community-building tool, because it engenders a sense of trust and class camaraderie—findings that are consistent with earlier research (Makos et al., 2013).

DISCUSSION

Overall, our research suggests that students are strategically using cues such as emoticons, punctuation, and the Like button to help express their perspectives online. Students use these cues to express their feelings about the content and peer feedback, as well as to project a particular emotional tone in their online notes, in part to prevent misinterpretation and the unintentional escalation of negative feelings. Some participants reported feeling conflicted about using these cues (particularly emoticons and exclamation marks) in an academic setting, which traditionally has not used such devices. Neverthe-less, they felt cues gave them an opportunity to better express themselves and to forge more supportive emotional bonds with their classmates. Indeed, when reading their online discussions, one is struck by the sense that students prefer to err on the side of being too generous with their Likes, exclamation marks, and smiley face emoticons. Presumably this produces a classroom cul-ture that is likely to be safer and more supportive—and less likely to suffer from misunderstandings that can produce flaming.

Given these findings, it may be argued that non-verbal cues, which have been largely appropriated from social media, may indeed play a productive and necessary role in online courses. They provide students with tools for conveying emotions; much in the same way that students in face-to-face courses can temper their speech acts with facial expressions. In the past, some instructors have discouraged students from expressing emotions in OLEs, and indeed, some students today still worry that their instructors will disap-prove of smiley faces and exclamation marks. However, recent research (Derks, Bos, & Von Grumbkow, 2007; Derks et al., 2008; Makos et al., 2013 as well as ours) suggests that online learners have developed these tools as a reasonable, adaptive response to the challenges of communicating and interacting in a text-only medium. Efforts to curtail the use of these tools may, in fact, inhibit community building and may reduce the clarity of student communication.

The availability of non-verbal supports may be particularly important, given the commonly reported phenomenon of students feeling separated or isolated from their peers in distance education courses (Rovai, 2002). Students tend to feel insecure in online environments because they lack the visual and aural information that is available in a traditional classroom. When sharing their ideas in a regular class, students can watch other people's faces to see if they nod, say "uh huh," or provide other forms of backchannel communication. This backchannel information is largely missing in online contexts. In fact, it is not unusual for an online learner to write a note and receive no response at all, a situation that often heightens the learner's feelings of insecurity. This is why the invention of the Like button is important: it serves as a low-cost, low-effort feedback mechanism that reassures the author that others have read and appreciated their writing.

Face-to-face classes are different from online classes in another important respect. When talking in a face-to-face class, you can monitor how people are reacting to you, and modify what you say, if you feel people are confused or upset. Online environments lack this capacity. When you engage in discourse in an online community, you contribute an entire passage without having any feedback to guide you. We suspect this is why many students have developed a strategy of infusing their messages with positive emotional cues (such as exclamation marks and smiley faces). These cues are an attempt to convey the positive intent of the author, and minimize the likelihood that their writing will unintentionally offend someone else in the class.

In conclusion, our research suggests that the social cues used by some online students are effective in terms of helping them express themselves more accurately to others. They help students bond with each other, better express their feelings, and portray who they are to their classmates (Duthler, as cited in Sherblom, 2010). They also provide students with new avenues for expressing emotion so they can better support their peers and engage more effectively with the content. Unfortunately, some instructors are still promoting a culture of formal academic writing, devoid of the emotional cues that can be instrumental in the development of a supportive, collaborative learning community. Future research should focus on the instructor's role in nurturing non-verbal cues in an OLE and the impact this can have on student engagement and learning.

REFERENCES

Alonzo, M., & Aiken, M. (2004). Flaming in electronic communication. *Decision Support Systems, 36*(3), 205–213.

Aragon, S. R. (2003). Creating social presence in online environments. *New Directions for Adult and Continuing Education, 2003*(100), 57–68.

Berenson, R., Boyles, G., & Weaver, A. (2008). Emotional intelligence as a predictor for success in online learning. *International Review of Research in Open and Distance Learning, 9*(2), 1–17.

Bryman, A. (2004). *Social research methods.* Oxford: Oxford University Press.

Cleveland-Innes, M., & Campbell, P. (2012). Emotional presence, learning, and the online learning environment. *International Review of Research in Open and Distance Learning, 13*(4), 269–292.

Derks, D., Bos, A. E., & Von Grumbkow, J. (2007). Emoticons and online message interpretation. *Social Science Computer Review, 26*(3), 379–388.

Derks, D., Fischer, A. H., & Bos, A. (2008). The role of emotion in computer-mediated communication: A review. *Computer Human Behavior, 24*, 766–785.

Feenberg, A. (1989). The written world: On the theory and practice of computer conferencing. In R. Mason & A. Kaye (Eds.), *Mindweave: Communication, computers, and distance education* (pp. 22–39). Elmsford, NY: Pergamon Press.

Gunawardena, C. N., & Zittle, F. J. (1997). Social presence as a predictor of satisfaction within a computer-mediated conferencing environment. *American Journal of Distance Education, 11*(3), 8–26.

Hiltz, S. R. (1986). The ëvirtual classroomí. Using computer-mediated communication for university teaching. *Journal of Communication, 36*(2), 96–104.

Kiesler, S., Siegel, J., & McGuire, T. W. (1984). Social psychological-aspects of computer-mediated communication. *American Psychologist, 39*(10), 1123–1134.

Linnenbrink-Garcia, L., & Perrun, R. (2011). Student emotions and academic engagement. *Contemporary Educational Psychology, 36*(1), 1–3.

MacFadden, R. J. (2005). Souls on ice: Incorporating emotion in web-based education. *Journal of Technology in Human Services, 23*(1-2), 79–98.

MacFadden, R. J., Maiter, S., & Dumbrill, G. C. (2002). High tech and high touch: The human face of online education. *Journal of Technology in Human Services, 20*(3-4), 283–300.

Makos, A., Oztok, M., Zingaro, D., & Hewitt, J. (2013, April). Use of a like button in a collaborative online learning environment. *Poster presentation in the "online teaching and learning posters: Interaction and collaboration; social media and mobile approaches" session. American Education Research Association annual conference*, April 26th-May 1st, 2013. Presented May 1st, 2013, San Francisco, CA, USA.

O'Regan, K. (2003). Emotion and e-learning. *Journal of Asynchronous Learning Networks, 7*(3), 78–92.

O'Sullivan, P. B., & Flanagin, A. J. (2003). Reconceptualizing 'flaming' and other problematic messages. *New Media & Society, 5*(1), 69–94.

Oztok, M. (2013). Tacit knowledge in online learning: Community, identity, and social capital. *Technology, Pedagogy and Education, 22*(1), 21–36.

Oztok, M., & Brett, C. (2011). Social presence and online learning: A review of the research. *Journal of Distance Education, 25*(3), 1–10.

Oztok, M., Lee, K., & Brett, C. (2012). Towards better understanding of self-representation in online learning. In G. Marks & T. Bastiaens (Eds.), *Proceedings of E-learn 2012. Presented at the world conference on E-learning in corporate, government, healthcare, and higher education, Montréal, QC* (pp. 256–262).

Palloff, R. M., & Pratt, K. (2007). *Building online learning communities: Effective strategies for the virtual classroom.* San Francisco, CA: Wiley.

Rojas, S. L., Kirschenmann, U., & Wolpers, M. (2012). We have no feelings, we have emoticons;-). In *Advanced learning technologies (ICALT), 2012 IEEE 12th international conference on, IEEE* (pp. 642–646).

Rovai, A. P. (2002). Building sense of community at a distance. *International Review of Research in Open and Distance Learning, 3*(1), 1–16.

Rovai, A. P., & Wighting, M. J. (2005). Feelings of alienation and community among higher education students in a virtual classroom. *The Internet and Higher Education, 8*(2), 97–110.

Sherblom, J. C. (2010). The computer-mediated communication (CMC) classroom: A challenge of medium, presence, interaction, identity, and relationship. *Communication Education, 59*(4), 497–523.

Shuck, B., Albornoz, C., & Winberg, M. (2013). *Emotions and their effect on adult learning: A constructivist perspective.* Miami: Florida International University.

Switzer, J. S. (2009). Impression formation in computer-mediated communication and making a good (virtual) impression. In C. Ang & P. Zaphiris (Eds.), *Human computer interaction: concepts, methodologies, tools, and applications* (pp. 1837–1848). Hershey, PA: IGI Global Snippet. http://dx.doi.org/10.4018/978-1-87828-991-9.ch120.

Tu, C. H., & McIsaac, M. (2002). The relationship of social presence and interaction in online classes. *American Journal of Distance Education, 16*(3), 131–150.

Vrasidas, C., & Zembylas, M. (2003). The nature of technology-mediated interaction in globalized distance education. *International Journal of Training and Development, 7*(4), 271–286.

Walther, J. B., Anderson, J. F., & Park, D. W. (1994). Interpersonal effects in computer-mediated interaction a meta-analysis of social and antisocial communication. *Communication Research, 21*(4), 460–487.

Weiss, R. E. (2000). Humanizing the online classroom. In R. E. Weiss, D. S. Knowlton, & B. W. Speck (Eds.), *Principles of effective teaching in the online classroom: 84* (pp. 47–51). San Francisco, CA: Jossey-Bass.

Zembylas, M. (2008). Adult learners' emotions in online learning. *Distance Education, 29*(1), 71–87.

SECTION II

Technology, Emotions, and Classroom Use

CHAPTER 5

Using Errors to Enhance Learning Feedback in Computer Programming

Man-Wai Chu, Jacqueline P. Leighton
University of Alberta, Edmonton, AB, Canada

Learning is not only a cognitive, but also a highly social and emotional process (Damasio, 2001). To facilitate the experience of learning for students as well as the successful acquisition of knowledge and skills, instructors should understand how human emotions and social interactions enhance or hinder learning, and use this information to build learning environments accordingly (Lajoie, 2008). Creating learning environments that are experienced by students as emotionally safe could facilitate their sense of ease when experimenting with ideas, making errors as they learn, and interpreting feedback meaningfully to correct errors without fear of looking silly or feeling unintelligent (Leighton, Chu, & Seitz, 2013; see also Bustos Gomez & Leighton, 2013). In meeting the goal of building learning environments that are sensitive to the emotions and social interactions of students, technology may be a powerful ally. For example, technology can facilitate the anonymous expression of ideas via online posts, and permit constructive and respectful feedback to be crafted in response to ideas (Roed, 2003). Although we were unable to find empirical research articles focused specifically on using technology to increase students' perceptions of safety in the classroom (however, see Roed, 2003), we expect that just as technology has facilitated the instruction of diverse learners (e.g., assistive technology for learning disabilities; see Lewis, 1998), it could also facilitate instructional interventions such as feedback delivery to create emotionally safe learning environments for students; however, this remains an empirical question.

Submitted to editors Dr. Sharon Tettegah & Dr. Michael McCreery. To appear in *Emotions and Technology: Communication of Feelings for, with and through Digital Media*

Although the content and delivery of feedback has been investigated previously (e.g., Bangert-Drowns, Kulik, Kulik, & Morgan, 1991; Kluger & DeNisi, 1996, for a historical review and meta-analysis; Shute, 2008), one issue that remains relatively unexplored is student preferences over the mode in which feedback is delivered following assessment activities. Surprisingly, not much research has focused on learners' emotional responses to feedback (Shute, 2008). A recent learning model attempts to address the complex relationship between feedback and students' emotional responses. The model, called the Learning Errors and Formative Feedback (LEAFF), focuses on students' mental models of their learning environment, including assessment activities (Leighton et al., 2013). One reason to investigate student preferences over the mode in which feedback is delivered rests with increasing the likelihood that students (1) experience productive emotional responses in relation to feedback; (2) acknowledge and accept the feedback given; and (3) use it to modify their learning in constructive ways. The objective of this chapter is to investigate the effects of an instructional intervention based upon the LEAFF model within a technology-rich learning environment. More specifically, the research questions guiding this study include: (1) Does an intervention based upon the LEAFF model have an effect on students' feelings of well-being as they learn computer programming? (2) Does an intervention based upon the LEAFF model have an effect on the number of errors students report? And (3) Does an intervention based upon the LEAFF model have an effect on students' preference of feedback delivery and use? The chapter is divided into four sections. We begin with a description of the LEAFF model, followed by the method and procedures of the quasi-experimental study we conducted to test aspects of the LEAFF model, along with the results. In the final section, we summarize and discuss the findings and conclude with the implications of this work.

LEAFF MODEL

The LEAFF model (Leighton et al., 2013), shown in Figure 5.1, involves three parts. The first part focuses on the instructional climate within classrooms, where instructors engage in pedagogical behaviors that either explicitly or implicitly promote safety or risk for learners experimenting with new knowledge and skills. Behaviors that explicitly promote safety might include verbal expressions about showing respect for others' views; for example, a teacher might say "we must be considerate of each other's values and

Formative Feedback In Computer Programming   1

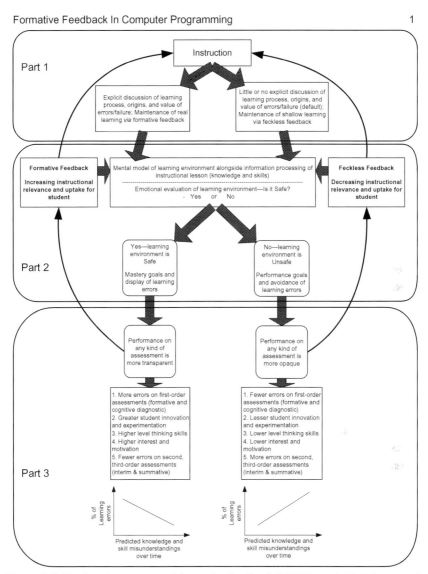

Figure 5.1 The learning errors and formative feedback (LEAFF) model (Leighton et al., 2013).

opinions during the discussion today." Behaviors that implicitly promote safety might include showing patience in body language (e.g., not tapping a finger or making facial expressions to indicate urgency) when a student is struggling to understand a concept.

One approach that is hypothesized to facilitate the creation of a safe learning environment is to explicitly discuss the value of "learning" errors with students. Learning errors are made in the formative stages of acquiring new knowledge and skills. Learning errors (from here on, simply called errors) signal student misunderstandings and can be used constructively to enhance future learning. Instructors are encouraged to discuss and help students understand that errors are a natural and necessary part of learning. It is expected that over time and with continued discussion of the value of errors, students may come to experience greater mastery-learning orientations, where errors are viewed as opportunities for clarification and pathways to deeper understanding. Further, students may come to experience increasingly positive emotions in learning environments where errors are viewed as opportunities for growth—a sense that the stakes are lower when errors are made during the learning process because they are viewed as a necessary part of learning complex skills. The explicit discussion of errors is designed to challenge students' assumptions about how innate intelligence limits learning potential and, instead, encourage a "growth" mindset (Dweck, 2006).

The second part of the LEAFF model focuses on students' mental models of the emotional (affective) and cognitive components of the classroom environment. Mental models (Johnson-Laird, 1983) are internal representations that reflect an individual's perception and understanding of the world around him or her for the purposes of reasoning and problem solving. Mental models contain information, as perceived by the individual, which allow judgments and inferences to be made about people, actions, events, and outcomes. Students employ their mental models to engage in metacognition about their own learning, including cognitive and emotional evaluations of their environment and decisions on courses of action. A student who views a learning environment to be emotionally safe would be expected to possess a mental model that provides an internal sense of ease in learning new knowledge and skills. Mental models that contain multiple positive aspects associated with the learning environment would also be expected to facilitate students' receptivity to feedback (see Kluger & DeNisi, 1996). For example, students who possess positive mental models about their teacher as a caring and trustworthy agent within a learning environment that supports errors as avenues for growth are expected to interpret formative and even summative feedback as genuine and relevant. According to the LEAFF model, when students feel at ease showing what they do not understand, thus revealing mental models that are positive about their learning environment, teachers can better address misconceptions because students are more likely to let their guard down and feel freer to show which aspects of the material they find challenging. When students possess positive mental models, feedback designed to address misconceptions is likely to be viewed as more relevant and informative by students (see Shute, 2008). This pathway is shown in the left side of Figure 5.1.

By contrast, shown in the right side of Figure 5.1, another path is depicted in the LEAFF model. This path reveals what is expected to happen when students appraise their learning environment, based upon their mental models, as emotionally unsafe. An emotion that might prevail in a classroom viewed as unsafe is fear—in particular, fear that revealing what is not understood might lead to the assignment of labels such as unintelligent, lazy, or slow. This fear would be expected to reduce students' comfort level in revealing potential mistakes and misunderstandings, and thus create missed opportunities for a teacher to provide remediation. In addition, when students do not feel a sense of well-being or safety in their learning environment, the errors they exhibit may not fully reflect what they fail to understand and, in fact, be more reflective of efforts at disguising areas of confusion. Thus, an instructor's feedback to remedy these contrived errors may be interpreted by students as irrelevant or off-target in relation to what students need.

Students' perceptions about the feedback they receive from teachers, whether it is viewed as formative or feckless, can function to reinforce the mental models created about the learning environment. For example, students who have generated mental models that promote a sense of safety in the learning environment and well-being may be expected to perceive feedback as formative and relevant, reinforcing a positive evaluation of the environment; however, students who have generated models that indicate a lack of safety in learning and sense of unease may be expected not only to perceive and receive feedback as feckless and irrelevant, but also to reinforce a negative emotional evaluation of the environment. Students' mental models are central in the LEAFF model because they set the cognitive and emotional parameters from which students interpret their environment and guide their actions for future learning.

The final part of the LEAFF model focuses on student performance. According to the LEAFF model, students are more likely to exhibit superior academic performance over time when they deem the learning environment to be safe (i.e., they possess positive mental models). When students deem their environment to be safe and feel at ease demonstrating their misunderstandings, that is, showing more errors on early assessments, they are expected to interpret the formative feedback they receive about their performance as more relevant and useful in guiding their learning. In contrast, when students view the learning environment as unsafe, they are more likely to interpret the feedback they receive from instructors as feckless, based upon inauthentic performances, thus creating ambiguity about the relevance of the feedback. In addition, students who appraise the learning environment as unsafe are expected to exhibit less intellectual risk taking and experimentation in their problem solving, fewer higher-order thinking skills, and more errors over time on summative assessments as they forego the opportunities to clarify misunderstandings early in the learning process to build a solid foundation of knowledge and skills. In relation to the latter, students who perceive the environment as unsafe are expected to make more errors over time on summative assessments; however, early on in the learning process, they may actually exhibit an equal number or even fewer errors on formative assessments compared with students who perceive the environment as safe as they rely on test-wise strategies and other shortcuts.

The LEAFF model reflects a way to use the discussion of errors strategically in instructional practice. By having the teacher discuss the formative value and necessity of errors during learning, he or she is in effect removing the stigma associated with errors for students, and thereby promoting greater exposure in the knowledge and skills students are willing to expose to the instructor. The LEAFF model suggests that when students are willing to expose what they do not know within a safe learning environment, they are more likely to be receptive to the feedback they receive from an instructor following any assessment activity to modify their learning.

METHOD

Participants

Thirty undergraduate students who enrolled in one of two sections of a 13-week, senior undergraduate course, focused on video-game development as a teaching tool, participated in the study. The students who served as participants did so voluntarily and therefore comprised a sample of convenience. Sixteen students self-identified as male (53.3%), 10 as female (33.3%), and 4 did not disclose gender (13.3%). Students ranged in age from 22 to 35 years; their mean age was 24.9 years, with a standard deviation of

2.8 years. Precautions were taken to ensure that students' willingness or unwillingness to participate in the study did not influence their course grade as per research ethics guidelines. A consent and information form about the study was provided to students, along with a verbal explanation to ensure students' comprehension of, and voluntary participation in, the study.

Quasi-Experimental Design

A quasi-experimental design was used to conduct the study. A single between-subject independent variable was manipulated, namely, an instructional intervention based upon the LEAFF model. The instructional intervention consisted of the presence of an explicit discussion of errors, described in greater detail momentarily, or the absence of an explicit discussion of errors. In other words, one section of the course received the intervention and one section did not. Students in each section of the course were unaware of the specific manipulations of the study. Further, to minimize any instructional differences between the two sections, aside from the manipulated LEAFF intervention, the two instructors and two teaching assistants involved with delivering the course material in the two sections met regularly to ensure consistency of instruction.

Dependent variables used to measure the effects of the intervention included measures of students' perceived well-being in the learning environment, frequency of self-reported errors, and preference of feedback delivery and use. We also collected students' demographic information, project marks, and final grades. Students enrolled in the section of the course receiving the intervention were designated as the experimental group ($n = 18$), while those in the other section of the course constituted the comparison group ($n = 12$), which did not receive the intervention. It was not possible to randomly assign students to each of the two groups or sections because of students' programmatic course timetables.

As shown in Table 5.1, the demographic composition and educational technology background of students in both sections were relatively comparable. For example, although the experimental group had slightly more male students (60%) than the comparison group (40%), ethnic composition was comparable; the largest proportion of students was Caucasian in both sections. Also, in both sections, the majority of students were enrolled in a Bachelor of Education program and reported a similar distribution of cumulative GPA. Furthermore, most students in the two sections had not previously enrolled in an educational technology class. Approximately 55% of students in the experimental group had taken at least one computing course,

Table 5.1 Demographic characteristics of the experimental and comparison groups

	Experimental		Comparison	
	Number of students	Percent of students (%)	Number of students	Percent of students (%)
Gender				
Female	5	27.8	5	41.7
Male	11	61.1	5	41.7
Ethnicity				
Caucasian	11	61.1	6	50.0
Other	4	16.8	4	33.3
Enrolled Faculty				
Faculty of Education	11	61.1	8	66.6
Other	5	27.8	1	16.6
Computing experience				
Previously took one or more Education— Instructional Technology class(es)	3	16.7	3	25.0
Previously took one or more Computing Science class(es)	10	55.6	4	33.3
Cumulative GPA				
C+	1	5.6	0	0.0
B-	2	11.1	1	8.3
B	7	38.9	3	25.0
B+	4	22.2	4	33.3
A-	1	5.6	1	8.3
A/A+	0	0.0	1	8.3
Estimated GPA for course				
B	0	0.0	1	10.0
B+	6	37.5	4	40.0
A-	7	43.8	3	30.0
A/A+	3	18.8	2	20.0

whereas only 33% of students in the comparison group had taken at least one computing course. Some participating students chose not to respond to these demographic questions.

The course on video-game development as a teaching tool involved a weekly three-hour lecture (delivered in two blocks of 90 min per week) and a three-hour interactive laboratory (delivered in two blocks of 90 min per week). The present study focused upon the interactive laboratory of the course in which the teaching assistant guided students through a laboratory challenge during the 90-minute session to teach specific programming skills. Although the course spanned 13 weeks, there were only 10 weeks of laboratories, because the first week and the last two weeks of the course did not have laboratory sessions. Further, the 13 weeks of laboratories were split into two parts; the first half of the laboratories (i.e., weeks 2-6) were focused upon the programming language Scratch, while the second half focused on the language Kodu (i.e., weeks 7-11). The objectives and activities of each laboratory are listed in Appendix A. The laboratory assistant in the experimental group administered the LEAFF-based intervention at the beginning (first 5-7 min) and in the middle (after 40 min) of each laboratory session. The LEAFF intervention was deliberately brief and involved a discussion about the importance of making errors when learning to program. This intervention was administered in a previous study with statistically significant effects (see Bustos Gomez & Leighton, 2013). More specifically, the following describes verbatim the intervention that was administered in the first 5-7 min (and then later after 40 min) in each laboratory session.

> You might have experienced in past classes that learning is a rewarding experience, but it also can be risky. Learning takes us from a state of not knowing to a state of coming to know, and this complex process involves several elements such as making mistakes. Making mistakes is part of learning. Actually, psychologists tell us that—in most cases—making mistakes help us learn.
>
> Mistakes help our brain clearly separate what is correct and incorrect. In the process of learning, being able to identify mistakes, where they can happen, and talking about them can help us learn better. You may recall an experience when you were learning something and made mistakes and this helped you learn that knowledge or skill really well. With that said, learning computer programming involves making mistakes, because this process requires continually testing out your code to ensure it works. We encourage you to make mistakes, ask questions, and test your code regularly, because these are necessary aspects of learning.

The experimental group received the LEAFF intervention and the comparison group did not. Instead, during the first 5-7 min (and after 40 min) of the laboratory, the comparison group focused upon the laboratory challenge activity. Both groups responded to all dependent measures, which included a set of questionnaires and scales. These are described next.

MATERIALS

Participating students responded to a combination of questionnaires and scales, at three time points: before, during, and after the study. First, a pre-intervention instrument was administered only once before the initiation of the intervention to collect demographic and background information on affective and motivational variables from all participants. This was done to evaluate the comparability of the groups at the outset given that random assignment was not possible. Second, an interim instrument was administered repeatedly during every laboratory session at 10-min intervals, for a total of nine times (90 min divided by 10 min intervals) within a single laboratory session to measure students' self-reported errors and well-being. Third, a post-intervention instrument was administered twice: once at the end of the Scratch programming unit (i.e., week 6) and then again at the end of the Kodu programming unit (i.e., week 11) to measure preferences on feedback delivery and use. These materials are described in greater detail in the next section and all are shown in Appendices B–D.

Pre-Intervention Instrument

This instrument included items from four pre-existing scales as well as demographic questions.

(1) *Motivated Strategies for Learning Questionnaire* (MSLQ; Pintrich, Smith, Garcia, & McKeachie, 1991). The MSLQ is designed to measure students' motivational orientation and use of different learning strategies. Participating students responded to only 16 of the full set of 81 MSLQ items using a 7-point Likert-type scale ranging from "1: Not at all true of me" to "7: Very true of me." The Likert-type scales used in the present study were retained from the original MSLQ. Of the 16 items, four items measured intrinsic goal orientation (items #1-4; Cronbach's $\alpha = 0.74$), four items measured extrinsic goal orientation (items #5-8; Cronbach's $\alpha = 0.62$), and eight items measured self-efficacy for learning and performance (items #9-16; Cronbach's $\alpha = 0.97$; Duncan & McKeachie, 2005). Instructions for completing the scale are shown in Appendix B.

(2) *Patterns of Adaptive Learning Scale* (PALS; Midgley et al., 2000). PALS is designed to measure students' mastery, performance-approach, and performance-avoid goal orientations, which are dispositions related to achieving academic goals in learning environments. Participating students in our study responded to only 14 of the full set of 94 items using a 5-point Likert-type scale ranging from "1: Not true at all," "3: Somewhat true," to "5: Very true." Again, the Likert-type scale was retained from the original PALS. Five items reflected measures of mastery goal orientation (items #17-21; Cronbach's $\alpha = 0.74$), five items reflected measures of performance-approach goal orientation (items #22-26; Cronbach's $\alpha = 0.89$), and four items reflected measures of performance-avoid goal orientation (items #27-30; Cronbach's $\alpha = 0.74$). Instructions for completing the scale are shown in Appendix B.

(3) *Self-Efficacy for Self-Regulated Learning* (Bandura, 2006). This scale is designed to measure students' perceived capability of using a variety of self-regulated behavioral strategies during learning (e.g., "finishing homework assignments by deadlines?"). Participating students responded to 10 items (Cronbach's $\alpha = 0.84$), which are a subset of the original 54 items in the Children's Self-Efficacy Scale. Participating students responded to the instrument using a 7-point Likert-type scale ranging from "1: Not well at all" to "7: Very well." The original Likert-type scale was changed from 100 points to 7 points, which made it more comparable to other scales used in the present study and in line with previous LEAFF intervention studies (Bustos Gomez & Leighton, 2013). Instructions for completing the scale are shown in Appendix B.

(4) *Student Trust in Faculty Scale* (Forsyth, Adams, & Hoy, 2011). This scale is intended to measure students' trust in an instructor (e.g., "Instructors are/appear always ready to help"). The 13 items used (Cronbach's $\alpha = 0.90$) are a subset of the Collective Trust in Schools instrument. Students in our study responded to the instrument using a 4-point Likert-type scale ranging from "1: Strongly disagree," "2: Disagree," "3: Agree," to "4: Strongly Agree," which was retained from the original scale. Instructions for completing the scale are shown in Appendix B.

The final seven items in the pre-intervention instrument (i.e., #55-62) invited students to provide demographic information such as gender, age, ethnicity, degree program, previous computer class experiences, cumulative GPA, and expected GPA in the course.

Interim-Intervention Instrument

This instrument was used to collect data about students' well-being and self-reported errors. During each laboratory, students were asked approximately every ten minutes (9 times during the 90 minute laboratory) to indicate (1) the frequency of their learning errors during the preceding ten minutes of the laboratory session; and (2) their feelings of well-being using a feeling scale (Hardy & Rejeski, 1989). The feeling scale involves a single item that is administered repeatedly throughout a session to measure the progression of an individual's feeling of comfort or wellness during an activity. Participants respond to this single-item scale using a 10-point Likert-type scale, ranging from "-5: Very bad," "-3: Bad," "-1: Fairly bad," "0: Neutral," "1: Fairly good," "3: Good," and "5: Very good." To measure the frequency of errors, students were invited to report a tally of their errors by filling in a box at the top of the questionnaire. The instructions for the interim instrument are shown in Appendix C.

Post-Intervention Instrument

This instrument was developed to collect information about students' preferences related to feedback delivery and use from teaching assistants/instructors, colleagues, and computers (e.g., "I had timely feedback when I asked the teaching assistant and instructor for help"). The instructions and items are shown in Appendix D. Students responded to items #1-10 in the post-intervention instrument using a 4-point Likert-type scale ranging from "1: Strongly disagree," "2: Disagree," "3: Agree," and "4: Strongly agree." Another four questions were included in the post-intervention instrument to collect behavioral evidence about students' feedback preferences and frequency of feedback use. Students were also given the opportunity to elaborate on their responses to preference and frequency ratings. Instructions for completing the instrument are shown in Appendix D.

RESULTS

The results are presented in two parts. Descriptive statistical results are outlined first, including preliminary statistical analysis of pre-existing differences between the groups, followed by inferential statistical results in line with the research questions posed. All statistical analyses were performed using Statistical Package for the Social Sciences (SPSS) version 21.0 (IBM SPSS, 2013). Shown in Table 5.1 are the demographic characteristics by group, and shown in Tables 5.2–5.4 are the sample sizes by group, means, and

Table 5.2 Sample size, means, and standard deviations in parenthesis of pre-intervention instrument

	N		Mean	
	E	C	E	C
Motivated strategies for learning questionnaire				
Intrinsic goal orientation*	16	10	4.83 (0.69)	5.43 (0.62)
Extrinsic goal orientation*	16	10	5.28 (1.30)	4.40 (1.58)
Self-efficacy for learning and performance*	16	10	5.63 (0.89)	5.21 (1.22)
Patterns of adaptive learning scale				
Mastery goal orientation**	16	10	4.06 (0.56)	4.04 (0.57)
Performance goal orientation**	16	10	2.68 (1.02)	2.20 (0.81)
Performance-avoid goal orientation**	16	10	3.01 (0.77)	2.85 (0.77)
Self-efficacy for self-regulated learning+	16	10	4.38 (1.08)	4.85 (0.89)
Student trust in instructor scale++	16	10	3.34 (0.38)	3.13 (0.20)

Notes: E = Experimental group, C = Comparison group; *7-point Likert scale ranging from "1: Not at all true of me" to "7: Very true of me"; **5-point Likert scale ranging from "1: Not true at all," "3: Somewhat true," to "5: Very true"; +7-point Likert scale ranging from "1: Not well at all" to "7: Very well"; ++4-point Likert scale ranging from "1: Strongly disagree," "2: Disagree," "3: Agree," to "4: Strongly agree."

Table 5.3 Sample size, means, and standard deviations in parenthesis of interim instrument

	N		Mean	
	E	C	E	C
Week 2-6 Average feeling scale	16	10	3.66 (1.14)	3.50 (0.99)
Week 7-11 Average feeling scale	16	10	3.54 (1.36)	2.15 (1.67)
Week 2-6 Average error tally	16	8	12.30 (19.53)	5.92 (5.57)
Week 7-11 Average error tally	13	5	10.98 (8.91)	2.58 (1.77)

Notes: E = Experimental group, C = Comparison group; Ratings occurred approximately every ten minutes during the laboratory session.

standard deviations for the pre-intervention, interim, and post-intervention instruments, respectively. Achievement outcomes for the groups are shown in Table 5.5. In particular, four types of achievement outcomes were collected for the course: Scratch project mark, Kodu project mark, final paper mark, and final course grade. The final course grade was comprised of the project marks and the final paper.

Table 5.4 Sample size, means, and standard deviations in parenthesis of post-intervention instrument

	N		Mean	
	E	C	E	C
Use of teaching assistant (Scratch)	17	11	6.94 (3.80)	5.82 (6.97)
Use of colleagues (Scratch)	17	10	5.00 (4.82)	3.30 (3.95)
Use of computer (Scratch)	17	10	34.47 (41.84)	53.60 (49.21)
Use of teaching assistant (Kodu)	15	9	7.47 (3.62)	6.11 (2.85)
Use of colleagues (Kodu)	15	9	6.93 (8.41)	3.44 (3.01)
Use of computer (Kodu)	15	9	27.13 (38.69)	45.44 (51.78)

Notes: E = Experimental group, C = Comparison group; Responses were self-reported frequencies

Table 5.5 Mean grades of students in experimental and comparison groups on assignments and course

	N		Mean	
	E	C	E	C
Scratch project	18	10	80.09 (8.64)	77.29 (14.08)
Kodu project	18	10	82.41 (9.18)	86.74 (8.35)
Final paper	18	11	81.39 (6.12)	87.95 (6.85)
Final grades	18	10	84.32 (3.45)	82.40 (2.84)

Notes: E = Experimental group, C = Comparison group; Final grade comprised marks for the Scratch project, Kodu project, and the final paper. There was no final exam for the classes.

In order to determine whether there were any pre-existing differences between students in the experimental and comparison groups, a cross-tab analysis of the categorical variables in Table 5.1 was conducted and no statistically significant differences were found. Further, students' responses to the pre-intervention instrument (e.g., MSLQ) were statistically assessed using a nonparametric independent sample Mann-Whitney U-test. A nonparametric test was used because of the small sample sizes of both the experimental ($n = 16$) and comparison ($n = 10$) groups (Fagerland, 2012). Across all four sections of the pre-intervention instrument, the Mann-Whitney U-test revealed no statistically significant differences in the responses between the two groups. Therefore, at least on the demographic characteristics and measures administered before the initiation of the intervention, the groups can be considered equivalent in their overall demographic composition, motivation, adaptation to learning, self-efficacy, and trust in the instructor (see Table 5.2).

To address the first research question—whether the LEAFF intervention had an effect on students' feelings of well-being compared to a comparison group, a repeated-measures analysis was conducted on students' feeling-scale ratings. We conducted a repeated-measures analysis, a parametric statistical test instead of a nonparametric test, because we were able to capitalize upon multiple data points from participants to maintain statistical power even with the smaller sample size. Furthermore, to increase the validity and reliability of students' ratings in response to distinct programming languages (Scratch and Kodu), we averaged Scratch and Kodu ratings separately. First, we averaged students' ratings for weeks 2-6 (time 1) when students worked on learning the computer programming language Scratch. Second, we averaged ratings for weeks 7-11 (time 2) when students worked on learning the computer programming language Kodu. Individual students' ratings were averaged at these time points to (1) increase the reliability of students' self-reported ratings and address individual cases of missing data, and (2) control for the effect of learning a different computer programming language. With respect to missing data, in some cases, students did not complete all feeling-scale ratings during a laboratory session, because they finished the laboratory activity early, before the allotted 90 min, and were allowed to leave class. The repeated measure analysis revealed a statistically significant interaction between group membership and time, $F (1, 22) = 5.922$, $p < 0.05$, partial eta squared $= 0.212$, indicating that students' self-reported feelings of well-being from time 1 to time 2 changed depending upon whether they were in the experimental or comparison group. In particular, as Figure 5.2 shows, the experimental group stayed fairly consistent in their self-reported feelings at both times 1 and 2, but the comparison group declined during that time period, indicating a reduction in well-being.

To answer the second research question—that is, whether the LEAFF intervention had an effect on students' self-reported errors during laboratory sessions—we intended to conduct another repeated-measures analysis to capitalize on multiple data points over time. As with students' feeling-scale ratings, students' self-reported errors were averaged for weeks 2-6 and for weeks 7-11. Again, this was done to increase the reliability and validity of reported errors, given the presence of missing data and to control for the learning of two distinct programming languages, Scratch and Kodu; however, we did not conduct the repeated-measures analysis, opting instead to conduct a nonparametric analysis for the following two reasons. First, the sample of students providing data on self-reported errors decreased compared to the number of students providing feeling-scale ratings. For example, for feeling-scale ratings, 16 students in the experimental group and 10 in

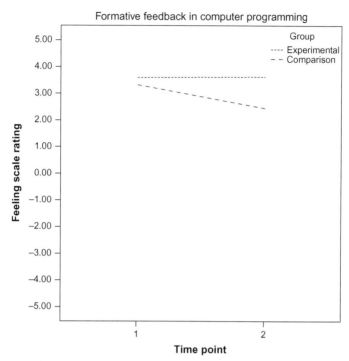

Figure 5.2 Feeling scale ratings for experimental and comparison groups.

the comparison group provided data; however, for self-reported errors, only 13 students in the experimental group and 5 in the comparison group (see Table 5.3) provided data. We explore possible reasons for this attrition in the comparison group in the discussion section. Second, the distribution of self-reported errors was skewed compared to feeling-scale ratings, probably given the smaller sample size, thus rendering the repeated-measures analysis potentially insensitive to any treatment effects, given the violation of normality. For this reason, a nonparametric, independent samples Mann–Whitney U-test (one-tailed) was conducted to evaluate the frequency of self-reported errors between the experimental and comparison groups at time 1 and then again, independently, at time 2.

Although self-reported errors decreased for both groups from time 1 to time 2, as shown in Figure 5.3, the experimental group self-reported more errors than the comparison group at both time 1 and time 2. The frequency of self-reported errors was not statistically different between the groups at time 1 (weeks 2-6), but it was at time 2 (weeks 7-11), ($E = 10.98$

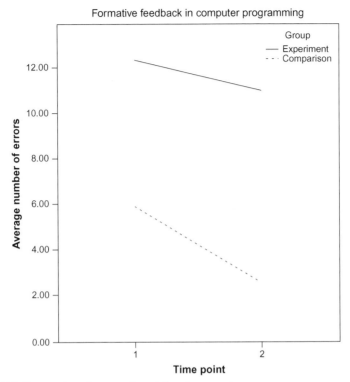

Figure 5.3 Error ratings for experimental and comparison groups.

versus $C=2.58$), $U=7.0$, $z=-2.52$, $p<0.01$. The experimental group self-reported more errors, in spite of indicating more computing experience on the demographic section of the pre-intervention instrument. Although having more knowledge about a content area could lead to greater confidence in self-reporting errors, it could also just as easily work against doing so, if students feel they should know more than they do. This interpretation requires more study; however, we do not think that participants in the experimental group self-reported errors simply because they had more pre-existing computing knowledge. This is corroborated by the fact that we found no statistically significant differences between the groups in computing experience (as measured by the pre-intervention instrument). In addition, achievement outcomes revealed that the experimental group did not perform consistently better than the comparison group. In particular, a Mann-Whitney U-test revealed that the comparison group performed better than the experimental group on the final paper,

$U=45$, $z=-2.44$, $p<0.01$, but the experimental group performed better than the comparison group in terms of the final grade in the course, $U=50$, $z=1.92$, $p<0.05$.

To answer the third research question—whether the LEAFF intervention had an effect on students' preferences for feedback delivery and use—two analyses were conducted. First, to test the effect of the intervention on preferences for feedback delivery, a crosstab analysis was conducted given the categorical response scale (i.e., whether they preferred feedback from a teaching assistant, colleague, or computer). The results showed no statistically significant difference between the two groups of participants with regard to preferences for feedback delivery. Second, to analyze students' use of different types of feedback delivery, Poisson loglinear regressions were conducted given students reported use of feedback as a frequency count. The experimental group reported using colleagues' feedback significantly more often than the comparison group when learning to program using Scratch, $b=0.42$, SE, 0.21, $p<0.05$. This was again observed with the computer program Kodu; the experimental group reported using colleagues' feedback significantly more often than the comparison group, $b=0.70$, SE, 0.20, $p<0.01$. In contrast, the comparison group reported using computer-generated feedback significantly more often than the experimental group when learning Scratch, $b=0.44$, SE, 0.06, $p<0.001$. This was again observed with Kodu with students in the comparison group reporting the use of computer-generated feedback more often than the experimental group, $b=0.52$, SE, 0.07, $p<0.001$. There were no statistically significant differences between the groups on any other part of the post-intervention instrument.

Missing data were also analyzed to examine the impact on the findings, and to explore differential completion rates across the experimental and comparison groups as an index of student engagement. Following a similar procedure as Bosnjak and Tuten (2001), survey completion was defined as (1) the percentage of surveys each student completed fully, and (2) the percentage of items students completed during the course. Using the Mann–Whitney U-test, the results indicated a statistically significant difference between students' instrument completion rates by group membership, namely, students in the experimental group completed more surveys than the comparison group, $U=48.00$, $z=-2.57$, $p<0.01$. Moreover, students in the experimental group completed a higher percentage of items than the comparison group, $U=52.00$, $z=-2.37$, $p<0.05$. The next section of this paper will discuss these results.

DISCUSSION AND CONCLUSION

The objective of the present research was to investigate the effects of an instructional intervention based upon the LEAFF model within a technology-rich learning environment. In this section, we discuss the results of the educational intervention we conducted, namely, the explicit discussion of errors, and its effects on students' sense of well-being, self-reported errors, and preferences related to distinct modes of feedback delivery and use.

The first question focused on the effects of the LEAFF intervention on students' sense of well-being. The results indicated that students in the LEAFF intervention group maintained feelings of well-being, while the comparison group declined in its feelings of well-being through the duration of the course. That the experimental group was able to maintain its positive feelings of well-being could be attributed to the intervention facilitating a more trusting learning environment, in which making errors is viewed as an integral aspect of the learning process (Leighton et al., 2013). This may have helped create a climate in which students felt at ease making mistakes and did not feel discouraged as they acquired new knowledge and skills (Boekaerts & Corno, 2005). The experimental group did indicate a greater level of computing experience, but this level of experience was not statistically different from the comparison group. Further, this reported level of computing experience did not give the experimental group a consistent advantage in achievement outcomes (see Table 5.5). In fact, the comparison group, which reported less computing experience, performed statistically better than the experimental group on the final paper. This finding may be accounted for in the LEAFF model—when students feel safe to report what they do not understand and the errors they are making—performance on proximal assessments such as a final paper may be lowered, as students are attempting to gain deeper knowledge and not simply learning for the exam. One of the predictions of the LEAFF model is that students in LEAFF-based interventions may see a temporary drop in their performance, but eventually observe improvement as their foundational knowledge is solidified. This was observed in our results; the experimental group performed less well on the final paper relative to the comparison group, but in terms of their overall final grade, the experimental group exhibited superior performance. Based upon the LEAFF model, we speculate that when students form mental models that help them perceive their learning environment to be safe and supportive, the fear of tackling more difficult and challenging concepts and the stigma of producing errors as these new knowledge and skills are learned might be lessened. In this type of learning environment, we would expect students to feel at ease about their learning, leading to feelings of well-being about learning and the course.

The second question focused on the effects of the LEAFF intervention on the number of self-reported errors made by students during class. Results indicated the self-reported errors decreased generally for both groups from time 1 to time 2, but the difference between errors reported by the experimental group and comparison group was statistically significant at time 2 (i.e., weeks 7-11). That the frequency of self-reported errors was significantly different between the groups only at time 2 could be due to a variety of reasons, deserving further study. One explanation could be that the LEAFF-based intervention over time was able to help maintain the experimental group's focus on reporting errors; however, the comparison group, which did not receive the intervention, did not have a similar focus and therefore exhibited a steeper reduction in the errors reported at time 2. We speculate that students in the comparison group might have withheld reporting their errors not only because they were not focused on their importance, but also because they may not have felt at ease disclosing them to the degree encouraged in the experimental group. It is also worth noting that fewer students in the comparison group were willing to self-report errors compared to the experimental group; 13 out of 16 students in the experimental group self-reported errors, but only 5 out of 10 in the comparison group did the same (see Table 5.3). Further, we noted statistically significant differences between the percentage of students in the comparison and experimental groups who completed items and full-survey instruments, again suggesting potentially differential levels of involvement and engagement (Frijda & Mesquita, 1994). This positive evaluation of the course might have helped experimental-group students feel more invested in the learning process, the course, and willingness to share their feelings, frequency of errors, and feedback preferences with study investigators (Leighton et al., 2013).

The third question focused on the effects of the LEAFF intervention on students' preferences for delivery and use of feedback. Students from the experimental group tended to use their colleagues' feedback significantly more often than students in the comparison group. This may be explained on the grounds that students in the experimental group felt a greater sense of well-being within the learning environment compared to the comparison group. As indicated in the LEAFF model, students in the experimental group would have had the typical unpleasantness associated with making mistakes in front of colleagues attenuated given the focus of the intervention on the necessity of errors for learning. Thus, the LEAFF-based intervention may have helped students in the experimental group experience greater willingness to use colleagues' feedback than students in the comparison group. Conversely, students in the comparison group tended to use computer-generated feedback significantly more often than the experimental group. Lacking the intervention, students in this group might have felt more of the typical stigma associated with making errors than the experimental group. Hence, they might have found it more comforting to use the non-judgmental computer-generated feedback to enhance their learning performance.

In short, our findings are in line with previous research (Bustos Gomez & Leighton, 2013) indicating that brief interventions based upon the LEAFF model may be beneficial in terms of helping students maintain positive feelings of well-being during learning. Further, as expected, the intervention resulted in students identifying more of their mistakes, and indicating their preference for human feedback (i.e., input from colleagues) to inform their learning. By removing the stigma associated with errors and facilitating the formative aspects of feedback, a brief LEAFF-based intervention could facilitate student outlooks on learning now and into the future. Interestingly, students in the comparison group, which did not receive the LEAFF-based intervention, indicated preferences for using computer-generated feedback more often than the experimental group. This latter finding needs to be investigated further, but it suggests that technology might facilitate feedback precisely in those situations where the learning environment is viewed as less safe and students feel more vulnerable as they learn new skills. This study used a traditional computer-programming classroom to investigate the LEAFF model, but there is a need to consider different types of learning environments, such as massive open online courses (MOOCs) or distant learning classrooms. The use of classrooms often creates the limitation of using a sample of convenience, because it is difficult to randomly assign students to different classes without altering students' preferred timetables. In addition, this study employed a quasi-experimental framework, and our results should be investigated using experimental frameworks, if possible. Although understanding the environmental conditions that can facilitate student learning and uptake of feedback is vital to helping students acquire new knowledge and skills, greater empirical and experimentally based research into interventions is required.

ACKNOWLEDGEMENT

Preparation of this chapter was supported by a grant to the second author from the Social Sciences and Humanities Research Council of Canada (SSHRC Grant No. 410-2011-0811). Grantees undertaking such projects are encouraged to express freely their professional judgment. This paper, therefore, does not necessarily represent the positions or the policies of the Canadian government, and no official endorsement should be inferred. Correspondence pertaining to this chapter should be directed to Man-Wai Chu or Jacqueline P. Leighton by airmail at 6-110 Education North, Centre for Research in Applied Measurement and Evaluation (CRAME), Dept. of Educational Psychology, Faculty of Education, University of Alberta, Edmonton, Alberta, CANADA T6G 2G5 or email at manwai@ualberta.ca or jacqueline.leighton@ualberta.ca.

APPENDIX A

Weeks	Laboratory Objective and Activity
1	Students will learn basic game-design elements and fundamental steps involved in creating and executing Scratch applications such as importing characters, moving characters using arrow keys, sensing character position, controlling environment settings, and storing and retrieving data
2	Students will learn advanced game design elements such as developing applications that can manipulate numeric data (e.g., add, subtract, multiply, divide, and generate random numbers), implementing loops and conditional programming logic, controlling the actions, appearance, and behavior of both characters and the background during different stages of a game
3	Students will learn role-playing game-design elements such as adding background music to the game and changing the appearances of the characters and background during the game
4	Students will practice all of the above elements in a laboratory challenge designed to utilize most of the skills listed above
5	Scratch assignment due—students presented their assignments
6	Students will learn the fundamental steps involved in creating and executing Kodu applications such as creating an environment, moving characters using the remote controller, and automating character movements
7	Students will learn to develop water and three-dimensional environments such as a lake ecosystem and obstacle course
8	Students will learn to change the appearance of characters and environments such as creating a first-person shooter game and allowing characters to switch vehicles and weapons during the game

Weeks	Laboratory Objective and Activity
9	Students will learn to increase difficulty levels of a game such as creating characters who can teleport to different locations of the environment and allowing "level-up" during the game
10	Kodu assignment due—no surveys administered

APPENDIX B

Pre-Intervention Instrument

Motivated Strategies for Learning Questionnaire (Pintrich et al., 1991)

Using the scale below and *thinking about your classes in general*, please rate the following items. Please answer all items, even if you are not sure. Please select only a single rating for each item.

1. I prefer class material that really challenges me so I can learn new things.
2. I'm certain I can understand the most difficult material presented in the textbook for the class.
3. The most satisfying thing for me in class is trying to understand the content as thoroughly as possible.
4. When I have the opportunity in class, I choose topics of class projects that I can learn from even if they don't guarantee a good grade.
5. Getting a good grade in the class is the most satisfying thing for me right now.
6. The most important thing for me right now is improving my overall school average, so my main concern in the class is getting a good grade.
7. If I can, I want to get better grades in the class than most of the other students.
8. I want to do well in the class because it is important to show my ability to my family, friends, or others.
9. I believe I could receive an excellent grade on an exam.
10. I'm certain I can understand the most difficult material presented during lectures.
11. I'm confident I can understand the basic concepts taught in lectures.
12. I'm confident I can understand the most complex material presented during lectures.
13. I'm confident I can do an excellent job on the assignments and tests.
14. I would expect to do well in this course and future ones.
15. I'm certain I can master the skills being taught during lectures.

16. Considering the difficulty of this course, I think I will do well in this course.

   Patterns of Adaptive Learning Scales (Midgley et al., 2000)

   Using the scale below and *thinking about your classes in general*, please rate the following items. Please answer all items, even if you are not sure. Please select only a single rating for each item.

17. It's important to me that I learn a lot of new concepts this year.
18. One of my goals in class is to learn as much as I can.
19. One of my goals is to master a lot of new skills this year.
20. It's important to me that I thoroughly understand my class work.
21. It's important to me that I improve my skills this year.
22. It's important to me that other students in my class think I am good at my class work.
23. One of my goals is to show others that I'm good at my class work.
24. One of my goals is to show others that class work is easy for me.
25. One of my goals is to look smart in comparison to the other students in my class.
26. It's important to me that I look smart compared to others in my class.
27. It's important to me that I don't look stupid in class.
28. One of my goals is to keep others from thinking I'm not smart in class.
29. It's important to me that my teacher doesn't think that I know less than others in class.
30. One of my goals in class is to avoid looking like I have trouble doing the work.

   Self-Efficacy for Self-Regulated Learning (Bandura, 2006)

   Using the scale below and *thinking about how you normally behave in terms of your schoolwork,* please rate the following items. Please answer all items, even if you are not sure. Please select only a single rating for each item.

31. Finish homework assignments by deadlines?
32. Study when there are other interesting things to do?
33. Concentrate on school subjects?
34. Take class notes of class instruction?
35. Use the library to get information for class assignments?
36. Plan your schoolwork?
37. Organize your schoolwork?
38. Remember information presented in class and textbooks?
39. Arrange a place to study without distractions?
40. Motivate yourself to do schoolwork?
41. Participate in class discussions?

Student Trust in Faculty Scale (Forsyth et al., 2011)

Using the scale below and *thinking about your course experiences in general*, please indicate how much you agree or disagree with each of the following statements. Please answer all items, even if you are not sure. Please select only a single rating for each item.

42. Instructors are/appear always ready to help.
43. Instructors are/appear easy to talk to.
44. Students are/appear well cared for in classes.
45. Instructors always do what they are supposed to.
46. Instructors really listen to students.
47. Instructors are/appear always honest with me.
48. Instructors do a terrific job.
49. Instructors are/appear good at teaching.
50. Instructors have high expectations for all students.
51. Instructors DO NOT care about students.
52. Students can believe what the instructor tells them.
53. Students learn a lot from the instructor.
54. Students can depend on instructors for help.

Demographics

55. Please indicate your gender:
    ☐ Male ☐ Female ☐ I prefer not to respond
56. Please indicate your birth date: _____ (month)/_____ (day)/ _____ (year)
57. Please indicate one or more of the following groups to which you self-identify in terms of ethnicity:
    ☐ Caucasian
    ☐ Chinese
    ☐ South Asian (e.g., East Indian, Pakistani, Sri Lankan *etc.*)
    ☐ African American
    ☐ Filipino
    ☐ Latin American
    ☐ Southeast Asian (e.g., Cambodian, Indonesian, Laotian, Vietnamese, *etc.*)
    ☐ Arab
    ☐ West Asian (e.g., Afghan, Iranian, *etc.*)
    ☐ Japanese
    ☐ Korean
    ☐ Other: _____
58. How many EDIT (Education Instructional Technology) class(es) have you previously taken: _____

59. How many CMPUT (Computer Science) class(es) have you previously taken: _____

60. In what university degree program are you presently enrolled in (e.g., Bachelor of Education)?

   _____

61. What is your approximate overall GPA up to now in university courses? Mark one option only.
   ☐ A+/A
   ☐ A-
   ☐ B+
   ☐ B
   ☐ B-
   ☐ C+
   ☐ C
   ☐ C- or lower

62. What is an approximate potential grade you think could receive from a class based upon this type of lecture? Mark one option only.
   ☐ A+/A
   ☐ A-
   ☐ B+
   ☐ B
   ☐ B-
   ☐ C+
   ☐ C
   ☐ C- or lower

APPENDIX C

Interim-Intervention Instrument
Tally of Learning Errors
During the "lab challenge" portion of the lab please tally how often you made a mistake/error, asked a question, tested your program, or had a misconception in the box below:

Feeling Scale
As part of this study, we are interested in knowing how you are feeling at different moments during the class. Please rate your overall feeling of comfort each time the instructor or teaching assistant asks you to do so. You will be asked to rate your feelings throughout the "lab challenge" task.

I FEEL

−5	−4	−3	−2	−1	0	1	2	3	4	5
Very bad		Bad		Fairly bad	Neutral	Fairly good		Good		Very good

APPENDIX D

Post-Intervention Instrument

Using the scale below and *thinking about your experiences working on your programming assignment*, please indicate how much you agree or disagree with each of the following statements. Please answer all items, even if you are not sure. Please select only a single rating for each item.

1. I had timely feedback when I asked the teaching assistant and instructor for help.
2. Feedback from the teaching assistant and instructor were helpful when I had a question.
3. Feedback from my colleagues was helpful when I had a question.
4. Feedback from my computer was helpful when I had a question.
5. I preferred to ask the teaching assistant and instructor for help when I had a question.
6. I preferred to ask my colleagues for help when I had a question.
7. I preferred to solve my problems using the computer feedback when I had a question.
8. I often asked the teaching assistant and instructor for help when I had a question.
9. I often asked my colleagues for help when I had a question.
10. I often used the computer feedback to solve the problem when I had a question.
    While working on this video game programming assignment:
11. Rate your most preferred form of feedback: (1 = most preferred and 3 = least preferred)
    _____ Teaching Assistant and Instructor
    _____ Colleagues
    _____ Computer-generated
12. Describe why you prefer your 'most preferred' form of feedback instead of the other two forms of feedback.

    _____

    _____

13. How often did you utilize each form of feedback: (e.g., 8 times)

_____ Teaching Assistant and Instructor

_____ Colleagues

_____ Computer generated

14. Describe why you utilized one form of feedback more often than the other two forms of feedback.

_____

_____

REFERENCES

Bandura, A. (2006). Guide for creating self-efficacy scales. In F. Pajares & T. C. Urdan (Eds.), *Self-efficacy beliefs of adolescents* (pp. 307–337). Charlotte, NC: Information Age Publishing.

Bangert-Drowns, R. L., Kulik, C. C., Kulik, J. A., & Morgan, M. T. (1991). The instructional effect of feedback in test-like events. *Review of Educational Research, 61*(2), 213–238. http://dx.doi.org/10.3102/00346543061002213.

Boekaerts, M., & Corno, L. (2005). Self-regulation in the classroom: A perspective on assessment and intervention. *Applied Psychology: An International Review, 54,* 199–231. http://dx.doi.org/10.1111/j.1464-0597.2005.00205.x.

Bosnjak, M., & Tuten, T. (2001). Classifying response behavior in web-based surveys. *Journal of Computer Mediated Communication, 6*(1), 1–14. Retrieved August 10, 2001, http://archive.is/kI8i.

Bustos Gomez, M. C., & Leighton, J. P. (2013). A classroom intervention for a safe learning environment: A test of the LEAFF model. In *Presentation delivered at the symposium (organizer J. Leighton) assessment and measurement of learning in light of learners' affective and cognitive states at the annual meeting of the Canadian Society for Studies in Education (CSSE), Victoria, BC, Canada.*

Damasio, A. (2001). Emotion and the human brain. In A. R. Damasio, A. Harrington, J. Kagan, B. S. McEwen, H. Moss, & R. Shaikh (Eds.), *Unity of knowledge: The convergence of natural and human science* (pp. 101–106). New York City: New York Academy of Sciences.

Duncan, T. G., & McKeachie, W. J. (2005). The making of the motivated strategies for learning questionnaire. *Educational Psychologist, 40*(2), 117–128. http://dx.doi.org/10.1207/s15326985ep4002_6.

Dweck, C. S. (2006). *Mindset.* New York: Random House.

Fagerland, M. W. (2012). T-test, non-parametric tests, and large studies—A paradox of statistical practice? *Medical Research Methodology, 12*(78), 1–7. Retrieved from, http://www.biomedcentral.com/1471-2288/12/78.

Forsyth, P. B., Adams, C. M., & Hoy, W. K. (2011). *Collective trust: Why schools can't improve without it.* New York, NY: Columbia University Teachers College Press.

Frijda, N. H., & Mesquita, B. (1994). The social roles and functions of emotions. In S. Kitayama & H. R. Markus (Eds.), *Emotion and culture* (pp. 51–88). Washington, DC, USA: American Psychological Association.

Hardy, C. J., & Rejeski, W. J. (1989). Not what, but how one feels: The measurement of affect during exercise. *Journal of Sport and Exercise Psychology, 11,* 304–317.

IBM SPSS for Windows 21.0 [Computer software]. (2013). Chicago, IL: SPSS Inc.

Johnson-Laird, P. N. (1983). *Mental models.* Cambridge, MA: Harvard University Press.

Kluger, A. N., & DeNisi, A. (1996). The effects of feedback interventions on performance: A historical review, meta-analysis, and a preliminary feedback intervention theory. *Psychological Bulletin, 119,* 254–284. Retrieved from, http://awalmsley.info/?p=83.

Lajoie, S. P. (2008). Metacognition, self regulation, and self-regulated learning: A rose by any other name? *Educational Psychology Review*, *20*, 469–475. Retrieved from, http://cocurricular-design.wikispaces.com/file/view/Metacognition.pdf.

Leighton, J. P., Chu, M. -W., & Seitz, P. (2013). Cognitive Diagnostic assessment and the learning errors and formative feedback (LEAFF) model. In R. Lissitz (Ed.), *Informing the practice of teaching using formative and interim assessment: A systems approach* (pp. 183–207). Charlotte, North Carolina: Information Age Publishing.

Lewis, R. B. (1998). Assistive technology and learning disabilities: Today's realities and tomorrow's promises. *Journal of Learning Disabilities*, *31*, 16–26.

Midgley, C., Maehr, M. L., Hruda, L. Z., Anderman, E., Anderman, L., Freeman, K. E., et al. (2000). *Manual for the patters of adaptive learning scales*. University of Michigan. Retrieved from, http://www.umich.edu/~pals/PALS%202000_V13Word97.pdf.

Pintrich, P. R., Smith, D. A. F., Garcia, T., & McKeachie, W. J. (1991). *A manual for the use of the motivated strategies for learning questionnaire (MSLQ)*. Ann Arbor, MI: University of Michigan, National Center for Research to Improve Postsecondary Teaching and Learning. Retrieved from, http://files.eric.ed.gov/fulltext/ED338122.pdf.

Roed, J. (2003). Language learner behaviour in a virtual environment. *Computer Assisted Language Learning*, *16*(2-3), 155–172. http://dx.doi.org/10.1076/call.16.2.155.15880.

Shute, V. (2008). Focus on formative assessment. *Review of Educational Research*, *78*, 153–189. Retrieved from, http://myweb.fsu.edu/vshute/pdf/shute%202008_b.pdf.

CHAPTER 6

Emotions in Learning with Video Cases

Martin Gartmeier[a], Tina Hascher[b]
[a]TUM School of Education, München, Germany
[b]University of Bern, Bern, Switzerland

INTRODUCTION

In our modern age of 3-D glasses, computer games, and immersive virtual environments that resemble motion pictures, videos no longer represent the cutting edge of multimedia technology. Nonetheless, never before has it technically been so easy to produce and publish videos, and to use them for a multitude of purposes. Along with this immense increase in their availability, videos have become a common element of a range of instructional strategies, educational programs, and institutions (e.g. de Leng, Dolmans, van de Wiel, Muijtjens, & van der Vleuten, 2007; Maclean & White, 2007).

In-line with this increased use of videos for educational purposes, educational researchers are challenged to deepen our understanding of how to integrate videos into instructional environments in ways that positively affect learning processes and outcomes (Balslev, 2011; Karppinen, 2005). Drawing upon Clark (1983), we do not mean to suggest that learning can be achieved merely by watching a video. Instead, what matters is how learners interact with and make sense of the video material. This sense-making process has not only a cognitive dimension, but also an emotional one.

Theoretically, videos provide a wide range of possible scenarios to influence learning processes. One of these scenarios is the use of videos serving as a basis for reflecting on particular situations of professional practice, such as when medical students watch and analyze a video of a physician-patient conversation. So far, existing studies have conceptualized and empirically investigated the effects of the integration of videos in learning environments, mainly on the cognitive and behavioral level (Balslev, 2011; Blomberg, Stürmer, & Seidel, 2011; Romanov & Nevgi, 2007). Videos, however, not only address cognitive aspects such as information perception and processing, they also stimulate emotions (Karppinen, 2005). Nevertheless, the emotional dimension of learning with videos has not yet received much attention from researchers.

Before addressing this topic, some clarification is necessary on what we mean when talking about videos in the present chapter. The term "video" today is a label used for a huge variety of material, from blurry mobile phone videos to expensively produced music videos. In our analysis, we focus on video cases as one particular form of instructional video (Digel, Goeze, & Schrader, 2012; Stephens, Leavell, Fabris, Buford, & Hill, 1999). Instructional video cases show scenes from a particular professional practice, such as a sequence taken from a physician-patient dialog or a school lesson, whereby the focus is on the professional actor(s). Mostly, video cases show one particular and self-contained scene, for example, one conversation. Video cases can also show *authentic* scenes (e.g. a *real* teacher teaching a *real* class) or *staged* scenes (involving actors or a script)—a differentiation that will later be relevant at several points of the present analysis.

We argue that video cases provide rich sources for learning because they can make learners reflect on professional practices and ways to solve specific work-related problems (Fertleman, Gibbs, & Eisen, 2005; Wetzel, Radtke, & Stern, 1994). The way in which video cases are used in profession-related curricula such as in university or in continuing education is an interesting area in which to explore the connection between emotions and learning.

Due to the richness and narrative quality with which videos can showcase work processes, professional behavior, and interpersonal interaction, they have great potential to induce emotional reactions in recipients (Karppinen, 2005) and add an emotional dimension to learning processes. For example, a viewer might feel surprise and curiosity when recognizing that his usual strategy of solving a particular professional task is rather poor compared with the strategy showcased in a video case. Accordingly, a video case can encourage or motivate professionals to learn certain behaviors. Anger could emerge from the viewer's impression that the showcased behavior is inappropriate or that an aspect of the practice is depicted in a way that is considered poor compared with the accepted standards established by a certain profession.

The given examples describe emotional reactions caused by watching a video case. We argue that these emotions can affect associated learning processes. As a rough systematization, a video case may first cause an array of spontaneous, unreflected, and immediate emotional reactions. Second, this initial reaction may be transformed into a more cognitive, comparative evaluation of things shown in a video case as well as one's own competencies or experiences. Third, the resulting emotions may affect any further learning processes; they might be enriched or intensified, entirely obviated, controlled, or changed in other ways. This systematization ties in well with established psychological theories (e.g. Pekrun, Frenzel, Goetz, & Perry, 2007) that assume emotions have a mediating role with regard to learning processes. Beyond this assumption, it is an important goal for research to unveil the processes and circumstances under which particular emotions have a more facilitating or a rather inhibiting effect on learning.

In this chapter, we will discover which roles emotions play in learning with video cases. In order to establish a conceptual framework as a basis for this, we first explicate the emotion-concept we draw upon in the current analysis. We then elaborate on how video cases can induce emotions in the learner, and thereby focus the more surface-oriented characteristics of the video material, which may influence immediate and spontaneous emotional reactions. We also outline theories apt to model emotional reactions to video cases. We go on to analyze the potential of videos to bring learners to empathize with the characters portrayed therein and finally, we draw conclusions for further research and educational practices.

EMOTIONS CONCEPTUALIZED

We understand emotions as subjective, conscious, multifaceted phenomena, which may involve characteristic sets "of coordinated psychological processes, including affective, cognitive, physiological, motivational, and expressive components" (Pekrun & Linnenbrink-Garcia, 2014, p. 2). Compared with *moods*, emotions are of higher intensity and are distinctively *relational* phenomena. Emotions are directed toward a specific focus, such as a particular event, a person, or an object (Shuman & Scherer, 2014). Drawing on this conception, we now focus on two understandings of emotions that are especially suitable to analyze the interrelation between emotions and learning with video cases: first, the aforementioned idea that emotion consists of components; and, second, the episodic character of emotions.

Components of Emotions

Describing them as multifaceted phenomena, Shuman and Scherer (2014) focus emotions as consisting of different components (Scherer, 1984). Besides the subjective feeling itself (the affective component), emotions can involve a cognitive or appraisal component, describing the mental process of individual meaning related to the emotion (e.g. feeling desperate because of having to communicate a terrible diagnosis to a patient).

Additionally, they involve a physiologic component (e.g. to shiver or to feel sick); an action tendency or motivational component (e.g. the tendency to turn from or toward another person); as well as a motoric or expressive component (e.g. smiling, crying, or frowning) (*cf.* Russell, 2003).

This notion of emotions consisting of components has several consequences. First, a particular emotion is not only an idiosyncratic, individual phenomenon, but is in some way externalized and expressed—if it is not masked due to, for example, a person's unwillingness to show shame or envy. This externalization usually follows learned and culturally shaped, emotion-specific patterns, which other individuals are able to decode—however reliably. This is an important notion, as the idea of each emotion involving a specific pattern of meaning-making, action-tendencies, physiological, and expressive elements underlines the inter-subjective, relational element of emotions. On the one hand, it raises the question after how or how well other individuals are able to recognize emotions. On the other hand, it shows that there is something like a *language* of emotions—meaning a psychologically grounded and culturally shared signal-system that serves to express and decode emotion-related messages (e.g. Niemeier & Dirven, 1997). We assume that dynamic media formats such as videos can convey complex emotional messages in a way that is reliably understandable between individuals who share relevant aspects of their background, such as a common profession.

Episodes and Emotions

A strong connection exists between emotions and the situational context. Researchers conceptualize emotions as temporal phenomena that are evoked by particular stimuli (Pekrun & Linnenbrink-Garcia, 2014). These stimuli can be actually occurring ones such as observing a traffic accident, or mere intra-psychological phenomena such as remembering a particular episode that is connected to an emotional experience. This means emotions are strongly event-focused phenomena, which often have a specific (concrete or imagined) situational reference point (Scherer, 2005). As Breithaupt (2009) argues, understanding another person's emotions involves understanding the role an emotion plays in a specific narrative in which the person is involved. This relates to the procedural or episodic character of emotions: (1) emotions emerge from a certain stimulus or situation; (2) emotions are one aspect of a person's processing and sense-making of the stimulus or situation; (3) emotions also (partly) explain immediate reactions in the situation, as well as the further courses of action.

Video as a medium has the potential to show sequences of actions and to capture situations in their timely nature. Hence, it is specifically suitable to add an emotional component to learning processes. Additionally, a video clip may convey a specific emotional message, but it ultimately depends on the embedding of the video clip and on the observer how this message is decoded and what emotions emerge from watching the clip.

EMOTIONAL POTENTIAL OF VIDEO CASES

Not every video induces emotions. There are complex interrelations between the videos and the emotions of viewers which, in our case, are assumed to be learners. Hence, in the next section, we explore what factors influence the potential of video cases to show emotions and to evoke emotional reactions in a viewer.

Emotionally Relevant Characteristics of Video Cases

In analyzing the emotion-inducing potential of surface-level aspects of video cases, we focus on the cinematography and the narrative of such material.

Cinematography

The emotion-inducing quality of video cases can be influenced by an array of cinematographic means (Wetzel et al., 1994). The most general of these, the *mise en scene*, describes all aspects of what can be seen in a video. For example, the space or room in which a scene is played out (a classroom or an outside open space), the characters visible on the screen, and the sequences of interactions displayed.

A well-described psychological effect documenting the influence of such surface visual aspects on the reception of video material is called the "Kuleshov-effect" (e.g. Prince & Hensley, 1992). This effect describes different interpretations of a human face with a neutral facial expression, depending on what is shown in a sequential frame. The combination of the neutral face with a food item—such as a plate of soup—in the subsequent frame leads viewers to interpret the face as expressing hunger. Showing a dead person or a luscious woman in a subsequent frame induces interpretations of the person's face as expressing sadness or lust, respectively. This means, a viewer takes contextual information, which is emotionally salient, into account when drawing inferences on the emotions of a person. This effect has been verified, for example, in a study that uses neurobiological measurement strategies (Mobbs et al., 2006).

For the present analysis, we conclude that cinematographic means can be used in video cases to stress certain emotional aspects of a situation and make certain interpretations by learners more probable (Cohen, Sebe, Garg, Chen, & Huang, 2003; Töpper, 2010). Making use of these stylistic means is more difficult in authentic video material, such as classroom videos, than in fictional video material. One reason for this is that a person's emotions are best captured on video by showing the person's facial expression in a close-up perspective. As classroom settings are usually shot with one or more cameras that adopt long-shot or medium-shot perspectives (Seidel, Prenzel, & Kobarg, 2005), clearly capturing significant emotional expressions by any actor involved is rather difficult. In contrast, the repertoire of cinematographic means can easily be enlarged in fictional video cases. For example, actors can be instructed and camera perspectives chosen in ways that allow the director to very clearly show particular facial emotional expressions. Moreover, fictional video cases can be improved stepwise and repeated as necessary.

Narrative

With narrative aspects of video cases, we mean aspects relating to the situation and context depicted in a video case and the "story" told therein. Video cases can provide very rich narrative representations. Depending on the cinematographic quality with which a video case is produced, they can give insights into cognitive or emotional states and dynamics experienced by individuals. This is because video cases show emotional expressions embedded in sequences of interactions, which are related as causes and effects. These can be depicted either by verbalizing emotions explicitly or by expressing them through non-verbal messages, such as tone of facial expression. The latter aspect can also be described as an *embodiment* of emotions (Lowe, Herrera, Morse, & Ziemke, 2007).

The potential of video cases to enrich the learning process with emotional aspects may be further described by drawing upon learning theory. In terms of constructivist theory, video cases may enrich learning processes by serving as a situational anchor (Cognition and Technology Group at Vanderbilt, 1990). The more learners are emotionally affected by video cases, the more this anchoring effect is emphasized, which could lead to deeper, more intensive learning processes. Video cases may also tie in with a learners' previous professional experience. For example, when a tenured physician watches a video case of a doctor-patient communication, it is likely that his/her existing knowledge and experience is activated and new knowledge can more deeply be integrated.

Thus, we argue that video cases are useful media for learning because they can very realistically *display* the emotions of individuals. In the previous sections, we reviewed various criteria that influence the depiction of emotions in video cases. In the next step, we review theories that will help us to better understand the emotional reactions a viewer might experience when engaging with video cases.

Modeling Emotional Reactions to Video Cases

Two theoretical approaches are especially promising with regard to modeling emotional reactions to video cases: the appraisal approach and the control-value theory.

Appraisal Approach

Drawing upon the appraisal approach (Arnold & Gasson, 1954), we assume that the perception and evaluation of any event or situation (appraisal) are key sources of emotions (*cf.* Stein & Oatley, 1992). In an initial appraisal, a rough tendency is established that leads either to turning toward or away from the situation. In the former case, the appraisal is associated with positive emotions and based on interest or curiosity; in the latter case, negative emotions prevail, such as displeasure or discomfort (Töpper, 2010). This emotional reaction, caused by an observed event, influences further courses of action in a situation.

Due to the subjectivity of any appraisal, this interrelation is not stable or linear, i.e., it is impossible to say that a particular event (e.g. a particular sequence of a video) will cause a certain emotion. Here, the individuality of the observer comes into play when he or she evaluates an event in the light of preceding experiences or actual mood, of existing knowledge, of learning goals, or the attitudes toward a specific topic. Thus, when aiming to analyze how video cases affect a learner emotionally, we argue that three aspects are proximate: the attributes of the case, the characteristics of the learner, and the situational circumstances. Basically, it is difficult to imagine a viewer watching a video with no emotional predisposition whatsoever. So, the emotional starting point with which a viewer sets out to watch a particular video case may also influence *what* the person sees in a video and *how* the material is perceived.

Control-Value Theory

As we focus on emotional reactions in *learning* settings, the control-value theory of achievement emotions (Pekrun et al., 2007) is a relevant approach in our context. Achievement emotions are emotions that emerge in goal directed activity. That is, at some point, evaluated against an applying standard. Such an evaluation process occurs, for example, when a learner watches a video case and evaluates the events displayed against the learner's own professional competencies and practices. According to the control-value theory, achievement emotions mainly originate from two sources: the activities, which are undertaken, and the outcomes of these activities. In brief, the key assumption behind this theory is that individuals' emotional experiences are related to the degree of perceived *control* of their activities and to the *value*, which is attributed to the achievement *outcomes*. Following these assumptions, the most positive emotional experiences will result from activities that are highly controllable for individuals and that result in highly valued outcomes.

This has consequences for learning with video cases. In the best of cases, learners can adopt the perspective of the people in the situation and hence watch a video case from a vicarious point of view. The more this is the case, the stronger the emotional impact of a video case will be. This is because viewers will evaluate how well they would have been able to *control* the situation and what *outcomes* would have been achieved if they had been involved in it themselves. As was already hinted at in this chapter, the emotions a learner experiences when working with a video case may directly lead to the activation of cognitive resources. Besides, emotions may influence a learners' motivation, the application of learning strategies, and the degree to which learning occurs in a self-regulated way (Pekrun et al., 2007).

In the following section, we focus on empathy as an emotion-related psychological phenomenon, which a viewer may experience as one possible reaction to watching a video case.

Video Cases and Empathy

We regard empathy as a specific emotional reaction to video cases. Empathy is understood as a phenomenon of emotional resonance regarding the emotions of another person. Empathy means *to sense an emotional impression that originates from and mirrors emotions felt by another person presented in a particular situation* (Davis, 1996; Gibbons, 2011). Compared with perspective-taking (see above), as a more cognitive phenomenon, we assume empathy is a distinct and clear vicarious emotional impression. Basically, empathy is a general human disposition which, in the last few years, has been traced back to the very neurological structures that allows this ability in humans, the so-called "mirror-neurons" (Zaboura, 2009). More specifically, empathy can also be viewed as a profession-specific ability that plays an important role in the context of social professions, which implies a high degree of "other-focusedness". Examples of these professions are teaching and medicine. In teaching, empathy is a prerequisite for taking the emotions of learners into account when designing instruction (Parsons & Brown, 2001); in medicine, it helps to give optimal advice and care while respecting and attending to the emotions of clients (Coffmann, 1981). We argue that many professionals, such as physicians and teachers, need to delicately regulate their degree of empathy during their everyday work. If they are too emotionally detached, they will probably miss important emotional messages from their counterparts and act in ways that do not meet the needs and current dispositions of their "clients" (patients, students). In being overly empathic, professionals may lose their ability to work effectively and be overly strained by the constant need to deal with the sometimes challenging emotional situations of others. To our knowledge, this ability is a hitherto poorly researched aspect of professional competence. With regard to learning with video cases, we argue that it can allow for the creation of learning environments that help to discover what degree of empathy is appropriate and functional for professionals in everyday work situations.

Research has uncovered the fact that individuals tend to mimic the facial expressions of their counterparts and also describe their own emotions, which correspond to those of their counterparts (Dimberg, 1988; Lundqvist & Dimberg, 1995). This means that empathy is directly linked to the visual stimuli an individual receives from another person. As video cases can give clear impressions not only of another person's facial expression or emotion but also of his gestures and posture, we argue that they can provide a suitable basis for perceiving emotions and for evoking empathy.

In this respect, the situation represented in the narrative quality of videos is equally relevant. As has been advanced above, the core of an emotion is the inner feeling a particular person senses in a moment. Beyond this discrete feeling, different emotions have characteristic patterns of externalization. In a situation where a video case prompts a viewer to take over the perspective or even to empathize with a character shown in it, the possibility is created to connect a unique emotional or empathic impression with the narrative and situation presented. When the "story" told in a video case is a relevant one, a learner is allowed to understand typical challenges a professional faces in a particular field while also empathically experiencing the emotional states and impressions connected with it.

CONCLUSIONS ON LEARNING WITH VIDEO CASES

"Does what we feel affect what we learn?" (Sansone & Thoman, 2005, p. 507) is a key question that poses the vantage point of the present analysis. In answering this question with a general "yes", we seek to elucidate "how" this influence can be theoretically described and conceptually framed in learning with video cases. Basically, there is a mutual relationship of emotions and learning (*cf.* Hascher, 2010) as emotions can affect learning as well as result from learning episodes (Sansone & Thoman, 2005). In this chapter, we focus on the potential of emotions to stimulate learning.

Emotional Content

Video cases as stimuli may trigger emotional reactions. These, in turn, may influence learning processes. Drawing on what has already been advanced, two scenarios are plausible in this respect. First, a video is a direct stimulus in which emotions or emotional scenes are shown that may lead a learner to reflect upon or to empathize with the characters portrayed (Lundqvist & Dimberg, 1995). Second, a video is a very rich source of information that can activate a learner's previous experiences and the emotions associated with these (Dobson, 2004; Karppinen, 2005). To revisit the doctor-patient video example, the video may transport an obvious and direct emotional message, such as when showing the immediate reaction of a patient on the delivery of bad news. It also may elicit emotions that are related to the professional challenges associated with such a situation. Basically, it offers opportunities to empathize with both characters portrayed and may activate experiences in a viewer that relate to the depicted scene (Shuman & Scherer, 2014). Additionally, emotions can arise when evaluating the portrayed situation (e.g. as authentic).

Emotions emerging from watching a video case influence how learners perceive the case, as well as how they engage with it. *"Emotions may initiate, terminate or disrupt information processing and result in selective information processing, or they may organize recall"* (Gläser-Zikuda, Fuß, Laukenmann, Metz, & Randler, 2005). Imagine an experienced teacher watching a video case showing a parent-teacher conversation. The way in which the teacher perceives and feels about the video case will be strongly influenced by previous experiences of working with parents and the emotions associated with these. In that sense, already existing cognitions and emotions form a backdrop against which a particular video case is viewed. If a teacher has developed primarily pessimistic attitudes and negative emotions—such as frustration—in working with parents, and watches a video case showing an enthusiastic teacher talking to an open-minded and cooperative parent, it is very likely that the teacher will perceive the video from a critical, perhaps even cynical point of view. The discrepancy between experience and example may also trigger emotional reactions in the teacher, such as anger or disappointment which, in turn, would strongly influence any learning processes related to the video case.

Beyond the emotions that result from experiences accumulated across longer time periods, situation-specific emotions and moods can also affect learning processes (Efklides & Volet, 2005). This is because they may influence how learners engage in learning activities and how intense they engage in those learning activities. Obviously, emotions can support or impede learning with video cases. Hence, in the following portion of this chapter, we analyze how videos can *supportively* be implemented in emotion-related learning processes in the light of the theorization unfolded here thus far.

Showing Emotions

Drawing upon the above-described components approach to emotions (Scherer, 1984; Shuman & Scherer, 2014), any emotion can be seen as a specific, typical pattern of such components. In relating this approach to learning with video cases, the potential benefit is to provide a rich impression of how certain emotions are expressed by individuals and how they are embedded in situations typical for a particular professional context.

For example, in a medical video case, in which bad news is being broken to a patient, the patient's shock and desperation can be very realistically depicted in its multiple components. The patient may show a spontaneous shock-reaction clearly visible in the facial expression (physiological component); may initially refuse to accept the diagnosis (action tendency); may express the emotion through gesture and body language (motoric component); and may verbalize thoughts relating to the diagnosis (appraisal component).

As already mentioned, video cases can show emotions relevant in a professional situation in their multifaceted nature and, at the same time, acknowledge the episodic character of emotions. This unique potential provides opportunities to enrich learning processes. As will be shown subsequently, respective learning goals may be related to recognizing emotions in the first place, to understanding emotions regarding their genealogy, phenomenology, and consequences, and to promising strategies of handling and managing emotions in work processes.

Recognizing, Understanding, and Reacting to Emotions

Recognizing relevant phenomena in pertinent work situations is a crucial component of competence in many professions (e.g. in teaching, see Blomberg et al., 2011). Accordingly, students who wish to become professionals should develop their ability to *recognize* emotional phenomena experienced by relevant others (patients, pupils, clients, etc.).

For recognizing emotions, as well as for understanding and reacting to them, one major challenge is that they have a *general* as well as *specific* aspect. As an example, the grief a particular person feels in a situation surely is not so different from the grief felt by others who have similar experiences. Besides, psychological theories may abound about grief or about how this emotion can be handled by professionals (Baile, 2000). This means that there is generalized knowledge available to professionals about how to handle particular emotions in a concrete professional situation.

However, emotions are private and idiosyncratic phenomena, shaped by the individuals' unique life history, attitudes, knowledge, and personality. This strongly contrasts to notions of emotions relating to general categories or of recipes existing for professionals to deal with the particular emotions of their clients. Despite this duality, one could assume that the initial *recognition* of a particular emotion might be relatively easy and straightforward, given the idea that relatively stable and typical patterns of indicators for emotions exist.

Going one step further, from recognizing toward *understanding*, a particular emotion requires both: *general* knowledge about how a particular emotion is externalized by others; and *specific* insights into an individual's personality, goals, social situation, and the reasons behind the specific emotion. The professional teachers and physicians in the focus of this chapter should know what competencies they need in order to handle the emotions and deficiencies of their patients/pupils. In this respect, several learning goals may be targeted by drawing upon a case presented in video format: (1) *untangling* the different aspects of an actor's behavior that expresses emotions (*cf.* the idea of components of emotions; Shuman & Scherer, 2014); (2) *understanding* prevailing emotions in their genealogy and as resulting from processes and events in the past (*cf.* emotions as part of narratives; Breithaupt, 2009); (3) *describing* the way in which the professional actor visible in a video case copes with and handles the counterpart in its emotional constitution (*cf.* action tendency resulting from initial appraisal; Arnold & Gasson, 1954); (4) *evaluating* the presented situation against a learners' conception of what could be an adequate or an inadequate way to solve the exemplified situation, of the learners' own abilities as well as against the value the learner puts on the situation (*cf.* the control–value approach; Pekrun et al., 2007).

Empathy and Professionalism

As has been shown, regulating and balancing their empathy is a key challenge for many professionals. Imagine the problems a teacher must face when he or she empathizes with students too deeply. Some students might try to take advantage of this and make use of a teacher's willingness to react to their emotions. On the other hand, a total lack of sensibility for the emotions of pupils might result in the alienation of students, and in classroom activities failing to be perceived as relevant by students (Hascher & Hagenauer, 2010). Hence, teachers, physicians, and many other professionals should develop their ability to empathize with pupils, parents, and patients, but also to fine-tune their empathy so that it does not impair, but support their professional practice (e.g. Pedersen, 2009).

DISCUSSION AND OUTLOOK

In this chapter, we have explored interrelations between emotions and learning with video cases in the process of professional learning. Our main argument has been that video cases have the potential to show the emotional aspects of work situations. They open up a promising possibility to relate *surface-level* phenomena in personal interaction to *internal* emotional processes experienced by the actors involved in the situation. A research question emerging here is how learning environments can be designed to allow individuals to look into and reflect on both the surface-level *and* the emotional aspects of a situation. We argue that video cases can be useful for establishing knowledge about situation-specific challenges that professionals face on an emotional level.

The relevance of this can be exemplified in a medical situation that physicians find particularly challenging: the breaking of bad news (Kurer & Zekrim, 2008). Here, physicians face several challenges. They need to recognize the emotions of the patients and empathize with them. Beyond that, they need to control their own empathy and stay in charge of the conversation while attending to the requirements of the situation and the needs of the patient in an appropriate manner. This means, the challenge for the professional is to handle the situation while also managing and regulating his or her own emotions.

REFERENCES

Arnold, M. B., & Gasson, J. A. (1954). Feelings and emotions as dynamic factors in person-ality integration. In M. B. Arnold & J. A. Gasson (Eds.), *The human person* (pp. 263–278). New York: Ronald.

Baile, W. F. (2000). SPIKES. A six-step protocol for delivering bad news: Application to the patient with cancer. *The Oncologist, 5*(4), 302–311.

Balslev, T. (2011). *Learning to diagnose using patient video cases in paediatrics: Perceptive and cognitive processes.* Maastricht: Maastricht University Library.

Blomberg, G., Stürmer, K., & Seidel, T. (2011). How pre-service teachers observe teaching on video: Effects of viewers' teaching subjects and the subject of the video. *Teaching and Teacher Education, 27*, 1131–1140.

Breithaupt, F. (2009). *Kulturen der empathie [Cultures of empathy].* Frankfurt: Suhrkamp.

Clark, R. E. (1983). Reconsidering research on learning from media. *Review of Educational Research, 53*(4), 445–459.

Coffmann, S. L. (1981). Empathy as a relevant instructor variable in the experiential classroom. *Group and Organization Management, 6*(1), 114–120.

Cognition and Technology Group at Vanderbilt. (1990). Anchored instruction and its relationship to situated cognition. *Educational Researcher, 19*(6), 2–10.

Cohen, I., Sebe, N., Garg, A., Chen, L. S., & Huang, T. S. (2003). Facial expression recognition from video sequences: Temporal and static modeling. *Computer Vision and Image Understanding, 91*(1–2), 160–187.

Davis, M. H. (1996). *Empathy. A social psychological approach.* Boulder: WestviewPress.

de Leng, B., Dolmans, D., van de Wiel, M., Muijtjens, A., & van der Vleuten, C. (2007). How video cases should be used as authentic stimuli in problem-based medical educa-tion. *Medical Education, 41*(2), 181–188.

Digel, S., Goeze, A., & Schrader, J. (2012). *Aus videofällen lernen: Einführung in die praxis für lehrkräfte, trainer und berater [Learning from video cases: A practical introduction for teachers, trainers and consultants].* Bielefeld: Bertelsmann.

Dimberg, U. (1988). Facial electromyography and the experience of emotion. *Journal of Psychophysiology, 3*, 277–282.

Dobson, R. (2004). Can medical students learn empathy at the movies? *BMJ, 329*, 1363.

Efklides, A., & Volet, S. (2005). Emotional experiences during learning: Multiple, situated and dynamic. *Learning and Instruction, 15*(5), 377–380.

Fertleman, C., Gibbs, J., & Eisen, S. (2005). Video improved role play for teaching commu-nication skills. *Medical Education, 39*, 1155–1156.

Gibbons, S. B. (2011). Understanding empathy as a complex construct: A review of the lit-erature. *Clinical Social Work Journal, 39*(3), 243–252.

Gläser-Zikuda, M., Fuß, S., Laukenmann, M., Metz, K., & Randler, C. (2005). Promoting students' emotions and achievement—Instructional design and evaluation of the ECOLE-approach. *Learning and Instruction, 15*(5), 481–495.

Hascher, T. (2010). Learning and emotion—Perspectives for theory and research. *European Educational Research Journal, 9*(1), 13–28.

Hascher, T., & Hagenauer, G. (2010). Alienation from school. *International Journal of Educa-tional Research, 49*(6), 220–232.

Karppinen, P. (2005). Meaningful learning with digital and online videos: Theoretical per-spectives. *AACE Journal, 13*(3), 233–250.

Kurer, M. A., & Zekrim, J. M. (2008). Breaking bad news: Can we get it right. *Libyan Journal of Medicine, 3*(4), 200–203.

Lowe, R., Herrera, C., Morse, A., & Ziemke, T. (2007). The embodied dynamics of emo-tion, appraisal and attention. In L. Paletta & E. Rome (Eds.), *Lecture notes in computer science. Attention in cognitive systems. Theories and systems from an interdisciplinary viewpoint* (pp. 1–20). Berlin: Springer.

Lundqvist, L., & Dimberg, U. (1995). Facial expressions are contagious. *Journal of Psychophysiology, 9,* 203–211.

Maclean, R., & White, S. (2007). Video reflection and the formation of teacher identity in a team of pre-service and experienced teachers. *Reflective Practice, 8*(1), 47–60.

Mobbs, D., Weiskopf, N., Lau, H., Featherstone, E., Dolan, R. J., & Frith, C. D. (2006). The Kuleshov effect: The influence of contextual framing on emotional attributions. *Social Cognitive and Affective Neuroscience, 1*(2), 95–106.

Niemeier, S., & Dirven, R. (1997). *The language of emotions: Conceptualization, expression, and theoretical foundation.* Amsterdam: John Benjamins.

Parsons, S. C., & Brown, P. U. (2001). Educating for diversity: An invitation to empathy and action. *Action in Teacher Education, 23*(3), 1–4. http://dx.doi.org/10.1080/01626620.2001.10463068.

Pedersen, R. (2009). Empirical research on empathy in medicine. A critical review. *Patient Education and Counseling, 76*(3), 307–322.

Pekrun, R., Frenzel, A., Goetz, T., & Perry, R. (2007). The control-value theory of achievement emotions: An integrative approach to emotions in education. In P. A. Schutz & R. Pekrun (Eds.), *Emotions in education* (pp. 13–36). Amsterdam: Academic Press.

Pekrun, R., & Linnenbrink-Garcia, L. (2014). Introduction to emotions in education. In R. Pekrun & L. Linnenbrink-Garcia (Eds.), *International handbook of emotions and education* (pp. 1–10). New York: Routledge.

Prince, S., & Hensley, W. E. (1992). The Kuleshov effect: Recreating the classic experiment. *Cinema Journal, 31*(2), 59–75.

Romanov, K., & Nevgi, A. (2007). Do medical students watch video clips in eLearning and do these facilitate learning? *Medical Teacher, 29*(5), 490–494.

Russell, J. A. (2003). Core affect and the psychological construction of emotion. *Psychological Review, 110*(1), 145–172.

Sansone, C., & Thoman, D. B. (2005). Does what we feel affect what we learn? Some answers and new questions. *Learning and Instruction, 15*(5), 507–515.

Scherer, K. (1984). On the nature and function of emotion: A component process approach. In K. Scherer & P. Ekman (Eds.), *Approaches to emotion* (pp. 293–317). New Jersey: Lawrence Erlbaum.

Scherer, K. R. (2005). What are emotions? And how can they be measured? *Social Science Information, 44*(4), 695–729.

Seidel, T., Prenzel, M., & Kobarg, M. (Eds.), (2005). *How to run a video study: Technical report of the IPN video study.* Münster: Waxmann.

Shuman, V., & Scherer, K. (2014). Concepts and structures of emotions. In R. Pekrun & L. Linnenbrink-Garcia (Eds.), *International handbook of emotions and education* (pp. 13–35). New York: Routledge.

Stein, N., & Oatley, K. (1992). Basic emotions: Theory and measurement. *Cognition and Emotion, 6*(3), 161–168.

Stephens, L., Leavell, J., Fabris, M., Buford, R., & Hill, M. (1999). Producing video-cases that enhance instruction. *Journal of Technology and Teacher Education, 7*(4), 291–301.

Töpper, J. (2010). *Der filmische James Bond und sein musikalisches Leitmotiv: Ein kognitionspsychologisches Experiment zur Bildung von Inferenzen über die Emotionen des Hauptdarstellers [The cinematic James Bond and his musical leitmotif: A cognitive-psychological experiment about the establishment of inferences on the emotions of the main-actor].* Saarbrücken: VDM.

Wetzel, C. D., Radtke, P. H., & Stern, H. W. (1994). *Instructional effectiveness of video media.* Hillsdale, NJ: Erlbaum.

Zaboura, N. (2009). *Das empathische Gehirn. Spiegelneurone als Grundlage menschlicher Kommunikation.* Wiesbaden: VS.

CHAPTER 7

Identifying and Tracking Emotional and Cognitive Mathematical Processes of Middle School Students in an Online Discussion Group

Amos Lee, Sharon Tettegah
University of Illinois at Urbana-Champaign, Urbana, IL, USA

Traditionally, in K12 schools, communicating mathematical ideas was done orally or through written word/symbols in a classroom environment. Yet, as K12 schools continually upgrade their uses of information and communication technologies, the social emotional nature of teaching and learning math also is changing with the use of online environments (O'Dweyer, Carey, & Kleimen, 2007). While the concepts taught within math might be the same, how one learns and understands these concepts may differ based on the environment in which they are discussed and learned (Azeem & Ashfaq, 2010). As schools continue to use online environments to enhance their academic offerings and provide opportunities for students with a wide range of needs, it is important to understand students math cognitive and social emotional interactions online in order to better address learning needs (Oliver, Kellogg, & Patel, 2010).

When thinking about discussions, the nuances of who speaks, the order of speech, and the related emotions are important when considering math discussions. Anxiety and frustration are common in math learning in the U.S. Sierpinska, Bobos, and Knipping (2008) argue that fast pace courses focused on achievement with inefficient learning strategies all contribute to the frustration students experience with math learning. This frustration can be seen inside the classroom as students who have varying levels of self-efficacy engage in mathematics curriculum. As seen from the findings of this research, these frustrations also take place online as students use words and exclamation points to describe their frustrations to their classmates when they struggle with understanding math material. To better address the frustrations and confusion that students have with mathematics learning in an online environment, this research sought to understand how math discussions take place online and provide useful scaffolding tools to help enhance these discussions.

LITERATURE: ONLINE LEARNING AND MATH DISCUSSIONS

Online learning is expanding in all sectors of education from elementary schools to higher education promising reform and innovation (Watson & Johnson, 2010). In 2010, 48 states offered online learning programs that supplemented what students were learning in the classroom or offered an entire education online (Watson, 2010). Florida Virtual School, Illinois Virtual School, and the Michigan Virtual High School are just a few examples of fulltime online educational opportunities that did not exist a decade ago (Watson & Johnson, 2010).

More K12 schools are employing online classes to meet the varying needs of a diverse student body. For example, students in the inner city and rural schools can still have an expanded range of classes to take even if they are not offered in a traditional classroom setting at their schools (e.g., college prep, Mandarin Chinese) by extending their learning opportunities online (Watson & Johnson, 2010). Online learning also affords more opportunities for students at risk or students who cannot attend class due to health reasons. Non-native speakers also have more time to think about, plan out, and respond to other students. They can also imitate academic words used by other students in the online discussion (Sfard & Kieran, 2001; Graham & Hodgson, 2008). Kanuka and Anderson (1998) also note the benefits of having online participants from different geographical regions. They argue that diverse life experiences and cultural backgrounds can provide for a richer discussion. Yet, even with these general benefits, the nuances behind how students learn specific academic content in an online environment are important for educators and students to better understand for ways in which educational institutions can provide positive emotional scaffolding when students have difficulties with experience.

Therefore, this research addresses the need to understand how math content is understood and discussed in an online context (Oliver et al., 2010). When thinking about math in an online context, the content does not fundamentally change from what is taught in class; the major difference is the medium in which students learn math (O'Dweyer et al., 2007). This research, therefore, focuses on how math discussions, which are a crucial part of math learning, happen and progress in an online environment (Cobb, Wood, & Yackel, 1993; Oliver et al., 2010).

Practitioners and researchers maintain that discussion aids the learning process as students better acquire knowledge when in dialogue with others (Cazden, 2001; Gee & Green, 1998; Green & Dixon, 2008). Yet, the nature of classroom discussions is complex and varied. Cazden (2001) considers these complexities and variations by writing about the different types of negotiations that occur in the classroom through different discussion patterns (e.g., initiate, response, evaluate). She argues that classroom discussion can both aid and hinder a student's learning process based on the type and degree of discussion that occurs, thereby creating stimulation or frustration. For example, traditional approaches to instruction employ an initiation, response, evaluate (IRE) discussion pattern, in which the student's role is merely to respond to the teacher's initiation of a topic.

In an IRE discussion pattern, teachers may ask students questions they already know the answer to (i.e., "display questions") in order to elicit student response (Cazden, 2001, p. 46). This type of communicative event can be deemed inauthentic since the teacher already knows the answer to the question he or she is asking. Non-traditional discussion patterns, however, elicit more authentic, open-ended questions that allow student responses to take a greater role in class discussion and allow for co-negotiation enriching the learning process (Cazden, 2001; Gee & Green, 1998; Green & Dixon, 2008; Herbel-Eisenmann & Cirillo, 2009; Nystrand, 1991).

These non-traditional discussion patterns are useful, as Cobb et al. (1993) note, in helping students develop their conceptual understanding. They propose that children need time to discuss and reflect on past classroom activities and other social processes related to math. The resulting discussion provides opportunities for students to learn by actively constructing their understanding of mathematical concepts. However, to achieve a high level of discussion with everyone participating is difficult to accomplish. Specifically the management and implementation can be difficult as the discussion is co-developed and negotiated between all those involved (Cobb et al., 1993; Nystrand, 1991; Stein, 2007). These difficulties can also hinder students' efforts in better understanding a mathematical concept causing feelings of frustration and anxiety (Sierpinska et al., 2008).

This co-developed and negotiated discussion becomes even more complex when situated in an online environment and similarly, the frustrations experienced by students in math classrooms can also take place online. Students talking to each other online can create interactions where feedback and response can come from multiple peers rather than the traditional IRE pattern that occurs between a teacher and a student in the traditional classroom (Cazden, 2001). This feedback and response from multiple peers simultaneously can create multiple threads of conversation. To add to the complexity, students in an online environment are not limited to one topic, but each student can pursue multiple topics. These multiple threads create a heightened interconnectivity that cannot occur in the classroom (Cazden, 2001) but also can cause "dangling conversations" due to the changed structure of interaction that takes place online (Black, Levin, Mehan, & Quinn, 1983, p. 62).

In the classroom face-to-face interactions provide a speaking order and thematically ties together discussions (Cazden, 2001; Swan, 2003). However as Kim, Anderson, Nguyen-Jahiel, and Archodidou (2007) points out the order of online discussion are not always coherent or in sequential order. Many topics can be discussed in a parallel manner to each other, which creates multiple threads of discussion that a participant needs to track (Black et al., 1983; O'Halloran, 2000). This contingency of online discussion can make it difficult for participants to understand. Further, in an online environment where everyone can comment at the same time, post new entries or reply to other entries, the chronological order and thematic ties of the conversation no longer exist (Kim et al., 2007). What remains are multiple strands of intertwined conversation that participants discuss and track in a parallel manner (Black et al., 1983; O'Halloran, 2000). These communication difficulties in an online environment can aide in the frustration and anxiety that is associated with U.S. mathematics education. Due to lack of coherence and sequential order, students may associate negative feelings with the content of mathematics instead of the mode of communication (Black et al., 1983; Kim et al., 2007; Oliver et al., 2010).

METHODS

In order to make sense of the multiple strands of intertwined conversation in an online discussion, students must keep track of the conversation to complete an assigned task. Identification analysis, within systemic functional linguistics (SFL), is a useful analytic tool because it tracks participants and processes throughout the text from point of entry and every time they reoccur in the discussion (Martin & Rose, 2003). Identification analysis also makes it easier to keep track of what is being said at any given point and how the tracked participant or process progresses throughout the discussion. Further, choosing which participants or people to track throughout the conversation is important when making sense of a group discussion.

In an online context, students use written text as a means to communicate, since they do not speak to each other face-to-face. However, the nature of the interaction changes, as traditional turn taking no longer appears in an online context when multiple turns can be taken simultaneously (Black et al., 1983; Blanchette, 2009; Kim et al., 2007). Therefore, students may experience challenges when trying to keep track of comments stated by their peers in an online discussion. When looking specifically at discussions online, how can students keep track of the conversation that is occurring through multiple threads with different peers, and ideally reduce frustration and anxiety? O'Halloran (2000) proposes a method in her study where she used the identification analysis to track symbols representing mathematical processes. She noted that students chose and used these symbols to represent important operations and processes throughout the problem. She tracked these symbols throughout the oral and written discussions in order to investigate how students made sense of the math problem.

Further, the ability to understand how students make sense of math terms is important as they represent key processes when solving a problem (O'Halloran, 2000). Whether in class or in an online environment, students use of specific mathematical terms are important as they represent important processes or operations that are useful in thinking about a math problem. When text is the primary source of communication online, being able to track these terms as they are used throughout the discussion helps peers better understand the reasoning behind their mathematical explanations and may limit confusion and frustration (Martin & Rose, 2003).

Participants

The participants, in this study, were from an eighth grade middle school algebra class in a small urban community. All students who participated were 12 or 13 years of age ($N=10$). This convenience sample consisted of seven male students and three female students returned active consent forms signed by their parents. No money was offered for their participation and no grades were assigned. The participants, in this study, were based on one algebra class, where students ($N=20$) had access to a computer and Edmodo (see below). The participants were divided into three groups. Group 1 had two male students and two female students. Group 2 had three male students and Group 3 had two male students and one female student.

Learning Environment

Each participant in the class had a computer with Internet access. The interface chosen for this study was Edmodo. Students logged into Edmodo on a daily basis to answer any questions or to see the directions for the day. Edmodo provides a safe and easy way for classes to connect and collaborate; share content; and access homework, grades, and school notices. Nic Borg and Jeff O'Hara created Edmodo in 2008 with the goal of helping educators harness the power of social media to customize their classroom for each and every learner. Edmodo provides a controlled environment where students' online discussions can either be synchronous or asynchronous and is recorded for future viewing by allowing students to post and reply to others' posts as well.

Procedures

This study was presented to the algebra class with the premise of investigating students' math discussion in an online environment. If students chose to participate, they were asked to return their consent and assent forms. After 2 weeks, 10 students chose to participate. These 10 students were then randomly assigned into three small groups.

Each group was assigned a team discussion page on Edmodo where only members of specific student group could hold a discussion together online. The function of the online groups allowed each small group to see posts and replies from their team members only. The entire activity ran one 80-min class period. Students were distributed in different areas of the classroom so that they did not sit next to their group members during their online math activities.

The problem was posted, in Edmodo, in the following way:

Pat was in a fishing competition at Lake Pisces. She caught some bass and some trout. Each bass weighed 3 pounds, and each trout weighed 1 pound. Pat caught a total of 30 pounds of fish. She got 5 points in the competition for each bass, but since trout are endangered in Lake Pisces, she lost 1 point for each trout. Pat scored a total of 42 points.

The students were provided with the following directions to the problem:

1. Write a system of equations representing the information in this problem.
2. Solve this system to find out how many bass and trout Pat caught.
3. Check you answer by substituting your solution into the original equation.
**Remember you are working as a group to solve this problem. Discuss what you think should be done and read your group member's comments. Everyone must agree on the same solution.

Students used the discussion features in Edmodo to communicate with one another. They also collectively discussed and agreed on a solution. Students posted their thoughts and replies to each other's responses using their Edmodo group page.

Finding Common Terms

Based on participant transcripts from online discussions, multiple threads of conversation appeared to be intertwined with each other due to a lack of speaking order in the online forum. Identification analysis was employed to track students' use of specific terms that represented mathematical processes throughout their discussion. Students, at times, introduced these terms and at other times appropriated them from the other members of their group in order to explain key processes in solving the problem.

During the solution process, students used the terms in Table 7.1 to represent the mathematical processes of conversion, substitution, addition, subtraction, and division. All of the online discussions were transcribed first and then all the mathematical terms (Table 7.1) that were used to represent key processes needed to solve the problem were identified. These terms were then tracked throughout the discussion in all three groups to better understand how students used them to better understand and keep track of the conversation.

Students Use of Terms

From the terms listed in Table 7.1, each term was tracked throughout the transcript and recorded to see how many times they were used in Order 1 entries and Order 2 replies (explained below). In order to transcribe the discussion using the Edmodo interface, a distinction was made between Order 1 posts and Order 2 replies to distinguish the multiple threads of conversation. Order 1 refers to students making new entries in the discussion. Order 2 is when students, instead of new entries, replied to other students'

Table 7.1 Terms representing key mathematical processes

Mathematical processes	Terms
Equation conversion	Change, changed, convert, converting
Substitution	Substitution, substitute, substituted, plugged, put
Division	Divided
Addition	Added
Subtraction	Subtracted, subtracting

Note: These were the key processes needed to solve the problem.

entries. Appendix B shows Order 1 entries and Order 2 replies in the online discussion.

Entries and replies were transcribed based on the order of appearance from the online discussion forum (see Appendix B). A tally was made in the Order 1 and Order 2 columns depending on whether the text was from an entry thread or from a reply thread of the discussion (see Table 7.2). Then the terms were tracked throughout the text. The italized words are the mathematical terms that represent equation conversion. The bold words are the tracked terms that represent the process of substitution.

As these terms appeared in the discussion, the terms were tallied into the appropriate category and aggregated. Then, each student's use of the math terms were tallied and aggregated within each group. The aggregate of the different terms (see Table 7.3) is important because it shows the importance of mathematical terms in explaining processes as well as using them to communicate mathematical ideas in an online setting. However, one student may be the only one using the term, so the aggregate of the terms within the total transcript were compared with an aggregate of which students used which terms (see Table 7.4). The terms in Table 7.1 were also tracked using a diagram in order to visually display which terms were used throughout the discussion. The visual diagram helps display how the students used and kept track of the mathematical processes throughout their discussion.

Table 7.2 Example of coding

Speaker	Text	Equation conversion	
		Order 1	Order 2
Gabe	What steps did u take to get this?		1
Brad	First, I *changed* the equation $5b - t = 42$ int $y = mx + b$ then I used *substitution* and mixed it with the $3b + 5b - 42$. I solved to get $b = 9$ and then **plugged** that **in** to $t = 5b - 42$ to get $t = 3$		1[a]
Gabe	$5b - 1(-3b + 30) + 44 = t$ I don't think this is right what I did was *changed* the first problem to slope intercept form the I **plugged** that into the second equation	1[a]	
Gabe	Help me!	1	

Note: Pseudonyms used for student names.
[a] Mathematical terms used in text.

Table 7.3 Aggregate of terms

	Group 1		Group 2		Group 3	
Operations	Order 1[a]	Order 2[b]	Order 1[c]	Order 2[d]	Order 1[e]	Order 2[f]
Equation conversion	1	1	1	3	1	2
Substitution	6	0	3	5	1	2
Division	3	0	0	0	0	0
Addition	4	0	0	0	0	0
Subtraction	2	0	0	0	0	0

Note: Footnotes represent the actual number of Order 1 entries and Order 2 replies that students made throughout the entire discussion.
a = 15, b = 9, c = 6, d = 10, e = 9, f = 8.

Table 7.4 Percentage of mathematical terms used by each participant in the discussion

Groups	Equation conversion (%)	Substitution (%)	Division (%)	Addition (%)	Subtraction (%)
1					
Cathy	100	14.3	0	0	0
Amy	0	14.3	0	0	0
Dillon	0	42.8	67	75	100
Bob	0	28.6	33	25	0
2					
Fred	50	0	0	0	0
Brian	50	87.5	0	0	0
Mel	0	12.5	0	0	0
3					
Gabe	67	33	0	0	0
Brad	33	67	0	0	0
Eliza	0	0	0	0	0

Order of Terms in the Discussion

Appendix C shows a breakdown of the colors, shapes, and arrows used to help organize how the mathematical terms were used and tracked through multiple threads of discussion. Terms representing equation conversion is in red ink and also contains the terms listed in Table 7.1, surrounded by a rectangle box and connected by dashed arrows. The terms representing substitution are tracked using blue ink and using the list of terms available in Table 7.1, an oval shape surrounding the text, and a solid arrow. These distinctions are made to isolate the two different types of terms being tracked and to show a comparison between the two terms that represented the necessary mathematical processes to solve the problem.

RESULTS

Table 7.3 shows the aggregate of all the terms used for the respective mathematical processes. Table 7.3 also shows all three groups compared to one another.

When viewing Table 7.3, Group 1 uses terms conveying equation conversion twice and terms conveying substitution six times. The same terms occur in Group 2 and in Group 3. The mathematical processes of division, addition, and subtraction occur in Group 1's discussion, but are not used in Group 2 or in Group 3's. So the only terms used in all three groups represent equation conversion and substitution, which were key processes in solving the problem. While Table 7.3 shows the aggregate of the terms used for each particular mathematical process, Table 7.4 shows the percentage and number of times each student used the operative terms in their text contributions.

In Group 1, Cathy is the only one to introduce and use terms that represent equation conversion. Amy, Dillon, and Bob do not use any terms dealing with equation conversion; but all Group 1 members use the substitution term at least once. Dillon and Bob together use the substitution marker 70% of the time. When looking at the division, addition, and subtraction markers, Bob and Dillon are the only one in Group 1 who uses them.

In Group 2, Brian and Fred both use the equation conversion terms equally, but Brian uses the substitution term 87.5% of the time and only Mel uses the term once in his contributions. Group 3 has Gabe and Brad using the equation conversion and substitution terms in their text contributions while Eliza did not. While the percentages are useful to compare who used the terms more, it is equally important to view it in light of the number of times the terms were used in order to not over account for a term that may have only been used once in the discussion by one student.

Figure 7.1 shows the tracking process for Group 1 (see Appendix C for tracking symbols).

Cathy, in Figure 7.1, used terms twice to represent equation conversion but these terms were not appropriated by any of her peers in the same discussion. In Figure 7.1, all the students used terms related to substitution (i.e., plugged, substituted, put in) in their text contribution. Cathy simplified her explanation by using terms related to equation conversion and substitution only without actually going into detail of all the other processes she used to convert the equation. While Amy used the same term that Cathy introduced to represent substitution (i.e., plugged), she does not use the terms she used for equation conversion (i.e., changed). Dillon and Bob used similar terms

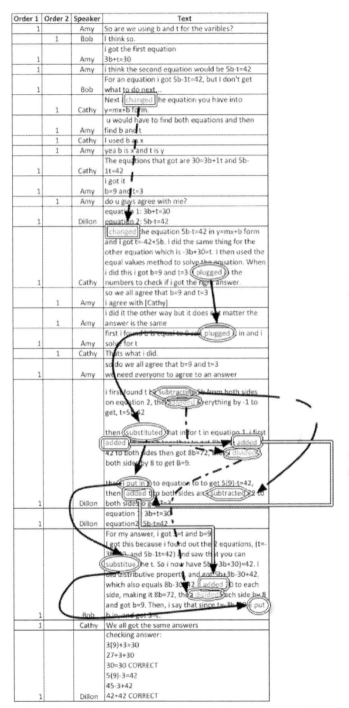

Order 1	Order 2	Speaker	Text
1		Amy	So are we using b and t for the varibles?
	1	Bob	I think so.
			i got the first equation
1		Amy	3b+t=30
1		Amy	i think the second equation would be 5b-t=42
			For an equation i got 5b-1t=42, but I don't get
1		Bob	what to do next...
			Next i changed the equation you have into
	1	Cathy	y=mx+b form.
			u would have to find both equations and then
	1	Amy	find b and t
	1	Cathy	I used b as x
	1	Amy	yea b is x and t is y
			The equations that got are 30=3b+1t and 5b-
1		Cathy	1t=42
			i got it
1		Amy	b=9 and t=3
	1	Amy	do u guys agree with me?
			equation 1: 3b+t=30
1		Dillon	equation 2: 5b-t=42
			changed the equation 5b-t=42 in y=mx+b form
			and i got t=-42+5b. I did the same thing for the
			other equation which is -3b+30=t. I then used the
			equal values method to solve the equation. When
			i did this i got b=9 and t=3 i plugged the
1		Cathy	numbers to check if i got the right answer.
			so we all agree that b=9 and t=3
	1	Amy	i agree with [Cathy]
			i did it the other way but it does not matter the
	1	Amy	answer is the same
			first i found to to equal to 42 plugged in and i
1		Amy	solve for t
	1	Cathy	Thats what i did.
			so do we all agree that b=9 and t=3
1		Amy	we need everyone to agree to an answer
			i first found t by subtracting 5b from both sides
			on equation 2, then divided everything by -1 to
			get, t=5-42
			then substituted that in for t in equation 1. i first
			added 42 to both sides then got 8b=72, i divided
			both sides by 8 to get B=9.
			then i put in b to equation to to get 5(9)-t=42,
			then added t to both sides and subtracted 42 to
1		Dillon	both sides to get t=3
			equation 1 3b+t=30
1		Dillon	equation2 5b-t=42
			For my answer, i got t=t and b=9
			i got this because i found out the 2 equations, (t=-3b+30 and 5b-1t=42) and saw that you can
			substitue the t. So i now have 5b-(-3b+30)=42. i
			did distributive property and got 5b+3b-30=42,
			which also equals 8b-30=42. i added 30 to each
			side, making it 8b=72, then divided each side by 8
			and got b=9. Then, i say that since t=-3b+30, i put
1		Bob	b in and got t=
1		Cathy	We all got the same answers
			checking answer:
			3(9)+3=30
			27+3=30
			30=30 CORRECT
			5(9)-3=42
			45-3=42
1		Dillon	42=42 CORRECT

Figure 7.1 Group 1's mathematical process terms tracked throughout the discussion.

for substitution; they chose to explain more in detail the operations needed to convert the equation and to answer the problem after substitution. For Group 1, tracking the term all students used for substitution helps show that this important mathematical process was used and tracked throughout their solution process.

In Figure 7.2, the substitution terms appear all throughout the multiple threads of discussion.

Brian used all but one of them in his Order 1 entries and his Order 2 replies. Mel used the substitution term once toward the end of the discussion but chooses to use "replace" instead of "substitute" which was used six times by Brian. Fred used the equation conversion term the first two times in the text and then the term was appropriated by Brian and used twice more. Notice Brian's statement asking what the equations meant and verbalizing his frustration and confusion in the text in Figure 7.2. Yet, he continued by explaining what he did know about the problem using key terms to explain his rationale. These same terms were then used and appropriated by his classmate Mel in his explanation of the problem.

In Figure 7.3, Gabe, Brad, and Eliza had a short conversation about how to solve the system of equations. In this text, Gabe introduced an equation conversation term (i.e., change) in the beginning of the conversation and then Brian used the term followed by Gabe repeating it. Brad introduces the substitution term (i.e., substitution, plugged) first in an Order 2 reply and then Gabe uses the term in his Order 1 entry. Also, Eliza and Gabe are both expressing their confusion and frustration through words such as "Hooowww?" and "help me!!!!!!!!!." These emotions related to mathematics are also seen in an online context and conveyed through text as they continue to try and make sense of the problem using key terms to explain their thinking.

Figures 7.1–7.3 show that the mathematical processes of conversion and substitution were important to solving the problem. Students chose terms to represent these processes and used those terms throughout the discussion as the visual diagrams show.

DISCUSSION

Understanding student's discussion patterns in online environments provides data to improve scaffolding, possibly reduce frustrations and help students learn math when engaged in online math discussions (Swan, 2003; Tallent-Runnels et al., 2006; Watson, 2010; Watson & Johnson, 2010). Online discussions, based on text, can cause multiple threads of conversation

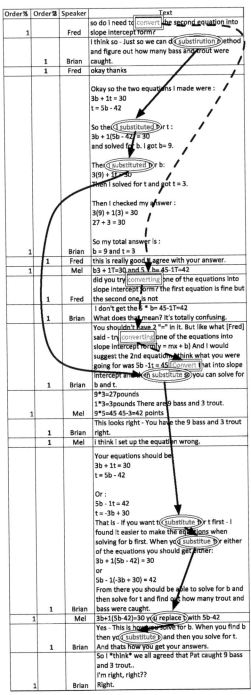

Order%	Order%	Speaker	Text
1		Fred	so do I need to convert the second equation into slope intercept form?
	1	Brian	I think so - Just so we can do substitution method and figure out how many bass and trout were caught.
	1	Fred	okay thanks
1		Brian	Okay so the two equations I made were : 3b + 1t = 30 t = 5b - 42 So then I substituted for t : 3b + 1(5b - 42) = 30 and solved for b. I got b= 9. Then I substituted for b: 3(9) + 1t = 30 Then I solved for t and got t = 3. Then I checked my answer : 3(9) + 1(3) = 30 27 + 3 = 30 So my total answer is : b = 9 and t = 3
	1	Fred	this is really good I agree with your answer.
1		Mel	b3 + 1T=30 and 5 * b= 45-1T=42
	1	Fred	did you try converting one of the equations into slope intercept form? the first equation is fine but the second one is not
	1	Brian	I don't get the 5 * b= 45-1T=42 What does that mean? It's totally confusing.
	1	Brian	You shouldn't have 2 "=" in it. But like what [Fred] said - try converting one of the equations into slope intercept form(y = mx + b) And I would suggest the 2nd equation, I think what you were going for was 5b -1t = 45 Convert that into slope intercept and then substitute so you can solve for b and t.
1		Mel	9*3=27pounds 1*3=3pounds There are 9 bass and 3 trout. 9*5=45 45-3=42 points
	1	Brian	This looks right - You have the 9 bass and 3 trout right.
	1	Mel	i think I set up the equation wrong.
	1	Brian	Your equations should be 3b + 1t = 30 t = 5b - 42 Or : 5b - 1t = 42 t = -3b + 30 That is - If you want to substitute for t first - I found it easier to make the equations when solving for b first. When you substitue for either of the equations you should get either: 3b + 1(5b - 42) = 30 or 5b - 1(-3b + 30) = 42 From there you should be able to solve for b and then solve for t and find out how many trout and bass were caught.
1		Mel	3b+1(5b-42)=30 you replace t with 5b-42
	1	Brian	Yes - This is how you solve for b. When you find b then you substitute and then you solve for t. And thats how you get your answers.
1		Brian	So I *think* we all agreed that Pat caught 9 bass and 3 trout.. I'm right, right?? Right.

Figure 7.2 Group 2's mathematical process terms tracked throughout the discussion.

Order 1	Order 2	Speaker	Text
1		Gabe	1.3b+1t=30 5b-1t+42
	1	Gabe	do change both into slope intercept form?
1		Brad	Equation 1 : 3b+1t=30 2: 5b-t=42
1		Eliza	1.) 3b+t=30 5b-t=42 b represents the amount of bass caught, t represents the amount of trout caught.
1		Gabe	what step do i do next?
1		Eliza	Question on #2, how do you make these equations equal each other if the y is different?
	1	Gabe	thats what i dont get. who else is in our group
	1	Eliza	I think it's just the three of us. [Brad] you and I?
1		Brad	3b+5b-42=30 b=9 t=3
	1	Gabe	what did u do 2 get this
	1	Eliza	Hooowww?
	1	Brad	the system or the answer
	1	Gabe	what step did u take to get this?
	1	Brad	first, i changed the equation 5b-t=42 int y=mx+b then i used substitution and mixed it with the 3b+5b-42 i solved to get b=9 and then plugged that in to t=5b-42 to get t=3
1		Gabe	5b-1(-3b+3)+44=t i dont think this is right what i did was changed the first problem to slope intercept form then plugged that into the 2nd equation
1		Gabe	help me!!!!!!!!!
1		Gabe	i agree with grant should we turn it in?

Figure 7.3 Group 3's mathematical process terms tracked throughout the discussion.

that may or may not be related or ordered thematically (Kim et al., 2007). The lack of a clear speaking or typing order and the ability to post responses simultaneously can create multiple intertwined threads of conversation (Black et al., 1983; Cazden, 2001), which can in turn contribute to confusion and frustration (Oliver et al., 2010; Sierpinska et al., 2008). The conversations in online environments are different when compared to discussions that are held in traditional classroom settings, where speakers' turns are tied thematically. Due to these differences, participants in online settings need to find ways to keep track of conversations, reduce frustrations, and increase stimulation as they progress through these multiple threads.

Discussions are useful in the learning process as students interact through the process of sharing ideas and their thinking processes (Bransford, 2000; Bruer, 1994). However, within face-to-face class discussions the ability to either help or hinder the learning process depends on how discussions are orchestrated (Cazden, 2001; Lampert, 2002). Online discussions offer a different medium compared to traditional speaking orders that are prevalent in face-to-face classrooms. The online environments can be beneficial for the participants, yet the lack of turn taking and the ability to simultaneously write and submit responses can cause feelings of confusion and frustration as multiple intertwined threads of conversation are created (Azeem & Ashfaq, 2010; Black et al., 1983; Kim et al., 2007).

In this study, students sought to make sense of each other's explanations of how the problem should be solved. When solving math problems, the operations and mathematical processes are important and useful in explaining one's cognitive and emotional learning (O'Halloran, 2000). This study revealed that when students are engaged in online environments without a clear speaking order, students needed to somehow make sense of the discussion. The patterns that appeared in all three groups show the importance of certain math terms over others. Students chose terms that represented mathematical processes in the areas of substitution and equation conversion, which are key components in solving the system of equations. Students also used and tracked these terms (see below) to better understand how their peers were solving the problem. A shared understanding of these terms was apparent in the discussions as they appear and reappear in the text. Sometimes other students appropriated these terms for use in their own explanations after the introduction of the term by another student. At other times, students had their own terms to explain operations, but these terms also seemed to be understood by their peers.

Textual math resources that help students navigate solving problems online are useful in explaining one's cognitive and emotional dispositions. When students needed to explain their thinking to their peers, having a common understanding of these mathematical terms was important; therefore, teachers should teach and scaffold the use of these terms to enhance online math discussions. Further, to limit student frustrations, disconnections emotionally and cognitively with the content, the teacher can scaffold by teaching the students how to write and explain their math reasoning using common words learned in class or presented online. The ability to communicate mathematically is an important skill in mathematics education, so more time should be allotted for helping students make sense of mathematical terms that represent key processes and operations. Further, scaffolds online are necessary in order to help students keep track of multi-threaded conversations. Perhaps having students create a list of common words and provide an explanation to what those words mean in the online discussion would help equip them with a vocabulary that can help limit frustration and anxiety and possibly provide better communication during the process online.

Limitations

One limitation of this study is the sample size of students, and these findings while generalizable to these 10 students only, have much to say about the importance of mathematical discussions in an online setting. With the increasing trend of online courses as ways to supplement, support, and provide content not available in certain places, it is important to critically analyze students social emotional learning needs and how students communicate and make sense of math talk in an online setting. More research is needed in the area of online math discussions to better understand the ways students make sense of online math content and how they use the textual resources to convey their understandings of different mathematical processes.

Further, the question of how to promote rich mathematical discussions online is a pressing question, especially in regards to different prompts. This particular study was to solve a system of equations together online, but online discussions can also be more conceptual in nature. As teachers set the stage for in class discussions, prompts also play a large role for how discussions ensue online. Future studies should look at how discussions are held with different prompts (e.g., computational problems, multi-step problems, reflections, math explorations, writing math rationales). Other future studies should focus on online discussions when other semiotic resources are available for student use, such as free draw or a web cam.

APPENDIX A

Example of Edmodo Interface

APPENDIX B

Order 1 Entries and Order 2 Replies in the Online Discussion

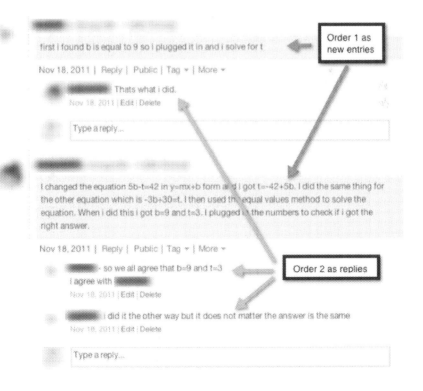

APPENDIX C

Symbols used to track terms that represent mathematical processes

Operative processes	Color used	Shape used	Arrow used
Equation Conversion	Red	Rectangle	Dashed arrow
Substitution	Blue	Oval	Solid arrow

REFERENCES

Azeem, M., & Ashfaq, M. (2010). Unintentional implicit mathematics values: Utilization of information and communication technology in mathematics. *The International Journal of Technology, Knowledge, and Society*, 6(6), 29–46.

Black, S., Levin, J., Mehan, H., & Quinn, C. N. (1983). Real and non-real time interaction: Unraveling multiple threads of discourse. *Discourse Processes*, 6, 59–75. http://dx.doi.org/10.1080/01638538309544554.

Blanchette, J. (2009). Characteristics of teacher talk and learner talk in the online learning environment. *Language and Education*, 23(5), 391–407.

Bransford, J. (2000). *How people learn: Brain, mind, experience, and school*. Washington, DC: National Academy Press.

Bruer, J. T. (1994). Classroom problems, school culture, and cognitive research. In K. McGilly (Ed.), *Classroom lessons: Integrating cognitive theory and classroom practice* (pp. 273–290). Cambridge, MA: MIT Press.

Cazden, C. B. (2001). *Classroom discourse*. Portsmouth, NH: Heinemann.

Cobb, P., Wood, T., & Yackel, E. (1993). Discourse, mathematical thinking, and classroom practice. In E. A. Forman, N. Minick, & C. A. Stone (Eds.), *Context for learning: Sociocultural dynamics in children's development* (pp. 91–119). New York: Oxford University Press.

Gee, J. P., & Green, J. L. (1998). Discourse analysis, learning, and social practice: A methodological study. *Review of Research in Education*, 23, 119–169.

Graham, J., & Hodgson, T. (2008). Speaking math: Using chat in the multicultural math classroom. *Learning & Leading with Technology*, 35(5), 24–27.

Green, J. L., & Dixon, C. (2008). Classroom interaction and situated learning. In M. Martin-Jones, A. M. de Meija, & N. H. Hornberger (Eds.), *Encyclopedia of language education: Discourse and education* (pp. 1–12). New York: Springer.

Herbel-Eisenmann, B., & Cirillo, M. (Eds.), (2009). *Promoting purposeful discourse*. Reston, VA: NCTM.

Kanuka, H., & Anderson, T. (1998). Online social interchange, discord and knowledge construction. *Journal of Distance Education*, 13, 57–74.

Kim, I. H., Anderson, R. C., Nguyen-Jahiel, K., & Archodidou, A. (2007). Discourse patterns during children's collaborative online discussions. *The Journal of the Learning Sciences*, 16(3), 333–370.

Lampert, M. (2002). Appreciating the complexity of teaching and learning in school: A commentary on cobb; forman and ansell; mcclain; saxe; schliemann; and sfard. *The Journal of the Learning Sciences, 11*(2), 365–368.

Martin, J. R., & Rose, D. (2003). *Working with discourse*. New York: Continuum.

Nystrand, M. (1991). On the negotiation of understanding between students and teacher: Towards a social-interactionist model of school learning. Paper presented at the annual meeting of the American Educational Research Association, Chicago, IL.

O'Dweyer, L. M., Carey, R., & Kleimen, G. (2007). A study of the effectiveness of the Lousiana Algebra I Online Course. *Journal of Research on Technology in Education, 39* (3), 289–306.

O'Halloran, K. L. (2000). Classroom discourse in mathematics: A multisemiotic analysis. *Linguistics and Education, 10*(3), 359–388.

Oliver, K., Kellogg, S., & Patel, R. (2010). An investigation into reported differences between online math instruction and other subject areas in a virtual school. *Journal of Computers in Mathematics and Science Teaching, 29*(4), 417–453.

Sfard, A., & Kieran, C. (2001). Cognition as communication: Rethinking learning-by-talking through multi-faceted analysis of students' mathematical interactions. *Mind, Culture, and Activity, 8*(1), 42–76.

Sierpinska, A., Bobos, G., & Knipping, C. (2008). Sources of students' frustration in pre-university level, prerequisite mathematics courses. *Instructional Science: An International Journal of the Learning Sciences, 36*(4), 289–320.

Stein, C. C. (2007). Let's talk: Promoting mathematical discourse in the classroom. *Mathematics Teacher, 101*(4), 285–289.

Swan, K. (2003). Learning effectiveness online: What the research tells us. In J. Bourne & J. C. Moore (Eds.), *Elements of quality online education, practice and direction* (pp. 13–45). Needham, MA: Sloan Center for Online Education.

Tallent-Runnels, M. K., Thomas, J. A., Lan, W. Y., Cooper, S., Ahern, T. C., Shaw, S. M., et al. (2006). Teaching courses online: A review of research of the research. *Review of Education Research, 76*(1), 93–135.

Watson, J. (2010). *Keeping pace with K-12 online learning*. Evergreen, CO: Evergreen Education Group.

Watson, J., & Johnson, L. K. (2010). Online learning: A 21st century approach to education. In G. Wan & D. M. Gut (Eds.), *Bringing schools into the 21st century* (pp. 205–223). Dordrecht: Springer. http://dx.doi.org/10.1007/978-94-007-0268-4_10.

CHAPTER 8

Online Learning, Multimedia, and Emotions

Mathew Swerdloff
Hendrik Hudson School District, Montrose, NY, USA

DEFINING EMOTIONS

Prior to our discussion of emotions, learning, and technology, we should understand how the term "emotions" is operationalized in this chapter. Damasio (2014) defines emotion as a reaction to an "action program" in the brain. He proposes that, as the brain processes our environment and the external stimulus that we are receiving, we associate the stimuli with a stored feeling state and react accordingly (fear, anger, anxiety, etc.). In this model, emotions are felt in the body but created by the brain, as a result of the environmental stimuli we experience, and our own internal thought processes which interprets the stimulus. Another way to define emotions is as a variance from a normal or neutral state to one of psychological arousal (Graesser & D'Mello, 2012). In this model, we can literally measure emotions using psychological indicators and physical arousal. This is useful when trying to determine how online learning and multimedia (OLaM) affects emotions, but quantifying emotions is necessarily problematic. People, and in particular young students, often have difficulty identifying their own emotions in the moment, and a retrospective recollection process can be risky in terms of validity.

Another way to examine emotions is through ancient spiritual traditions. Both scientific descriptions of emotions were preceded by Buddhist teachings, which tell us that emotions are merely a creation of the mind, and that as the mind creates, so it can dissipate. Thus, in the Buddhist tradition, the brain is used to manage emotions and attain equilibrium (De Silva, 2007). Emotions arise from either attraction or repulsion to all manner of external stimuli (physical or mental) and exist within the mind but are manifested in the body. The body reacts with set patterns as to how the mind processes the external stimuli of our world. This is another way of seeing emotions as a reaction to something "other."

Emotions, Technology, and Learning
http://dx.doi.org/10.1016/B978-0-12-800649-8.00009-2

155

In all cases, we see emotions as a reaction to external stimuli or thoughts about those stimuli, and as something that can be managed. This is a useful notion to understand as educators. Rather than see ourselves as helpless in the face of our students' emotional states, we can help them manage and channel emotions to support learning. In the traditional classroom, it is generally possible for an experienced teacher to see or intuit the emotional state of a student. When a student is sitting alone in front of a computer, this is not the case. The machine, as of now, does not have the emotional intelligence of a good teacher.

For this discussion, emotions are a reaction to the environment (in this case, OLaM), and the nature of the emotional state can affect how learning happens and the association that the student has with the learning environment in general, and OLaM in particular. In the school setting, we naturally want students to feel comfortable and safe, as well as experience emotional states that support academic growth. The focus here is an understanding of how OLaM affects emotions, how we can use OLaM to support academic growth, how emotions affect the use of OLaM, and how these factors interact.

LEARNING AND EMOTIONS

OLaM was designed to emulate instruction delivered in person, by a teacher, as a means of offering more instructional contact without the confines of place, time, and expense. To this end, it has been very successful in moving beyond those limitations. Students can literally learn anywhere, anytime, on any device, using OLaM. However, what is lacking in OLaM is the interplay of instructor and student, specifically with regard to the emotional state of the learner. The ability of a human instructor to interact with a student and adjust instruction based on academic progress and emotional state is quite important. When using OLaM, software can adjust based on algorithms that analyze academic status, but not based on emotional state. With human instruction, teaching is a dynamic process based on the "whole child". With OLaM, this is not the case. How is cognition affected by the learner's emotional state, and vice-versa?

As educators, it is essential that we consider how the student's emotional state is affected by OLaM, and how OLaM can affect the emotional state. In both cases, learning, growth, and student wellbeing can be influenced.

An individual's emotional state can affect memory, cognition, attentiveness, attitude, and boredom with the content (Pekrun, 2005). Motivation, effort, and drive are also effected by the emotional state of the learner. Pekrun (1992) analyzed the variety of emotional states experienced by learners and organized them into four groups: positive-activating, positive-deactivating, negative-activating, and negative-deactivating. Each group of emotional states carries with it a factor on two scales: positive-negative and activating-deactivating. The organization in terms of these factors allows us to quantify emotions in terms of the effects on the learner and the learning process. Table 8.1 describes each group in further detail.

According to Pekrun (1992), emotional states skewed toward those in the positive-activating category are beneficial for learning, while negative-deactivating states are least beneficial. Positive-deactivating emotions can be expected at the completion of successful work, and negative-deactivating emotions appear when work is not or cannot be completed. Thus, enjoyment, hope, and pride can be used as a precursor to and a by-product of successful use of OLaM. This is essential for educators to realize. Students are not "machines" that can be placed in front of a computer to "learn." As educators, we must consider the whole child in all situations. As we shall see later in the chapter, emotions can have a profound effect on learning.

Another area of interest involving emotions and technology is the notion of *anticipated emotions* and learning outcomes (Chan, Caputi, Jayasuriya, & Browne, 2013). Effective teachers know that goal-setting at the commencement of a lesson can be an effective strategy for learners. Similarly, reflection on *anticipated emotions* can bolster learning outcomes. The term "anticipated emotions" refers to a conscious process the learner undergoes at the beginning of a lesson or activity, wherein she reflects on how she would feel at the end of the lesson or activity if certain learning outcomes were or were not met (Chan et al., 2013). Notably, this reflective process can increase learning outcomes. By placing herself in the desired emotional state, the learner is reinforced, in advance of the outcome, to work toward that same outcome. In effect, the learner is giving herself the emotional reward as a motivator to achieve the outcome that will be rewarded. In the classroom, this can be

Table 8.1 Emotional groups as defined by Pekrun

Positive-activating	Positive-deactivating	Negative-activating	Negative-deactivating
Enjoyment	Relief	Anger	Boredom
Hope	Relaxation	Anxiety	Hopelessness
Pride	Contentment	Shame	Despair

Note: Adapted from Pekrun (1992).

applied to learners of all ages. One simple strategy for the classroom teacher is to allow student's a few moments to reflect on the pride and joy they *will* feel when the project or task is complete. With younger students especially, immediate gratification is the status quo, and the ability to defer gratification is learned as one ages. By using anticipated emotions to support delayed gratification, teachers can help students achieve academically and grow emotionally.

Much has been said about the lack of empathy and the "deadening" of emotions as a result of technology use in general, and OLaM in particular (Goleman, 2006). Although the mass media does report often on this phenomenon, taking up the cry after every school shooting or incident of school violence, there is a dearth of empirical evidence to support the claim that technology use limits emotional response. For "digital immigrants" (Prensky, 2012), the notion that technology is antithetical to emotional awareness is a common assumption. Many of those who grew up without today's pervasive technology still find it foreign, even after two decades of using the Internet, e-mail, and multimedia tools. The tendency to see technology as "other" is natural. However, for "digital natives" (Prensky, 2012), OLaM is quite natural, and with it, comes the emotions of face-to-face encounters. It is a grave mistake for adults to assume that their students are like them in the way they react to and interact with technology and OLaM. Our students are vastly different from us in terms of how they see, use, and relate to technology tools. For these "digital natives," technology, and by extension OLaM, is just another facet of "real life." There is less and less of a distinction between "virtual" and "real." "Talking" with a friend can mean many things; a video chat, mobile texting, a phone-call, or an in-person conversation. There is no distinction between mediums.

There is enough relevant research to support the notion that the use of OLaM is often a rich experience both in terms of academics and emotions. In fact, in some situations, some students are more "emotionally connected" when in an OLaM environment than when in the "real world." In one study, the interactions of students participating in online courses through their school were measured (Meyer & Jones, 2010).

The researchers measured the emotional state of 67 college students during their participation in an online course and while engaging in non-course-related activities. The research found the highest statistical means were in the "sometimes" category for expressing emotions during the online class. Emotions measured included anticipation, wonder, interest, anger, surprise, and amusement. Interest, surprise, and anger were expressed most often, but all emotions measured were expressed to some degree when in the online course environment. Also important, the study measured emotional empathy of students when online. The study measured the emotional empathy when in the course environment as compared with when in a non-course environment, and found the expression of empathy to be significantly higher ($p = 0.007$) when in the course environment (Meyer & Jones, 2010). This correlates with the statements above regarding the lack of distinction between mediums. Students today "feel" all the time, and their emotions can be as vivid and real when texting or chatting as when talking in person. In another study, Cleveland-Innes and Campbell (2012) observed a sample of 217 college students and found similar results. Specifically, students experienced a rich emotional life when in the online learning environment, including many of the emotions (anger, sadness, joy, disappointment, anxiety) that they experienced in face-to-face classes. Both of these studies appear to contradict Goleman's assertion (Goleman, 2006) that engaging or teaching and learning in online environments creates social isolation and lack of empathy. This poses many interesting questions for instructional designers, who previously focused solely on the domain of content and delivery, and now, as with the classroom teacher, must consider the emotional lives of their students. Next, we focus on the justification of using OLaM as an instructional methodology, and how it can benefit our students.

THE CASE FOR THE USE OF OLaM TO IMPROVE ACADEMIC ACHIEVEMENT

While it may seem a foregone conclusion that OLaM is a valuable tool for students, it is worth noting some of the research in this area. There is enough research to support the claim that OLaM can have a positive effect on academic achievement when used with fidelity.

Specifically, Soe and Chang (2000) have asserted that the use of OLaM has led to positive growth in reading achievement and reading comprehension. In their meta-analysis, Soe and Chang reviewed 17 studies completed between 1982 and 1998. All of the studies included the use of OLaM as an independent variable and reading comprehension or reading achievement as a dependent variable, and were implemented in grades K-12. A majority of the studies (88%) used standardized measures of achievement, and 65% took place over a period of 5-12 months. In all, 41% of the studies were published after 1994, and most students (66%) were ethnic minorities, educationally challenged, or economically disadvantaged. Sample sizes ranged from a low of 20 to a high of

558 students per study. Statistical analyses were completed on the sample data. The researchers found a significant increase on achievement scores between students using OLaM and those that did not. Soe and Chang then completed an additional analysis to determine if the variables of sample size, duration of treatment, and grade level of students had an effect on individual results. Their statistical analysis revealed that the effects were so large that over 800 new studies that showed no effect of OLaM would need to be added to the calculations in order to change the outcome of the study. The researchers concluded that there is in fact good reason to believe that OLaM can have a positive impact on achievement in the K-12 setting. The interaction of OLaM and emotions was not studied.

A second meta-analysis conducted in Turkey (Camnalbur & Erdogan, 2008) evaluated the effect size of studies which took place between 1998 and 2007. The authors sought to determine if OLaM was more effective than traditional, in person methods. The pool was 78 studies based on specific selection criteria, including date of original study, minimum sample size, publication status, duration of treatment, and research design. Total sample size for the combined treatment group was 2536 and for the control group 2560. Using these data, Camnalbur and Erdogan (2008) determined a significant effect, and indicated that academic achievement was higher for students receiving OLaM. The authors suggested that OLaM is indeed an effective method of instructional delivery and did have a significant effect on learning when compared to traditional methods.

These two meta-analyses, and many other individual studies, support the claim that OLaM can be a positive tool for academic growth in our schools. It is clear that the effect of OLaM was positive in the majority of these cases, in terms of academic achievement. In addition, these studies covered a variety of cultures, student ethnicities, school settings, student socioeconomic backgrounds, and grade levels. Many other studies have examined the effect of a technology-rich classroom on academic achievement. In many of these cases, the results are positive.

The above meta-analyses show that OLaM can have a significant effect on academic achievement. OLaM offers the promise of delivering instruction in a shorter time with greater academic gain. These studies highlighted the potential for using OLaM to customize instruction to meet the needs of individual learners, deliver differentiated and self-paced instruction, and to manage diverse learners efficiently. Next, we turn our attention to the design of OLaM and how a consideration of mental processes can improve the efficacy of OLaM.

ON OVERVIEW OF THE COGNITIVE THEORY OF MULTIMEDIA LEARNING

Multimedia learning is a form of computer-aided instruction that uses two modalities concurrently (Mayer, 2002). The use of visual learning (pictures, written text, animations, and videos) and verbal learning (spoken narration) as discrete channels for delivering content is different from the traditional classroom practice of lecturing to students or having students read silently. Multimedia learning can be delivered by a teacher, but is often delivered by a computer running a software application. In the text that follows, multimedia learning is included as a part of OLaM.

Essential to the cognitive theory of multimedia learning (CTML) is the notion that the brain processes information using two discrete channels and two discrete memory paths (Mayer & Moreno, 1998). According to Mayer and Moreno, the verbal (auditory) channel is responsible for processing music, sound accompanying video, and spoken words. The visual (ocular) channel processes written text, animation, still images, and moving video images. This is an essential part of the CTML and is displayed graphically in Figure 8.1.

Figure 8.1 illustrates how words can be assimilated through the ears or the eyes, depending on whether or not the words are spoken or printed. Pictures are assimilated through the eyes only.

Richard Mayer states that there are a number of distinct principles at work in multimedia learning (Moreno & Mayer, 2000). The *Multiple Representation Principle* indicates that meaningful learning occurs when both channels (verbal and visual) are used at the same time. This process involves the learner connecting the information from each channel and mentally cross-referencing it in working memory, which improves learning. The *Spatial Contiguity Principle* states that any text and visual content should be

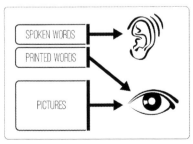

Figure 8.1 Processing of information using the visual and verbal channels. *Figure credit: Adin Gold.*

contiguous; that is they should be close to each other on the page or screen. The *Temporal Contiguity Principle* states that verbal and visual content should be contiguous in time; both forms of content should be presented together in time rather than asynchronously. Placing both words and pictures explaining the same content into working memory at the same time is beneficial. If this information is out of synch, the brain is less able to connect the information from the two channels. The *Split Attention Principle* states that when showing visual content, it is preferable to present words as verbal content rather than as text on the screen. This method is preferable because the written text is processed visually with the images, while the verbal text is processed through the ears with the verbal processing system (Mayer, 2002). The *Modality Principle* states that students learn better when text is presented in verbal form (as narration) rather than in visual form (as written text). Mayer suggests that this is due to the fact that when processing visual images and written text, the learner is using the same channel, resulting in cognitive overload. However, if the learner processes the same visual images with verbal text (narration), he or she is using two distinct channels and thus better able to process the information. The *Redundancy Principle* further refines the description of how multimedia learning is most effective. Mayer states that while two channels of content can be more effective, too much content can be counter-productive. In fact, presenting animation and narration and written text is not more effective than animation and narration alone. The final principle outlined is the *Coherence Principle*. Mayer states that background sounds and music take away from the learner's experience rather than adding to it. These verbal distractions can overload the auditory channel and take away from the ability to process essential auditory content.

Figure 8.2 provides a detailed overview of the CTML; it depicts content presented as words and pictures. Pictures are processed through the sensory memory via the eyes as visual stimulus and are then processed by the brain in

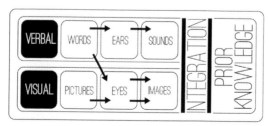

Figure 8.2 Cognitive theory of multimedia learning. *Figure credit: Adin Gold.*

working memory. Words can be processed in one of two ways. Spoken words are processed through the sensory memory via the ears as verbal stimulus. Written words are processed through sensory memory via the eyes as visual stimulus. This graphic is a clear example of how educators can customize delivery of instruction to maximize learning by choosing the correct channel for the words. It also helps us understand how multimedia information is processed in the brain.

Mayer's theory attempts to explain how multimedia applications can be best designed and utilized. It is important to consider this when implementing instructional programs for use in schools. There are in fact other theories that explain cognitive load and processing as well, but Mayer's ideas are well accepted and solidly based on sound research, and are thus worth considering closely. In addition, cognitive load is an important consideration when examining emotions. Students who cannot learn well using OLaM will experience frustration; students who are using poorly designed multimedia, without regard for cognitive load theory, will experience emotional states that do not support learning.

The flowchart depicts how information is processed through both the verbal and visual channels through two memory spaces. Considered next is the effects of OLaM on emotions, and how emotions and technology interact in the school setting.

EMOTIONAL STATE AND ADOPTION OF NEW COMPUTER INITIATIVES

Motivation is a key factor in success at school and in the workplace. Very often, OLaM is deployed in the school setting without proper consideration for staff and student anxiety. It is important to consider how the use of OLaM will affect the teacher and the student before they use it. While for most students the transition to OLaM is seamless, this is not always true for teachers, many of whom find technology to be foreign and imposed upon them. In addition, we do need to be cognizant of how the deployment of OLaM affects students who may be emotionally fragile or disconnected, or may use technology as a way to "hide" from their daily reality. Just as we react *after* new computer initiatives are implemented, we can react *before* the new initiatives are implemented, to the idea, if not the actual implementation. Beaudry and Pinsonneault (2010) examined this phenomenon with bank employees before a new software program was deployed. They looked at how the emotional state of the employees before the initiative was implemented affected the implementation and adoption of the initiative. The study focused on four emotions; anger, anxiety, excitement, and happiness, and the ramifications for educators in the school setting.

Simply put, people will tend to follow their directives at work despite their own anger or frustration. The authors found that of the angry employees, those who sought social support showed a higher level of software use. The angry employees who sought assistance ended up using the software more than those who were self-isolated. This has implications for schools in terms of students as well as teachers, and how OLaM is deployed in the school setting. We need to ensure that both students and staff are supported in learning to use new technology tools.

When employees were anxious about the project, there was a correlation with reduced use of the software. Anxiety in the school and the workplace is not conducive to learning. However, when anxious employees sought social support, they too showed higher software adoption rates, revealing a similar pattern as seen with the angry staff. In both cases, seeking support from co-workers helped to reduce isolation and increase assimilation and adoption of the new software. For the school setting, we must address teacher and student anxiety about technology use, in order for it to be effective. Anxiety can be a destructive emotion that is detrimental to the learning process in many ways.

Happiness and excitement as precursor emotions also show interesting results in this study. Happiness, as expected, showed a positive correlation to adoption of the program. People who reported feeling happy prior to the project showed a higher software adoption rate than those who reported being unhappy. However, those who were excited about the project showed no significant correlation with higher adoption rates if they did not pursue additional strategies. If the excited users adapted the task to meet their needs and also sought social support, they too showed higher adoption rates than non-excited users.

In grouping the four emotions into pairs of (anger and anxiety) and (happiness and excitement), additional data analysis revealed that anger and anxiety accounted for 14% of the adoption rate of the users, while happiness and excitement accounted for 47% of the adoption rate (Beaudry & Pinsonneault, 2010). The positive emotions had a much larger effect on adoption rates than the negative ones; positive emotions had over three times the impact of negative ones. The implications for education are interesting, and the importance of positive emotions on the learning process cannot be underestimated.

THE EFFECT OF COMPUTER-AIDED INSTRUCTION ON EMOTION IN THE SCHOOL SETTING

While the research on OLaM and emotions is not as prolific as the research on OLaM and academics, there are some studies about the interplay of emotions and technology. What are the emotional domains that we can examine around student computer use? In the section that follows, attitude toward computers and attitude toward school were examined, as well as student feelings about both school and computer use. These studies support the author's research, which is reviewed in detail later in this section.

It is reasonable to expect that enjoyment is correlated with the use of computers. Specifically, as educators, we hope that by increasing student enjoyment of an experience, in this case OLaM, students will increase their use, thus increasing the benefit to them. Knezek, Miyashhita, and Sakamoto (1996) purport that exposure to computers at an early age improves children's attitude toward school. Three researchers conducted research in Japan and the USA to support this claim. Their research defines attitudes toward computers as a combination of computer importance and computer enjoyment, both subscales of their Young Children's Computer Inventory (YCCI) instrument that defines the attitudes toward computers construct. Computer enjoyment is an emotional state regarding the use of computers, an expression of joy or happiness associated with computer use. Computer enjoyment remains high or rises for students exposed to computers in the primary grades. Computer importance does decline each year from Grades 1-3 but the change is not significant. Most educators can support this claim with anecdotal evidence from their own experiences as teachers. Further, there appears to be no specific type of computer use that is more appealing to students. All computer use generates an improved attitude toward computers. There are some changes between attitude levels when using drill and practice versus discovery learning situations but the difference is not significant (Knezek et al., 1996). Also worth noting in this study is how the frequency of computer use affects anxiety. As one might expect, the more students use computers, the less anxious they are about computer use, and the more positive the emotional experience of the student. In practical terms, the earlier we introduce students to computers, the more they will enjoy using them, and the greater the exposure they have, the more positive their attitude will be.

Enjoyment is a positive emotion that benefits students and a positive attitude supports enjoyment, thus creating a cycle that will benefit both students and staff.

THE NEW YORK GRADE THREE STUDY ON FEELINGS, ATTITUDE, AND ACHIEVEMENT

We now turn our attention to a recent study conducted in the school setting specifically designed to measure student feelings about computer use. In the Fall of 2012, a study of Grade 3 students' attitudes and feelings about computers and school was conducted (Swerdloff, 2013). This study also measured the academic effect of using multimedia software designed according to Mayer's CTML. The site of this study was a medium-sized (<2500 students) suburban New York school district, within commuting distance of a major metropolitan area. The study commenced in September of 2012 and was completed by January 2013. Students from 10, 3rd grade classrooms, formed the population of the study. Five classrooms were randomly selected as a control group and the remaining five served as the treatment group. All students completed the 2008 New York State English Language Arts (NYS ELA) Exam Part 1 and the YCCI as pretests. Following the pretests, the treatment group was given instruction in the use of Destination Reading (2007), the multimedia software used to deliver targeted ELA instruction. The students used the software for 10 weeks in the classroom. During this 10-week period, the control group students continued to receive traditional targeted ELA instruction. After the treatment was complete, both groups received the 2009 version of the NYS ELA and a re-ordered version of the YCCI instrument.

Once the groups were formed and the pretest was administered, it was determined that there was no statistically significant difference between treatment and control groups for the three variables being measured (attitude toward school, attitude toward computers, and reading comprehension).

Post-test data were analyzed and five students (one from each treatment class) were selected based on their gain in ELA exam scores. The student from each treatment class who showed the largest positive academic gain on raw scores from pretest to post-test was selected to be interviewed. The researcher conducted one-on-one semi-structured interviews (Bogdan & Biklen, 2007) with each student to determine the effect of the use of the software on attitude toward school and attitude toward computers, in a manner that differed from that which the YCCI instrument could provide. Five questions and appropriate follow-up questions were asked of each student, aimed at gaining a fuller sense of how the software use affected student attitudes and feelings. Data from the interviews were coded, analyzed, and triangulated with the quantitative data (Table 8.2).

Table 8.2 Number of students in each demographic class by group

Group	Count	Poverty	ELL	SpEd	Male	Female
Treatment	69	5	5	12	29	40
Control	57	8	2	4	26	31

Swerdloff (2013).

Two instruments were used, as well as semi-structured interviews. The 2008 and 2009 versions of the NYS ELA Exam Part 1 measured reading comprehension. The YCCI measured attitude toward computers and attitude toward school. Following the post-test, the five selected students met with the researcher during the school day and the interview took place with specific questions follow-up as needed.

Both the 2008 and 2009 versions of the NYS ELA exam were comprised of two parts. Part 1 included several short passages and a series of 20 multiple choice questions designed to assess a student's comprehension of the passages. Part 2 assessed a student's listening and writing skills. Part 2 was not used for this study. The vendor reports that this is a highly reliable instrument, Cronbach's alpha 0.84 (New York State Testing Program, 2009). Each test was examined by an independent auditor for content and construct validity, and was determined to measure the desired standards in a valid manner (New York State Testing Program). The YCCI contains 51 items using a 4-point Likert-type scale in survey format (Knezek, 1992). It was designed for elementary children and can be administered online or on paper. Regarding validity of the instrument, the authors stated that the YCCI is valid as a result of three specific actions that were taken in the development of the instrument. Content validity was assessed by approximately 12 content-area experts in the field who reviewed the wording and selection of the questions in the YCCI. Construct validity was determined using factor analysis, and the YCCI was deemed stable over time and consistent across cultures. Criterion validity was assessed using analysis of variance and discriminant function results, which indicated that the YCCI does in fact distinguish between groups of students with differing attitudes (Knezek & Miyashita, 1993).

Semi-structured interviews are designed to allow the researcher to address certain topics while allowing space for the interviewee to embellish or add information as needed (Creswell & Plano Clark, 2011). Five interview questions were developed for this study to accomplish this goal. The questions were designed to develop a clear understanding of the feelings

Table 8.3 Interview questions for five students in New York study
Qualitative interview questions

Please describe what it was like for you to use the Destination Reading software
Do you think the use of the software changed how you feel about school? How?
Do you think the use of the software changed how you feel about computers? How?
Do you think the software helped you to learn to read? How?
Is there anything you would like me to know about using the software?

Swerdloff (2013).

of the students regarding how the use of OLaM in this study affected their emotions, learning, and attitude, and to ensure that each child could speak freely about the entire process. Semi-structured interviews took place in order to facilitate the data analysis process with 3rd grade students. The interviewer used warm-up questions that were designed to relax the interviewees (Bogdan & Biklen, 2007) and recorded each session in order to be able to transcribe all data at a later date (Table 8.3).

The treatment took place over a 10-week period in the Fall of 2012. Each of the five classes was scheduled to use the computer lab in their school for three, 30-min sessions per week. After the first session with the researcher, teachers brought their classes to the lab independently. Students logged on to the network and the software using unique usernames and passwords provided by the researcher. After accessing the software, students used headsets to listen to the audio portion of the software and used the mouse and keyboard to interact with the software (Table 8.4).

A significance level above 0.05 indicated that the scores of the treatment group were not significantly higher than those of the control group.

Table 8.4 Posttest descriptive statistics for both groups and all variables

	Reading comprehension	Attitude toward computers	Attitude toward school
N	117.00000	117.00000	117.00000
Mean	14.45300	36.05130	10.51280
SE of mean	0.35214	0.55162	0.31177
Median	15.00000	37.00000	11.00000
Mode	15.00000	38.00000	14.00000
SD	3.80901	5.96664	3.37234
Range	17.00000	24.00000	12.00000
Minimum	3.00000	20.00000	4.00000
Maximum	20.00000	44.00000	16.00000
Sum	1691.00000	4218.00000	1230.00000

Swerdloff (2013).

A MANOVA was conducted to compare post-test scores of students in the control and treatment groups on the variables reading comprehension, attitude toward computers, and attitude toward school. The MANOVA data revealed that the multivariate score of the treatment group was significantly higher than that of the control group and that approximately 8.1% of the variance in the composite dependent variable (reading comprehension, attitude toward computers, and attitude toward school) was due to the independent variable (type of instruction). Effect size for these data was small (Table 8.5).

The quantitative portion of the study was used to explore whether or not there was a significant difference in the reading comprehension, attitude toward computers, and attitude toward school of students who received targeted ELA instruction using multimedia applications and those who received targeted ELA instruction without multimedia applications. The sample of students was divided into a treatment and a control group. Each group received the NYS ELA and YCCI exams as pretests and an ANOVA was carried out on each variable to determine group equivalency. Two groups were equivalent, with no significant differences between treatment and control groups on the variables.

The treatment group then received 10 weeks of targeted ELA instruction using OLaM. The control group received traditional ELA instruction in the classroom without OLaM. After the treatment period ended, all students were assessed using the NYS ELA exam and the YCCI instrument in order to determine the effect of the treatment.

A MANOVA was calculated after the removal of outliers and missing cases. The analysis revealed that the treatment group scored significantly higher than the control group, indicating that the use of the OLaM in this study improved scores on the matrix of variables measured by the instruments used in the study.

This qualitative portion of the study question addressed the affective domain through the following question: What are the perceptions of students who use multimedia applications in school and show the greatest gain in reading comprehension after the study treatment period? To address this

Table 8.5 Multivariate test comparing treatment and comparison posttest groups for reading comprehension, attitude toward computers and attitude toward school scores
MANOVA

	Value	F	Hypothesis df	Error df	Sig.	Partial η^2
Wilks' lambda	0.919	3.313	3.00	113.00	0.025	0.081

Swerdloff (2013).

question, the researcher identified one student from each treatment class using purposeful sampling (Creswell & Plano Clark, 2011). Purposeful sampling is used to develop a broader understanding of the quantitative data. In this research, the purposeful sampling protocol was used to identify students who showed the greatest gain in reading comprehension, a key focus of the study, and to elucidate details from the students about the treatment. The sample was selected to best address the research question. This selection was made based on quantitative data results. Specifically, it was posited that the students who showed the greatest quantitative gain on the comprehension measure would be able to describe the process of the treatment protocol and how it affected them in terms of emotions and attitudes.

Analysis of scores in each class produced a list of five students. The researcher contacted each teacher to arrange an appointment to interview each student in a private setting. All interviews took place within the same week. Students assented to the interview and the interviews were recorded using a digital voice recorder in the first week of January, 2013, and transcribed for analysis (Table 8.6).

The identification of themes in qualitative research is a valuable method of analysis (Gall, Gall, & Borg, 2007). Three themes emerged after the interview text was analyzed using HyperRESEARCH. Themes and codes were not pre-determined but emerged organically from the coding process. The most prominent theme to emerge, "having fun", was a clear expression of an emotional state by the students. "Learning content" was the second most common theme and referred to an understanding that although they were enjoying the process, it was still "school work" and the students were

Table 8.6 Samples of emotions described in interview transcripts
Theme

Having fun	Learning content	Expressing emotions
It was really, really fun	I learned a lot	I feel good
I like it so much and that was all new	It tells you about a lot of interesting things like space	I feel different
I liked everything, it was fun	It tells you a lot of things about the things	It changed the way I feel in a good way
Yes it was fun	It made me realize school is a good way to have you learn	I feel perfect now
I liked that a lot	I felt like I was learning	Interesting … yes

Swerdloff (2013).

Figure 8.3 Depiction of three themes of student interview responses. *Figure credit: Adin Gold.*

learning as they "played." Finally, "expressing emotions" was common. Students spoke about excitement, feelings, feeling good, and feeling different when using the software.

Figure 8.3 depicts the three themes that emerged from the qualitative analysis of the interviewee responses.

A total of 47 keywords or phrases were identified, coded, and related to three themes that were identified and were focused on during the interview analysis.

Qualitative analysis revealed three common themes that all students expressed in the interviews: having fun, learning content, and expressing emotions. All students found the software to be fun, exciting, and engaging, and had positive feelings about using it. They felt that it supported learning and school work, and enjoyed using the software and computers. These data supported the quantitative gains in reading comprehension scores achieved by all of the interviewees.

Given that teachers had to bring their students to the computer lab, or assign them to use the computers in the classroom, teacher attitude and investment in the treatment had a profound impact on the outcome. With any treatment involving children, it is essential that the adult participants are committed to the research. This was the case in the present study; however, sometimes the realities of life in a 3rd grade classroom impinged on the best intentions of teachers.

In addition to the total number of hours spent using the software, the overall duration of the entire treatment is worth noting. While Kulik and Kulik (1991) state that shorter treatment duration can be more effective, it is worth considering that there was limited access to the OLaM in the 10-week period in this study. Had the treatment lasted longer, perhaps the increased use of the software would have increased the effect size for the MANOVA scores. This extended treatment period may have compensated for the reduced time per week spent using the software.

DISCUSSION

In this chapter, we have examined research and practice with regard to the use of OLaM in the classroom. We have seen examples of how the use of OLaM can have a positive effect on student academic growth, student attitude, and student emotions. We have also seen how the design of multimedia is important; how an understanding of cognitive load theory can help us to select and design OLaM that can benefit our students. We know that emotions can have a profound effect on our students prior to engaging in learning, and how the learning process itself can create and foster a rich emotional life for our students. As educators, it is essential that we consider the whole child when planning instruction, and that in so doing, we are cognizant of the emotional state of our students.

The primary research in this chapter indicated that students enjoy and have fun using OLaM, and that this transfers to a positive attitude and fosters learning. Certainly, as we design our classroom learning opportunities, it is worth considering how we can support the emotional state of our students in order to achieve academic growth in a positive, nurturing environment.

SOME IMPLICATIONS FOR EDUCATION

Educators today have come to rely on technology tools to help them manage many daily tasks in their classrooms. Teachers are quite familiar with using e-mail, searching the web, word processing, using online grade books and report cards, and presenting lessons with various software packages. However, many teachers still remain reluctant to give up their role as "chief content provider" and to use OLaM as an assistive tool. This research, and other research like it, demonstrated that OLaM can be an effective means of delivering ELA content and can improve reading comprehension. In addition, students expressed strong, positive emotions toward school and computers that they associated with the use of this OLaM program. Further examination by school leaders and teachers is warranted. In particular, it is worth considering how schools can best leverage their already large investment in technology tools to deploy effective teaching and learning solutions. While many schools have well-developed instructional technology programs, it is not common for schools to measure the effectiveness of their investments in terms of actual student learning. Parents and students have come to expect the availability of these tools for student collaboration, productivity, and communication, but have not yet demanded that these tools demonstrate increased academic achievement for students. Schools should demonstrate this before it is required of them by their stakeholders.

The increased pressure on today's teacher is very real. Teachers are being asked to do more and more, with fewer resources and less time. OLaM can be a valuable tool in the struggle to better educate our students. By using high quality multimedia software and the power of the Internet, educators could extend the school-day and ensure that students have more time on tasks with approved educational content. This new paradigm could have profound effects on children and educators. Online multimedia applications may offer a cost-effective way to achieve this goal. If online multimedia instruction can effectively ensure learning, as this study indicates, then it is reasonable to assume that it can also do so from home. Schools should actively investigate ways to deliver asynchronous instruction to students through applications such as Destination Reading, blogs, wikis, and teacher websites.

CONCLUSION

In the era of high-stakes testing, teacher accountability, and market driven school reforms, school leaders and teachers are forced each day to make decisions of priority and attention. They are asked to do more with less, and need to decide which program, resource, or person to eliminate. These are difficult decisions and are often made in haste or under pressure. Often overlooked is the "whole child," specifically the emotional wellbeing of the student. Students bring rich emotional and social experiences to our schools. They have years of successes and defeats that they live with, and a history of both positive and negative emotions. As educators, it behooves us to acknowledge this, and work with it in our classrooms. Specifically, an examination of the research in this chapter indicates that the emotional state of the child can have a profound impact on learning and attitude, that the use and design of multimedia applications can support learning and positive emotions, and that the experiences students have in schools and at home with OLaM can be beneficial. When evaluating such program and products, we need to look at the whole picture: academic gains, functional skills, and emotional benefits. The use of OLaM can be of great benefit to students from a variety of demographic backgrounds. It is associated with positive emotions about school and can help support the work of educators in many ways.

REFERENCES

Beaudry, A., & Pinsonneault, A. (2010). The other side of acceptance: Studying the direct and indirect effects of emotions on information technology use. *MIS Quarterly, 34*(4), 689–710.

Bogdan, R. C., & Biklen, S. (2007). *Qualitative research for education: An introduction to theories and methods.* Boston, MA: Allyn and Bacon.

Camnalbur, M., & Erdogan, Y. (2008). A meta-analysis of effectiveness of computer-assisted instruction: Turkey sample. *Educational Sciences: Theory and Practice, 8*(2), 498–505.

Chan, A. Y. C., Caputi, P., Jayasuriya, R., & Browne, J. L. (2013). Counterfactual thinking and anticipated emotions enhance performance in computer skills training. *Behavior and Information Technology, 32*(4), 387–396.

Cleveland-Innes, M., & Campbell, P. (2012). Emotional presence, learning, and the online learning environment. *The International Review of Research in Open and Distance Learning, 13*(4), 269–292.

Creswell, J. W., & Plano Clark, V. L. (2011). *Designing and conducting mixed methods research.* Thousand Oaks, CA: Sage Publications.

Damasio, A. (2014). Q + A: Antonio Damasio. *MIT Technology Review, 117*(4), 48–51.

De Silva, P. (2007). The psychology of emotions in Buddhist perspective. Access to Insight, November, 2013.

Destination Reading. (2007). Boston, MA: Houghton Mifflin Company.

Gall, M., Gall, J., & Borg, W. (2007). *Educational research: An introduction.* Boston, MA: Allyn and Bacon.

Goleman, D. (2006). *Emotional intelligence.* New York: Bantam Dell.

Graesser, A. C., & D'Mello, S. (2012). Moment-to-moment emotions during reading. *The Reading Teacher, 66*(3), 238–242.

Knezek, G. (1992). *Young children's computer inventory.* Retrieved from University of North Texas website: http://www.iittl.unt.edu/surveys/demos/ycci.htm.

Knezek, G. A., Miyashhita, K. T., & Sakamoto, T. (1996). Information technology from the child's perspective. In *Children and computers in school* (pp. 69–103). Mahwah, NJ: Lawrence Erlbaum.

Knezek, G. A., & Miyashita, K. (1993). *Handbook for the young children's computer inventory.* Denton, TX: Texas Center for Educational Technology.

Kulik, C., & Kulik, J. (1991). Effectiveness of computer based instruction: An updated analysis. *Computers in Human Behavior, 7*, 75–94.

Mayer, R. E. (2002). Cognitive theory and the design of multimedia instruction: An example of the two-way street between cognition. *New Directions for Teaching and Learning, 89*, 55–71.

Mayer, R. E., & Moreno, R. (1998). A split-attention effect in multimedia learning: Evidence for dual processing systems in working memory. *Journal of Educational Psychology, 90*(2), 312–320.

Meyer, K., & Jones, S. J. (2010). Do students experience "social intelligence", laughter, and other emotions online? *Journal of Asynchronous Learning Networks, 16*(4), 99–111.

Moreno, R., & Mayer, R. E. (2000). A coherence effect in multimedia learning: The case for minimizing irrelevant sounds in the design of multimedia instructional messages. *Journal of Educational Psychology, 92*(1), 117–125.

New York State Testing Program. (2009). *English language arts grades 3–8.* Monterey, CA: CTB.

Pekrun, R. (1992). The impact of emotions on learning and achievement: Towards a theory of cognitive/motivational mediators. *Applied Psychology: An International Review, 41*(4), 359–376.

Pekrun, R. (2005). Progress and open problems in educational emotion research. *Learning and Instruction, 15*, 497–506.

Prensky, M. (2012). *From digital native to digital wisdom*. Thousand Oaks, CA: Corwin.

Soe, K., & Chang, J. M. (2000). *Effect of computer-assisted instruction on reading achievement*. Monograph No. RS0001. Retrieved from Pacific Resources for Education and Learning website: http://www.prel.org/products/Products/effect-OLaM.htm.

Swerdloff, M. (2013). *The effects of targeted English language arts instruction using multimedia applications on grade three students' reading comprehension, attitude toward computers, and attitude towards school*. Danbury, CT: Western Connecticut State University.

CHAPTER 9

New Media, Literacy, and Laughter: LOL in the English Classroom

Beth A. Buchholz[a], Julie Rust[b]
[a]Appalachian State University, Boone, NC, USA
[b]Millsaps College, Jackson, MS, USA

In the current school climate, which often prioritizes standards and test scores over student experience, humor in the classroom is often labeled as diametrically opposed to the serious academic goals in place. This same pedagogical paradigm also views technology as potentially distracting in classrooms, despite the fact that young people's interactions, relationships, and identities outside of school are largely mediated by technology (e.g. Buckingham, 2011; Ito et al., 2009; Vasudevan, Schultz, & Bateman, 2010). It appears that both humor and technology, two powerful meaning-making vehicles for young people, are often unwelcomed within school spaces. This chapter explores the potential and pitfalls associated with the three-way intersection of new media, humor, and learning, by probing at the functions of digitally mediated humor observed in two separate classroom contexts.

In this chapter, we highlight the ways a range of digitally mediated school experiences implicitly and unexpectedly invited humor into classrooms. Humor and new media go hand-in-hand; digital technology opens up communicative pathways for humor to be shared, amplified, and networked in ways that were not previously possible. Our data point to the fact that even in classroom spaces, young people are increasingly engaging in the "mediatization of humor" (Kuipers, 2008, p. 391). This has specific implications for learning: this "funny" digital participation often involves the production and consumption of new textual forms, reflecting a range of complex literacy practices which are largely ignored in traditional English classrooms.

By exploring two distinct classroom contexts, a sophomore English classroom utilizing a Facebook-like platform for academic purposes and an upper-elementary classroom in the first year of a district-wide 1:1 iPad

Emotions, Technology, and Learning
http://dx.doi.org/10.1016/B978-0-12-800649-8.00008-0

initiative, we highlight the ways in which humor—mediated by students' interactions with technology—emerged as a powerful, productive, and often overlooked force in the classroom. We also consider the problematic nature of some of this humorous participation, of this blurring of the lines between in-school and out-of-school norms. In this chapter, we share our findings based on two research questions: (1) How do students use humor in new media spaces situated within classrooms? (2) In what ways do these functions create tensions within traditional classroom expectations?

THEORETICAL FRAMEWORK

For many years, scholars and researchers tended to discuss humor only in terms of laughter (i.e. humor's expressive manifestation), emphasizing the individual-centered, cognitive workings that produced this laughter. However, more recently scholars (e.g. Martin, 2007) have begun to explore the *emotional* underpinnings of humor, suggesting that laughter is the way we communicate our "mirthful" pleasure to those around us. This notion of laughter as a communicative tool frames humor as necessarily situated within human interaction. In our work, we define humor as a socially situated "*form of play* that comprises cognitive (nonserious incongruity), emotional (mirth), and expressive (laughter) components" (Martin, 2007, p. 114). Individuals use humor as they participate in their social worlds.

Sociocultural theory (Vygotsky, 1978) is particularly posed to contribute to an exploration of humor in the English classroom, given its theoretical emphasis on learning as situated in and mediated by social and cultural interactions and tools. This theoretical framing opens up a space to explore humor as a situated practice that rests on the evolving understanding youth and teachers co-construct in the classroom. What makes a particular discursive action "funny" is not determined by an individual's cognitive intentions, but is always influenced by and negotiated within the ongoing interpretive process engaged in by the community (i.e. classroom). The sociocultural edge in literacy studies is productive when exploring humor in classroom spaces because of its insistence on situating emotions as socially "constructed through language, culture, and power" (Lewis & Tierney, 2011, p. 321), rather than as merely sensations located within the bodies of individuals. From this vantage point, "being funny" in the classroom is a mediated action that is produced socially in relation to histories, practices, and identities (Micciche, 2002).

Humor is a form of play enjoyed by people of all ages for its own sake, but research has shown that it also serves important social functions. "Although it is playful and non-serious, and is often seen as frivolous and unimportant, humor can be used for a number of 'serious functions,' extending into every aspect of social behavior" (Martin, 2007, p. 150). In this way, humor is a complex social "tactic" used by individuals to accomplish a range of conscious and subconscious goals (Francis, 1994; Keltner, Young, & Buswell, 1997; Martin, 2007; Meyer, 2000). Previous research on humor in the classroom (e.g., Corsaro, 1994; Walker & Adelman, 1976) has often focused on *teachers' use of humor* as a "tactic"—specifically how teachers use humor to denigrate or support students' academic identities. Whereas this work positioned teachers as agentic subjects who tactically wielded humor to control students, our research worked to reposition students as the agentic subjects, opening up questions about the tactical "functions" of their playful use of humor in the classroom setting.

For as readily as humor is a part of everyday social interactions, both face-to-face and online, it is important to note that humor's place in the English classroom is contested. Young people's emotions—like their bodies—remain under tight surveillance in classrooms (Eagleton, 1985-1986). The expected "student state" allows for only a very narrow range of acceptable emotions (McLaren, 1999, p. 91). Certain emotions, for example, empathy, enthusiasm, and admiration, are considered desirable and productive for learning in the English classroom, reflective of our larger cultural milieu that positions these emotions as signs of refinement and class (Lewis & Tierney, 2011). Emotions such as anger, jealousy, and humor, on the other hand, are often pushed out of classrooms so that the focus can remain on the "serious" endeavor of learning (Lewis & Tierney, 2011).

It is in the contested classroom context—here specifically in relation to humor—that the notion of "Third Space" (Gutiérrez, 2008) becomes generative. This construct differentiates between official teacher classroom spaces/purposes (i.e. "first space") and purely student spaces/purposes (i.e. "second space") and makes room for a potential merging or meeting of the two spaces in what is called "Third Space." By acknowledging power relations and "unofficial" participation structures in classrooms, Third Space paves the way for "a view of classrooms as having multiple, layered, and conflicting activity systems with various interconnections"(Gutiérrez, 2008, p. 152). We find in our data that humor is both produced in Third Space and productive of Third Spaces, and that digitally mediated learning opens up Third Spaces in more profoundly visible ways than those possible within only face-to-face participation classroom structures.

RECONSIDERING READING & WRITING IN THE ENGLISH CLASSROOM

Advances in technology are shifting long-standing practices and structures in English classrooms. As new media (e.g. smart phones, laptops, tablets) become a critical part of how youth make meaning in and make sense of their lives outside of school, educators must reconsider what kinds of literacy practices are valued as part of the English classroom curriculum (Knobel & Lankshear, 2007). The traditional print-centric curriculum now stands in stark juxtaposition to youth's everyday experiences with digitally mediated, socially situated composing events outside of school (e.g. texting a friend, designing a blog, posting Facebook updating, Tweeting a link, creating a meme, remixing a YouTube video). This disconnect between everyday engagement in digitally mediated spaces and classroom literacy experiences often makes school feel "out of sync" for many youth (Sheridan & Rowsell, 2010, p. 5).

In youth's everyday lives, print is intertwined *with* other modes such as images, video, audio, and music, to represent complex meanings. As new digital affordances change the way youth play, think, live, and communicate in everyday life, pedagogy in the English classroom is being revised to include the multimodal and interactive experiences that define how youth consume and produce media outside of school (Jewitt, 2009). Many of the initial technology-in-literacy empirical studies have focused on young people's creation of multimodal texts (Hull & Nelson, 2005; Jocson, 2008; Pahl & Rowsell, 2010). This work emphasizes the identity work that is often embedded in these serious compositions, which have the potential to create transformative spaces for "imagining selves, constructing texts, acquiring new literacies, and evoking possibilities for social change" (Jocson, 2008, p. 171). In other words, youth use these digital compositions to be recognized as particular kinds of people in a particular context (Gee, 2001, p. 99).

Other literature highlights the ways that new media can be used more playfully in the classroom, through perspective-taking, performance, and taking on other roles (Gerber & Price, 2011; Nichols, 2008; Schechter & Denmon, 2012). In particular, the playful integration of popular culture texts with English class is reported as increasing both engagement and learning (Bucolo, 2011; Kremer & Sanders, 2012). This is of particular interest to us, as play often calls upon humor to mediate social interaction and engagement.

The two classrooms at the center of this chapter offer illustrative examples of the diverse ways that educators are integrating technology into the English curriculum. The addition of technology in the classroom necessarily adds new layers of, and spaces for, interaction as youth engage in a range of platforms, and produce complex, multimodal texts. Specifically, by focusing on the ways that humor has surfaced in our students' social interactions via technology, we build on the important work that has already been done in the literacy studies field regarding the sometimes clashing intersection between students' and teachers' purposes for new media in the classroom.

METHODS

Research Questions

This section draws from two distinct classroom settings to answer the following questions:

- (RQ1) How do students use humor in new media spaces situated within classrooms?
- (RQ2) In what ways do these functions create tensions within traditional classroom expectations?

Context 1: Upper Elementary

The first author's data draws from a multi-year classroom ethnography in a public elementary school. The second year of the study offered the opportunity to observe and document the lived experiences of teachers and children as they negotiated a district-wide 1:1 iPad initiative. The introduction of iPads into the classroom heightened tensions between teachers and students, as children's playful practices and relationships with technology outside of school came into conflict with schooled expectations of using the iPad as a "serious" learning tool. Drama pedagogy (O'Neill, 1995), a performative teaching method emphasizing the playful process of building drama worlds as a complex learning medium, was employed as part of the literacy curriculum as a way for children to playfully explore their own experiences with technology in school. One drama invitation asked children, working in small groups, to create short commercials (filmed and edited using their iPads) that argued either for or against schools implementing 1:1 technological initiatives. The group of 5th and 6th graders highlighted in this chapter chose to create a satirical commercial for a hypothetical parent advocacy group that opposed technology integration into schools. Data sources include video recordings of the production process, the edited commercials, and reflective student interviews.

Context 2: High School

The second author's data draws from a research partnership utilizing ethnographic methods with a High School English teacher who agreed to collaborate to intentionally integrate more new media platforms into her traditional

Honors Sophomore English class. The data highlighted in this piece draws from their use of a "Facebook-like" social networking site (called a "Ning"), during which adolescents spontaneously engaged in consistently humorous discourses (such as by uploading silly profile pictures or using hashtags in a witty way) without being explicitly prompted to do so. Data also includes a discussion between the classroom teacher and researcher, while collaborating to grade digital movie adaptations students' made after reading *Wuthering Heights*. Data sources include contributions on the Ning site (including written text, uploaded images, videos, etc.) as well as informal interviews and focus groups with the collaborating classroom teacher and the 16 student participants.

Analytic Methods

Across the two datasets, we utilized our definition of humor: a socially situated "form of play that comprises cognitive (nonserious incongruity), emotional (mirth), and expressive (laughter) components" (Martin, 2007, p. 114) and identified moments of laughter or young people's attempts to elicit laughter in others. Laughter or the online equivalent ("LOL," "ha ha ha," winking emoticons) were used as identifiable markers for humor, given the difficulty of ascertaining participants' internal feelings of mirth. We then employed open coding (Strauss & Corbin, 1990) to categorize the foregrounded functions that each of these moments of humor seemed to accomplish. For example, we first looked through our data and marked instances that we interpreted as students' deliberate uses of humor, such as posting amusing cat profile pictures or the employment of an ironic "thumbs up" for parody. We then coded each instance with the foregrounded potential purpose driving the students' humorous participation. Collapsing overlapping labels and narrowing down our coding terms, we simplified the humorous class participation as accomplishing affiliation-building, critique, and, at times, unsettling. We selected illustrative cases from each of the sites to highlight each of our main findings. Findings were triangulated with field notes and informal interviews collected at our respective research sites. Our ethnographic work in each classroom afforded us comprehensive knowledge of each participant, which supported the validity of the coding process.

Findings

By situating humor as a tactic across our very distinct datasets, we identify three common themes that emerged as powerful functions of the socially embedded act of "being funny" with new media in the classroom: (1) humor as affiliation-building; (2) humor as critique; (3) humor as unsettling. These three functions often worked in concert, overlapping and merging in ways sometimes unanticipated by the teachers and researcher in the classroom. While all three themes are certainly present in classroom spaces, regardless of whether technology is integrated, the increased prevalence of explicit humorous participation when digital devices are involved suggests that there may be more space for students to re-invent spaces when the in-school platforms evoke participatory learning possibilities.

Humor as Affiliation-building (RQ1)

It is a sleepy Tuesday afternoon. Participants from American Literature had just returned from lunch, and they followed me (second author), happy to be free from class duties, to the circle of chairs I had set up in a nearby classroom. The following conversation ensued:

> Trisha: [The Ning] was definitely interesting because I'm so used to just typing it down on a piece of paper and turning it in or writing it and not putting it on the blog for everyone could see.
>
> Elsa: Yeah, I don't think I like that … I mean, I like that if I'm on Facebook because I can say what I WANT to say in a humorous way … not like an assignment … but in writing an assignment on there and you're like, you read someone else's and you're like "Oh my God. I look like an idiot."

One key tension that students described experiencing in the high school context involved the clash of interaction norms evoked in the Third Space opportunities constructed when the classroom teacher and I brought in typically informal, out-of-school social networking sites, such as Ning and Twitter, for classroom purposes. Finding themselves at the intersection of the first space of academic pursuits and the second space of social play, students wrestled with how best to build affiliations among their virtual audience of teacher and peers. Livingstone, Van Covering, and Thumin (2008) comment:

> [A]lthough it indeed appears that, for many young people, social networking is 'all about me, me, me', this need not imply narcissistic self-absorption. Rather … social networking is about 'me' in the sense that it reveals the self embedded in the peer group, as known to and represented by others, rather than the private 'I' known best by oneself. (p. 401)

It comes as no surprise that students were concerned with the construction of their social selves on this *social* networking site. However, it is interesting that they experienced ambiguity about how best to build social ties through virtual participation; successful and appropriate interaction norms on the Ning were perceived by the 10th graders as conflicting, somewhere in the middle of the spectrum between "traditional school" purposes and "Facebook" social purposes. On the class-based Ning, students wanted to maintain academic face in these spaces, while also appealing to their friends and the informality norms of the platforms.

Humor emerged consistently among Ning participation, as an affiliation-building strategy, and it was often framed uniquely for the purpose of social play (Second Space) rather than academic (First Space). One 10th grader, Trey, explains: "On the Ning I usually have to post serious and like have to act all smart for the *honor's* class … You can't be all joking around … but I still add a little joking around, but I have to get a good grade and be serious about it sometimes." Trey's words reveal that his experience of the Ning rarely veered into Third Space; instead, he decompartmentalized his "for-school" moves away from his "social" moves.

Known as a "class clown," Trey was remarkably adept at a variety of social media. His posts, nearly always humorous or sarcastic in tone, received a great deal of attention, and served to strengthen his already-existing social ties in the physical classroom. Figure 9.1 shows one of Trey's many posts that earned him virtual "likes," the equivalent of a "high five." Students chose to "like" a blog or status update most often when the post was funny/witty/creative, judgmental about a character that it was popular to dislike, or inclusive of a popular culture allusion (to signal that they are "in" on the joke).

A perfect example of humor-powered affiliation-building can be found in Trey's sarcastic creation of The "Exclusive Club of Exclusiveness for Exclusive People" featured in Figure 9.2. As teachers, we did not even know students could create their own forums on the Ning, and Trey co-opted the space to engage in some social banter with his friends, who all happened to sit with him in the same physical corner of the classroom. Here, Trey's wit is in direct tension with the intended "academic" use of the Ning. Instead of doing the official school business, he created this forum to strengthen social ties, as a platform for social play.

Figure 9.1 Trey uses humor to virtually build affiliations with his sarcastic profile picture (featuring popular culture icon, Kim Kardashian) and his use of informal slang in posts.

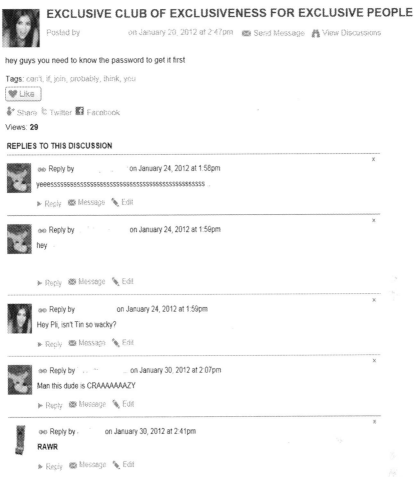

Figure 9.2 Trey uses the time he has been given to write a literary blog to strengthen already-existing social ties through the spontaneous creation of the "Exclusive Club of Exclusiveness."

Nevertheless, just because Trey ignored the teacher's direction to do the literary blog in favor of creating this humorous forum does not mean that learning is not occurring. Vygotsky (1978, p. 104) warns against over-trivializing such social play, explaining that it "bears little resemblance to the complex, mediated form of thought and volition it leads to," inferring that play always serves to meet a young person's need (perhaps in this case, affiliation-building), thus paving the way for change and development.

Other times, however, students embraced teacher invitations to use humor in their literary blogs to simultaneously fulfill the academic objective while also building social affiliations. This generative juxtaposition opened up the possibility for a Third Space in which student cultural capital collided with teacher-driven curricular objectives. Kelly, for instance, found that combining the affordances of Facebook with school-like objectives created a "more interactive" experience than the traditional English class assignments. She went on to explain:

> It's kind of cool to make more references to our social world of like media and stuff…I know that's one thing that was encouraged in the blog. And also being like funny, like I never write about funny things really but I'm trying to do that more in the blog. And so like that's kind of nice…

While Kelly's comments about deliberating and attempting to insert more humor into her posts opened up Third Space potential, a closer look into her Ning participation revealed she often operated in the realm of First Space, academic objectives. Although Kelly had a well-established "successful face-to-face English class student" identity, she did not garner as many "likes" on her blogs and status updates as many other, less traditionally successful students in her English 10 Honors class. Affiliation-building was simply not her main priority. In an interview, she shared that she chose not to participate much on social media outside of school, which reveals her lack of interest or experience in affiliation-building via online networking platforms. Later on in the semester, when her peers were using the witty hashtags on the status update function on the Ning to comment on a film they were watching in class, Kelly anxiously asked me to help her learn how to do hashtags.

Perhaps a truer version of Third Space emerged when students *hijacked* "serious academic" virtual spaces and purposes to "joke around" while still skillfully meeting both the expectations of the teacher and their peers. Figure 9.3 illustrates one such occasion. Because students seemed to have trouble relating to the characters in the novel *Letters to Werther*, the classroom teacher strategically planned to assign each student a character in the novel and to have them write letters to another main player in the book "in-character." Then, students were asked to find the blogs with letters written to them, and to respond with a letter of their own. Kevin and Rick, two friends who sat near each other in the physical classroom, began by first completing the required assignment. Kevin wrote an initial letter in-character, using all the typical old-fashioned letter conventions, and Rick, following assignment directions, responded with a traditional letter of his own. Then, Rick noticed that Kevin had intentionally manipulated/played with the number of views (circled in Figure 9.3) for his blog post, and this conversation followed, all in the "Comments" section of the initial blog:

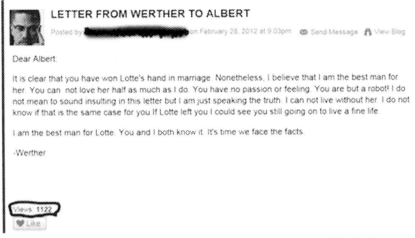

LETTER FROM WERTHER TO ALBERT

Posted by ▓▓▓▓▓▓▓▓▓▓ on February 28, 2012 at 9:03pm   ✉ Send Message   🔗 View Blog

Dear Albert:

It is clear that you have won Lotte's hand in marriage. Nonetheless, I believe that I am the best man for her. You can not love her half as much as I do. You have no passion or feeling. You are but a robot! I do not mean to sound insulting in this letter but I am just speaking the truth. I can not live without her. I do not know if that is the same case for you. If Lotte left you I could see you still going on to live a fine life.

I am the best man for Lotte. You and I both know it. It's time we face the facts.

-Werther

Views: 1122

♥ Like

Figure 9.3 Rick and Kevin fulfill the requirements of an assignment while simultaneously reappropriating the space to engage in humorous banter and manipulation of view count.

> Rick: You seem to be quite the popular man with all these views!
> Kevin: People like my stuff I guess
> Rick: Indeed, that would be as it seems.
> Kevin: Yes, indeed it is
> Kevin: By the way how is Lotte?
> Rick: Ah she is fine and doing quite well, and yourself?
> Kevin: Good, how are the kids?
> Rick: Kids, if you did not realize, Lotte is in a chastity belt.
> Kevin: She was not when we were together;

Kevin and Rick chose to "continue" the sanctioned assignment in very interesting ways. Rather than sticking with the old-fashioned letter genre, they are reappropriating the assignment to better fit the platform they are using—a virtual blog that can facilitate real-time chat conversation. But they are also reappropriating the assignment from a "serious" one to a more "humorous" one that incorporates a discourse of two young men joking around to establish affiliation ties. Rick begins the back-and-forth with a sarcastic jab at noting that Kevin has manipulated his "view count" to make it appear as though it has been the most popular blog in the class. Rick confessed in an interview to me that he put a rock on the keyboard to create a huge number of hits for one of his blogs. This manipulation of view count recurred multiple times with multiple students throughout the semester, and became less about looking popular and more about flaunting one's ability to humorously hack the system.

Kevin ends the exchange by making an allusion to sleeping with Lotte, which is consistent with his character, but somewhat outside the bounds of sanctioned classroom humor. Their banter parallels the kind of sexualized heteronormative banter that adolescent males often engage in, and it reveals the very tactical ways that they re-made the for-class space into something that more closely resembled their informal social-virtual affiliation-building spaces.

Humor as Critique (RQ1)

A small group of 5th and 6th graders sat in the corner of the classroom, planning out their "anti-iPad" commercial. Laughter punctuated the conversation as they playfully tried out different voices and mannerisms for the proposed dialogue and characters. At one point, the group debated the use of an "abused cat" as the spokesperson, to elicit sympathy from the audience, but ultimately they decided on a parodic version of an infomercial depicting exaggerated interactions between two students and a teacher in a 1:1 iPad classroom. Specifically, the group discussed using the structure of an "infomercial fail" for their commercial, a well-documented infomercial convention online with gifs, YouTube compilations, Tumblrs, and blogs committed to collecting the most laugh-inducing examples. An "infomercial fail" begins by presenting a problematic situation marked with large red Xs flashing on top of the "fail." The advertised product is then presented with the promise of miraculously solving the problem. The children decided to remix the "infomercial fail" genre conventions by presenting iPads as the problem-inducing rather than problem-solving product.

The commercial as a genre is particularly interesting given that it is considered a type of "old humor" (Shifman, 2007), but one that now has a prominent place online as part of viral advertising campaigns. Whereas humor was/is an optional part of television commercials (Weinberger, Spotts, Campbell, & Parsons, 1995),

> In viral Internet-based commercials, humor is an integral, almost obligatory component. Since humorous content is by far the most dominant content type in pass-along/viral emails (Phelps, Lewis, Mobilio, Perry, & Raman, 2004), it is not surprising that humor plays such an important role in viral commercials... (Shifman, 2007, p. 196)

In other words, humor is now a critical tool of advertisers looking to persuade Internet users to not only purchase a product or engage in some kind of desired behavior, but humor is also leveraged to persuade users to pass the commercial along to others via e-mail and social networks. Given the cultural significance of humorous commercials online, it should be of little surprise that given the opportunity to film a commercial, every group of children utilized humor as a persuasive tool. The focal group of children discussed here, however, went even further, using humor as a tactic to critique larger adult discourses around children, technology, and schools.

The use of humor as a tactic to engage in social critique is well-documented as part of everyday interactions outside of schools (e.g., Gilbert, 2004; Martin, 2007; Meyer, 2000; Mulkay, 1988). Martin (2007) posits that humor has been "co-opted" as a tool (i.e. tactic) as a way for people to communicate with one another about issues about which they disagree: "By simultaneously expressing opposite meanings, the humorous mode provides a shared conceptual framework that embraces contradictions, rather than avoiding them, and thereby enables people to negotiate otherwise difficult interpersonal transactions" (p. 115). This tactic is particularly salient for classroom interactions where inherent power differentials between teachers and youth often allow few opportunities for more serious forms of student critique. Humor invites youth and teachers to communicate about important issues that may be silenced in classrooms where only the serious mode is recognized as an accepted form of interaction.

The group's final edited 2 minute long anti-iPad commercial opened with a familiar scene: two children sitting at table in a classroom, looking down and swiping at the screens of their iPads. After 12 s of silence, the female student pushes a pencil cup off the table in anger after losing a game on her iPad. A teacher runs into the scene:

Teacher: What's all this noise about?

Female student: Oh nothing. [gaze remains on iPad; she returns to playing the game]

Teacher: That game looks so **educational**.

Female student: [without looking up] Yeah, it is.

Teacher: Do you just connect the dots?

Female student: Yeah.

Teacher: [Looks straight into camera, smiling] Very **educational** [thumbs up]. [Red X appears across the teacher's face.]

The humor in this scene emerges in part from the playful incongruence between the ways the teacher character is portrayed compared with children's everyday interactions with their own classroom teachers. One of the main concerns of teachers was the triviality of the apps that came preloaded on the iPads from the district, especially the games, many of which were simplistic forms of test preparation. But the commercial presents a caricature of an uncritical teacher who appears unaware of what children are doing on their iPads. The student and teacher's dialogue humorously hints at some of the larger discourses surrounding educational technology, particularly discourses that imply that adding 1:1 devices will instantly "fix" classrooms. The commercial's parodic interaction between the students and the teacher raises critical questions around what is considered an "educational" use of iPads in the classroom as well as highlighting teachers' general lack of experience with new media compared with the students they are teaching.

At the midpoint of the commercial, what began as a semi-realistic series of events (exaggerated and parodic but plausible) suddenly takes on the conventions of the horror genre: dark lighting, eerie noises, moaning, and possessed and potentially violent children. During the group's planning sessions, they satirically discussed iPads "sucking out [children's] brains and souls" and transforming children into "empty shells of their former selves." In the commercial, the narrative suggestion is that adults have decided to remove the iPads from the classroom, and in response, the children have transformed into possessed, zombie-like beings. The dark screen is illuminated and the viewer sees that the setting has changed to a small office with bookshelves on each wall. The female student is curled up in a rocking chair, while the male student sits crouched against the wall. Both students moan, "iPad... iPad... iPad" with growing intensity. The teacher frantically hands a book to one of the students, but the student throws it back at her face. Both students scream, "NO! NO!" as a large X appears over the whole scene (see Figure 9.4). Through the use of exaggerated horror conventions, the scene humorously speaks from a critical stance in response to the fears and fierce

Figure 9.4 Children employ genre conventions of an infomercial (large red X) to humorously critique public discourses about iPad use in schools.

debates that adults wage over children's "screen time." The scene offers an exaggerated version of adults' fears (e.g. children won't want to read "real" books anymore), emphasizing the absurdity of such scenarios. In effect, children metaphorically smile and wink at the circulating discourses around evil technology and childhood innocence.

The final scene begins with a black screen and a very serious voiceover: "Do you want your kids winding up like this? No! Help us ban iPads before chaos starts." The setting for the finale returns to the classroom, but now five students stand on chairs in a circle in the middle of the room. The teacher stands in the middle of the chairs frantically turning in circles trying to find a way out. The students hold pencils and forks in their hands (representative of flaming torches), as they chant, "We want iPads. We want iPads. We want iPads." In the closing moments, the teacher falls to the ground as the students jump off of the chairs and attack her lifeless body. Most of the children in the class agreed that this was the funniest scene in any of the commercials that were made. The humor here stems from the outrageousness of the proposed classroom scene—sporks and all, but in a more critical sense for children, the humor and fun arises from the playful reversal of the typical power relations in classrooms. In other words, humor as a tactic within the commercial allowed children to critique and rupture the status quo of bodies in the classroom. This final scene is the only scene of the commercial where students physically positioned themselves on a higher level than the teacher. In the other scenes, the students were seated while the teacher stood and had the ability to move in and out of the scene. Standing on top of the chairs represents a complete break with the expected "student state" or the "gestures, dispositions, attitudes and work habits expected of 'being a student'" (McLaren, 1999, p. 91). Chairs, often used as a tool for controlling student behavior, were moved out from behind the tables and repurposed as platforms to stand on. Children's lifeless bodies from the previous scenes have been injected with energy as they chanted and jumped on top of the chairs before jumping down on the teacher. Chaos, rather than control, now defines the classroom space.

For readers asking, "Isn't this *just* a case of children playing around?" The simple answer is: yes, this is a case of children playing around. But in this Third Space, children were playing around with complex meanings, while protesting against adult discourses that constrain them as passive users of technology. Critique is too often situated as an exclusively "serious" undertaking, while humor can be an equally powerful tool of critique. The children's anti–iPad commercial demonstrates how the tactical use of humor has the ability to open up "a discursive space [i.e., a Third Space] within which it becomes possible to speak about matters that are otherwise naturalized, unquestioned, or silenced" (Goldstein, 2003, p. 10). Importantly, this discursive, Third Space invites youth and adults to communicate diverse perspectives and knowledge, opening up unique opportunities for all participants to engage in the learning process.

Humor as Unsettling (RQ2)

In many cases, there is a reason that teachers are reluctant to embrace humor in classroom spaces. What is mirth-inducing for some can be cringe-inducing for others. In both of our datasets, adult-teacher/researcher-figures felt uncomfortable at various times because of the ways in which technology-mediated humor was too noisy, too distracting, or too messy in light of existing neat curricular goals. In addition, young people often tactically use humor to push the boundaries of what may or may not be deemed "appropriate" in the classroom. It is the "multiplicity and ambiguity of meaning in humor" (Martin, 2007, p. 123) that allows a young person to withdraw and say he/she was "just joking" and "didn't mean it." While young people in the classroom can wield the ambiguity and multiplicity as a powerful social tool, teachers are often left feeling vaguely or even deeply unsettled by the ideas, beliefs, and values that joking can provoke. If one function of humor is often to build affiliations among peers in the classroom, a natural question arises … who is excluded here? (The authors write in first person here to reflect their own unsettling experiences researching humor in the classroom.)

　　Unsettling the official curriculum. Although humor is not necessarily at odds with academics, in the high school context, the classroom teacher and I (J.R.) often found ourselves pitting the two against each other. Below is a snippet of a transcript taken when we were discussing how to grade 10th graders' movie adaptations of *Wuthering Heights*. The particular movie we are addressing below was composed by four males in the class who were cited most heavily previously as using the Ning platform for social affiliation building purposes. In the transcript, references to humor are in bold.

　　Julie: Huh … so [the group's reflection] is really interesting to read isn't it … I think it's smart—I feel like he's kind of defending some of their decisions … he's anticipating some of things I would have addressed like …

　　Allison: the mood—

　　Julie: Like it got too **silly** or—…

　　Allison: I do think a lot of the things they chose to do seem to be for **entertainment value** versus, right

Julie: Right. I do think the mood, even though they said they did it on purpose … that's a spot I think we can take off a little because we did feel like we all were **laughing** kind of and again …

Allison: Yeah, so like, I think we can say "we appreciated the **comedic aspect of your film, but in some places it overshadowed the goals**."

Julie: Yep- And so now I'm thinking … A lot of people were **laughing** a lot … I know when we get to [another movie composed by members of the same social group] … we run into the same issue …

Notice that in the transcript above, Allison and I set up socially driven peer humor and comedy (Second Space) as directly incompatible with classroom academic goals (First Space), thus denying the possibility for Third Space to emerge. While we experienced some types of humor in other movies as sanctioned and compatible with learning, it is clear that we were especially uncomfortable when humor was foregrounded rather than the assigned categories in the rubric for the assignment. The various words we use to describe the source of our unease include "comedic," "entertainment," "laughing," and "silly." Even more interesting is the fact that the group's written reflection for the teacher on the design decisions they made in creating the movie explicitly defends their humorous tone as purposeful and effective. They seemed to anticipate teachers' objections to the humor in advance and sought to directly confront those concerns in the reflection.

Unsettling bodies and space. In the case of the children producing the anti-iPad commercial, I (B.A.B.) was the researcher, but at times I was also positioned as the authority figure in the room—a role typically reserved for the classroom teacher. Due to state standardized testing in the mornings and afternoons, some children wanted to use time during their lunch period to work in the classroom on filming their commercials. I was the lone adult in the classroom during this time, which created some unexpected moments of tension as I negotiated the line between my roles as a researcher and supervising adult. One significant moment of tension involved schooled expectations about noise: I heard screaming coming from the small library/office that connected two classrooms and assumed something was wrong. I rushed in only to ruin the filming of a scene in the commercial where the student throws the book back at the teacher and screams. Below is an excerpt from reflective notes taken after leaving the field site for the day:

> *My main worry today was that there were other classroom teachers eating in the lunch in a nearby classroom. I was concerned with what they would think was happening—what I was allowing to happen in this classroom. The children agreed to try and be quieter. (B. Buchholz, field notes, March 23, 2013)*

A second moment of tension involved schooled expectations of bodies and space. Children asked whether they could run around and jump on top of the tables to film the final scene of the commercial. Again, an excerpt from my reflective notes:

> I wanted to say, "Yes, of course, run around on top of the tables…," but instead I repeated the traditional school script, "No. No running on top of tables, even if it is for your commercial." My "No" came from a deeply paranoid part that every teacher can identify with—that part that imagines another teacher or the principal walking by the classroom window, peering in to see children laughing and screaming excitedly and questioning whether any "serious" learning is actually happening. I worried that I would be judged as an incompetent adult who allowed children to run around wildly, reflecting one of the biggest sins an elementary school teacher can make: to be seen as incapable of controlling children's bodies and behaviors. (B. Buchholz, field notes, March 23, 2013)

These tensions, related to children's bodies and voices, are evocative of Heathcote's (1984) warning that, "You cannot make drama sound academic" (p. 117), only here we might revise it to say, "You cannot make all technology use sound (or look) academic." The reality was that this invitation to create a commercial, strategically placed at the intersection of technology, literacy, and drama, sounded and looked a lot like that which schools consider as "off-task" or "out of control" behavior. Children's desire to experience humor in the process using technology and the goal of inducing humor in others can ultimately lead the adult in the classroom space to experience much different emotions: anxiety, worry, and fear.

IMPLICATIONS

Our investigation into the main tactics our young participants used when employing technology-mediated humor in English classrooms revealed three main functions: affiliation-building, critique, and unsettling, as described above. Humor as affiliation-building reveals students' deliberate cultivation of their social self through a variety of methods ranging from the creating "exclusive clubs" on a social networking site to the parodic remixing of infomercial conventions when composing digital texts. Humor as critique emphasizes the ways in which students agentically manipulate conventions, school assignments, and teacher invitations, to creatively "mash-up" in-school and out-of-school norms and parodically critique schooled expectations related to technology. Finally, humor as unsettling, hints at the ways that digital technology enables students to disrupt teacher-assigned school-purposes in pursuit of other, more pressing social purposes that may clash with what is seen as appropriate for school. From this exploration, three important implications result: legitimize humor in school, leverage the "funny" in technology, and let them play.

Legitimize Humor in Schools

Technology is often pushed into classrooms under the pretense that these new tools will be unproblematic and simply additive to an already stable curriculum. However, our two classroom contexts suggest that the layering of digital and face-to-face spaces requires constant exploration and negotiation on the part of teachers and students. It is as Neil Postman (1998, p. 4) warned over a decade ago: "Technological change is not additive; it is ecological … A new medium does not add something; it changes everything." Integrating technology into English classrooms creates ruptures within the histories and norms that have come to define what it means to be a "good" student. While these ruptures powerfully open up spaces for a wider array of possible literate identities, there are also serious tensions that arise as out-of-school norms and identities are invited into classroom spaces. Rather than rushing to close these ruptures by labeling them as misbehavior, teachers and researchers need to work collaboratively to explore how students' use of humor in technologically mediated spaces may be regarded as an acceptable and even "genuine" emotion in the English classroom (Lewis & Tierney, 2013).

Leverage the "Funny" in Technology

Whether filming digital commercials or commenting on the class Ning, our work builds on nearly two decades of research on Third Space by exploring classrooms where new forms of digital tools and modes reframe interactions between teachers and students. Our research findings suggest that new media spaces seem to create more pronounced opportunities for youth to humorously engage in the learning process in ways that are personally and socially meaningful. Teachers can deliberately "leverage the funny" in the new media tools they invite into the classroom by thinking-aloud and modeling appropriate, effective, rhetorically guided uses of humor via technology. While students' humorous contributions are often experienced as unsettling by teachers, more research needs to be done to unearth whether or not this "unofficial" or "off-task" work could also involve contingent connections with the official work of the class (Maybin, 2007). It is no surprise that where two or more social actors are involved, the expected uses of a space become contested. What is surprising is just how generative these spaces of seeming opposition, in which teacher purposes meet student tactics, often became. The blurring of boundaries, the juxtaposition of objectives, and even the mixing of selves (the school self and the out-of-school self) often resulted in connection-making and bridge-building.

Let Them Play

By focusing on the realities inherent in classroom spaces intentionally working to integrate technology, this chapter contributes to critical conversations in the field about the collaborative and contextual nature of technology. Our work suggests that rather than removing the body from the English classroom, digital spaces and tools invite the body—and specifically emotions—to be unveiled and recognized as part of students' literate identities within schooled spaces. Researchers and teachers must begin to understand humor as a way that humans continue to play over the course of their lives and that this play can often serve "serious functions." Young people's mediatization of humor in the English classroom can serve as a tactical form of play; a form of play that serves important social, emotional, and critical thinking functions (Bateson, 2005). Reframing young people's humorous and playful participation with technology as a tactic, an agentic means of re-making their learning space can allow us to begin to see empowering possibilities, where we once saw only meaningless play and disruptive laughter.

REFERENCES

Bateson, P. (2005). Play and its role in the development of great apes and humans. In A. D. Pellegrini & P. K. Smith (Eds.), *The nature of play: Great apes and humans.* New York: The Guilford Press.
Buckingham, D. (2011). *The material child.* Buckingham, UK: Polity Press.
Bucolo, J. (2011). Survivor: Satis House: Creating classroom community while teaching Dickens in a reality-TV world. *English Journal, 100*(5), 29–32.
Corsaro, W. (1994). Discussion, debate and friendship processes: Peer discourse in U.S. and Italian nursery schools. *Sociology of Education, 67*(1), 1–26.
Eagleton, T. (1985-86). The subject of literature. *Cultural Critique, 2,* 95–104.
Francis, L. E. (1994). Laughter, the best mediation: Humor as emotion management in interaction. *Symbolic Interaction, 17*(2), 147–163.
Gee, J. P. (2001). Identity as an analytic lens for research in education. In W. G. Secada (Ed.), *Review of research in education: Vol. 25* (pp. 99–125). Washington, DC: American Educational Research Association.
Gerber, H., & Price, D. (2011). Twenty-first-century adolescents, writing, and new media: Meeting the challenge with game controllers and laptops. *English Journal, 101*(2), 68–73.
Gilbert, J. R. (2004). *Performing marginality: Humor, gender, and cultural critique.* Detroit, MI: Wayne State University Press.
Goldstein, D. (2003). *Laughter out of place: Race, class, violence, and sexuality in a Rio shantytown.* Berkeley, CA: University of California Press.

Gutiérrez, K. D. (2008). Developing a sociocritical literacy in the third space. *Reading Research Quarterly*, *43*(2), 148–164.

Heathcote, D. (1984). Drama and learning. In L. Johnson & C. O'Neill (Eds.), *Collected writings on education and drama* (pp. 92–102). Evanston, IL: Northwestern University Press.

Hull, G. A., & Nelson, M. E. (2005). Locating the semiotic power of multimodality. *Written Communication*, *22*(2), 224–261.

Ito, M., Baumer, S., Bittanti, M., Boyd, D., Cody, R., Herr, B., et al. (2009). *Hanging out, messing around, geeking out: Living and learning with new media.* Cambridge, MA: MIT Press.

Jewitt, C. (Ed.), (2009). *The Routledge handbook of multimodal analysis.* London: Routledge.

Jocson, K. (2008). Situating the personal in digital media production. In M. L. Hill & L. Vasudevan (Eds.), *Media, learning, and sites of possibility* (pp. 167–199). New York: Peter Lang.

Keltner, D., Young, R., & Buswell, B. N. (1997). Appeasement in human emotion, personality, and social practice. *Aggressive Behavior*, *23*, 359–374.

Knobel, M., & Lankshear, C. (2007). *A new literacies sampler.* New York: Peter Lang Publishing.

Kremer, N., & Sanders, H. (2012). Shakespeare in 3D: Bringing the bard to life through new (old) media. *Voices from the Middle*, *14*(9), 57–64.

Kuipers, G. (2008). The sociology of humor. In V. Raskin (Ed.), *The primer of humor research* (pp. 361–398). Berlin: Mouton de Gruyter.

Lewis, C., & Tierney, J. D. (2011). Mobilizing emotion in an urban English classroom. *Changing English*, *18*(3), 319–329.

Lewis, C., & Tierney, J. D. (2013). Mobilizing emotion in an urban classroom: Producing identities and transforming signs in a race-related discussion. *Linguistics and Education*, *24*(3), 289–304.

Livingstone, S., Van Covering, E., & Thumin, N. (2008). Converging traditions of research on media and information literacies. In J. Coieo, M. Knobel, C. Lankshear, & D. Leu (Eds.), *Handbook of research on new literacies* (pp. 103–132). New York: Routledge.

Martin, R. A. (2007). *The psychology of humor: An integrative approach.* Burlington, MA: Elsevier Academic Press.

Maybin, J. (2007). Literacy under and over the desk: Oppositions and heterogeneity. *Language and Education*, *21*(6), 515–530.

McLaren, P. (1999). *Schooling as a ritual performance: Toward a political economy of educational symbols and gestures.* London: Rowman & Littlefield.

Meyer, J. C. (2000). Humor as a double-edged sword: Four functions of humor in communication. *Communication Theory*, *10*(3), 310–331.

Micciche, L. R. (2002). More than a feeling: Disappointment and WPA work. *College English*, *64*, 432–458.

Mulkay, M. (1988). *On humor: Its nature and its place in modern society.* Cambridge: Polity Press.

Nichols, R. (2008). Kind of like emerging from the shadows: Adolescent girls as multiliteracy pedagogues. In M. L. Hill & L. Vasudevan (Eds.), *Media, learning, and sites of possibility* (pp. 119–156). New York: Peter Lang.

O'Neill, C. (1995). *Drama worlds: A framework for process drama.* Portsmouth, NH: Heinemann.

Pahl, K., & Rowsell, J. (2010). *Artifactual literacies: Every object tells a story.* New York, NY: Teachers College Press.

Phelps, J. E., Lewis, R., Mobilio, L., Perry, D., & Raman, N. (2004). Viral marketing or electronic word-of-mouth advertising: Examining consumer responses and motivations to pass along email. *Journal of Advertising Research*, *44*(04), 333–348.

Postman, N. (1998). Five things we need to know about technological change. In *Conference in Denver, CO.* Retrieved November 4, 2013, from, http://www.mat.upm.es/~jcm/neil-postman–five-things.html.

Schechter, A., & Denmon, J. (May 2012). How do I earn buy-in from digital natives? *Voices from the Middle*, *19*(4), 22–28.

Sheridan, M. P., & Rowsell, J. (2010). *Design literacies: Learning and innovation in the digital age.* London: Routledge.

Shifman, L. (2007). Humor in the age of digital reproduction: Continuity and change in internet-based comic texts. *International Journal of Communication, 1*(1), 23.

Strauss, A. L., & Corbin, J. M. (1990). *Basics of qualitative research.* Newbury Park, CA: Sage.

Vasudevan, L., Schultz, K., & Bateman, J. (2010). Rethinking composing in a digital age: Authoring literate identities through multimodal storytelling. *Written Communication, 27*(4), 442–468.

Vygotsky, L. S. (1978). *Mind in society: The development of higher mental process.* Cambridge, MA: Harvard University Press.

Walker, R., & Adelman, C. (1976). Strawberries. In M. Stubbs & S. Delamont (Eds.), *Explorations in classroom observation.* London: Wiley.

Weinberger, M. G., Spotts, H. E., Campbell, L., & Parsons, A. L. (1995). The use and effect of humor in different advertising media. *Journal of Advertising Research, 35*(3), 44–56.

CHAPTER 10

"I'm White Trying to Play a Black Dude": The Construction of Race, Identities, and Emotions in Actual and Virtual Spaces

Mary Beth Hines, Michael L. Kersulov, Chuck Holloway, Rebecca Rupert
Indiana University, Bloomington, IN, USA

INTRODUCTION

During the World Cup soccer match between Ghana and Germany on June 21, 2014, several French and German light-skinned fans painted in blackface lit up Twitter, Instagram, and other social media sites (Heim, 2014). Commentators essentially spanned the spectrum of emotional reactions. Some claimed indignation at the racist portrayal, while others argued that the blackface caused no harm. Supportive fans suggested that it was innocent fun, while others registered anger, shame, and/or disgust. Dubois (2014) of the *New Republic* explained that the phenomenon "triggered a rapid response on social media and a debate about what was happening, and what should be done." The potentially racist undertones of the act did not go unnoticed.

A month later, a baseball fan appeared in redface at a Cleveland Indians game in "grotesque homage" to the club's logo. In response, the founder of Eradicating Offensive Native Mascotry, Jacqueline Keeler, said:

> It is not acceptable to wear blackface in this country and never should have been. ... We need to make the same case about redface. We need people to think of it in the same way and see why it's wrong in the same way (Brady, 2014).

Despite the best intentions of antiracist advocates such as Ms. Keeler, these images went viral.

Online discussion continued when a Michigan social studies teacher was suspended for two weeks after showing students a 29-second video about the use of blackface in early twentieth century American history (Fox News, 2014). Posted on websites and circulated *via* social media, the story led onlookers to chat about whether the Michigan teacher was a racist or an "innocent" history teacher just doing his job.

Although these incidents occurred in a variety of contexts, the blackface/redface images of 2014 began trending, fanning commentary and fueling emotions as they spread. Digital witnesses asked, Were the painted faces paying "grotesque homage" and thus racist, or were they innocent images of American history and culture, produced and circulated by people who didn't know the history of blackface in this country? On the one hand, it might be argued that the blackface incidents were idiosyncratic, isolated experiences. On the other hand, it might also be argued that these moments—when situated socially, historically, and culturally—were symptomatic of our collective anxieties and ambivalences about what counts as racism. If so, then we need to consider the ways in which new technologies should have been implicated in escalating racial tensions, not only because the images circulated globally, but also because the emotional reactions to them went viral as well.

This cycle was brought into bold relief when riots in Ferguson, Missouri ignited after social media announced that an African-American teenager, Michael Brown, was allegedly shot by a white police officer. Tense emotions burst into violence in the streets of Ferguson and spread to Atlanta, Houston, San Francisco, and elsewhere. At the same time, a group of girls on a powder puff football team made the news, playing in blackface 60 miles away from the Missouri riots. The story and related pictures went viral. In addition, other blackface images materialized in 2014. A blackface man in a Michael Brown costume lit up Twitter and online news feeds, and a Kanye West blackface shocked Kim Kardashian at a social event. Both stories and related images went viral. In December 2014, a Google search using the words "Michael Brown" brought this array of widely dispersed images and news feeds together on the screen. Viewers saw the screen filled with a pastiche of articles about Michael Brown's death: images of protests in cities across the country appeared; and a series of blackface images and storylines—including the powder puff team in blackface, the Kanye West blackface interloper, and the young man in Michael Brown blackface and costume—were mashed together. Thus, it could be argued that digital media discursively reflected, constructed, and reproduced representations of race. Moreover, it is equally possible to argue that the montage of representation and social practices reflected and triggered the emotions of actual and virtual witnesses who, at times, engaged in violent social action. Race, representation, emotion, and social action were inextricably and dynamically linked in discursive digital practices, and the potency of the blackface incidents became all the more palpable with each additional viewer's typing of Michael Brown's name in the Google search engine.

For several decades, feminists and other scholars in cultural studies, as well as the mass media, have explored this relationship between discourse and lived experience (Ahmed, 2004; Belsey, 1980; Butler, 1989; Butler & Athanasiou, 2013). As one reporter argued, if we situate the events of Ferguson, Missouri and the attendant replay *via* social media, against the backdrop of American history and culture, then the riots should be seen as the legacies of segregation (Washington, 2014).

While it is important to examine digital media for the ways in which texts and images conveyed issues of race, it seems equally important to consider the social construction and circulation of emotions around race. In the case of Michael Brown, social media generated and circulated emotional responses so virulent that they led to violence. That is, the escalation of events in Ferguson, Missouri were fueled in part by digital media capturing local events and circulating them globally, accumulating emotional responses along the way. This phenomenon highlights the role that new technologies play in the culture, enabling local experiences to instantly become part of transnational flows.

After the grand jury's decision not to indict the white police officer who shot Michael Brown, Washington (2014) wrote:

What was behind the wave of emotions? … Interviews around the U.S. show that these roiling emotions spring as much from America's troubled racial history … as from a rational examination of the evidence.

Washington's words suggest that some Americans were situating the grand jury's decision against a tableau of systemic racism. Tying race to colonial legacies, Washington's statement raises an important question about the role of social media in shaping culture and history: How should "rational," socially responsible citizens react to digital media, to images, and information that potentially broker racism and embody enactments of violence?

In this chapter, we explore these questions in relation to a blackface incident that occurred in one English classroom around the same time the blackface images previously discussed went viral on social media. Shelly, a white English teacher at a predominantly white midwestern alternative high school, Last Chance High School (pseudonym; LCHS), found herself face-to-face with a blackface character in her own classroom. During a group project related to *Monster* (Myers, 1999), three students used iPads to create a video that featured a white student in blackface. Shelly was completely caught off guard when the trio proudly presented their video to her, she said in an interview later that day. She was horrified at the blackface specter, but pleased to see students finally engaged in a classroom activity, she reported. Furthermore, she was keenly aware of the potential for dissemination of a potentially racist image, for the video not only was constructed with digital media, but it also was capable of being dispersed with digital media, she added. Conflicting emotions in play, Shelly struggled with what she should have said in the moment, she conceded later that day. Declaring her initial response unsatisfactory, she then asked colleagues to weigh in on what she should have said and done. They did, and this chapter explores the emotional, political, and cultural valences of Shelly's possible options for responding to a twenty-first century blackface incident.

This chapter draws from a 4-year critical qualitative study of one English class at an alternative high school that for many was the last stop before incarceration or expulsion. Shelly invited her English class combined of ninth and tenth grade students to read the young-adult novel *Monster* (Myers, 1999), about an African-American young male who is incarcerated and waiting for trial. For the final project, students were to create multimodal texts, that is, texts that use multiple sign systems, including visual, audio, graphics, and/or print to produce meaning (Coiro, Knobel, Lankshear, & Leu, 2008; Hull & Schultz, 2002; Lankshear & Knobel, 2006). The iPad videos were to engender interest in the book's characters. Then students were to post them as Vine videos on Google+. One group of three white students responded by painting a white male in blackface to resemble the person portrayed on the book cover. Before turning to Shelly's classroom, we provide a brief summary of our conceptual framework, the historical genesis of blackface, the role of technology and twenty-first century literacies in the workplace and school, and a brief overview of social justice orientations to literacy education. From there, we will describe the larger study, our methods of data collection and analysis and our findings.

CRITICAL SOCIOCULTURAL PERSPECTIVES

We use a critical sociocultural framework informed by New Literacy Studies to explore the role of technology in eliciting and fanning the production of emotions on race issues at both micro- and macro-levels (Dunsmore & Fisher, 2010; Gee & Hayes, 2011; Lewis, Enciso, & Moje, 2009; Li, 2009). We examine the blackface incident as a local, transnational, and cultural digital media practice. With this approach, discourses and social practices can be examined for the ways in which they support and/or challenge the status quo. From a sociocultural perspective, meaning and identity are not constructed in the mind, but are cultivated as dynamic social practices nested in particular social, cultural, and historical contexts. Signifying practices both reflect and create meaning that is contingent and variable (Dunsmore & Fisher, 2010; Gee & Hayes, 2011; Li, 2009; Lewis et al., 2009). Using a critical sociocultural framework, we can examine the interplay of race, class, power, and privilege in literacy practices related to the blackface video. We can explore what is at stake for producers and viewers, and whose interests prevail. Moreover, we can look at the interplay between emotions and technology as a social and cultural construction with political consequences.

To explain these principles, we turn to researchers working within the New Literacy Studies traditions and to policy statements issued by literacy professional organizations, foregrounding the role of technology in and out of twenty-first century classrooms.

TWENTY-FIRST CENTURY LITERACIES: DIGITAL MEDIA IN LANGUAGE AND LEARNING

Digital media has been of great interest to educational researchers. Researchers have investigated how technology can be used to motivate and engage students (Coiro et al., 2008; Gee & Hayes, 2011; Jenkins, 2009). New Literacy Studies research has explored student interactions with digital media outside the classroom (Gee & Hayes, 2011; Hull & Schultz, 2002; Ito et al., 2010). As a result, many contemporary scholars have advocated for the adoption of digital tools used outside the classroom to entice young adults in the classroom (i.e., Gee & Hayes, 2011; Hagood, Alvermann, & Heron-Hruby, 2010; Hull & Schultz, 2002; Kajder, 2010; Thomas, 2007; Williams & Zenger, 2012).

The National Council of Teachers of English (NCTE) has called on teachers and educational policymakers to recognize the impact new media can have on the classroom (National Council of Teachers of English, 2013; Street, 1995). This is in part because new literacy practices have afforded multiple modes of expression (Kress & van Leeuwen, 2001) and have been linked to success in the twenty-first century workplace and classroom. This policy has stressed collaborative problem-solving inquiry as well as the production and reception of multimodal texts. Using digital media to produce and interpret multimodal texts has allowed students to move beyond the restrictive notion of texts created with print and language only (Gee, 2004; Sefton-Green, 2006). Multimodal digital texts have demanded an understanding of semiotics, or the meaning-making capabilities involved in the text, including linguistic, aural, and visual signs. To interpret multimodal texts, viewers have made connections among multiple modes, tapping into social, emotional, and cognitive aspects of the context for understanding (Nespor, 1994). New Literacy scholars, using sociocultural perspectives, have referred to these communicative situations as socially and culturally grounded literacy practices (Lewis & Fabos, 2005). In Shelly's class, students routinely produced and consumed multimodal texts. As the next section elaborates, young adults have used digital media not only to construct texts, but also to construct and convey emotions and identities.

INTERSECTIONS OF IDENTITY, EMOTIONS, AND DIGITAL MEDIA PERFORMANCES

From a critical, sociocultural perspective, identities are seen as constructed and enacted within social contexts. Identities are not static or inherent, but are dynamic and variable, changing with the circumstances. New Literacy Studies highlights this dynamicity both in and out of school literacies and technologies. It affords new spaces for investigating youth identities as youth traverse physical and virtual spaces in meaning-making activities. Leander has made an excellent point about the nature of those depictions in New Literacy Studies; young adults are depicted as "rational" designers of texts, "potentially missing how their moving, feeling bodies influence meaning-making in unpredictable ways" (Ehret & Hollett, 2014, p. 430). Indeed, at LCHS, the students' "rational" texts and selves were obscured by their subversive play in social networks as they performed identities designed to derail or minimally participate in "doing school." Young adults in this classroom strategically mobilized emotion to enact particular identities as they overtly or tacitly avoided doing school. Their embodied literacy practices literally spilled onto desks and floors as they simultaneously entertained onsite and virtual audiences. As we will see, for Shelly's students, "the rational" design was not on their list of priorities.

LCHS students fit the profile of teens reflected in recent research. Specifically, today's adolescents have been referred to as "digital natives," or individuals for whom being technologically literate comes as almost intuitive, as opposed to older generations who struggle to learn new technologies (Prensky, 2001). Ninety-two percent of adults in households with 15- to 34-year olds have reported owning computers. About 78% of young adults have said they owned cellphones, and almost half (47%) of those cell phone users had smartphones. In short, 37% of all teens possessed smartphones in

2013, up from just 23% in 2011 (Madden, Lenhart, & Duggan, et al., 2013). Moreover, young adults captured in the research on technology have used Facebook, YouTube, and Twitter as social events (Madden, Lenhart, & Cortesi, et al., 2013).

Many researchers have pointed to the need for updated pedagogical approaches in schools so as to not alienate these "digital natives" (Bennett, Maton, & Kervin, 2008; Palfrey & Gasser, 2013). Weber and Mitchell (2008) have argued that young people are attracted to digital media for social practices, because they can revisit their own work, observe how others respond, and gather community reflections. Additionally, users have been able to choose their level of anonymity when creating digital works (Palfrey & Gasser, 2013). The socialization, anonymity, and versatility of digital media has provided young people with "trying on of various identities" (Weber & Mitchell, 2008, p. 38) in a virtual setting without immediate consequences. Young adults "trying on" identities can mobilize a range of actual and feigned emotions in identity performances (Gee, 2000). Identity performances in the context of this study were entangled in the production and reception of off-task and off-color images and information that students sent to each other throughout the day *via* social media. Much of that identity production was engineered to produce emotional effects from friends—laughter, yelling, and anger—suggesting other ways that emotions and identities were socially constructed and mediated by technology.

THE EMOTIONAL AS POLITICAL: "SOCIALLY ASSIGNED DISPOSABILITY" IN SCHOOL SYSTEMS

We draw upon the work of Butler and Athanasiou (2013) to understand the emotional valences of youth at Shelly's school. These scholars argue that emotion is not exclusively an internal process, conceptualized as a phenomenon occurring inside the head of a young adult, but instead emerges as a response to "normative and normalizing powers" (p. 2). Dispossession occurs as a byproduct of individuals' interactions with others and with the culture, typically experienced when people are disowned or experiencing "painful injuries, painful interpellations, occlusions and foreclosures" (p. 2). Butler and Athanasiou (2013) argue that certain groups of people have been and can be relocated in the face of hunger, war, political struggle, unemployment, economic, or social conflicts. They consider such incidents acts of dispossession, forms of injustice, resulting in situations in which some groups are considered disposable while other groups are not.

In a parallel fashion, we argue that many LCHS students fit the profile of children and young adults who have not fared well in American mainstream schools. They are part of a larger population of nonmainstream students often relocated, dispossessed of home schools, and relegated to positions of "socially assigned disposability" when they don't meet academic or social expectations (Butler & Athanasiou, 2013, p. 19). Our case students consistently reported transferring to LCHS when they found themselves in institutional systems that were not a good fit. The processes of dispossession they reported include dropping out, suspension, probation, taking the GED, moving, transferring to LCHS and/or joining the workforce with minimum-wage jobs. They were angry and alienated at the "normative and normalizing powers" that brought them to LCHS (Butler & Athanasiou, 2013, p. 2).

WHITE PRIVILEGE AND BLACKFACE

While it is important to understand and respect the lived experiences of students who entered LCHS, it seems equally important to acknowledge our own privilege as researchers. We draw upon critical research theory (CRT) as a way to problematize our own positionalities as white, middle-class teachers and researchers working in a school that is predominantly white and low-income. As Kumasi (2011) explains, "CRT is one powerful weapon that can help us understand and fight the lingering effects of racism, both in school systems and in everyday life" (p. 125). CRT offers a tool to critique the role of white privilege in our lives and work. With critical race theory, we can problematize our own assumptions about race as we attempt to understand the nature of blackface at Shelly's school.

In order to understand the potentially racist dimensions of the multimedia project, the next section traces the history of blackface images in American media.

BLACKFACE LEGACIES IN THE CLASSROOM CONSTRUCTION OF RACE

Early performances of blackface and minstrel show began in the 1830s, becoming increasingly popular into the early twentieth century. Multiple caricatures arose from minstrel shows, ranging from a central figure that acted as a master of ceremonies to musicians. Minstrelsy provided what Mayo (2008) refers to as a vocabulary for white culture to define racial differences between white and black persons in ways that positioned whites as superior; however, such actions were enacted to satisfy a "white desire for black culture, yet whiteness disavowed its desire for blackness" (Mayo, 2008, p. 46). Blackface was "organized around the quite explicit 'borrowing' of black cultural materials" and it "brought to public form racialized elements of thought and feeling, tone and impulse, residing at the very edge of semantic availability, which Americans only dimly realized they felt, let alone understood" (Lott, 1995, p. 3). While the popularity of minstrel shows and blackface died down in the 1920s and maintained only a thin presence up until the 1960s (Lensmire & Snaza, 2010), there has been a resurgence of blackface performances not only in the news, but also in contemporary popular culture. The television show *The Chappelle Show* and Robert Downey, Jr.'s role in the film *Tropic Thunder* have promoted the casual presence of blackface in popular culture and could be dangerously misinterpreted to suggest that there is not necessarily any racial conflict in contemporary society. When such racially charged images have appeared in the classroom, as we saw demonstrated at LCHS, they carry with them the inaccurate and dangerous perception of a "post-racial" society. Thus, Alvarez and Johnson (2011) argue that educators are faced with the choice of either completely refraining from addressing racially charged pieces or focusing only on race. This binary does not seem adequate to the task of creating a culturally sensitive citizenry in a multicultural society, nor does it seem appropriate in the (black)face of technology's capability to take instant messaging images viral, potentially fanning the flames of incendiary emotions, as occurred in Ferguson, Missouri. It was against this backdrop that Shelly considered the role of digital media in her classroom and the larger implications in the culture.

THE LARGER STUDY

Data used in this chapter were culled from a larger, ongoing, 4-year qualitative case study. We examined the ways in which Shelly and her students engaged and resisted through literacy practices as students created texts and identities with digital media. The authors were participant observers in Shelly's classroom for multiple years, collecting data (e.g., field notes, observations, and audiotape) and providing member checks. The research team analyzed handouts and student work, including the class set of the Vine videos posted on Google+. Three of the researchers interviewed the students involved in producing the blackface video and an additional English teacher who had these same students in a class. We conducted 2 hours of focus group sessions with adult stakeholders, and the transcript became a springboard for additional analysis. Initially, we combed the dataset looking for preliminary emerging themes, such as student engagement and student resistance using processes suggested by qualitative researchers (Cresswell, 2013).

Analyzing more data, we attempted to nuance those general categories. For instance, student resistance was divided into four categories. These included: (1) active resistance through off-task disruptive behavior (shouting, belching, and throwing candy across the room); (2) active resistance without disruption (activities that didn't bother anyone, like texting or surfing the web); (3) indifference (not working and not bothering anyone, sleeping); and (4) passive aggressive resistance ("I don't know"). We followed the same procedure for determining degrees of the category of engagement (i.e., active engagement that involved consistently participating in activities and being on task, to sometimes engaging in on-task activities to sometimes being off-task). We used axial coding to identify relationships among categories. For instance, the passive-aggressive "I don't know" was linked to all categories of student resistance. We tested those codes and relationships with additional data and recursive data analysis, following methods of constant comparison (Glaser & Strauss, 1967). The categories became more nuanced, and we were able to develop potential hypotheses regarding engagement and resistance. The next section explores the context for the project, LCHS.

THE CONTEXT

This chapter focuses on a moment that occurred 3 years after the alternative school opened. Enrollment was open to any high school student in the district, although some students from the other three high schools enrolled when given the option of attending LCHS or being suspended or expelled. At the time of the blackface incident, a large percentage of applicants were referrals from the other high schools, students who were not succeeding in traditional settings. Shelly indicated that they had poor performance, either behaviorally, academically, or both. Student attendance for the semester of this incident was 65%. Given that this figure included daily attenders as well as daily nonattenders, teachers could essentially expect to see students only 3 of the 5 days per week. The students and teachers were predominantly white, and about 60% of students received free or reduced lunch.

Complicating matters more, one district administrator figured that 20% of LCHS students were designated or undiagnosed students with special needs. While the school did have funding for a part-time special education teacher, there was no funding for inclusion resources. In addition, Shelly found that over 60% of the students in her ninth and tenth grade combined "Foundation English" class were struggling readers, reading at between fourth or fifth grade levels when tested by NWEA and AIMS measures. For most of our case study students, if they graduated from high school, they would very likely be the first in their families to do so.

At the time of the study, teachers and staff at this "alternative to expulsion" school were keenly aware of the students' histories, and they rallied to make students feel welcomed, safe, and successful in their relocation. Despite the staff's good intentions, students frequently demonstrated mistrust of school personnel, acting out in anger, defiance, and unruly behavior, several teachers reported. In Shelly's class, students brought to the foreground their histories and hostilities as students who had been marked as struggling, failing, unable—dispossessed and disposable school subjects.

SHELLY'S COMMITMENTS TO DIGITAL MEDIA, THE STUDENTS, AND SOCIAL JUSTICE

Shelly, a veteran English 9-10 teacher at LCHS was a national board-certified teacher deeply invested in using digital media in the classroom. She was respected as a district leader in teaching English with technology and was routinely invited to participate in funded technology projects with university partners. Shelly wanted her students to have access and opportunities for digital proficiency, and these priorities dovetailed with her commitments to social justice, reflected in her choice to work at an alternative high school. For Shelly's participation in multiple grant-funded projects, she gained class sets of iPads, laptops, and Kindles.

THE *MONSTER* UNIT AND SHELLY'S CLASS

Shelly's students became highly engaged in *Monster* (Myers, 1999), a young-adult novel about Steve Harmon, a 16-year-old boy awaiting trial in jail, accused of complicity in a botched robbery that ended in murder. While in jail, he drafts a screenplay of the trial, the murder, and parts of his life that led to his predicament. The screenplay is interspersed with Steve's diary entries conveying his emotional response to the situation. The culminating assignment for the book was for students to analyze Steve's character development by creating a Vine (a brief video), using an iPad and the iMovie app. Vines had recently proliferated in the classroom as students frequently took out their cellphones to share short videos with one another. Shelly seized this moment to marry the students' ardor for trending cellphone apps with their interest in the social justice topics of the book. After creating Vines, students were to write formal character analyses in the form of blog entries posted on Google+. Students were to post their Vines and corresponding blog entries with hashtags indicators (e.g., #SteveHarmon, #character development, #Monster) that signified their topic and also allowed other students to easily find and navigate material online.

We witnessed the group's excitement about the invitation to make videos, and student engagement grew more intense as the days progressed. Shelly reported that the students responded well to the assignment, captivated by the process of creating Vines. It seemed that Shelly's efforts to entice the digital-native side of her students was paying off. Students worked with partners and in small groups, and the room was abuzz with plans, conversations, and filming. Shelly was delighted with the students' engagement, stating, "Everyone was on task, even students who had done nothing academic prior to this time, and there were several students who met this criterion." During the assignment, Shelly floated among the groups and pairs, helping students understand and use the iMovie app on their iPads and occasionally asking questions that might deepen their investigation of the characters. In side conversations, students shared experiences with the justice system that resonated with the protagonist's experiences. For instance, Steve Harmon's dilemma triggered several young women to talk about how much they missed their fathers who were in prison, and one young woman quietly explained that she hadn't seen her father in over a year. During the *Monster* unit, emotions and technology became inextricably linked in multiple ways. Students created videos designed to garner emotional responses from viewers as they disclosed their own emotions about the texts and their lives. The digital platform served as a springboard for the social construction of identities, emotions, and texts.

BLACKFACE AS CATALYST FOR EMOTIONAL TURMOIL

During the planning phase, we could hear students yelling ideas to one another about who would portray which characters and how they would capture needed scenes from the book in their multimodal videos. As we observed the students working with their iPads and cellphones, we could feel the teeming energy in the room and the growing sense of importance the students placed on the project. During the production and filming stage of the Vines, one group caught Shelly's attention. Gary, Josey, and Jamie (pseudonyms), three students who previously displayed little to no interest in academics were engrossed in making their Vine.

A small crowd of other students gathered around them. The three had moved aside tables and chairs so that Josey could apply makeup to her partners's faces. It was clear that Josey and her classmates were excited about the group project. Shelly commented, "This was the first time I had ever seen any of the three students engaged in any academic activity." Later Shelly mentioned, "These students characteristically—in unique and individual ways—had resisted my attempts to engage them." During our observations, Gary usually had his sweatshirt hood up and his head down, even though Shelly had tried multiple tactics to include him in discussions and activities. Josey was prone to declaring outright refusals to work, and Shelly often had to send her to the office for her behavior. Much to Shelly's exasperation, Jamie was habitually truant. Despite past avoidance of class activities, each student participated in this phase of the project, preparing for the video performance to come.

Finally, the day of the final production arrived. Jamie, Josey, and Gary hovered in the back of the room for most of the class and finally moved to the hall to film while Shelly worked in the classroom with students. A crowd of students quickly gathered outside the door to witness the students filming. Shelly came out in time to see the group finishing the video in front of their fans, who were clapping and high fiving. Turning the iPad to Shelly, Josey proudly pointed to the image of Gary on the screen, declaring that her artistic handiwork was proof that she should go to cosmetology school. At the same time, when Gary turned to face the coauthor, she observed that Josey had used a tawny shade that made Gary's face more orange than tan. It was at that moment that Shelly and the coauthor realized that Gary was in blackface. He looked garish with large pale lips, black circles around his eyes, and a caked, orange-brown complexion that contrasted with his blonde hair. The students were excited, and the adults were speechless. The students wanted them to watch the video right then and there. The adults did and Shelly managed to stammer something to the students as they left for their next classes.

Immediately after class, Shelly and a coauthor discussed their emotional responses to the events of the day. A coauthor explained that she had been shocked to see Gary as a spectacle of blackness, a mocking rendition of the "Blackie" characters of early television played by white males. A coauthor tried to process the fact that there had been a case of blackface in Shelly's classroom. She remembered feeling a myriad of emotions all crashing upon her simultaneously: horror, fear, dread, anger, sadness, and shock. Was she imagining this? Did students REALLY make a blackface video? Did they know about blackface? She was concerned about Shelly, because she knew how proud she was of her reputation as a teacher committed to social justice and how problematic this would be for her. She felt horrified as she imagined the video being posted on social media.

Shelly expressed similar emotions about the incident and the video. "Was that really happening in my class?" Shelly asked. Thinking aloud, she tried to make sense of what she had witnessed, saying that the students surely wouldn't have used blackface if they had known about its history. Shelly also acknowledged the students' pride in the makeup and the video, and she didn't want to crush that pride. The irony of the situation was palpable. That is, as Shelly stated later, she recognized that the text and digital tools that she had mobilized for exploring social inequity—the wrongful incarceration of the African-American protagonist, Steve Harmon—had become the very means by which students produced and consumed racist images. Moreover, as a teacher committed to social justice and to supporting her students, she felt paralyzed by the rush of conflicting emotions.

DRAWING A LINE OR CROSSING A LINE? ANOTHER TEACHER'S PERSPECTIVE

In the course of considering the consequences of the blackface incident in Shelly's classroom, we interviewed Sarah, another English teacher at LCHS. Sarah and Shelly shared the same commitments to social justice and to using digital media and twenty-first-century literacies in the classroom. Sarah was struck by the difficult situation in which Shelly had to weigh her priorities and responsibilities as a teacher against her personal values. Sarah emphasized the delicate nature of the event, saying, "When teachers see students who resist the routine of the classroom become engaged and excited about learning, teachers jump at the chance to invoke the teachable moment, but it's not a time to quell students' enthusiasm." Sarah's comments further complicated our understanding of Shelly's role during "touchy" situations, noting that she did not know how comfortable she would have been with allowing other students in the classroom to see the video. "My educational background and experience as a teacher motivate me toward the teachable moment here," Sarah related, "perhaps leading the class in an investigation of the comment on race and identity that surfaced due to the application of makeup on Gary's face."

Sarah saw the vulnerable position Shelly was experiencing. Like Shelly, she was adamant about not wanting to accuse the students of doing something malicious or of doing the assignment incorrectly. Regardless, she would have felt compelled to call attention to the blackface.

> I do not deny the trickiness of the situation. At some point, though, one must draw a line and say, "Here's my view, and I cannot allow that," and then follow with a class discussion of the very themes involved regarding racial depictions and representations.

Reminiscent of Alvarez and Johnson's (2001) warning that educators find it difficult to have conversations about race, Sarah suggested that educators should invite students to consider their own values and behaviors in relation to those of the larger society. Such classroom exercises encourage critical thinking and promote recognition and contemplation of social justice, Sarah explained.

Sarah commented that if she were in Shelly's place while the students were applying makeup on Gary, she would have wanted to interrupt their plans and say, "That is so racist. That's so wrong in so many ways." She recognized that her initial reaction was highly motivated by her emotional investment in a teaching style influenced by social justice. She also acknowledged that such a response would have further complicated the situation. Sarah added that she would have considered a follow-up lesson if the incident had occurred in her classroom, one focusing on the historical presence of blackface. After asking students to research examples of blackface, she would have asked students to compare them to representations of whites/dominant figures. Class discussions would have generated ties between past and present stereotype depictions and agendas. As Sarah explained, "Without understanding the history, it is impossible for young people to see contemporary incidents as part of a longer continuum of degradation and racist constructions." Such a lesson would have satisfied Sarah's desire to "respond to such remarks by taking my students to places of questioning and reflection and guide them to a place of understanding and acceptance." That inquiry would have exposed, rather than imposed, multiple perspectives on the incidents because, as she said, "I know I cannot tell them what to think, what to believe, how to live their lives, no matter what."

Sarah's views highlighted the symbiotic nature between technological practices and emotional reactions that occurred in response to digital images at LCHS. Many times, students brought in examples of racial insensitivity they had picked up from popular culture. Frequently they shared them through digital means, using videos, cellphones, and laptops. The plight that vexed Shelly and Sarah is that with every new racially charged image (e.g., students making a video with blackface), they were compelled to generate untested responses on the spot and couldn't always rely on previous practices.

Rather than lecture to students about the topic, Sarah would have encouraged students to be part of the meaning-making process of the class, a tactic familiar to digital natives who are accustomed to creating content in online arenas (Lenhart, Madden, Macgill, & Smith, 2007). By including students in this inquiry, Sarah would have turned students away from a sense of dispossession and toward an engagement in local and global race issues, exploring their roles and views on such issues. By inviting them to reflect on popular culture, she hypothesized that they would have been able to reflect on the Vine postings, thereby performing identities as socially responsible citizens.

SHELLY'S SOCIAL CONSTRUCTION OF EMOTION IN RESPONSE TO THE BLACKFACE GROUP

Unlike social media respondents who have the luxury of responding in hindsight and at a distance, Shelly had to respond in the moment, on her feet, facing the video's proud creators. She could have squelched the group's performance by calling out its possible ties to racism and reinforced student identities as dispossessed and alienated students, or she could have used the occasion to reward their engagement and give them a glimmer of what success in school might look and feel like. Social justice advocacy was a central part of her identity performances as a teacher, and supporting marginalized students was part and parcel of that identity. In this case, the two goals seemed at odds to her. Hence, she froze.

CONFLICTING EMOTIONS: PERSPECTIVES FROM A FORMER ADMINISTRATOR

One coauthor had been a principal at LCHS and another alternative high school before retiring. He served as a consultant to the other coauthors on this project because of a long history as an administrator. Although the coauthor was not the principal at the time of the incident, he knew many of the students. In an interview, the coauthor provided perspectives on the incident.

> For the first time in the school year, [Shelly] had three previously very disengaged students actively participating in an assignment. ... Although these students were finally engaged in a class activity, their engagement may have crossed the lines of good taste, social consciousness, and racial bigotry. The dilemma was balancing the fact that students were engaged in an activity when they have never been engaged before against the "teachable moment" that might need to be addressed to let them know what they were doing was potentially highly culturally and/or socially unacceptable. Additionally, the three students were seeing firsthand how participating in academics could enhance their social standings; other students began surrounding them and encouraging them to continue their efforts. If Shelly confronts them (the "teachable moment") about the impropriety of the blackface piece of their project, is she risking squashing their enthusiasm? Such a comment would sound to them something like, "Your engagement is cool, but it's all wrong." And no matter how she says it, she runs the risk of now sabotaging the fact that for the first time in three months, those students are doing something in the class that is benefiting them.

The coauthor's perspectives offered a complex consideration of the issues at stake in Shelly's dilemma. As she attempted to delicately negotiate the emotions of her students with the possibility that they had created a racist image that could have gone public, Shelly had to balance between two equal but unsavory options. As the coauthor explained, the situation called upon Shelly to engage the "teachable moment" while juggling multiple emotionally charged factors among students: the plight of the fictional character, Steve Harmon; students' memories of loved ones who were incarcerated; some students' newly found interest in academic work; the group's increasing social standing among peers; and the issue of blackface and its ties to social injustices.

As the coauthor explained, if Shelly had confronted the students to see if they understood the social justice issues and the possible social consequences of blackface, the students might have reacted to that with the sensibilities of dispossession. The coauthor drew from his experiences with at-risk students, knowing that taboo subjects (e.g., death, substance abuse, or suicide) were often realities in the everyday lives of LCHS students. They also recognized that students might have been censored for writing about controversial subjects at previous schools, where they also might have been sent to the vice principal or school counselor to be punished or to discuss their issues. The coauthor's point was that students with such histories were sensitized to failure, so a teacher's negative response—"That's wrong" or "You're not allowed to write that"—would only teach students to be mistrustful, defensive, and reluctant to participate. As the coauthor said, what was more important at the time: supporting and fostering student participation and engagement in an environment where it has been monumentally difficult to cultivate such engagement, or exploring social-justice issues? These were identity issues for Shelly. If she were to opt for endorsing student engagement, did that mean ignoring the inappropriate aspects of the student work and its possible collusion with racism? If she were to make a point about social justice, would it undermine student engagement with future classroom assignments? If she questioned the students' intentions, would she inadvertently be teaching the rest of the class that the appropriate response to racial and emotionally charged situations is to embarrass and criticize their classmates?

SHELLY: BUILDING A "SAFE AND INCLUSIVE COMMUNITY" ONSITE AND ONLINE

In an interview several weeks after the blackface incident, Shelly reflected on the blackface activity as well as Sarah's and a coauthor's perspectives.

In retrospect, I think I acted in the best way possible at that time and in that situation. I didn't want to shut down their creativity, even for a moment. It was that fragile. It is also true that if other students, black or white, had taken offense at their video, we would have had to talk about the issue as a class. I was prepared to do that, but glad I didn't have to. At that point, early in the year, I was still attempting to build a safe and inclusive community, and such a conversation might have been volatile.

I don't believe there was necessarily a right or wrong choice here … Helping me to make such a decision would be whether I believed there was intent to "cross lines" or whether this was done moreso out of lack of knowledge and understanding. Knowing the ages of these students, their educational backgrounds, and their relative understanding of social justice issues would help in any decisions about challenging their work at the risk of dampening their newfound work ethic. In the case of these particular students, I don't believe there was any malicious intent in their focus. I believe they most likely really had no clue that what they were doing might be offensive.

From Shelly's perspective, the students were most likely behaving innocently, unaware of the history of blackface as a form of racism, so calling them out still did not seem to be the most appropriate response. They didn't appear to "cross the line." Had they, she would have gladly engaged the class in a discussion on the topic. Beyond that, in the alternative school context, she was painfully sensitized to the experiences of "the dispossessed" and wanted her classroom to offer a space of community.

STUDENTS' PERSPECTIVES ON THE BLACKFACE PRODUCTION

We interviewed the three students in the blackface group to get their perspectives, but did not get much feedback. When asked why she applied dark makeup to the student playing Steve Harmon, Josey explained that she wanted Gary to look as realistic as possible. Gary, elaborated, "I'm white trying to play a black dude. It just don't seem right." These comments suggest that the students viewed their actions as pragmatic.

After reading the interview data from students, Shelly commented:

Teaching and learning are simultaneously messy and fragile. What I wish I would have done was to have had a subsequent lesson, one not in any way connected with the Monster module, one much later in the year when our classroom community was such that difficult issues could respectfully be discussed. I would have focused this lesson on language, on the current black and white appropriation of the "N-word" and on its racist uses in history. I would have tied into the lesson the related history of blackface. At some point during the lesson, I would have taken Gary, Josey, and Jamie aside privately. I would have gently reminded them of their video and of the ways others might have viewed it as offensive, but I would be clear to point out that I had faith they had not intended that sort of offense.

Shelly would have created a unit taking an historical approach, highlighting the ways in which linguistic and visual signs were implicated in issues of social justice. She would have conducted a side conversation with the group members that would have "gently reminded" them that some viewers of the blackface video would have considered it racist, just as some people would have considered the use of the N-word racist.

THE POLITICAL AND SOCIAL CONSTRUCTION OF EMOTIONS MEDIATED BY TECHNOLOGY

It was Gary's comment that was most chilling to us: "I'm white trying to play a black dude. It just don't seem right." While his intentions may have been innocent, Gary seemed to view race as biological, static, and innate. When he looked at Steve (or anyone who doesn't look like him) he could easily say, "I'm white; he's not; we are far more different than the same." Such a perspective distanced him from any kind of engagement with or nuanced understanding of difference and its concomitant social responsibility.

We considered further the possible consequences of the event, especially since the event was captured digitally. Such an emotionally and racially charged video could have found its way online, shared by hundreds, if not thousands, in a matter of days. The video could have undermined Shelly's goals by inadvertently promoting blackface as it reinforced the identity performances of students as "rational designers of text (Leander & Boldt, 2013), potentially missing how their moving, feeling bodies influence meaning making in unpredictable ways" (Ehret & Hollett, 2014, p. 430). That is, if posted, viewers might have presumed that blackface was a rational explicit expression of racism rather than a pragmatic, though misguided, attempt to portray identity that inadvertently "crossed a line," as a coauthor said. Additionally, if the video had found notoriety among an online community, it could have become a permanent stain on the lives of the three students who made the video. Shelly was convinced that Gary's identity performance suggested that he might not have known about the connotations of racism attached to blackface and was simply trying to complete a school assignment. Such a response suggests the need for difficult, emotionally charged conversations with students about what counts as racism and what counts as social responsibility.

As it turned out, the day after the videotaping took place, Shelly tried to view the Vine Gary, Josey, and Jamie made on their iPad, but the video had mysteriously disappeared from the iPad they had used. A coauthor and Shelly examined a number of iPads, hoping they could find it before the other students did. Curiously, no one seemed to know what had happened to it. After thoroughly searching, Shelly assumed the three students had erased their assignment, but she never found out for sure. Even though it was a relief to Shelly that the video never appeared on the class's Google+ page or on another class iPad after its production, that didn't stop Shelly from considering how she should have handled the issue.

CONCLUSION

To recap, researchers, teachers, and students expressed a number of emotions issuing from their respective political perspectives on whether the digitally captured image of blackface promoted racism. Shelly and a coauthor had been taken aback while standing witness to the initial presentation of the video and Gary's painted face. Initially shocked, then horrified, they both froze momentarily, keenly aware of the perceived racism, their respective social justice commitments, and wondering how to negotiate discussion of the video's perceived racism with the emotional fallout from students who took pride in the video. Two of the group members, who were new to the school, garnered attention from multiple students in the classroom and in the hall, so the event provided the new students with some important social recognition. Moreover, Shelly later admitted she could have praised the students for producing the video. When she didn't, she denied them an opportunity to accrue more social affirmation. Nonetheless, in class and in the hall, the budding cosmetologist gained additional acclaim for the makeup job, thus reinforcing Josey's talents as a beautician.

While shutting down the group project to avoid potential conflict might have been another option, this pathway offered the risk of completely shutting down the students, given their vulnerability as new students and their histories with schooling. That is, in this context, students carried legacies of dispossession with them, and being told that the project was unacceptable was in effect telling them that they were unacceptable, that they should go elsewhere.

The three students played with notions of race and identity as they constructed a fabricated persona that would exist separate from their own in two physical senses: the co-constructed characterization of Gary as a racialized black man moving through the classroom, and the new blackface persona created for and captured by the digital space within the Vine video. The digital tools, it could be argued, provided Gary, Josey, and Jamie with a safe way to try on a new racialized identity with neither the repercussions of any type of loss of one's own identity nor with a sustained consequence—but only if, in fact, they did not know the history of blackface.

What should Shelly have done in the classroom? The importance of the question is rooted in the various interests of the groups involved, the cultural history of the event, and the possible social and political comment being made due to the classroom teacher's reaction or lack of reaction. While Sarah insisted that the students would have benefited from a teacher-led investigation of the racial overtones enacted in the preparation and production of the video, Shelly indicated that she would have waited for the students to first address the topic. In any case, it is possible that there was not one single or simple "best practice" to be had in Shelly's classroom. We argue that what was more productive was the collaborative inquiry of educators investigating the dilemma through the cooperative exchange of ideas, viewing pedagogy as an act of refinement, not perfection, for both students and teachers alike. The conflict inherent in this event is less about what Shelly should have done in relation to student behavior and more about how to read her students, how to discern what they know, what they need to know, and how to facilitate a teachable moment in the face of a controversial subject. As Alvarez and Johnson (2011) argue, educators struggle with classroom discussions of race, as the topic is emotionally charged, and all participants in the conversation have a stake in the argument. Additionally, discussions of race, particularly in the classroom, are uncomfortable for teachers and students alike, as somebody is likely to be more politically aware or sensitive to the issue than someone else.

From a CRT standpoint, the hypothetical choices being explored here bring to the forefront the privilege of whiteness, and the four of us have to continually interrogate our own teacher and researcher assumptions on this issue. That is, from our standpoint, is it that we, as white teachers and researchers, have the luxury of assessing such choices from a distance, and in hindsight, away from the emotionally charged event? Does our whiteness permit us to confidently enter an investigative conversation or wait for the luxury of the teachable moment, depending upon our reading of the situation?

In light of the Ferguson, Missouri riots, we are reminded that social actions are mediated and propelled by both emotions and digital media. Digital media provided both the platform for the world to bear witness to Michael Brown's death and to register outrage about it. In a similar fashion, as social media lit up, as the USA Today and blackface/redface images went viral, so, too, did reactions of outrage. It is the critical unpacking of relationships among technology—its capacities to create and circulate images and information and emotions, the socially constructed responses to images and information—that enables teachers to create space for students to examine issues of race, power, and privilege. Whether responding with a teachable moment or a newly developed curriculum on language and culture, teachers can leverage students' construction of texts, identities, and emotion to redirect the production and circulation of emotions in socially responsible and productive ways.

REFERENCES

Ahmed, S. (2004). The cultural politics of emotion. New York: Routledge.
Alvarez, N., & Johnson, S. (2011). Minstrels in the classroom: Teaching, race, and blackface. Canadian Theatre Review, 147(1), 31–37.
Belsey, C. (1980). Critical practice. New York: Routledge.
Bennett, S., Maton, K., & Kervin, L. (2008). The 'digital natives' debate: A critical review of the evidence. British Journal of Educational Technology, 39(5), 775–786.
Brady, E. (2014). Native American activists seek to eliminate "redface". USA Today. Retrieved from, http://www.usatoday.com/story/sports/2014/07/21/native-americans-redface-san-francisco-giants-washington-redskins/12967437/.

Butler, J. (1989). *Gender trouble: Feminism and the subversion of identity.* New York: Routledge.

Butler, J., & Athanasiou, A. (2013). *Dispossession: The performative in the political.* Malden, MA: Polity Press.

Coiro, J., Knobel, M., Lankshear, C., & Leu, D. J. (Eds.), (2008). *Handbook of research on new literacies.* New York, NY: Routledge.

Cresswell, J. (2013). *Qualitative inquiry and research design: Choosing among five approaches* (3rd ed.). Thousand Oaks, CA: Sage.

Dubois, L. (2014). *Why are these fans showing up in blackface? And what is FIFA going to do about it?.* The New Republic. Retrieved from, http://www.newrepublic.com/article/118382/why-are-these-fans-showing-world-cup-matches-blackface.

Dunsmore, K., & Fisher, D. (Eds.), (2010). *Bringing literacy home.* Newark, DE: International Reading Association.

Ehret, C., & Hollett, T. (2014). Embodied composition in real virtualities: Adolescents' literacy practices and felt experiences moving with digital, mobile devices in school. *Research in the Teaching of English, 48*(4), 428–452.

Fox News (2014). *Michigan teacher suspended after using blackface video in a history lesson.* Retrieved from, http://www.foxnews.com/us/2014/06/01/michigan-teacher-suspended-after-sho.

Gee, J. (2000). Identity as an analytic lens for research in education. *Review of Research in Education, 55*, 99–125.

Gee, J. (2004). *Situated language and learning: A critique of traditional schooling.* London: Routledge.

Gee, J., & Hayes, E. (2011). *Language and learning in the digital age.* New York, NY: Routledge.

Glaser, B., & Strauss, A. (1967). *The discovery of grounded theory: Strategies for qualitative research.* Chicago, IL: Aldine.

Hagood, M., Alvermann, D., & Heron-Hruby, A. (2010). *Bring it to class: Unpacking pop culture in literacy learning.* New York, NY: Teachers College Press.

Heim, M. (2014). *Selma native takes viral pic in Brazil if fans in blackface, compares SEC and kick six to world cup.* Retrieved from, http://www.al.com/sports/index.ssf/2014/06/selma_native_took_viral_pic_in.html.

Hull, G., & Schultz, K. (Eds.), (2002). *School's out! Bridging out-of-school literacies with classroom practice.* New York, NY: Teachers College Press.

Ito, M., Baumer, S., Bittanti, M., Boyd, D., Cody, R., Herr-Stephenson, B., et al. (2010). *Hanging out, messing around, and geeking out: Kids living and learning with new media.* Cambridge, MA: MIT.

Jenkins, H. (2009). *Confronting the challenges of participatory cultures: Media education for the 21st century.* Cambridge, MA: The MIT Press.

Kajder, S. B. (2010). *Adolescents and digital literacies: Learning alongside our students.* Urbana, IL: National Council of Teachers of English.

Kress, G., & van Leeuwen, T. (2001). *Multimodal discourse: The modes of media and contemporary communication.* London: Edward Arnold.

Kumasi, K. (2011). Critical race theory and education: Mapping a legacy of scholarship and activism. In B. A. U. Levinson (Ed.), *Beyond critique: Critical social theories and education* (pp. 196–219). Boulder, CO: Paradigm Publishers.

Lankshear, C., & Knobel, M. (2006). *New literacies: Changing knowledge and classroom learning* (2nd ed.). Philadelphia, PA: Open University Press.

Leander, K., & Boldt, G. (2013). Rereading "a pedagogy of multiliteracies" bodies, texts, and emergence. *Journal of Literacy Research, 45*(1), 22–46.

Lenhart, A., Madden, M., Macgill, A. R., & Smith, A. (2007). *Teens and social media: The use of social media gains a greater foothold in teen life as them embrace the conversational nature of interactive online media.* Pew Internet & American Life Project. Retrieved from, http://www.pewinternet.org.

Lensmire, T. J., & Snaza, N. (2010). What teacher education can learn from blackface minstrelsy. *Educational Researcher, 39*(5), 413–422.

Lewis, C., Enciso, P., & Moje, E. (2009). *Reframing sociocultural research on literacy: Identity, agency, and power.* New York, NY: Routledge.

Lewis, C., & Fabos, B. (2005). Instant messaging, literacies, and social identities. *Reading Research Quarterly, 40*(4), 470–501.

Li, G. (Ed.), (2009). *Multicultural families, home literacies, and mainstream schooling.* Charlotte, NC: Information Age Publishing.

Lott, E. (1995). *Love and theft: Blackface minstrelsy and the American working class.* New York, NY: Oxford University Press.

Madden, M., Lenhart, A., Cortesi, S., Gasser, U., Duggan, M., Smith, A., et al. (2013a). *Teens, social media, and privacy.* Pew Internet & American Life Project. Retrieved from, http://www.ris.org/uploadi/editor/1363164043PIP_TeensandTechnology2013.pdf2013.

Madden, M., Lenhart, A., Duggan, M., Cortesi, S., & Gasser, M. (2013b). *Teens and technology.* Pew Internet & American Life Project. Retrieved from, http://www. pewinternet.org/2013/03/13/teens-and-technology-2013.

Mayo, C. (2008). Being in on the joke: Pedagogy, race, humor. In R. Glass (Ed.), *Philosophy of education yearbook* (pp. 244–252). Urbana-Champaign, IL: University of Illinois at Urbana-Champaign.

Myers, W. D. (1999). *Monster.* New York, NY: HarperCollins.

National Council of Teachers of English (2013). *NCTE framework for 21st century curriculum and assessment.* Retrieved March 1, 2013 from, http://www.ncte.org/library/ NCTEFiles/Resources/Positions/Framework_21sCent_Curr_Assessment.pdf.

Nespor, J. (1994). *Knowledge in motion: Space, time and curriculum in undergraduate physics and management.* London: Routledge.

Palfrey, J., & Gasser, U. (2013). *Born digital: Understanding the first generation of digital natives.* New York, NY: Basic Books.

Prensky, M. (2001). Digital natives, digital immigrants part 1. *On the Horizon, 9*(5), 1–6.

Sefton-Green, J. (2006). Youth, technology, and media culture. *Review of Research in Education, 30,* 279–306.

Street, B. (1995). *Literacy in theory and practice.* Cambridge: Cambridge University Press.

Thomas, A. (2007). *Youth online: Identity and literacy in the digital age 19.* New York, NY: Peter Lang.

Washington, J. (2014). *Reactions based on both emotion and evidence.* Retrieved from, http:// bigstory.ap.org/article/5af714f8b338446eb4eb1442d9dd4ce0/anger-ferguson-case-based-emotion-evidence.

Weber, S., & Mitchell, C. (2008). Imaging, keyboarding, and posting identities: Young people and new media technologies. In D. Buckingham (Ed.), *Youth, Identity, and Digital Media* (pp. 25–47). Cambridge, MA: The MIT Press.

Williams, B., & Zenger, A. (Eds.), (2012). *New media literacies and participatory popular culture across borders.* New York, NY: Routledge.

Exploring Affect With and Through Technology: Research and Practice

CHAPTER 11

Leveraging the Social Presence Model: A Decade of Research on Emotion in Online and Blended Learning

Aimee L. Whiteside[a], Amy Garrett Dikkers[b]
[a]Department of English and Writing, University of Tampa, Tampa, FL, USA
[b]Department of Educational Leadership, University of North Carolina Wilmington, Wilmington, NC, USA

INTRODUCTION: THE POWER OF EMOTIONS FOR LEARNING

About 7 years ago, we met Sara, a student in an online Human Rights Education (HRE) class, who forever changed our relationship as teachers and researchers to the emotional aspects of learning in all types of learning environments. Sara had just finished writing a heart-wrenching, lengthy, online discussion passage about the discrimination she faced as a student:

> Okay, so I just wrote a book about my own experiences and maybe it sounded a little mad ... sorry about that, but I get kind of passionate about that topic, and my own personal experiences are largely what have led me to my [graduate] program. All people have worth and should be valued for their differences and are deserving of the respect of others and I am going to do whatever I can to make that happen. And THAT is why Human Rights are important.
>
> *Whiteside and Garrett Dikkers (2012).*

Sara's disclosure unleashed a flood of empathy and other emotions from her classmates and simultaneously encouraged other students to open up about their experiences and observations. From that point forward, the online learning environment seemed to transform from a course to a true community of learners.

Through Sara, we began to understand how the reflective qualities of online learning can create a powerful emotional experience for students; one that can, in fact, be greater than in a face-to-face course (Whiteside & Garrett Dikkers, 2012). This chapter condenses a decade of our case study research on *social presence*, or the level of connectedness among students and instructors, within online and blended learning environments. It addresses

Emotions, Technology, and Learning
http://dx.doi.org/10.1016/B978-0-12-800649-8.00013-4

the power of emotion for learning, defines the concept of social presence, outlines and explains the Social Presence Model (SPM), offers evidence from students and instructors in multiple case studies in K-12 and Higher Education, and summarizes the key findings of over a decade of research.

SOCIAL PRESENCE AND THE SPM

The concept of social presence originated during the telecommunication era of the late 1960s and 1970s, as that which was lost in the remote communicative experience (Short, William, & Christie, 1976). As various interactive and other communication media evolved in the coming decades, such as interactive television, videoconferencing, and online learning environments, the concept of social presence gained complexity, depth, and prominence (Tammelin, 1998). Rettie (2003) divides early social presence research into two very distinct categories: (1) research that addresses social presence as a "property of a medium in mediated communication," and (2) research that "refers to the perceptions, behaviors, or attitudes of the participants in a mediated interaction" (p. 1). Contemporary researchers often extend Rettie's research to a new category that views social presence as focused on creating more meaningful and significant online learning experiences (Whiteside, 2007, 2015).

Today, social presence draws from a rich basis of literature in social psychology, literacy, cooperative learning, computer-mediated communication, and online and blended learning to focus on the social dimensions of online learning (Allen & Seaman, 2011; Gunawardena & Zittle, 1997; Lowenthal, 2009, 2012; Lowenthal & Dunlap, 2014; Picciano, 2002; Picciano & Seaman, 2009, 2010; Richardson & Swan, 2003; Rourke & Anderson, 2002; Rourke, Anderson, Garrison, & Archer, 1999; Rovai, 2002; Shea, Pickett, & Pelt, 2003; Stacey, 2002; Swan, 2002; Swan & Shih, 2005; Tu, 2001, 2002a, 2002b).

Much of the research on the social dimensions of online learning diverged in two different but complementary directions: the Community of Inquiry (COI) Model and the SPM. The COI explores learning experiences as a careful combination of social presence, teacher presence, and cognitive presence (Garrison, Anderson, & Archer, 2000, 2010), while the SPM examines social presence as a powerful, overarching concept with five interconnected components: Affective Association, Community Cohesion, Instructor Involvement, Interaction Intensity, and Knowledge and Experience (Garrett Dikkers & Whiteside, 2008,

2013; Garrett Dikkers, Whiteside, & Lewis, 2012, 2013; Whiteside, 2007, 2015; Whiteside & Garrett Dikkers, 2008, 2009, 2010, 2012; Whiteside, Garrett Dikkers, & Lewis, 2014; Whiteside, Hughes, & McLeod, 2005). The SPM views social presence as a "master conductor that synchronizes the instructor, students, norms, academic content, learning management system (LMS), media and tools, instructional strategies, and outcomes within a learning experience" (Whiteside, 2015).

This chapter focuses on a decade of research through four different research projects employing the SPM as a theoretical framework.

LESSONS LEARNED: A DECADE OF SPM RESEARCH

Our journey of exploring emotion and learning began in July 2003, when a team of 17 school administrators came together to kick-off an intensive blended graduate certificate program at a large Midwestern University and quickly became connected to each other. Whiteside (2007) researched how those connections were impacted by the online learning experiences of the cohort. Next, we moved from this programmatic research to exploring 3 years' content of an online course at a large Midwestern University. In recent years, we have moved to researching social presence in a virtual public school in the Southeast and, finally, a blended learning high school program in the Midwest. We discuss each of these case studies in an effort to illuminate the power of social presence and emotion for learning in various online and blended learning environments.

Higher Education: School Technology Leadership Program (2002-2007)[1]

We first came to study emotions and learning with experiences as participant-observers in a graduate-level certificate program designed to help K-12 educational leaders integrate technology into their schools and districts. The focus involved the School Technology Leadership (STL) Certificate Program at a large Midwestern University (McLeod, 2012). The STL Certificate consisted of 15 one-credit courses taught over 13 months (Hughes, McLeod, Garrett Dikkers, Brahier, & Whiteside, 2005; Garrett Dikkers, Hughes, & McLeod, 2005). In this low-residency model, each cohort of students began their first face-to-face session in July,

---

[1] Excerpted in part from *Journal of Online Learning*, 2015, A. L. Whiteside, *Introducing the Social Presence Model to explore online and blended learning experiences.*

when they completed their first four, one-credit courses during an intensive 6-day session. The cohort then transitioned to two (2) 15-week terms of online coursework using a LMS, and, finally, they returned to campus the following summer for a 4-day, face-to-face facilitation of their final three credits.

The data collection process for this study began in Summer 2003 and ended in Spring 2007. The students in this program included superintendents, principals, technology coordinators, media specialists, teachers, and other K–12 school leaders. The first cohort, Cohort 1, consisted of 17 consenting participants, and the second cohort, Cohort 2, consisted of 5 consenting participants. The research questions explored were as follows: (a) How can coded online discussions, face-to-face observation notes, and interview transcriptions illustrate social presence in a learning community? (b) How does social presence affect blended learning programs and vice versa?

Specifically, this study examined face-to-face observation notes for several courses, interview transcriptions (for two instructors and four students), and students' online discussion messages for eight courses using the pre-established Social Presence Coding Scheme developed by Rourke et al. (1999) and extended by Swan (2002). This Social Presence Coding Scheme divides social presence into three categories: affective, cohesive, and interactive, and offers 14 codes to help capture instances of social presence. Data spanning 26 months were coded across face-to-face and online courses for two cohorts of students.

Coding data from the first cohort's interactions showed they were more connected, used more emotion and self-disclosure, and were more often challenged and supported each other's learning. Through the codes alone, the second cohort demonstrated less social presence in their online interactions. Figure 11.1 compares the number of social presence codes for each student in the two cohorts.

As Figure 11.1 illustrates, the average number of codes per participant for Cohort 1 suggests that they are nearly twice as socially present as Cohort 2. However, this data conflicts with numerous other data artifacts. These artifacts, which included interview transcriptions from instructor and student interviews coupled with researcher observation notes, tell a much different story: one where Cohort 2 seemed far more socially present and connected to one another as a small cohort of five individuals.

The instructor interviews also suggest Cohort 2 to be much more socially present. One instructor, Dr Mike Stanley, commented, "The second group

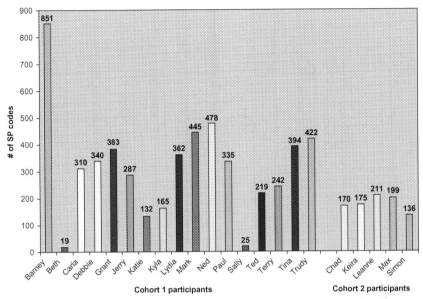

Figure 11.1 Comparison of social presence codes among individuals and cohorts.

was very, very tight. I think mostly because they were such a small group; there were basically just five of them" (Whiteside, 2015). Another instructor, Dr Sarah Finch, also found that the smaller size of Cohort 2 impacted their level of social presence. She stated, "I think everybody in the second cohort participating in the classes were socially present" (Whiteside, 2015). Finch explained that "they did a good job" and their level of social presence "was probably based on the fact that there was" so few people in the cohort. In regard to Cohort 1, Finch explained that she was "kind of surprised at times" when "even in the last day, they didn't know each others' names." Overall, she stated, "I don't think that there was as deep or as much connected[ness] in the first cohort as there was in the second cohort." Thus, the social presence coding data conflicted significantly with the face-to-face observation notes and the interview data, which led to a second, deeper analysis of the data.

Further analysis determined two key components of social presence emerging that were missing from the Coding Scheme (Whiteside, 2015). The first involved the difference in the leadership expertise of the two groups. If you have less experience to share, there is less discussion, which was the case in Cohort 2. Second, because there was less overall leadership expertise for participants in Cohort 2, the instructors adjusted the online discussion fora to make them less situated in their schools and to allow them to write a more reflective response. As a result, students found the online discussion to be "academic" and began to lose the level of connectedness within the formal learning environments (Whiteside, 2015).

Therefore, two important components were added to social presence: (a) the collective knowledge and experience of the participants and (b) the instructors' involvement with their choice of instructional strategies. These two new components, Knowledge and Experience and Instructor Involvement, were added to the existing coding elements: Affective Association, Community Cohesion, and Interactive Intensity, to form the SPM. See Figure 11.2 for a graphic representation of the intersecting elements of the SPM.

In sum, the SPM centers on five integrated elements (*Affective Association, Community Cohesion, Instructor Involvement, Interaction Intensity, Knowledge and Experience*) that together determine a participant's motivation to take an active role in their own and their peers' meaning-making processes (Whiteside, 2015).

This study was significant because it showed a delicate, interconnected, and emotive relationship among instructors, learners, and social presence; additionally, it introduced the SPM, which we continue to employ in our research today. This study and the resultant definition of social presence led to a series of case studies in higher and secondary education in three different locations with participants from varied sociocultural and international backgrounds. Armed with a new model, we first moved on to test it with three iterations of a university-level HRE course.

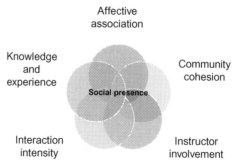

Figure 11.2 The Social Presence Model.

Higher Education: Human Rights Education (2008-2012)[2]

From 2008 to 2012, we explored social presence in three subsequent iterations of a HRE course (Spring 2008, Spring 2009, and Spring 2010). Although the majority of the students in the course were based in and around a large Midwestern University in the United States, some students were located outside the metropolitan area and around the world. They enrolled in the course because of an interest in the topic and because it was offered entirely online.

One of the main tenets of HRE is that it is participant-guided and context-driven. As such, the course instructors created an authentic HRE experience for students by bringing in as many real-life experiences of HRE advocates and practitioners from around the world as possible, creating a professional development opportunity to train locally, and engage community resource people around the globe in the learning process (Garrett Dikkers & Whiteside, 2011). This online course engaged human rights educators from Canada, Chile, and Mongolia into discussions.

The majority of the coursework was conducted asynchronously with posts in discussion forums and blogs, as well as the completion of activities through other websites. In each of the 3 years the course was taught, the course instructors integrated opportunities for additional online interactions, including synchronous sessions recorded through a conferencing software program and archived online for students to view asynchronously as their busy schedules allow. One unique aspect of this course is that experts from the community who are practitioners in the field (and not students in the course) voluntarily provided content for the students (lectures, PowerPoint presentations, articles, drafts of chapters), engaged in dialog with the students in discussion forums, and/or participated in the recorded synchronous presentations and discussions. Finally, the course culminated in a final project of the students' own choosing that situated their learning about human rights.

We coded a sampling of course-level data with the five components of the SPM. Ultimately, through students like Sara, who is featured in the opening lines of this chapter, we discovered a consistently high level of social presence in all three iterations of this course. The following example

---

[2] Excerpted in part from IGI Global, A.L. Whiteside and A. Garrett Dikkers, Using the Social Presence Model to maximize interactions in online environments. In K. St. Amant & S. Kelsey (Eds.), *Computer-mediated communication across cultures: International interactions in online environments*, pp. 395-413. Copyright 2012.

exemplifies the power of emotion by showing how one student's experience can help deepen the discussion:

> In my school right now, I think of a student who has her human rights violated daily by fellow staff members. This student is one of a handful of minority students in our school yet in a school of over 1000 students, she accounts for a third of all office referrals in our building—checked. When something happens, she is usually sought out and blamed for crimes she didn't commit. She's been kicked off a sporting team because she lost her uniform and doesn't have the money to replace it. Interestingly enough, three minority students have been kicked off teams in the last two years for one reason or another, while white students who lose their uniforms are still allowed to participate use without being reprimanded.
>
> **Whiteside and Garrett Dikkers (2012)**

The value of this emotive response is that it creates an open opportunity for other students to freely share their experience to support the entire learning community. HRE is a subject where individuals often have very strong opinions. Our analysis of the course content showed that the online environment in some ways enhanced the discussions as it allowed for greater reflection. Several students point out in the course evaluations how the technology made it "much easier to share personal information" and "feelings" that you may not want to share a "normal classroom setting." Another student commented that the rate of the sharing also increases with technology. This student explained, "This [technology], I think, let's people divulge more ... sooner [than they would] ... in a face-to-face environment" (Whiteside & Garrett Dikkers, 2012).

All aspects of the SPM were significantly present in this course. Overall, the data in this case study suggested that online learning environments provide important affordances for highly emotional topics.

Virtual High School: NCVPS (2011-Present)[3]

For the past several years, our social presence research shifted to focus on virtual public schools as an emerging newcomer to online education. In recent years, K–12 online learning and virtual public schools have increased across the country (Picciano & Seaman, 2009, 2010; Watson, Murin, Vashaw, Gemin, & Rapp, 2010, 2012, 2013). A 2013 review of K–12 online learning confirms all 50 states have some online learning opportunities at the K–12 level, 26 states have established virtual schools that are at least partially

---

[3] Excerpted in part from *Journal of Interactive Online Learning*, vol. 12(3), A. Garrett Dikkers, A. L. Whiteside, and S. Lewis, Virtual high school teacher and student reactions to the Social Presence Model, pp. 156–170. Copyright 2013, with permission from JIOL.

funded at the state level, and another 7 states have virtual learning opportunities in choice programs (Watson et al., 2013). As of 2013, four states also have requirements that students take an online course before graduation from high school (Watson et al., 2013). The most recent growth in K-12 online learning has come in the form of online charter schools, many of which are organized and managed by private and for-profit Educational Management Organizations (Molnar, 2013).

Although there is a growth in online learning at the K-12 level, there is still a distinct lack of research around teaching and learning in the K-12 online environment (DiPetro, Ferdig, Black, & Preston, 2008; Means, Toyama, Murphy, Bakia, & Jones, 2010). To address this gap in the research, we partnered with the North Carolina Virtual Public School (NCVPS) to research teachers' and students' online high school experiences. NCVPS, founded in 2007, offers coursework predominantly in grades 9-12 and offers "nearly 50,000 secondary students … over 150 Advanced Placement, Honors, Traditional, Credit Recovery, and Occupational Course of Study" course options (North Carolina Virtual Public School, 2013). Students enroll in NCVPS through the eLearning Advisor at their local public school or in their district, and they use the Moodle and Blackboard LMSs in a largely asynchronous learning experience. We explored whether the elements of the SPM served as a useful model for quality teaching and learning in K-12 online environments.

The open-ended survey comments and interview data from NCVPS teachers suggest they found great value in the SPM to support the work they already do to strengthen the online learning environment for their students. K-12 teachers also seemed to appreciate seeing a model to help them understand how to create high quality online learning experiences. Figure 11.3 depicts the degree to which NCVPS teachers agree that the components of the SPM promote quality teaching and learning in online environments.

Teachers elaborated on all aspects of the SPM and its applicability to their teaching and their students' learning in the NCVPS. Responses to an open-ended survey question asking teachers to list strategies they use to promote each aspect of the SPM yielded a list of course tools that NCVPS teachers find useful in promoting all aspects of the model. In regards to using synchronous contact as a strategy to promote Interaction Intensity, one teacher commented, "Between Facebook, Twitter, Google Voice, e-mail, phone-calls, and Pronto, I'd say that one cannot proactively or reactively have more interaction intensity than me!" And in using discussion fora as a strategy to promote Knowledge and Experience, another teacher

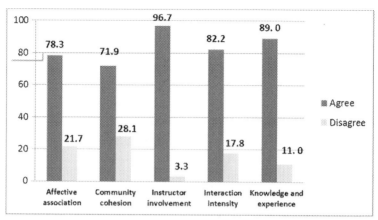

Figure 11.3 Perceptions of relevance of the Social Presence Model for NCVPS teachers.

commented, "Students with strong online learning or technological experience are provided a forum to share their tips and ideas; students with strong writing skills often model good writing for those who are struggling; students with a variety of content knowledge share this information on the [course] Wiki, which is very helpful for others with limited knowledge." (Garrett Dikkers et al., 2013).

Additionally, one NCVPS teacher explained the value of social presence for individualized student learning:

> *Synchronicity is individualized. Therefore, different plans for Social Presence is [sic] individualized too. The directive and requirement of specifics in how a teacher creates the social presence in their individual online course is different from course to course, teacher to teacher. The key is to have a social presence; it should not and cannot be a prescribed method. This prescription will be a loose-end of online instruction as 'click-click-teach' is not the essence of online instruction. Social Presence is not about a formula, but rather about a philosophy.*
>
> **Garrett Dikkers et al. (2013).**

Several responses aligned with this teacher's greater awareness about the importance of building connections with their students. One teacher mentioned s/he was "more aware of the need to build and maintain positive relationships with students." Another explained: "Since teaching online, I have come to understand the barriers that students believe exist between themselves and their teachers. I now distribute my cell phone number for text messages from face-to-face students ... On snow days or when they are sick or just need a quick question asked, they can ping me and it is just great."

Although all areas of the SPM intrigued teachers, they saw themselves (and *Instructor Involvement*) as key to their students' learning. One teacher suggested, "I think it is very important for students to recognize that the instructor is a real person that cares about their success in the course. They want to know that I am working as hard toward their success as they are." Additionally, teachers identify the importance of cultivating a relationship with their students and how important those relationships are in the learning process. One teacher notes:

> I think that ... the teacher has to believe in the students and the content. We have to be willing to take risks and share information about ourselves with our students. I truly believe that rapport is a vital part of education. If a student has a rapport with you, he/she is more willing to work harder for you! Students aren't going to be invested if they know their instructor isn't.
>
> **Garrett Dikkers et al. (2013).**

NCVPS students provided conflicting reports at times; they saw themselves as key to the process, but they still wanted the one-to-one access with their instructors. They liked the autonomy of online learning, but they still wanted guidance and deadlines from their instructors. One student commented, "A sense of community helps reduce stress and the sense of loneliness. The instructor absolutely needs to get involved in learning and the students absolutely need to be able to communicate!" Students overwhelmingly agreed that *Instructor Involvement* is important to their learning, specifically in regard to how the instructor works to meet their individual learning needs.

By applying the SPM to a new educational context with younger students, this project helped us understand the importance of models for teachers to connect to their students in online and blended modalities. This study led to several related sub-studies, including an exploration of students at-risk of dropping out and students with learning disabilities (Lewis, Whiteside, & Garrett Dikkers, 2014). In summary, this project helped us begin to understand a new audience of secondary school teachers and students in an online learning environment and how the components of the SPM may serve them. It also led to a new study of social presence in a secondary school blended learning initiative.

Blended High School: Huntley High Blended Program (2014-Present)[4]

In late 2013, we were approached to conduct research on a blended learning initiative in the Midwest at Huntley High School. Huntley High School is

[4] Excerpted in part from *eLearn Magazine*, 2014, A. Garrett Dikkers, A. L. Whiteside, and S Lewis, Do you Blend? Huntley Does.

one of nine schools that make up District 158 in McHenry and Kane counties of Northern Illinois. Consolidated School District 158 serves 9300 students in Pre-kindergarten through Grade 12. There are 2509 students attending Huntley High School (Illinois Report Card, 2014). Huntley High School started with three blended classes in 2011-2012 and currently has blended learning options for 17 classes, with 21 teachers, offering classes with a total of 835 seats in the 2013-2014 school year. Some of these classes are year-long; others are either Fall or Spring semester courses. There also is a mix of required courses such as English, Biology, or US History; advanced courses such as AP Psychology or AP Music Theory; and general electives, such as Intro to News Media, History of Sports, Personal Fitness, and Recent Reads.

This new project allows us to expand our research to explore connections between students, their peers, and their teachers in a program that blended online components and face-to-face instruction. The mission statement at Huntley is "Inspiring students to succeed, challenging students to achieve their potential, and empowering students to be contributing citizens in an ever-changing world" (Huntley High School, 2014). Blended learning at Huntley High School is a formal education program, in which students learn at least in part through online delivery of content and instruction and at least in part, at school with some element of student control over time, place, path, and/or pace.

One unique aspect of Huntley High School's blended learning model is the built-in flextime for students. Blended classes meet face-to-face two or three times a week, and on the non-meeting days, students have flextime. Students, parents, teachers, and administrators at Huntley see this flexibility as a significant benefit. Students use the flextime for their blended learning coursework, to get one-on-one time with their blended learning teacher, to set-up tutoring sessions, and for other purposes. Students also discuss the benefits of their flexible blended learning time as helping them learn to properly manage their time, forcing them to take responsibility for their own learning, allowing them to identify how they learn best, and gaining study habits they will need in order to be successful in college. One student in a focus group commented, "That's actually why I took this class ... [be]cause I wanted to prepare myself for the future where I'd be on my own and having to manage my time properly ... [to] feel a little more confident going into college" (Garrett Dikkers, Whiteside, & Lewis, 2014).

The vast majority of students (91.9%; $n = 247$) report themselves as satisfied or very satisfied with their blended learning experience

(Garrett Dikkers et al., 2014). As for emotion, students identified all aspects of social presence as being important or very important to their learning: Instructor Involvement (90.09%); Knowledge and Experience (75.94%); Interaction Intensity (74.40%); Community Cohesion (69.34%); and Affective Association (60.10%). In our analysis of students' open-ended survey responses, we discovered that students see *connections* as being important, but they do not necessarily equate connections with their peers and their instructor as being *emotional*. For example, one student explains in a survey response:

> *I think being connected to your classmates and teacher and being able to rely on them if you're struggling is more important than emotion or previous knowledge. If you have that connection, the emotion should just come and if you don't have any previous knowledge, that's why you're taking the class and you can aks [sic] your classmates or teacher to explain the material to you.*
>
> **Garrett Dikkers et al. (2014).**

Additionally, teachers suggest that the autonomy and college-like experience has led to a more mature, intellectual experience. One teacher indicates, "The interaction with the students [in the Blended Program] is different. They act more mature and responsible than in my traditional classes. Even though I only meet with them for 2 days during a normal week, I feel as though I have gotten to know these students better than the students in a traditional class" (Garrett Dikkers et al. (2014)).

One of our key findings of this most recent case study is that the administrators at Huntley High School have a close, emotional connection to their students. They truly care about their students and have expectations for their learning. And their students know it. Huntley's Superintendent explains the value of blended learning for meeting the needs of individual students:

> *The blended learning environment really allows kids to go faster, to go slower, to spend more time on things they need to get. To get more individual help from the teacher because the teacher's caseload is exactly the same as before. ... On the days when they're not meeting, the teacher has office hours, just like you'd do at the college level ... I think kids that need help are getting more attention.*
>
> **Garrett Dikkers et al. (2014).**

If teachers notice any individual student or group of students who need extra help, they can require that the students come in during their office hours for extra help and tutoring. As Principal Rowe explains, "That's what's special about it ... we can slowly take those scaffolds away and put them back if we have to." Upper administration also keeps close track of student progress. For every class that has a blended section, there is also a traditional section.

So, if students are not ready for blended or are struggling to keep up with the independent nature of the course, they can be placed back into a traditional section. As one administrator sums up, "Blended learning allows our students the opportunity to learn how they want to, when they want to. We give them the chance to use there [sic] time as they feel they need to, yet provide a safety net for them in case they stumble. It is a transition for them to begin learning as adults do, in the real world" (Garrett Dikkers et al., 2014).

In sum, this new project has opened our eyes to a new world of research on the emotion and connectedness at the core of blended learning programs for high school students. We also uncovered how a school community individualizes student learning with scaffolding to help students begin a transition into higher education with a head start on twenty-first century skills and innovative learning practices.

REFLECTIONS AND MOVING FORWARD

In conclusion, our research with the SPM over the past decade finds that emotions matter greatly in online and blended learning. The SPM grew out of a need to understand the experiences of connectedness among cohort members in a blended learning graduate program, the STL Program. We were then able to strengthen our understanding of the relationship among emotions, technology, and learning through HRE courses, as well as by applying the SPM to two different K-12 contexts, a state-level virtual school and a district-level blended learning initiative.

These case studies demonstrate the SPM's significance for teachers as they reflect on and adjust their instructional practices to create connections with and among their students. We now see a whole area of research opening up that explores the impact of connection and emotion for the learning experiences of youth. Finally, we also discovered the importance of a dedicated cadre of leaders, as we found in the Huntley Blended Learning Initiative, who individualize student learning to help their students to transition into higher education through the use of innovative instructional strategies and demonstrating genuine care and concern for their students. In short, emotional support is invaluable to all learning with technology, but it is particularly important for blended and online learning programs.

Moreover, our key finding over the years is that social presence embodies an essential literacy for cultivating emotions and relationships that enhance the overall learning experience. This literacy is akin to any influential literacy, such as technological literacy, rhetorical literacy, and digital literacy. It is a literacy that requires careful consideration, cultivation, and continued exploration. Social presence through the SPM represents an emotive quality that is essential to successful, meaningful online or blended learning experiences.

REFERENCES

Allen, I. E., & Seaman, J. (2011). *Going the distance: Online education in the United States.* Babson Park, MA: Babson Survey Research Group.

DiPetro, M., Ferdig, R. E., Black, E. W., & Preston, M. (2008). Best practices in teaching K-12 online: Lessons learned from Michigan Virtual School teachers. *Journal of Interactive Online Learning, 7*(1), 10–35.

Garrett Dikkers, A., Hughes, J., & McLeod, S. (2005). Bridging the no-man's land between school technology and effective leadership. *Technological Horizons in Education (T.H.E.) Journal, 32*(11), 20–22. 24.

Garrett Dikkers, A., & Whiteside, A. L. (2008). Using the social presence model to maximize online learning. In *Paper presented at the 24th annual conference on distance teaching and learning. Madison, WI.*

Garrett Dikkers, A., & Whiteside, A. L. (2011). Leveraging the technology-enhanced community (TEC) partnership model to enrich higher education. In M. Bowden & R. Carpenter (Eds.), *Higher education, emerging technologies, and community partnerships: Concepts, models and applications.* Hershey, PA: IGI Global.

Garrett Dikkers, A., & Whiteside, A. L. (2013). Creating social presence in asynchronous online learning. In *Paper presented at the Global learning technology conference, Wilmington, NC.*

Garrett Dikkers, A., Whiteside, A. L., & Lewis, S. (2012). Get present: Build community and connectedness online. *Learning & Leading with Technology, 40*(2), 22–25.

Garrett Dikkers, A., Whiteside, A. L., & Lewis, S. (2013). Virtual high school teacher and student reactions to the social presence model. *Journal of Interactive Online Learning, 12*(3), 156–170.

Garrett Dikkers, A., Whiteside, A. L., & Lewis, S. (2014, December). Do you blend? Huntley High School does. *eLearn Magazine.* Association of Computer Machinery (ACM). Retrieved from, http://elearnmag.acm.org/archive.cfm?aid=2686759.

Garrison, D. R., Anderson, T., & Archer, W. (2000). Critical inquiry in a text-based environment: Computer conferencing in higher education. *The Internet and Higher Education, 2*(2-3), 87–105.

Garrison, D. R., Anderson, T., & Archer, W. (2010). The first decade of the community of inquiry framework: A retrospective. *The Internet and Higher Education, 13*(1-2), 5–9.

Gunawardena, C. N., & Zittle, F. J. (1997). Social presence as a predictor of satisfaction within a computer-mediated conferencing environment. *The American Journal of Distance Education, 11*(3), 8–26.

Hughes, J. E., McLeod, S., Garrett Dikkers, A., Brahier, B., & Whiteside, A. L. (2005). School technology leadership: Theory to practice. *Academic Exchange Quarterly (Special Issue on Leadership), 9*(2), 51–55.

Huntley High School. (2014). *Student handbook.* Retrieved from, http://www.district158.org/hhs/Home%20Page%20Documents/13-14%20HHS%20Student%20Handbook.pdf.

Illinois Report Card. (2014). *Huntley high school.* Retrieved from, http://illinoisreportcard.com/school.aspx?schoolID=440631580220002.

Lewis, S., Whiteside, A. L., & Garrett Dikkers, A. (2014). Autonomy and responsibility: Online learning as a solution for at-risk high school students. *International Journal of E-Learning & Distance Education, 29*(2), 1–11.

Lowenthal, P. R. (2009). The evolution and influence of social presence theory on online learning. In T. T. Kidd (Ed.), *Online education and adult learning: New frontiers for teaching practices* (pp. 124–139). Hershey, PA: IGI Global.

Lowenthal, P. R. (2012). *Social presence: What is it? How do we measure it?* Unpublished doctoral dissertation, Denver, Colorado: University of Colorado Denver.

Lowenthal, P. R., & Dunlap, J. C. (2014). Problems measuring social presence in a community of inquiry. *E-Learning and Digital Media, 11*(1), 19–30. Retrieved from, http://patricklowenthal.com/publications/Problems_measuring_social_presence_in_a_community_of_inquiry.pdf.

McLeod, S. (2012). *Center for the Advanced Study of Technology Leadership in Education.* University Council of Educational Administration. Retrieved from, http://schooltechleadership.org/.

Means, B., Toyama, Y., Murphy, R., Bakia, M., & Jones, K. (2010). *Evaluation of evidence-based practices in online learning: A meta-analysis and review of online learning studies.* Washington, D.C.: U.S. Department of Education, Office of Planning, Evaluation, and Policy Development.

Molnar, A. (Ed.), (2013). *Virtual schools in the U.S. 2013: Politics, performance, policy, and research evidence.* Boulder, CO: National Education Policy Center.

North Carolina Virtual Public School. (2013). *Home.* Retrieved from, http://www.ncvps.org/.

Picciano, A. G. (2002). Beyond student perceptions: Issues of interaction, presence, and performance in an online course. *Journal of Asynchronous Learning Networks, 6*(1), 21–40.

Picciano, A. G., & Seaman, J. (2009). *K-12 online learning: A 2008 follow-up of the survey of U.S. school district administrators.* NY: The Sloan Consortium. Retrieved from, http://www.sloanconsortium.org/publications/survey/k-12online2008.

Picciano, A. G., & Seaman, J. (2010). *Class connections: High school reform and the role of online learning.* Boston, MA: Babson College Survey Research Group.

Rettie, R. (2003). Connectedness, awareness, and social presence. In *6th international presence workshop. Aalborg University.* Retrieved from, http://eprints.kingston.ac.uk/2106/1/Rettie.pdf.

Richardson, J. C., & Swan, K. (2003). Examining social presence in online courses in relation to students' perceived learning and satisfaction. *Journal of Asynchronous Learning Networks, 7*(1), 68–88.

Rourke, L., & Anderson, T. (2002). Exploring social presence in computer conferencing. *Journal of Interactive Learning Research, 13*(3), 259–275.

Rourke, L., Anderson, T., Garrison, D. R., & Archer, W. (1999). Assessing social presence in asynchronous, text-based computer conferencing. *Journal of Distance Education, 14*(2), 50–71.

Rovai, A. (2002). Building a sense of community at a distance. *International Review of Research in Open and Distance Learning, 3*(1). Retrieved from, http://www.irrodl.org/index.php/irrodl/article/view/79/152.

Shea, P., Pickett, A., & Pelt, W. (2003). A follow-up investigation of teaching presence in the SUNY Learning Network. *Journal of the Asynchronous Learning Network, 7*(2), 61–80.

Short, J., William, E., & Christie, B. (1976). *The social psychology of telecommunications.* Toronto, ON: Wiley.

Stacey, E. (2002). Social presence online: Networking learners at a distance, education and information technologies. *Education and Information Technologies, 7*(4), 287–294.

Swan, K. (2002). Immediacy, social presence, and asynchronous discussion. In J. Bourne & J. C. Moore (Eds.), *Elements of quality online education: Vol. 3.* Needham, MA: Sloan Center for Online Education.

Swan, K., & Shih, L.-F. (2005). On the nature and development of social presence in online course discussions. *Journal of Asynchronous Learning Networks, 9*(3), 115–136.

Tammelin, M. (1998). From telepresence to social presence: The role of presence in a network-based learning environment. In S. Tella (Ed.), *Aspects of media education: Strategic imperatives in the information age*: University of Helsinki. Media Education Publications. Retrieved from, *http://www.european-mediaculture.org/fileadmin/bibliothek/english/tammelin_telepresence/tammelin_telepresence.html*.

Tu, C.-H. (2001). How Chinese perceive social presence: An examination of interaction in online learning environment. *Education Media International, 38*(1), 45–60.

Tu, C.-H. (2002a). The impacts of text-based CMC on online social presence. *The Journal of Interactive Online Learning, 1*(2), 1–24. Retrieved from, http://www.ncolr.org/jiol/issues/PDF/1.2.6.pdf.

Tu, C.-H. (2002b). The measurement of social presence in an online learning environment. *International Journal on E-Learning, 1*(2), 34–45.

Watson, J., Murin, A., Vashaw, L., Gemin, B., & Rapp, C. (2010). *Keeping pace with K-12 online learning: An annual review of policy and practice*. Evergreen, CO: Evergreen Education Group.

Watson, J., Murin, A., Vashaw, L., Gemin, B., & Rapp, C. (2012). *Keeping pace with K-12 online and blended learning: An annual review of policy and practice*. Evergreen, CO: Evergreen Education Group.

Watson, J., Murin, A., Vashaw, L., Gemin, B., & Rapp, C. (2013). *Keeping pace with K-12 online and blended learning: An annual review of policy and practice*. Evergreen, CO: Evergreen Education Group.

Whiteside, A. L. (2007). *Exploring social presence in communities of practice within a hybrid learning environment: A longitudinal examination of two case studies within the School Technology Leadership graduate-level certificate program*. Unpublished doctoral dissertation, Minneapolis, MN: University of Minnesota.

Whiteside, A. L. (2015). Introducing the Social Presence Model to explore online and blended learning experiences. *Online Learning: Official Journal of the Online Learning Consortium, 19*(2). Retrieved from http://olj.onlinelearningconsortium.org/index.php/jaln/article/view/453/137.

Whiteside, A. L., & Garrett Dikkers, A. (2008). Social presence in online learning. In *Paper presented at the new media research conference*. Minneapolis, MN: University of Minnesota.

Whiteside, A. L., & Garrett Dikkers, A. (2009). Strategies for maximizing learning outcomes and student engagement in online and blended learning environments. In *Workshop presented at the academy of distinguished Teachers teaching and learning conference, Minneapolis, MN*.

Whiteside, A. L., & Garrett Dikkers, A. (2010). Strategies to maximize online interactions using the social presence model. In *Paper presented at the Sloan-C international conference on online learning, Orlando, FL*.

Whiteside, A. L., & Garrett Dikkers, A. (2012). Using the social presence model to maximize interactions in online environments. In K. St. Amant & S. Kelsey (Eds.), *Computer-mediated communication across cultures: International interactions in online environments* (pp. 395–413). Hershey, PA: IGI Global.

Whiteside, A. L., Garrett Dikkers, A., & Lewis, S. (2014). The power of social presence for learning. *Educause Review*. Online. Retrieved from, http://www.educause.edu/ero/article/power-social-presence-learning.

Whiteside, A. L., Hughes, J. E., & McLeod, S. (2005). Interconnecting cognition, contact, and comprehension: The influence of social presence in a hybrid-model certificate program. In *Proceedings of the new media research conference*, Minneapolis, MN: University of Minnesota.

CHAPTER 12

Technology and Human Cultural Accumulation: The Role of Emotion

Geoff Woolcott
Southern Cross University, Lismore, NSW, Australia

INTRODUCTION—EMOTION, TECHNOLOGY, AND EDUCATION

Technology has become a prominent issue in education, with developments in electronic data storage and computing facilitating increases in amounts of stored information and accessibility for learning. Individuals may now access interactive or static instructional devices that require only the learner and the device. Sophisticated adaptive online learning technologies enable devices to dynamically adjust instructional methods and procedures as a learner acquires knowledge (Kalyuga, 2008).

In the classroom, teachers are seeking to assist learning by engaging students through the electronic devices and media the students use for social communication (Westwell, 2008). Both classroom learning and self-learning, which occurs outside the classroom, have been supported by an increase in research into educational use of electronic media, which is reflected in the increasing number of research publications and journals dedicated to this area.

Studies have suggested that learning, and this necessarily includes online learning, is intrinsically intertwined with emotion and closely allied with drives and motivation (Damasio, 2003; LeDoux, 1996; Panksepp, 1998). Research on emotion and learning, and on motivation as a related issue, has been linked to developments in technology (e.g., Olguin, Gloor, & Pentland, 2009). Within the cognitive sciences, studies of emotions upon faces are being used to develop digital technologies (Baron-Cohen, Golan, & Ashwin, 2009).

It can be argued, however, that a view of technology that encompasses only digital or electronic devices may be obscuring broader considerations such as the conflict between human values and technological needs

Emotions, Technology, and Learning
http://dx.doi.org/10.1016/B978-0-12-800649-8.00006-7

243

(e.g., Pirsig, 1974). Additionally, since technology may be considered as both non-neutral and value-laden (Kruse, 2013), educators may need information about emotional involvement in learning in order to decide when technology may interfere with learning. Research that ties emotion to technology may be of particular importance (Woolcott, 2013a). There are acknowledged conflicts as to the nature of emotion (e.g., Damasio, 2003) and the nature of technology (e.g., Kruse, 2013; Lane, 2009), and these may need to be reconciled with modern views of learning in order for the field to consolidate research across disciplines (Woolcott, 2013b).

This theoretical essay focuses on the relationship between emotion, technology, and learning. It argues that human interaction with the environment through problem solving and learning (in the sense of Tonegawa, Nakazawa, & Wilson, 2003) requires the involvement of emotions, as well as drives (Grandin & Johnson, 2005; Panksepp, 1998). The chapter also argues that technology is an integral part of such human interaction (e.g., Lane, 2009). A view is elaborated that embraces technology as an integral part of this human accumulation of culture through environmental interaction and learning, with culture considered as the sum total of human knowledge (in the sense of Tomasello, 1999). This essay provides a generalized cognitive model based upon biological views of information processing that recognizes the links between learning and emotion, and the role of technology in human environmental negotiation and cultural accumulation (Woolcott, 2013a).

ACCUMULATING CULTURE

Within modern industrialized societies, each individual from 5 to 16 years of age may spend as many as 20 h a week in an educational institution, such as a school, college, or university, with some individuals continuing this type of education for many more years. Such institutionalized education has become an important way for individuals to learn complex cultural information that might otherwise not be learned from parents, society, or the natural environment (Sylwester, 1995). This style of education has become an important part of the accumulation of culture across society (in the sense of Tomasello, 1999), where the knowledge, skills, and experiences that constitute the cultural memory of each individual in human society are transferred from one human memory to another through teaching and learning environments.

Education and Cultural Accumulation

The process of cultural accumulation ensures that culture continues to be accumulated through person-to-person interactions, across generations, as well as through storage using such technological devices as books and electronic media. Although culture may be accumulated prior to or after schooling (Dehaene, 2007; van Merriënboer & Sluijsmans, 2010), school education has become an important part of the human cultural accumulation process, largely because such education may enhance the transmission and sharing of culture such that it increases overall across a society. This process is referred to here as cultural ratcheting (Boesch & Tomasello, 1998; Tomasello, 1999).

An awareness of the role of education in processing and transmitting environmental information underlies cultural accumulation and cultural ratcheting. These ideas are reflected in theories and teaching practices based upon connectionist models that arose from studies in information science and modern cognitive psychology (e.g., see Lachman, Lachman, & Butterfield, 1979; Miller, 2003). The sharing of this culture between individuals, and the use of such external storage devices may also constitute a major factor in human survival (Dehaene, 2007; Mesoudi, 2011). Such sharing of culture, for example, has contributed to the development of human society, particularly in industrialized countries, where it has had an impact on social and economic improvement (e.g., reduction in mortality rates, injury, and disease).

Cultural accumulation processes may involve, of course, some loss of knowledge, skills, and experiences. This loss may be due to human conflict or environmental catastrophe, for example. Additionally, culture may not be effectively passed on from one generation to another, particularly where the information is related to action within a specific context, such as in the knowledge, skills, and experiences related to hunting or craft.

Emotion and Cultural Accumulation

Cultural accumulation through learning, including learning in educational institutions, has been facilitated by a human nervous system, centralized within a complex brain. This nervous system allows each individual to learn and remember large amounts of information obtained and abstracted from their own environmental interactions (e.g., Edelman, 2007), and this includes interactions with other individuals. Ideally, this information is shared across society and contributes to cultural accumulation.

Some biological studies, generally referred to under the collective term "affective neuroscience," look at learning, memory, and emotion (e.g., Damasio, 2003; LeDoux, 1996; Panksepp, 1998). These studies indicate that pathways of internal connectivity in the nervous system, including assemblies of brain cells involved in learning and memory, may include those information pathways that are tied closely to the intrinsic somatic (bodily) chemical and energetic pathways identified with emotions and drives. The emotion pathways are tied to every learning experience (LeDoux, 1996), and emotions are sometimes referred to as brain-based motivators because of this involvement (Grandin & Johnson, 2005).

Technology and Cultural Accumulation

There may be a similarly close relationship between technology and emotion, given that learning and emotion have such a close relationship, and that learning and memory are in many ways a product of a nervous system that interacts with its environment. This is also the case because, in its broad sense, technology is considered to involve human manipulation of the environment (e.g., Kruse, 2013; Lane, 2009). Technology, then, is part of the human culture that develops and accumulates through learning based upon the process of problem solving.[1] That is, the process of the interaction with environmental stimulus mediated by attention and working memory. Emotion is, in this regard, integral to the development of technology through its role in environmental interaction, learning, and resultant human negotiation of the world. In addition, emotion can be involved in the activation of memory pathways, and can therefore be involved in remembering information related to environmental manipulation, and as a result in the use of technology.

LINKING EMOTION WITH LEARNING

Emotions, along with the drives that regulate bodily needs, are thought to play an integral role in processing environmental interactions, determining the information that is stored as long-term memory (LTM), and also in

---

[1] Problem solving is used here in the sense of Tonegawa et al. (2003) to mean interaction with environmental stimulus and not in the sense of solving a problem, such as a school mathematics problem (eg, see Sweller, van Merriënboer, & Paas, 1998).

determining responses to thought or action (e.g., see Damasio, 1999, 2003; LeDoux, 1996; Panksepp, 1998). Emotions and drives are thought to function in the formation and modification of all human memory through the development or activation of connected pathways in the nervous system (e.g., Damasio, 2003; LeDoux, 1996). Such pathways may contribute directly to concept formation. For example, through reinforcement of existing or newly formed connections in short-term memory (STM) or LTM, or in providing additional connectivity through pathways to memories in LTM (e.g., Coricelli, Dolan, & Sirigu, 2007).

Intrinsic Pathways and Intrinsic Emotions

Modern scientists have argued that an intrinsic system of chemical and energetic pathways, including those tied to emotions, serves as a basis for all memories accumulated during a lifetime. Some see such information pathways as fixed-action patterns (Llinás, 2001) or reflexes (Cotterill, 2001), as a common feature of organisms with a centralized nervous system. Minsky (2006) has suggested that some emotions enact biased activation in neuronal pathways of particular intrinsic pathways, and this view appears to be supported by Cotterill (2001), who has specified some of the links between emotional and other neuronal pathways.

Intrinsic pathways may be viewed as those arising from combinations of simple networks that are developed during growth, including growth prior to birth, through systemic interaction with environment (e.g., genetic interaction; LeDoux, 1996). Larger pathways and networks, almost all of which may have a component linked to intrinsic emotions (Panksepp, 1998), may develop from such simple networks through environmental interaction or through processes such as feedback from motor neurons and sensors in muscles (Calvin, 1996; Cotterill, 2001). Potentially, there may also be development of larger networks from neuronal pathways with activation bias due to their structure or spatial location, and influenced by their stage of development (Grillner, 2003; Turchin, 1977).

Arguments for the developed, and potentially developing, nature of some intrinsic pathways have been supported through modeling of reflexes considered to be inbuilt, such as facial recognition (e.g., Butko, Fasel, & Movellan, 2006). Some pathways considered as intrinsic may be considered in the overall context of memory as neuronal pathways constructed during the life of an organism through environmental interaction (e.g., learned fear; Damasio, 1999; Phelps & LeDoux, 2005).

Care must be taken, however, in any generalization of links between emotions and learning, as the description of emotions in cognitive psychology, and in everyday life, may vary considerably from those used in modern biology. Drawing from a background in affective neuroscience (Damasio, 1999, 2003; LeDoux, 1996; Panksepp, 1998), Grandin and Johnson (2005) describe only four intrinsic primal emotions: fear; seeking (curiosity/interest/anticipation); rage; and prey-chase drive. They refer to these as having a primary function as inbuilt brain-based motivators. Grandin and Johnson (2005) also describe four similarly intrinsic primary social emotions: sexual attraction and lust; separation distress; social attachment; and play and roughhousing. In recent times, power and disgust (see, e.g., Toronchuk & Ellis, 2012) have been added to the short list of intrinsic emotions developed by Panksepp (1998).

Other types of emotions, for example, those described in cognitive psychology and everyday life, may be considered as developing from these intrinsic pathways. It should be noted, though, that there might be considerable variation as to what is considered as emotion, intrinsic, or otherwise, even within affective neuroscience (e.g., Damasio, 2003; LeDoux, 1996). In any case, these intrinsic emotions, and the networks of association developed from them, may vary in intensity and probably frequency of expression between animal groups, and between animals within groups, including between human individuals (Grandin & Johnson, 2005).

Emotion and Learning Processes

Modern institutional education serves to teach control of learning processes, such as working memory (STM)[2] and attention, two of the key processes in learning (Tonegawa et al., 2003). A whole-system approach that provides connection between emotion and such processes, as well as connections to environmental interaction, does not appear to have yet played a prominent role in education (Woolcott, 2013b). Although educational theories and teaching practices may accommodate implicitly the view that teachers need to utilize environmental interactions and build memories in accordance with cultural knowledge, these theories and practices rarely combine this with a whole-system or connectivity approach (see, e.g., discussion in Siemens, 2008).

---

[2] Short-term memory (STM) may be seen, in a general sense, as being equivalent to working memory, representing the capability of a flexible nervous system in attending to different kinds of information (eg, Postle, 2006).

There is some support, however, for the awareness of attention and working memory (or STM) and related inhibitory processes in teaching and learning interactions (e.g., Postle, 2006). There is also an increasing awareness of the role of emotion in such interactions, and the place of inhibition or control, sometimes under the banner of emotional intelligence (e.g., Parker, Saklofske, Wood, & Collin, 2009) or motivation (e.g., Brooks & Shell, 2006; Shell et al., 2010).

It may be relevant for educators to be aware of the constraints dictated by the type and extent of interactions, including emotional interactions, across the human system. Such awareness may be useful in considering the effect on the entire system of such factors as amount of sleep, nutrient supply, emotional control, concentration, body position, and neuronal connectivity, or other factors that may interfere with the optimization of learning (Woolcott, 2011). These constraints have only recently been considered in educational studies, although they are recognized in the brain/mind/behavior model of Frith and others (e.g., Blakemore & Frith, 2000), where environmental factors are compartmentalized into those that affect the brain (e.g., oxygen and nutrition), mind (e.g., teaching), and behavior (e.g., teaching tools) to demonstrate the connectivity between biology, cognition, and behavior, in addition to any potential constraints that may result.

TAKING A BROAD VIEW OF TECHNOLOGY

Technology is sometimes seen exclusively as tools, from simple levers to more complex devices, such as printing presses and computers. Technology in a broad sense (e.g., Lane, 2009), however, might be better described as any human activity that can manipulate, through muscular contraction and resultant motor activity (bodily movement), an aspect of environmental interaction through problem solving (or utilization of new informational input). In the context of human learning, technology can be discussed with respect to environmental interactions that rely on use of a well-developed human nervous system that is efficient in dealing with new information and that has a large LTM. This means that technology can be discussed in terms of interaction with new information that, through deliberate manipulation, offers a reproductive or survival advantage.

The view of technology as tools or electronic media may, therefore, be masking the broader picture of environmental manipulation, and may hamper the application of technological thinking in terms of environmental interactions and emotions as brain-based motivators. Accumulated culture may give rise to improved technology, a view that has been developed with respect to media technology (e.g., Brynjolfsson & McAfee, 2012; Greenfield & Bell, 2010), but this may be because shared culture can lead to new ways of viewing environmental manipulation. It may be important to broaden the view of technology so that a restricted view of such interactions is removed.

Technology and Human Advantage

With a broad view of technology in mind, environmental manipulations, such as writing, could be described as technology; so could less tangible environmental manipulations, such as fanning a spark to start a fire, or cooling objects in water, or even persuading someone to complete a task (e.g., see discussion in Lane, 2009). In humans, technology may be linked to the addition of created information in LTM (Sweller, van Merriënboer, & Paas, 1998) and to creativity (Sweller & Mann, 2011), provided there is some kind of motor output in response to new environmental input. Humans can often respond more quickly than other large animals to short-term environmental change and, as a result, technological knowledge and emotional control may be central to the human advantage in such crucial activities as obtaining food, avoiding predators, and reproducing in safety.

In using such a broad description of technology, however, there may be some unresolved issues, including whether a given environmental interaction is a manipulation, whether such a manipulation offers an advantage, or whether an organism has intended any advantage. One argument in favor of advantage is that the accumulation of technology culture, as part of the build-up of a shared culture, is a major factor in human survival and reproduction. The sharing and storage of memories of individuals as technology culture can be considered to be partly responsible for advantaging human survival in cooperative societies (Mesoudi, 2011). The shared knowledge, skills, and experiences required for agrarian practices and animal husbandry that have facilitated human settlement is an example.

It may be that technology has allowed sufficient environmental information to be accumulated across particular societies such that self-sufficient communities could share information through cooperative education. The bodies of knowledge that have developed into modern education, and the subject categorization that has emerged within it, appear to be a development that occurred after the establishment of such self-sufficient communities.

Within societies, technology can be considered not only as development of a tool, but also as development of a farming practice, or a business practice, or other activity that involves an environmental interaction that acts to advantage an individual's survival or reproduction. Since education and teaching function in the communication of memories, they are an important mode of transmission of the part of the body of culture that is technology. In terms of neuronal connectivity, however, there may be little distinction between culture labeled as science or history, and culture labeled as technology. Although this has caused some dispute among theorists (Dehaene, 2004), any differences may lie in the access to LTM activated by input environmental information and to the contextualization and reorganization of information in LTM. Whether technology is a manipulation and whether this manipulation was a result of intention, therefore, may remain disputed issues.

Technology Through Emotion and Learning

Considered in the broad sense as environmental manipulation, technology has been part of human cultural accumulation longer than any culture resulting from modern industrial development and any associated changes in education. This is due, in large part, to the use of technological devices to store information external to the human body. For example, written records were used to store information in the earliest agrarian societies (Schmandt-Besserat, 1996) long before there was an industrialized society. The accumulation of technology as culture, and the transmission of this culture from generation to generation, forms part of the greater accumulation of culture obtained through learning and memory processes. This includes those processes involved in human environmental interactions and negotiation of the physical world, such as processes related to education, teaching, and social communication more generally.

Learning and memory processes are also associated with emotions, and this makes an obvious conjunction for technology and emotion, linked through learning. Consider the environmental manipulation or technology that a farmer may have used to improve the sowing of seeds. The emotion concerned may have been related to seeking or curiosity, and emotion may also be involved in this hypothetical case, in having an active and aim-related focus, sometimes summarized under the umbrella term of motivation (Brooks & Shell, 2006). Success of this technology may have resulted in its reuse, and a resultant activation of emotion pathways, associated learning and memory processes, and pathways in the nervous system, even where these may be concerned solely with the maintenance of a goal state (e.g., see Gray, 2004).

A concern, however, must be raised here associated with differentiating between learning and sensation. Greenfield has outlined the following differences in technology: on the one hand, there is technology that provides sensation, triggering and stimulating reward centers; but on the other hand, there is technology that aids the guided instruction and self-regulation of attention and working memory that is central to growth of LTM and which is essential to learning and the growth of expertise (e.g., see Greenfield and the opposing views expressed in the seminar of Greenfield & Bell, 2010). Greenfield argues that there is a good deal of modern media technology, including television, geared toward provision of sensation, with learning as a sidebar to such stimulation. Where this type of technology is used in education for learning, it can be potentially advantageous. This is largely because the technology can use the same emotions as would be used in real-world learning, by engaging these emotions in online contexts. This can also be disadvantageous in some situations, since the corresponding memories, actions, and thoughts may not lead to the learning expected, and there may be a distancing, in effect, from the natural environment context in such online environmental interactions (e.g., see discussion in Picard, 2010).

SURVIVING INVOLVES PROBLEM SOLVING

Humans, like many other primates, do not generally live in isolation, but rather in social groups where information about the environment, as knowledge, skills, or experiences, can be learned, stored as memories, and shared (Tomasello, 1999). The human nervous system allows for individual accumulation, or remembering, of large amounts of information from a large variety of environmental connections, including connections with other humans, as well as with nonhuman organisms (e.g., Edelman, 2007). The memories stored as LTM can be classified broadly in terms of declarative systems and nondeclarative systems (e.g., Squire, 1994). Declarative memory, the memory of everyday facts and events, can be divided as semantic memory (facts) and episodic memory (events). Nondeclarative memory, expressed through performance, rather than recollection, as is the case with declarative memory, is an umbrella term for a range of memory abilities that includes acquisition of skills, habits, and conditioned emotional responses (see summary in Howard-Jones, 2008).

Education and teaching are arguably built around conscious rather than implicit or nonconscious learning (e.g., see Schnotz & Kürschner, 2007). In storing memories through conscious learning and subsequent development of LTM, attended input information, held as working memory (or STM), may be processed as working memory and added as knowledge to LTM (e.g., Ericsson & Delaney, 1999; Miller, Galanter, & Pribram, 1960). During such learning, information in LTM may be added to or modified. Attention and working memory can be viewed as a collection of mechanisms that allows the comparison of new sensory information from the environment with memories in LTM and which add information to LTM in a limited way (Postle, 2006). Educators, either deliberately or through a basis in historical practice, manipulate this system to promote conscious learning (Sweller et al., 1998).

Environmental Interaction, Problem Solving, and Education

In biological terms, information storage is generally considered to lie within a centralized nervous system, including memory storage as STM or LTM. This system has a primary function of facilitating survival, including growth and reproduction, through the interaction of new environmental information with information in memory, considered here as problem solving (in the sense of Tonegawa et al., 2003). The term "problem solving" as used here is related to the function of the central nervous system and is not to be confused with the use of the term "problem solving" in the sense, say, of solving a written mathematical problem (e.g., Sweller et al., 1998). Emotion is a central component in problem solving (e.g., Cotterill, 2001; LeDoux, 1996), although the specialization of research in the biological sciences has perhaps limited the elaboration of this view, and it is not explicitly stated as a feature of educational theories (Woolcott, 2013b).

Problem Solving and Technology

In the process of problem solving (in the sense of Tonegawa et al., 2003), the environment, both internal and external to the organism, is thought to be represented as patterns of linked information, or pathways, in the nervous system of the organism (e.g., Edelman, 2007). The interaction of such patterns in STM and LTM allow development of behavioral responses through such fast-acting processes as predictive patterning, as well as through other slower processes (e.g., Bullock, 2002; Calvin, 2004; Cotterill, 2001). The cognitive system that promotes this problem-solving function in invertebrate and vertebrate organisms has been conserved and improved upon within evolutionary mutations and genetic recombination, resulting in the state seen in the modern human cognitive system (Calvin, 1996, 2004; Finlay, Darlington, & Nicastro, 2001).

Memories (as STM or LTM) formed through conscious problem solving, or environmental interaction, and through nonconscious processes, are considered to reside largely within the connections of the network of neurons and related structures linked to and within the brain (e.g., Edelman, 2007; Sporns, 2010). Humans appear to have developed a much greater degree of connectivity or association than other animals (Cotterill, 2001; Finlay et al., 2001). Such connectivity has been utilized in the learning that occurs through social interaction (Godfrey-Smith, 2002), including the structured interactions seen in education (Goswami, 2008), and has had an impact on cultural accumulation and cultural ratcheting in human societies (Woolcott, 2013a). Through cultural accumulation processes, human society has been able to use the rapid environmental assessment and predictive capability or planning seen in the human response to stimulus in problem solving (Calvin, 2002, 2004). The deployment of this capability to environmental manipulation is what is being considered here as technology (e.g., Lane, 2009).

EMBRACING TECHNOLOGY WITHIN A SYSTEMS VIEW

One of the ways to embrace the views described here of emotion and technology, and the link to the processes of learning and problem solving, which together contribute to cultural accumulation, is to consider a human as a single complex system. In such a system, cognition and behavior may be a result of the holistic interaction with environment of the entire system, not just the brain (Bakhurst, 2008; Squire & Kandel, 2008). In a biological sense, emotion and technology may rely on system connectivity, related learning, problem solving, and accumulation. An example of this connectivity would be the interaction of a centralized nervous system. This system interacts with a muscular system where these and other system components act together as an operational system directing survival-oriented activities associated with interaction and problem solving in a given environment (Cotterill, 2001; Sylwester, 1995).

This type of connectivity outlined above may also operate within component systems, such as the nervous system itself, where the connectivity of neurons in assemblies or networks is built from intrinsic neuronal networks

(Cotterill, 2001; Edelman, 2007; Llinás, 2001). This would include networks associated with drives and emotions (e.g., Damasio, 1999; LeDoux, 1996; Panksepp, 1998), even though these may not be considered as cognitive in some studies (e.g., see discussion in Patten, 2011). Such neural connectivity may be associated with features as motivation and reward (e.g., Murayama, Matsumoto, Izuma, & Matsumoto, 2010).

Holistic Interactions and the Human System

Some researchers consider that connections within learning and memory systems are relational and dynamically link individuals with the environment in a complex way. Network theory (a modern development associated with graph theory) and complexity theory have been used to investigate such connectivity and have been applied in recent times to educational theory (e.g., Davis, Sumara, & Luce-Kapler, 2008; Kop & Hill, 2008), as well as to teaching practices (e.g., Siemens, 2008) and educational leadership (e.g., Morrison, 2008). Such connectivity suggests that it may be useful to consider cognitive models that provide support for the treatment of individuals as learning systems that are adaptive and self-organizing, as studies in complexity theory suggest (Davis et al., 2008). Utilizing such models in an educational context may facilitate the examination of technology using concepts based upon human connectivity with environment. This may be done by examining networks and complex systems, versus linear systems, in exploring the relationship of technology to the subject content of courses in schools (Woolcott, 2013b).

Consideration of complex systems and networks may be extremely useful in reviewing the boundaries between technology and other learning domains, since all such domains may be linked through networks based upon remembered experiences of the physical environment (e.g., see discussion in Lakoff & Johnson, 1999). Some experienced educators with scientific research backgrounds are considering such connectivity in applying broader views to studies in education, including the use of generalist cognitive models (e.g., Lucas, 2005; Woolcott, 2011). Such models may also offer placement of educational concepts, such as emotion and technology, learning and problem solving, in a broader science-based framework that has relevance to evolutionary considerations of human environmental interaction (e.g., Squire & Kandel, 2008; Thelen & Smith, 1994; Woolcott, 2013a). Such models and frameworks may enable a broad view that embraces educational concepts across educational curricula, as well as including technology culture; this offers a way to integrate those concepts scientifically.

Some of these generalist models, or frameworks, are based upon embodiment and affective neuroscience, as well as in a new reconceptualization of information processing.

Embodiment and Emotion

One of the generalist cognitive models that has been well researched in integrative biology and that may be most easily understood when applied to education and teaching is related to the viewpoint of embodiment (Lakoff & Johnson, 1999). Embodiment, from this viewpoint, refers to the connection of abstract memories to motor scenarios, where conceptual knowledge is considered to develop through bodily experiences. Teachers of subjects based upon physical movement, such as physical education and the visual arts, may see this as a given, but this type of connectivity, which ties the human body to its environment through learning, has been applied more widely only recently in education through the use of embodied metaphors in mathematics (e.g., Mowat & Davis, 2010).

There is some disagreement over the degree to which learning is governed by either embodiment or intrinsic networks (Edelman, 2007). Despite this, embodiment broadly describes what teachers may refer to as learning development that moves from concrete to abstract, or content to process (Bruner, 1964), but also the implication that development is not linear and that complex networks of knowledge, skills, and experiences may be involved (Khattar, 2010). Emotional interactions are an integral part of such complex networks, since they are involved in all aspects of learning and memory (LeDoux, 1996). On arguments presented above, technology may also be involved, because the concrete and abstract learning development referred to above involves environmental interactions, which may be environmental manipulation. Embodiment, in particular, may embrace environmental manipulation as a basis for some of the information stored in LTM.

Several cognitive models, largely developed through studies in affective neuroscience, tie emotions closely to formation and modification of all learning and memory through neuronal pathways. These pathways bias preferentially, either temporarily or permanently, the formation and activation of neuronal assemblies as memories (LeDoux, 1996). These models appear to have close links with concepts of embodiment and with the concept of technology (Woolcott, 2013b), since all appear to relate physiology to neural connectivity as a way of describing the interactions of the entire human system, rather than just the interactions within some of its components.

Some research has applied remote observation of physiological characteristics to the construction of sociometric badges that, among other things, automatically measure individual and collective patterns of behavior and enhance social interactions through feedback (e.g., Olguin et al., 2009).

Reconceptualization of Information Processing

Information processing has been re-examined, based upon a much overlooked description of information as matter and energy (see Bates, 2005). Based upon this conceptualization of information, memory can be described in terms of the overarching range of possibilities or potentialities of any matter and energy within any described spatial entity. Learning can be described as any change to memory that results from input or output of information (e.g., Woolcott, 2011, 2013a). In organisms such as humans, learning may therefore be described in terms of the process of change in connectivity. This would include changes in number, strength, and type of connections, for example, within and between the structures representing the pathway between an environmental signal and an organismal response. On this basis also, the number, strength, and type of such connections may be described as memory.

Within this information framework, the nervous system can be described as a discrete component system that interacts with the entire system and the environment, in processes that are conventionally termed learning and memory. The nervous system, as a component system, includes subcomponent systems that can be related to emotion. The subcomponents of the nervous system act together as an adaptive and self-organizing system (e.g., Sporns, 2010), as does the entire system (e.g., Squire & Kandel, 2008), in interactions with the environment. Technology as environmental manipulation is in many ways a product of such system interaction. This system-wide view indicates that the nervous system does not act alone, and is always interacting with other internal systems, such as the circulatory and immune systems, as well as with the external environment (e.g., Thelen & Smith, 1994).

This informational framework may be useful in examining the links between science-based approaches to learning and memory, such as embodiment and affective neuroscience, as well as concepts such as technology (where these are described in scientific terms). It may be problematic, however, in that some descriptions of information have arisen partly from philosophies that see information, and in particular the cognitive processes, that deal with information, as not having chemico-energetic, that is, matter or energy involvement (e.g., see discussion in Bakhurst, 2008; Godfrey-Smith, 2007). Additionally, there is a long history of computational and probabilistic views of information processing being applied in education, rather than non-chemico-energetic views (Lachman et al., 1979; Miller, 2003).

Based upon the ideas above, all accumulated culture may be viewed from within the context of human system interaction with the environment, including the non-human world. This context may offer a way of resolving technology within the context of modern curricula, since the generalist models that describe human interaction may also incorporate a uniform and scientific description of concepts, such as learning and memory that apply across accumulated culture and to the description of technology. The reconceptualization of information processing outlined above suggests that informational connectivity between each individual and his environment is central to learning and memory processes. It further suggests that the transmission of matter and energy as information into and/or out of the system may be contributing to any potential change or processing of information over any given time interval.

In considering learning, emotion, and technology in education, individual informational connectivity may be particularly important. This is the case, as all three are related to the input and output of information processing as gaged by observed or reported changes in an individual's memory. Such a generalist view, in fact, may also provide a wider context for studies of learning and memory. This is because such system-wide processes, from which technology culture may have accumulated, may facilitate the development of educational theories and practices that embrace modern scientific empiricism.

CONCLUSION—WHAT THIS MEANS FOR EDUCATION

For each human individual, education involves learning that leads to the formation of memories, and some of that learning is based upon conscious interaction with new environmental input through the process of problem solving. Additionally, some of that learning involves interactions within the human system, such as interactions between the nervous and muscular systems. The key focus of educational institutions is in teaching individuals to consciously control the processes involved in optimizing the use of the subsystems of working memory and attention, along with related inhibitory processes. This control of processes should be well learned and automatic when applied to learning tasks in the classroom, such that learned information becomes, as shared memories, part of accumulated culture (e.g., Sweller et al., 1998; Woolcott, 2013a, 2013b). An important part of this process is in conscious control of cognitive aspects related to emotion, particularly in social contexts where information is being shared between individuals as part of cultural accumulation processes, but also in awareness of the role of emotion and self-regulation of learning (e.g., Posner, Rothbart, & Tang, 2013; Rothbart, 2011).

Technology, considered in terms of environmental manipulation, has always been a major component of cultural accumulation. The broad view of technology may be confounded in modern educational contexts by a narrower view of technology as tools, in particular of technology as electronic media. Emotion has arguably always been a component of learning, and memory, and resultant cultural accumulation. The role of emotion may also be confounded by the range of views of what constitutes emotion and also by the confusion in differentiating cognition and emotion within learning (e.g., Patten, 2011). Studies have tried to illuminate both the broad view of technology (e.g., Kruse, 2013; Lane, 2009) and a more rigorous treatment of emotion (e.g., Damasio, 2003; LeDoux, 1996; Panksepp, 1998). As a result, both technology and emotion are being reconsidered in some modern educational contexts, both in relation to each other and in relation to a broad systems view of human environmental interaction (Woolcott, 2013a, 2013b).

Every interaction with the environment that each individual makes in negotiation of their world can be viewed as a matter and energy interaction of the human considered as a system (Woolcott, 2011, 2013a). Human system-wide interactions may lead to storage as memories of some aspects of these interactions, where all such "learning" interactions may be influenced in some way by systems that engage emotions and drives and that may regulate other system interactions. Human civilization has benefited from such interactions, largely because resultant stored memories can be shared across society and passed from generation to generation as accumulated culture, such that it increases overall across a society, through the process of cultural ratcheting (Boesch & Tomasello, 1998; Tomasello, 1999). Technology should be seen as new knowledge, skills, and experiences, or culture, added to the human system. Technology may also be referred to in terms of component systems, including systems related to emotion, and systems related to problem solving (in the sense of Tonegawa et al., 2003), and the development of LTM (e.g., Cotterill, 2001).

The development of technology may benefit from consideration of both system and subsystem input and output that is involved, not just in individual learning and memory, but also in cultural accumulation. In an educational context, this may expand the treatment of technology in terms of environmental manipulation, since the exploration of technology will include not just tools and external information storage, but also systems and subsystems involved in learning. Emotional subsystems, for example, may become more of a focus for technology development, as is already being seen in some studies (e.g., Olguin et al., 2009; Picard, 2010). A major point of discussion relates to whether some technology is related more to learning or sensation, and a systems view might clarify which subsystems are interacting and whether any learning is contributing to cultural accumulation (e.g., see Greenfield & Bell, 2010; Woolcott, 2013a, 2013b).

Technology, like other culture derived from learning, needs to be considered in a context of value to the society in which it is being accumulated. It is important in modern education to maintain the connectedness of learning to environmental interaction and to develop teaching that is based upon a good grasp of operation of the human system. In this way, technology may become more fully integrated as a component of a human cultural accumulation that is based upon the negotiation of the environment. This negotiation also involves social interactions and is influenced by internal system operation, including emotions and drives.

REFERENCES

Bakhurst, D. (2008). Minds, brains and education. *Journal of Philosophy of Education, 42*(3–4), 415–432.
Baron-Cohen, S., Golan, O., & Ashwin, E. (2009). Can emotion recognition be taught to children with autism spectrum conditions? *Philosophical Transactions of the Royal Society of London B, 364,* 3567–3574.
Bates, M. J. (2005). Information and knowledge: An evolutionary framework for information science. *Information Research, 10*(4), 239. Retrieved from, http://InformationR.net/ir/10-4/paper239.html.
Blakemore, S. J., & Frith, U. (2000). *The implications of recent developments in neuroscience for research on teaching and learning.* London: Institute of Cognitive Neuroscience.
Boesch, C., & Tomasello, M. (1998). Chimpanzee and human cultures. *Current Anthropology, 39*(5), 591–614.
Brooks, D. W., & Shell, D. F. (2006). Working memory, motivation, and teacher-initiated learning. *Journal of Science Education and Technology, 15*(1), 17–30.
Bruner, J. S. (1964). *Towards a theory of instruction.* Cambridge, MA: Harvard University Press.
Brynjolfsson, E., & McAfee, A. (2012). *Race against the machine: How the digital revolution is accelerating innovation, driving productivity, and irreversibly transforming employment and the economy.* Lexington, MA: Digital Frontier Press.

Bullock, T. H. (2002). Biology of brain waves: Natural history and evolution of an information-rich sign of activity. In K. Arikan & N. Moore (Eds.), *Advances in electrophysiology in clinical practice and research* (pp. 1–19). Wheaton, IL: Kjellberg.

Butko, N. J., Fasel, I. R., & Movellan, J. R. (2006). Learning about humans during the first 6 minutes of life. In: *Proceedings of the fifth international conference on development and learning (ICDL06), Indiana, USA.*

Calvin, W. H. (1996). *The cerebral code: Thinking a thought in the mosaics of the mind.* Cambridge, MA: MIT Press.

Calvin, W. H. (2002). *A brain for all seasons: Human evolution and abrupt climate change.* Chicago, IL: University of Chicago Press.

Calvin, W. H. (2004). *A brief history of the mind: From apes to intellect and beyond.* London: Oxford University Press.

Coricelli, G., Dolan, R. J., & Sirigu, A. (2007). Brain, emotion and decision making: The paradigmatic example of regret. *Trends in Cognitive Sciences, 11*(6), 258–265.

Cotterill, R. (2001). Co-operation of the basal ganglia, cerebellum, sensory cerebrum and hippocampus: Possible implications for cognition, consciousness, intelligence and creativity. *Progress in Neurobiology, 64,* 1–33.

Damasio, A. R. (1999). *The feeling of what happens: Body and emotion in the making of consciousness.* London: Heinemann.

Damasio, A. R. (2003). *Looking for Spinoza: Joy, sorrow, and the feeling brain.* New York, NY: Harcourt.

Davis, B., Sumara, D. J., & Luce-Kapler, R. (2008). *Engaging minds: Changing teaching in complex times.* New York & London: Routledge.

Dehaene, S. (2004). Evolution of human cortical circuits for reading and arithmetic: The "neuronal recycling" hypothesis. In S. Dehaene, J.-R. Duhamel, M. D. Hauser, & G. Rizzolatti (Eds.), *From monkey brain to human brain* (pp. 133–158). Cambridge, MA: MIT Press.

Dehaene, S. (2007). A few steps towards a science of mental life. *Mind, Brain, and Education, 1*(1), 28–47.

Edelman, G. M. (2007). *Second nature: Brain science and human knowledge.* London: Yale University Press.

Ericsson, K. A., & Delaney, P. F. (1999). Long-term working memory as an alternative to capacity models of working memory in everyday skilled performance. In A. Miyake & P. Shah (Eds.), *Models of working memory: Mechanisms of active maintenance and executive control* (pp. 257–297). Cambridge, MA: Cambridge University Press.

Finlay, B. L., Darlington, R. B., & Nicastro, N. (2001). Developmental structure in brain evolution. *The Behavioral and Brain Sciences, 24*(2), 263–278. discussion 278–308.

Godfrey-Smith, P. (2002). Environmental complexity and the evolution of cognition. In R. Sternberg & J. Kaufman (Eds.), *The evolution of intelligence* (pp. 233–249). Mahwah, NJ: Lawrence Erlbaum.

Godfrey-Smith, P. (2007). Information in biology. In D. Hull & M. Ruse (Eds.), *The Cambridge companion to the philosophy of biology* (pp. 103–119). New York, NY: Cambridge University Press.

Goswami, U. (2008). *Cognitive development: The learning brain.* Philadelphia, PA: Psychology Press of Taylor and Francis.

Grandin, T., & Johnson, C. (2005). *Animals in translation.* New York, NY: Harcourt Books.

Gray, J. R. (2004). Integration of emotion and cognitive control. *Current Directions in Psychological Science, 13,* 46–48.

Greenfield, S., & Bell, V. (2010). What is the potential impact of technology, such as computer gaming, on the brain? In: *Transcript of the all-party parliamentary group on scientific research in learning and education seminar.* London: House of Lords.

Grillner, S. (2003). The motor infrastructure: From ion channels to neuronal networks. *Nature Reviews. Neuroscience, 4,* 573–586.

Howard-Jones, P. A. (2008). Philosophical challenges for researchers at the interface between neuroscience and education. *Journal of Philosophy of Education, 42*(3-4), 361–380.

Kalyuga, S. (2008). *Managing cognitive load in adaptive multimedia learning.* New York, NY: Information Science Reference. http://dx.doi.org/10.4018/978-1-60566-048-6.

Khattar, R. (2010). Brought-forth possibilities for attentiveness in the mathematics classroom. *Complicity: An International Journal of Complexity and Education, 7*(1), 57–62.

Kop, R., & Hill, A. (2008). Connectivism: Learning theory of the future or vestige of the past? *International Review of Research in Open and Distance Learning, 9*(3), 1–13.

Kruse, J. W. (2013). Implications of the nature of technology for teaching and teacher education. In M. P. Clough, J. K. Olsen, & D. S. Niederhauser (Eds.), *The nature of technology: Implications for learning and teaching* (pp. 345–370). Rotterdam, The Netherlands: Sense.

Lachman, R., Lachman, J. L., & Butterfield, E. C. (1979). *Cognitive psychology and information processing: An introduction.* Hillsdale, NJ: Lawrence Erlbaum.

Lakoff, G., & Johnson, M. (1999). *Metaphors we live by.* New York, NY: Basic Books.

Lane, A. (2009). *World around us—What is technology? [Television broadcast].* UK: BBC. Retrieved from, http://www.open2.net/sciencetechnologynature/worldaroundus/whatistechnology.html.

LeDoux, J. E. (1996). *The emotional brain: The mysterious underpinnings of emotional life.* New York, NY: Touchstone.

Llinás, R. (2001). *I of the vortex: From neurons to self.* Cambridge, MA: MIT Press.

Lucas, C. (2005). Evolving an integral ecology of mind. *Cortex, 41*(5), 709–726.

Mesoudi, A. (2011). Culture and the Darwinian Renaissance in the social sciences and humanities. *Journal of Evolutionary Psychology, 9*(2), 1–16.

Miller, G. A. (2003). The cognitive revolution: A historical perspective. *Trends in Cognitive Sciences, 7*(3), 141–144.

Miller, G. A., Galanter, E., & Pribram, K. H. (1960). *Plans and the structure of behavior.* New York, NY: Henry Holt & Company.

Minsky, M. L. (2006). *The emotion machine: Commonsense thinking, artificial intelligence, and the future of the human mind.* New York, NY: Simon & Schuster.

Morrison, K. (2008). Educational philosophy and the challenge of complexity theory. *Educational Philosophy and Theory, 40*(1), 19–34.

Mowat, E., & Davis, B. (2010). Interpreting embodied mathematics using network theory: Implications for mathematics education. *Complicity: An International Journal of Complexity and Education, 7*(1), 1–31.

Murayama, K., Matsumoto, M., Izuma, K., & Matsumoto, K. (2010). Neural basis of the undermining effect of monetary reward on intrinsic motivation. *Proceedings of the National Academy of Sciences of the United States of America, 107*(49), 20911–20916.

Olguin, D., Gloor, P. A., & Pentland, A. (2009). Capturing individual and group behavior with wearable sensors. In: *AAAI spring symposium on human behavior modeling, Stanford, CA, March,* Stanford, CA: AAAI.

Panksepp, J. (1998). *Affective neuroscience: The foundations of human and animal emotions.* New York, NY: Oxford University Press.

Parker, J. D. A., Saklofske, D. H., Wood, L. M., & Collin, T. (2009). The role of emotional intelligence in education. In J. D. A. Parker, D. H. Saklofske, & C. Stough (Eds.), *Assessing emotional intelligence: Theory, research and applications, Plenum series on human exceptionality, Part 3* (pp. 239–255). Dordrecht, The Netherlands: Springer.

Patten, K. E. (2011). The somatic appraisal model of affect: Paradigm for educational neuroscience and neuropedagogy. *Educational Philosophy and Theory, 43*(1), 88–97.

Phelps, E. A., & LeDoux, J. E. (2005). Contributions of the amygdala to emotion processing: From animal models to human behavior. *Neuron, 48,* 175–187.

Picard, R. W. (2010). Emotion research by the people, for the people. *Emotion Review, 2,* 250–254. http://dx.doi.org/10.1177/1754073910364256.

Pirsig, R. M. (1974). *Zen and the art of motorcycle maintenance: An inquiry into values*. London: Random House.

Posner, M. I., Rothbart, M. K., & Tang, Y. (2013). Developing self-regulation in early childhood. *Trends in Neuroscience and Education*, 2(3), 107–110. http://dx.doi.org/10.1016/j.tine.2013.09.001i.

Postle, B. R. (2006). Working memory as an emergent property of the mind and brain. *Neuroscience*, 139, 23–38.

Rothbart, M. K. (2011). *Becoming who we are: Temperament, personality and development*. New York, NY: Guilford Press.

Schmandt-Besserat, D. (1996). *How writing came about*. Austin, TX: University of Texas Press.

Schnotz, W., & Kürschner, C. (2007). A reconsideration of cognitive load theory. *Educational Psychology Review*, 19, 469–508.

Shell, D. F., Brooks, D. W., Trainin, G., Wilson, K. M., Kauffman, D. F., & Herr, L. M. (2010). *The unified learning model: How motivational, cognitive, and neurobiological sciences inform best teaching practices*. Dordrecht, The Netherlands: Springer.

Siemens, G. (2008). *Connectivism: A learning theory for today's learner*. Retrieved from, http://www.connectivism.ca/about.html.

Sporns, O. (2010). *Networks of the brain*. Cambridge, MA: MIT Press.

Squire, L. R. (1994). Declarative and nondeclarative memory: Multiple brain systems supporting learning and memory. In D. L. Schacter & E. Tulving (Eds.), *Memory systems* (pp. 203–231). Cambridge, MA: MIT Press.

Squire, L. R., & Kandel, E. R. (2008). *Memory: From mind to molecules* (2nd ed.). Greenwood Village, CO: Roberts & Company.

Sweller, J., & Mann, L. (2011). The psychology of creativity and its educational consequences. In L. Mann & J. Chan (Eds.), *Creativity and innovation in business and beyond: Social science perspectives and policy implications* (pp. 223–238). New York, NY: Routledge.

Sweller, J., van Merriënboer, J., & Paas, F. (1998). Cognitive architecture and instructional design. *Educational Psychology Review*, 10, 251–296.

Sylwester, R. (1995). *A celebration of neurons: An educator's guide to the human brain*. Alexandria, VA: Association for Supervision and Curriculum Development.

Thelen, E., & Smith, L. B. (1994). *A dynamic systems approach to the development of cognition and action*. Cambridge, MA: MIT Press.

Tomasello, M. (1999). *The cultural origins of human cognition*. Cambridge, MA: Harvard University Press.

Tonegawa, S., Nakazawa, K., & Wilson, M. A. (2003). Genetic neuroscience of mammalian learning and memory. *Philosophical Transactions of the Royal Society of London B*, 358, 787–795.

Toronchuk, J. A., & Ellis, G. F. R. (2012). Affective neuronal selection: The nature of the primordial emotion systems. *Frontiers in Psychology*, 3, 589.

Turchin, V. F. (1977). *The phenomenon of science*. New York, NY: Columbia University Press.

van Merriënboer, J. J. G., & Sluijsmans, D. M. A. (2010). Toward a synthesis of cognitive load theory, four-component instructional design, and self-directed learning. *Educational Psychology Review*, 21(1), 55–66.

Westwell, M. (2008). Mind over matter: The science of learning when teaching matters. Seminar at the University of New South Wales, August 2008, organized by Education.au, Australia. Podcast available from: http://educationau.edu.au/jahia/Jahia/home/mind_over_matter.

Woolcott, G. (2011). A broad view of education and teaching based in educational neuroscience. *International Journal for Cross-Disciplinary Subjects in Education, Special Issue*, 1(1), 601–606.

Woolcott, G. (2013a). Giftedness as cultural accumulation: An information processing perspective. *High Ability Studies*, 24(2), 153–170.

Woolcott, G. (2013b). Technology and education: A broad perspective. In: *Proceedings of the annual conference of the Australian association for research in education, Adelaide, Australia, 1-5 December*, Adelaide: AARE.

CHAPTER 13

Empathy, Emotion, Technology, and Learning

Bridget Cooper
University of Sunderland, Sunderland, UK

INTRODUCTION

This chapter considers research evidence from an in-depth study in empathy in learning relationships between teachers and students in England and how this relates to emotion, learning, and technology. The research is significant because the findings apply generically from 3 to 18 year olds, and although technology changes rapidly, the need for empathic interaction in the learning process remains constant. Empathy is a highly complex phenomenon, which appears in different degrees of profundity in different individuals and contexts and has been widely researched alongside concepts of emotional intelligence in recent years, through a range of disciplines and methodologies. Empathy is a crucial feature of human interaction in society and it facilitates understanding and communication between people, through both verbal and non-verbal interaction, and combines both affective and cognitive understanding, which are continually interrelated. At its most profound level, empathy has strong moral effects and a transformative impact on learning and development. In this chapter, it is argued that technology, given its increasingly central role in communication and learning, can both support and reduce the development of empathy between people. Knowing when, why, and how this occurs is crucial to the successful design and deployment of technology for learning.

The research study in this chapter gathered exceptionally rich data from teachers, students, and classrooms. The results reveal how educators can build high-quality relationships and transform learning through making deep, emotional connections with students. The importance of empathy and emotion in learning will be considered in relation to both the positive and negative effects of current technology, culminating in broad guidelines for the use of technology in learning and interaction.

Emotions, Technology, and Learning
http://dx.doi.org/10.1016/B978-0-12-800649-8.00011-0
265

After raising some initial questions, a range of literature involving learning processes and technology will be considered. Subsequently, features of fundamental and profound empathy in learning relationships will be examined and how technology can support or constrain their development (Cooper, 2011a, 2011b). The hyperbole and excitement around technology frequently lacks criticality. Potential effects of technology on interaction are revealed in the narrative account of an incident I observed recently when I visited my doctor, where three different types of technology intervened in moments of more conventional human interaction.

Reflecting on my technology experience:

I watched a mother and child arrive in the waiting room for doctor's appointments. The mother was interacting with the child in a very caring way, smiling, making eye contact, encouraging him to speak and interact. On arrival, each patient registers via a touch screen, so that receptionists can work uninterrupted. Incoming patients seemed to be happy with this. The mother and child sat down and waited to be called into the doctor's room by a large black computer screen, high up on a wall, which had rolling red messages moving across it. When a patient was invited to enter the doctor's room, the screen beeped to attract attention and printed the patient's name.

After a few moments, the mother took her internet-connected phone from her pocket. She became immediately engaged and fixated on the screen, immersed in the engaging nature of technology and the instant and varied interaction it provides. It was clearly absorbing, but sadly more engaging than her son. He was about three years old and was learning to master language and to understand the world around him; He became intrigued by the black screen near the ceiling. Suddenly it beeped and invited another patient into the doctor's room. 'Is it vat? Is it vat what beeped?' he asked his mother. Her eyes were focused on her phone. She said nothing. 'Is it vat? Is it vat what beeped?' he said again, looking towards his mother and back to the screen. Still there was no reply, not even an upward glance to give a nod of affirmation, nothing to acknowledge his question. Having seen their pleasant interactions when they arrived, I felt sure she would answer him but she did not. He asked about ten times, raising his voice and changing his sentence and jumping around to attract her attention but received no response. She continued to fixate totally on her phone. Occasionally her body twitched when he spoke, like an involuntarily response to a sound during sleep. Eventually the child's name appeared on the screen. The mother put her phone away, took his hand and they entered the doctor's room.

Technology increasingly pervades most of our human interactions and deep consideration is required to understand what is gained and lost in human interaction and learning in every instance. In the scenario above, the technology used to register arrival and entry into specific doctors' rooms can save time and money and aid more routine tasks. Doctors and receptionists have no need to divert from other tasks to register new arrivals but can concentrate on what may be perceived as more important or complex tasks. Patients also perhaps acquire a sense of satisfaction at entering their own data and responding successfully to the requests on the interactive touch screens.

However, because the receptionists do not interact with arriving patients on a more personal basis, opportunities are lost for creating more humane relationships. Casual, off-task conversation can build positive relationships and community (Klein, 1987), whereas relationships and a sense of community can be destroyed by the "I-it relationship," when people are reduced to the status of objects (Clark, 1996). Positive relationships are central to successful human interaction and learning. Knowing a person enables better quality interaction to take place. In the example above, patients arrive without any human acknowledgement and no-one welcomes them with human eye-contact or a simple smile or "hello," which are fundamentals of human interaction and central to building empathy, emotional connections, and relationships. Patients respond to the logic of the computer screens rather than human beings. This may seem efficient initially, but the human relationships may not be created, which may be necessary later for more complex interactions. Moreover, everyone in the doctor's waiting room watches the screen, or they will miss their turn. This may also deter or interrupt other casual conversations with fellow patients in the room.

As for the mother, the issue of mobile phones interrupting face-to-face interaction is widespread and this example shows the engaging power of the technology. However, the phone interaction conflicts with an opportunity for interaction with her son. Here, the mother's total engagement with technology seemed particularly problematic and could have negative consequences for the child's language, learning, and sense of self-worth. Does a child feel frustrated or even worthless if they ask a question 10 times with no response from their closest relative? Is their curiosity quashed or do they become angry and demand attention? What effect can these increasingly pervasive interactions with technology, in different times and places, then have on relationships and learning?

LEARNING AND TECHNOLOGY

Issues of self-worth, valuing, and formative feedback are central to our learning. Dialog is at the heart of learning (Vygotsky, 1978, 1986) and so is non-verbal feedback and human relationships (Cooper, 2011a). Responsiveness in interaction plays a key part in the development of self and learning. Of course, people require some personal, quiet time. Parents, particularly, require space for themselves when bringing up young children, but perhaps there are times and places for that. Mobile and pervasive technology has changed the times, the places, and the way that humans interact; questions need asking continually—when and where and how is technology working for the better? What improves and what problems are created? The aim for technology should be to improve learning and society, not to damage it. Technology can be life-affirming and liberating, giving access to global knowledge and enabling increasingly high quality communication and interaction with people and organizations, in both formal and informal ways. Conversely, technology can be intrusive, frustrating, and unreasonably demanding of both time and money. Increasingly, technology intervenes at the very moment of human interaction in a million ways. Good hardware and software can enable and encourage interaction and learning and poorer software can simply be a hindrance (Cooper, 2006). Increasingly, mobile and pervasive technology impacts on face-to-face interactions. Well-informed and ethical decisions need to be made at all levels of technological implementation and usage, which includes designers, commercial companies, educationalists, and individual users, as to the appropriateness of the technology, and the affordances and drawbacks in different contexts. If computers are highly engaging for all manner of interactions and learning, the negative effects they create may be subtle or hidden and need meticulous consideration.

Immediate responses from software applications or people down the line can provide adults with "intensive interaction" (Hewett & Nind, 1998). This can build a sense of self-worth and importance. If people are always communicating and responding, they need never feel alone or unimportant. However, by engaging in online interactions, they may disengage from face-to-face interactions with more immediate others, as in the example above, and these issues need careful thought, knowledge, and research and significantly an understanding of how human learning happens.

Interactive technology can offer us one-to-one support and can respond rapidly to our every keystroke and increasingly our voice or other sensual commands and signals. Technology now offers dynamic multimodal interaction. Pictures, color, sound, music, animation, and individual responsiveness and feedback can combine in many forms to make learning and interaction more diverse, enjoyable, accessible, and rapid.

Multisensory learning is very powerful in raising achievement. People can find pleasure and gain esteem from intensive interaction with technology and in some situations, technology facilitates greater human interaction. Students can experience constant feedback and response from a computer, which focus their mind on the activity, builds their sense of self, and gives a sense of value. Such interaction and learning can expand and satisfy the brain and the senses.

HOW LEARNING HAPPENS AND ITS RELATIONSHIP TO EMPATHY

Learning is an everyday process for human beings from birth to death. According to Greer (2010), most mothers (not all) become natural teachers and the intensely close contact with their infants leads them to know them intimately and to teach contingently to meet their learning needs. Increasingly, fathers or other carers take the role of the significant other and have to respond similarly to children's needs. Young babies learn faster within caring families than at any other time, during those nurturing, one-to-one relationships, where one-to-one time, love, and opportunities for constant verbal and non-verbal interaction feed learning and create "joint involvement episodes" (Anning & Edwards, 1999, p. 66) or intensive interaction (Hewett & Nind, 1998). This warm, close human interaction develops profound empathy and love between parents and children. They develop a strong sense of each other's feeling and thinking, beginning with close non-verbal interaction through cuddling, feeding, and playing, gradually introducing and sharing language through simple words, nursery rhymes, and lullabies. Both affective and cognitive development is intertwined. Children's brains grow when they feel cared for, according to Winkley (1996). Those unfortunate enough to lose their key carer after this intense interaction and emotional bonding can be severely damaged psychologically (Bowlby, 1951; Docker-Drysdale, 1990) and can struggle to develop and learn. Similarly, those who never receive personal nurturing because of absent or negligent parents may never be loved and responded to, and so never learn to love and respond, with damaging personal and societal consequences.

One-to-one intensive interaction similar to that experienced in infancy remains important throughout children's lives at home and school and for individuals generally throughout various educational phases, but is especially crucial for children with particular needs. "Intensive interaction" (Hewett & Nind, 1998) is a way of developing children with special educational needs and has also been referred to as "augmented mothering" (Ephraim, 1986) echoing the intense interaction of infancy. The high degree of attention, interaction, and response improves neural connections rapidly building trust, confidence, and self-esteem. In such relationships, emotional resilience is built, which Reay (2000) refers to as "emotional capital", describing it as,

> the stock of emotional resources built up over time within families and which children could draw upon (p. 572).

Neuroscience echoes psychology in its understanding of the significance of emotion to human interaction, development, and learning. Damasio (1999, 2003) argues that each interaction changes us and our understanding in an ongoing dynamic narrative. If the interaction is positive, humans are motivated to interact more, if not, they withdraw to a more defensive and less exploratory mode. The support of learning therefore requires the creation of positive, interactive environments. This understanding has been long-established in the literature of teaching and learning (Rowe, Wilkin, & Wilson, 2012).

Joy and pleasure support engagement and interaction, but they can also be addictive. When pleasure is gained at someone else's expense, or gratifies immediately at the expense of later benefits, then moral decisions have to be made. Who is the beneficiary of this technological interaction and who is disadvantaged by it and when? Technologists and educationalists need to consider deeply what impact pervasive technology has and hidden issues such as what it hinders and who it excludes, for example, in terms of age, gender (Gillard, Howcroft, Mitev, & Richardson, 2008) class, or the digital divide (Rudd, 2001). Mobile technology can exclude alternative face-to-face interactions and what are implications does this have in different contexts?

Education systems have always been problematic for learning and classic literature points out the disadvantages of large classes and normative assessment and testing, which can diminish self-esteem and restrict learning due to the controlling, depersonalized, and demoralizing nature of some students' experiences (Foucault, 1977; Freire, 1970; Goffman, 1961; Hargreaves, 1982; Illich, 1971). Similarly Noguera (2007) compared some schools in the United States with prisons, where the monitoring, surveillance, and searching of young people dominates and dehumanizes school life. However, technology has often enabled one-to-one support, which can raise self-esteem and boost confidence. Technology can facilitate the personalization of learning (Rudd, 2009) and indeed is excellent for personal research and its interactive nature excellent for engagement and motivation. Technology can support differentiation, both in terms of content and process. For example, it provides excellent and varied tools for literacy development through the use of music, photography, and film and animation. Pictures, sound, and knowledge from around the world pour into classrooms and homes. For early readers or children with special needs, technology can guide, repeat sounds and sentences combined with pictures, and tactile experience to maximize multisensory learning, offering intense interaction at an appropriate level and feedback, where none would have been available from the one teacher busily managing a large class. Technology can provide the timely, step-by-step reinforcement, which Skinner (1954) explained is simply not available from teachers in large classes. Technology can support early imagination, self-expression and creativity, and higher order skills with multimedia software, enabling children to bypass the often frustrating bottleneck of traditional writing (Cooper & Brna, 2002).

Routine and mechanical aspects of learning can be enlivened through games and music to create enjoyment, and technology can massively improve presentation skills, having much wider impacts than on the writing itself. For example, a child whose writing is illegible often feels a failure and gives up. They learn to despise a school system which relies on writing ability for achievement across the curriculum, feeling continually inadequate. Even a caring teacher unable to read a student's work can struggle to give positive feedback. The child may be dismissed by peers who may reject them academically and socially. Parents can also become frustrated and add to negative feedback, even if it is unconscious and non-verbal, and children are extremely alert to this (Cooper, 2011a). Reduced self-esteem and learning can spiral downwards. However, if a computer program can improve presentation and enable a student to produce legible text, they can then receive praise and constructive feedback from the teacher, which reverses the process. This can trigger a transformation in their ability to learn, creating a positive cycle in which peers also value them, giving the child higher social and academic status and affirmation. Communication with other staff or the head teacher can enhance the child's reputation and positive feedback grows in a wider, affirming circle. Parents may be delighted to see the development and the cycle of positivity increases further. In this way, more than just enabling learning, technology can act as a catalyst to enhance human relationships, which is much more important to learning than most research ever admits. Research frequently neglects the role of human relationships in learning and the impact that innovation has on those relationships. Here is a major area for research and is why technology must address its impact on relationships in learning, whether positive or negative.

Technology can also be very frustrating and disruptive to human interaction and learning. Faulty or ill-designed software and hardware or poor quality on-line systems, predominantly based around text, for example, without the sophistication and emotional nuances of multisensory face-to-face interaction, can hinder rather than support interaction and learning.

Human beings, although expensive in the learning process, can have a transformative effect. They love other people for their own sake, and treasure their development, not for their own status or profit but because they are developing human beings. Macmurray (1935) considers the central nature of emotion and sensitive awareness in human interaction and criticizes the use of the senses for merely intellectual or functional purposes. He argues the senses should be a source of joy in the world beyond the self, whereas the intellect is of a lower level and is self-centered. "Intellectual awareness is egocentric. It uses the senses as its instrument. But the direct sensual awareness has its center in the world outside, in the thing that is sensed and loved for its own sake" (Macmurray, 1935, p. 43). Hay (1997) also discusses heightened awareness and sensitivity, suggesting it is a physical state, which relates closely to Damasio's descriptions (Damasio, 1999, 2003) of a neurobiological state or process which enables an openness to others or an openness to the environment which is a precursor to learning. Noddings (1986) calls this way of being "receptivity" and Watson and Ashton (1995) call it "openness." If technology encourages selfishness and restricts openness and awareness of others because it is so mentally engaging, immediate positive effects may be negated by longer-term negative effects. A balance must be sought between developing individual and social beings.

For students struggling to learn in large classes and within a normative curriculum, intensive one-to-one support akin to that given in infancy is a powerful approach and has proven successful in a variety of areas, for example, Reading Recovery (US Dept. of Education, 2007). Parents with sufficient resources pay for one-to-one tuition in many subjects from music to advanced math. The Oxbridge one-to-one tutorial is considered the height of university education, based on the tutor's opportunity to know, assess, and scaffold their student most precisely (Gibbs & Simpson, 2004).

Intensive learning and emotional capital can therefore be enhanced by other people than families, by other carers, wider relatives, friends, peers, and significant people in children's lives, such as teachers, tutors, social workers, and health workers. However, emotional resilience can also be reduced by human beings, depending on their ability to respond and the time allotted to individual response within the environment in which they interact. Working environments can make a huge difference (Cooper, 2011a). Moreover, if off-task, friendly interaction is reduced to provide more complex on-task interaction for example, something is lost that is quite important for relationship building and emotional resilience. Gentle, introductory, or casual chat can reduce anxiety and tension and open doors for people to ask more difficult and challenging questions. Business-like interactions can be hurried and task-centered, at the expense of personal, caring interaction, such as "How are you?," "How's things," "Are you ok?," which open up interpersonal dialog and learning.

Marx argued that relationships can be destroyed by the "cash nexus" (Marx & Engels, 1888). When relationships are based on monetary exchange, the intrinsic value of others can be forgotten, a point recently reinforced by Sandel (2009). In a sense, the technology at the doctors represents the "cash nexus" but indirectly. Health services try to save money, so a human face and the complex humanity behind that face becomes a computer screen. This favors machine over human relationships and everyone needs to be keenly aware of its negative effects. Recently, American college students showed 40% less empathy on the same test than their counterparts 30-40 years ago (Konrath, O'Brien, & Hsing, 2010) which is worrying. Research is clearly needed into this issue. A depersonalized education system can certainly constrain empathy (Cooper, 2011a, 2011b), but these reductions may be to do with many factors, the breakdown of families, the fragmentation of communities and society, television or lack of family, and communal social activity. They may also be linked to the increase in pervasive technology, which replaces and disrupts more important human interaction.

The findings discussed below confirm that positive emotion and empathy generated through human relationships are central to the learning process and needs recognizing whenever the relationship between technology and learning is considered. Technology is likely to be most effective in supporting learning, where it can support a positive climate, empathy, and human relationships. Understanding in depth how empathy works in relationships should support understanding of how technology can or cannot assist in learning. The relationship with technology is considered below, after discussing the findings of empathy in teaching and learning.

UNDERSTANDING THE ROLE AND NATURE OF EMPATHY IN TEACHING AND LEARNING

A grounded theory approach to understand how teachers demonstrate empathy and how this impacts on learning was used to analyze the data in this research (Cooper, 2011a). After rigorous analysis of exceptionally rich and saturated data from lengthy interviews with teachers selected for their empathy, and approximately 50 h of observation in their classrooms, three new categories of empathy emerged: fundamental, functional, and profound. A fourth category "feigned empathy" was discussed by teachers in interviews but was not detected in classrooms. The two types particularly useful for individual learning are fundamental and profound empathy, which are discussed in detail below. Functional empathy, by contrast, was an adaptation of empathy used in large classrooms and is less relevant. Neither is feigned empathy relevant here, as it refers to pretend empathy (for details, see Cooper, 2011a). The validity of the data was also confirmed by young children interviewed in the pilot project, who revealed great sensitivity to non-verbal signals and disliked teachers who lacked authenticity, who said one thing but did another, or who said something which was belied by their facial expressions, body language, and voice tone, creating distrust (Cooper, 1997).

Fundamental empathy was described as the empathy required to initiate relationships and which "oils the wheels" of social interaction. Without an open approach, generally demonstrated by positive body language, voice tone, and verbal interaction, relationships and social interaction of any kind can be difficult. Even an exchange at a supermarket checkout can turn sour if suitable responses are not forthcoming from both parties. An introductory smile, given and received genuinely, which acknowledges the other as a fellow human being, enables most interaction to begin smoothly at least. Fundamental empathy requires the characteristics listed below, which can be shown through various means of communication (for further details, see Cooper, 2011a).

CHARACTERISTICS OF FUNDAMENTAL EMPATHY

1. *Initial characteristics*:
   * being accepting and open
   * giving attention
   * listening

* being interested
* taking a positive and affirmative approach
* showing enthusiasm.

2. *Means of communication*:
   * facial expression and interaction
   * gestures, body language, and movement
   * height and physical distance
   * language and tone of voice

Non-verbal interaction conveying emotional information such as eye-contact, voice tone, gesture, facial expression, and physical proximity are very important factors indicating empathy, not unlike the powerful non-verbal interactions required with infants. These teachers were enthusiastic and found positive time and attention for individuals and demonstrated their care by listening and taking an interest.

Teachers have to adapt massively to groups and individuals in different contexts and in the way they demonstrate their empathy. For example, a teacher can become very big and excited and enthusiastic in both voice tone, facial expression, and body language, in order to motivate and communicate with a whole class but equally, can visibly shrink in size and personality, and use a whisper when they address a young or nervous student (Cooper, 2011a). They become experts in reading verbal or non-verbal signals and in reading the moods and emotions of individuals and classes, picking up even slight fluctuations in voice tone, eye contact or body shape, or movement, which denote lack of understanding or concealed anxiety or low mood. Such signals comprise the essential feedback on the human aspects of learning, which enable the teacher to continue or to change course; to have a quiet word; move up a gear or slow the pace down; generate more enthusiasm or stimulate thinking, thus facilitating learning for all the children in their care. Contingent teaching is an enormous and highly skilled task, which improves with experience both of teaching and life in general.

CAN TECHNOLOGY SUPPORT FUNDAMENTAL EMPATHY?

Understanding how emotional bonding, the development of a sense of worth, and empathy, can support human interaction and learning, can also inform us about technological interaction and emotion. High quality technology can mimic some of the characteristics of fundamental empathy and can offer individual support and attention. The multisensory nature of increasingly high quality software and technology has some of the potential for multisensory interaction and responses that good human relationships create. Learning with technology can be highly personalized and responsive within a limited domain. Although the technology itself cannot feel how another human being feels, it does respond to whoever activates it. It can therefore be accepting and open, not judgmental in its responses, which non-empathic humans can also be. When students work on individual computers, the learning is personalized for them. Technology shows attention by responding and appears to be "listening" to what a student inputs. Increasingly, devices can actually "listen" and respond to simple human commands, though this is a developing technology. Of course the computer is not really "interested" but because it responds, it offers students more autonomy and control within the framework of each software application. Some software also responds positively, issuing praise or rewards for tasks completed and using friendly, enthusiastic, animated characters or images and sounds to show appreciation of an individual's efforts. In this way, technology can mimic to some extent some of the characteristics and means of communication of fundamental empathy and help to build esteem, understanding, and achievement. Animated characters use non-verbal and verbal communication, facial expressions, gestures, and body language and respond to students with a positive use of language and tone of voice. High quality technology can equalize traditional power relationships in classrooms, empowering students and helping teachers become facilitators rather than managers and instructors.

However, much software available for learning has limited adaptability, when it comes to emotional responses. Artificial intelligence, for example, can enable some tracking of facial and emotional signals but not in the sophisticated, group, and adaptive way of humans. Even voice recognition software on automated telephone menus, for example, reveals how primitive and annoying supposedly adaptive technology can be to humans needing to interact. In terms of learning and development for highly sensitive and malleable individuals such as children, the utmost sensitivity and an exceptionally responsive nature is required. One could argue that to overuse technology without human interaction to mediate its effects could be very dangerous.

PROFOUND EMPATHY

Over time and with frequency of interaction, fundamental empathy can develop into *profound empathy*. Relationships grow deeper, the quality of interaction and learning improves and the relationship becomes one of care and concern, promoting deeper levels of understanding, greater sharing of knowledge and pleasure in each other's company. In this way, teachers develop a more profound level of empathy and emotional bonding, knowing and understanding the child in every detail and being able to cater even more precisely for their needs. In teaching observations, this level of profound empathy was not seen generally in large classes, except in tiny pockets. Profound empathy was mainly observed in small groups and especially in one-to-one tutoring sessions, where the quality of the teacher/pupil relationship, the intensity of interaction, and the quality of teaching were extremely high. Seven large themes emerged from the data and are listed below. There is an extensive amount of detail on the nature and effects of profound empathy (see Cooper, 2011a). The categories listed below had many complex subthemes, which can only be addressed briefly here.

1. Developing positive emotions and interactions
2. Understanding self, others, and explaining understanding
3. Appreciation of all relationships
4. Breadth and depth of empathy
5. Act and take responsibility
6. Richly adaptive and integrated concept of themselves and others
7. Moral aspects.

The first theme, *Developing positive emotions and interactions*, was seen in interactions between teachers and students, where great pleasure emerged through the use of humor and fun. Students and teacher grew to know and like each other in relationships where time and attention was freely given and where positivity and personal achievement was stressed. Teachers explained in interviews how they knew themselves deeply and had deep knowledge of students both personal and academic, getting inside their thinking and feeling, drawing on all their historic personal experience to understand their pupils, and to explain issues to them. They were deeply aware of the importance of relationships in learning both with students, their peers, other staff, family and community and knew how relationships formed the climate of both the school and home environment, which impacted on learning and self-esteem. These teachers aimed to meet individual needs and knew which students needed more time and effort. They were prepared to work tirelessly with each student to support their development and achievement.

These close relationships led them to adopt a moral approach to their students. They saw themselves as moral models, where morality was developed through an interactive and caring process. This led teachers to care deeply for students, to do their very best for them, to seek solutions to meet their needs, to sacrifice their time and feelings for them, to protect them, to understand them even more deeply, and to have appropriate but increasingly high expectations for them. They understood the importance of the personal to the academic and they held a holistic view of life and teaching and saw part of their role as forming a bridge between their students and others, enabling their own knowledge to be shared for beneficial purposes. These teachers adapted massively to different individuals and environments. They were highly skilled, caring human beings, and excellent teachers.

From these categories, the most obvious way in which technology can support the characteristics of profound empathy therefore is by offering successful one-to-one, personalized attention, and creating positive emotions through the intense engagement of the brain in a multi-modal environment. This can lead to learning and pleasure. Closed software in classrooms can adapt to individual needs on specific topics and open software can support creativity and skills development and communication, therefore showing this first aspect of profound empathy at a superficial, but often useful level. The subthemes of this category are:

- Pleasure, happiness, fun, humor
- Liking, loving, seeing the good
- Mask negative emotions
- Time-givers
- Sole attention
- Physical contact
- Relaxed, comfortable, informal climate.

For example, very positive emotions and interactions can be easily engendered by software which can generate pleasure and excitement for learners through the use of humor and fun, though the computer cannot share the learner's emotions like a human teacher. Programs use songs, rhymes, and rhythm, and multicolored images and animations to generate pleasure, capture attention, and reinforce learning. Game-based learning software works hard, like an empathic teacher, to make learning enjoyable and create moments of laughter and of achievement and of shared positivity through the characters and activities. Software can intrigue and delight, stimulate curiosity, develop thinking, literacy and numeracy, and a wide range of skills in a positive atmosphere. Moreover, computer responses can be rapid and personalized, which is often not possible for teachers in large, busy classrooms. Computers mimic the giving of time and sole attention to learners, create a relaxed and informal climate, and because they cannot recognize negative emotions, they appear to mask them like empathic teachers, thus emphasizing the positive. Although the technology cannot form a deep personal relationship with a child, the child can develop a relationship with the technology and higher quality software can mimic some of the qualities seen in highly empathic teachers.

However, as far as all the other categories of profound empathy are concerned, even the most advanced artificial intelligence still struggles with anything at this level of caring interaction (Cooper, 2003). The complexity involved in human learning and interaction requires massive adaptability and intimate knowledge of both the cognitive and emotional states of individuals and how to respond to them successfully in dynamic, moment by moment interaction. The mental and emotional model of each individual and the response mechanisms required would have to be expansive and developmental and able to adapt to context.

Computers have some limited ability to mimic category two of profound empathy: *understanding self, others, and explaining understanding*. The sub-themes for this are:

- Self-knowledge
- Being me, being human
- Get inside
- Understanding, deeper knowledge
- Explain why.

Applications can be knowledgeable on particular topics, so they appear to have some internal knowledge of self, which is mostly academic, although this only covers the knowledge programmed in. Intelligent programs order and control academic knowledge but struggle with knowledge of learners and humanity, which is hard enough for empathic, probing teachers to discover. Good software is designed for certain types of users and certain types of learning and often have carefully graded steps or challenges, which respond to the level of the user and thus mimic user understanding and responsiveness (a form of scaffolding) taking the user one step at a time to maximize success and minimize failure.

Some software can facilitate deeper levels of understanding by responding to queries and explaining more difficult questions with references to websites. However, this can depend on the learner testing out various queries, rather than as a teacher would, by responding immediately through a range of explanation and questioning and gauging non-verbal signals until they are sure the student fully understands. Hence searches, either Internet-wide or on specific sites or applications, for example, which rely on users framing the question appropriately and getting a useful answer, can be unpredictable, despite the amazing speed of current search engines. More-over, the accuracy of any information found can be questionable, so the life experience and judgment of the knowledgeable expert is often missing in such searches and the responses are standard and not tailored to the individ-ual as a result of their specific knowledge. Technology is not generally able to "get inside" the users head and cannot tailor specific explanations or, for example, adapt to the knowing or blank look given by the learner. Never-theless, Internet-based software can take students beyond the knowledge of any specific classroom teacher and facilitates their ability to seek out knowl-edge for themselves, encourages autonomy and agency, building a powerful sense of achievement, which does not always happen in classrooms when teachers over-control curricular knowledge.

One of the weakest aspects of technology in relation to mimicking pro-found empathy before the advent of social media was in category three: *appreciation of all relationships.*

This encompassed the ability to understand and appreciate the impor-tance of all relationships in an individual's life. Thus, whereas profoundly empathic teachers know the individual personally, their families and peers and their relationships with other teachers and can use this knowledge to support them most appropriately. Learning software cannot attempt do this as the memory of all past interactions and all other students and all their cur-rent and past relationships would have to be stored and drawn upon.

However, social media, for example, does attempt to value and mimic the networks of relationships between people and build communication, though often it bases these networks on limited information and often sends inappropriate requests for friends and other connections. The inaccuracy and inappropriateness of its actions can create negative emotions and reluc-tance of some users to engage. Neither do these networks always relate to learning and often encourage performance rather than authenticity of interaction.

The final three categories, which function at a deeper, more personal and human level, are even harder for technology to mimic, though they may be embedded in the designers thinking or the attitudes and behaviors of people who work around and alongside the technology.

Category four: *breadth and depth of empathy* explains how empathic teachers know individual students deeply but also recognize differences and respond personally and appropriately to all students' needs, however easy or difficult they are to empathize with. Its subcategories are:

- All children
- Children who were easier to empathize with
- Children who were more difficult to empathize with
- Individual
- Meeting needs
- Difference.

Technology often attempts to address "the individual" in that, as a whole, it tries to meet the generic needs of users and cater for individual needs where it can. Personalization and the ability to update dynamically to changing individual requirements is central to this, and though many designers aim for a personalized approach, software cannot always meet all very specific needs and often bases its information on specific categories of user and limited information. In this sense, it often operates at a more functional level of empathy (Cooper, 2011a), targeting certain academic levels or basing its mental model for interaction on a whole age group or stereotypical sub-groups, such as gender, as might a teacher in a large class. Creating an extensive emotional and mental model of every student in software would be a challenging task and perhaps something to be dreamed of by science fiction writers rather than real-world technologists. Here, sophisticated human support around technology in specific contexts becomes vital.

Category five: *act and take responsibility* presents another set of elusive requirements:

- Solution-seeking
- Persistence, self-sacrifice
- Protect
- Perceive more deeply.

Technology is not able to mimic category five, unless it has human beings operating personally behind or alongside it. It cannot take responsibility and find real solutions for real individuals, is not able to sacrifice itself and protect vulnerable individuals personally or understand human learning at the very deepest emotional levels and uncover well-disguised or hidden needs and fears.

Category six: *richly adaptive and integrated concept of themselves and others*

- Adapt to both individual and environment
- High eventual expectations
- Personal, academic link
- Holistic view
- Bridging.

Computers and technology generally struggle to adapt simultaneously to the individual and the environment they find themselves in, which may be peopled with other individuals. However, mobile technology is more adaptable to a greater range of environments and can be used in and can adapt to certain changes in location. Technology can build high expectations through stepped gradation but is impotent in terms of emotional assessment, which empathic teachers become experts at and use to judge the right level for any particular student, so that confidence is built before higher expectations are voiced. The academic level alone is not always enough to provide contingent teaching. Teachers understand the dynamic levels of emotional resilience of students, which tempers their guidance and expectations at different times. Empathic teachers are experts at linking the personal to the academic, i.e. linking students prior or outside interests, and personal circumstances to what is learned in educational institutions. Technology for learning focuses on the academic content. Teachers tend to take a much more holistic view and are constantly developing the whole child, not just one specific area of knowledge. Teachers also see themselves as personal bridges between the student and other staff, parents, students, and the wider world and act as their students' advocates across all relationships and share their growing skills and confidence with others. This builds student self-esteem, enlightening and transforming negative perceptions and relationships into positive ones. However, computers can at times help to build bridges at a lower, more skills-based level and by enabling students to achieve can improve a whole series of relationships, as explained previously.

Perhaps the most difficult category of profound empathy for technology to mimic is category seven: *moral aspects*, which includes subthemes of:

- Conceptions of morality
- Moral, empathic link—an interactive process
- Modeling morality.

Teachers explained their own strong moral positions and the intrinsic link between empathy and morality. As they developed deeper levels of empathy, they constantly modeled morality to their students through their interactions. They envisaged their students' futures and took decisions, which might not produce instant gratification but would have long-term beneficial effects. Technology, without the quality of profound human empathy, could not start to offer a moral model. A mobile phone cannot say "Switch me off and talk to your little boy, he is more important." It would have to be aware of the whole real-world context and have an inbuilt moral imperative and long-term perspective. Catering for individual engagement, technology must necessarily be complimented by an understanding of wider social and emotional needs and relationships. Technology is more likely to work most effectively therefore, when it functions within warm, caring, and collaborative human environments where the crucial profound empathy and moral support of human beings are readily accessible.

Complex moral decisions are currently too challenging for technology to make, but empathic teachers have a strong moral compass, which continually drives their caring nature, attitudes, and actions. Morality, fairness, honesty, and a strong sense of care were all expressed by these teachers and formed a central tenet of their vocation.

BENEFITS OF PROFOUND EMPATHY

In addition to redefining the complexity of empathy, the benefits of empathic relationships were clearly identified in this research, especially in regard to profound empathy. Empathy facilitated talk and communication which supports learning and exchange of personal information, esteem-building, and emotional links which led to friendship. Teachers were able to deeply understand the child's perspective, notice hidden issues which affected learning, and became aware of the significance of empathy to achievement. When, empathy became profound, it built self-esteem and a sense of worth, a sense of security, and trust. Children emulated teacher's behavior, showing greater empathy themselves. Teachers became more knowledgeable about their students and the learning process, both in their teaching and in the wider learning relationships within their department, aiding their own personal and professional development. Moreover, as children emulated the empathy of their role models, the general climate for learning also improved and led to an optimization of learning through high quality assessment both emotional and cognitive and improved teaching methodology. For some students, profoundly empathic relationships were transformative in terms of self-esteem and achievement and impacted strongly on their wider relationships with peers, teachers, and family members.

In order to compensate for the aspects of empathy which technology struggles to mimic, a key strategy is to ensure it is both designed by and used with the support of caring, sentient human beings who will be able to fulfill the more human aspects of empathy and relationships. Learners need to experience a wide range of learning activities, which challenge them in multiple and differing ways, not just through large and small screens. Children and adults need to understand the addictive pleasure, which technology can afford and will need to think deeply about when best to use it or when human interaction is required.

PROBLEMS WITH TECHNOLOGY AND EMOTION

If technology can support positive emotions in many ways, what else does technology lack in relation to affect? Although technology can be a catalyst to improve human relationships and can rapidly engender positive feelings through interesting content and give pleasure and feedback in a multiplicity of multisensory ways, technology can also generate very negative emotion through poor software, hardware or connectivity, which makes the learning and communication harder or more frustrating than it should be. Human beings are exceptionally expert, multisensory communicators, and poor systems and software can frustrate a good communicator, as a speech impediment might (Cooper, 2006). Computers cannot feel like a human, or sense the feelings of others in the complex way that humans do naturally and continually. Mirror neurons in the brain enable humans to mimic the emotional dispositions of people they encounter (Preston & de Waal, 2002). Humans are, for the most part, social beings enjoying each other's company, as do many other mammals. Humor is a key aspect of this social enjoyment and even rats produce what Panksepp (2008) calls "ancestral laughter" when tickled. Technological tools might provoke laughter, but it cannot laugh along with humans or appreciate their jokes.

Even wonderfully designed, software cannot smile like a real person, or hug someone in an affectionate way, or place a hand on their shoulder when reassurance is needed, having known themselves, what it is to find learning difficult or challenging and to have felt frustrated or defeated. Even highly adaptive software is only pretending to know you and knows only a fraction of the whole person and works to its own (pre-coded) agenda for much of the time, mostly following serial pathways, rather than parallel ones. Caring human beings are highly adaptive because they can value and support almost any individual in any context, if they are given enough time, partly because of their own education and training but mostly because they are human too, and were raised to interact with, to value and to respond to other human beings. Of course some people can also be frustrating and confusing and uncaring, and they want to control and dominate, which can destroy self-esteem.

GUIDELINES FOR THE USE AND DESIGN OF LEARNING TECHNOLOGY

Many things can be understood through this discussion of empathy, emotion, learning, and technology. First, technology designed for learning requires empathetic design with an understanding of how learning happens. It is insufficient for the mechanics of software to work, the question is: "Can learning, interaction and relationships develop effectively through or around this technology, with these students and tutors, in this topic area, in this unique environment?" All participants need increased understanding of how human learning and interaction work and need to continually ask whether this technology will enhance higher levels of human interaction and learning. Learning contexts, tutors, and students are very unique and this affects how learning can happen. If design occurs with human beings in mind in all their cognitive and affective complexity, there is more chance of learning happening than if design is concerned with efficiency, control, or profit. Learning technologists also need to understand that technology is only as good as the education of tutors who use it, the conditions they have to work in, and the number of students they teach. Those complex decisions of when, where, and how to use technology are becoming increasingly complex, as technology and society evolve. The emotional climate created by such complexity and influenced by leaders and policy in society and education is particularly significant. New technology needs careful thought and introduction and human support and moral decision-making if it is to be really useful. Mere installation does not ensure it is used to full potential and, quite frequently, it is not used successfully at all. Even the most wonderful technology can be badly used through ill-planned introduction and lack of support to assuage anxiety, without time for experimentation. If technology is carefully designed to create an empathetic learning ambience with affordances, which permit sensual, emotional, and discursive communication, then users need support and time to understand why and how it can work.

GENERIC FEATURES REQUIRED FOR LEARNING WITH TECHNOLOGY

The following features might be useful for people designing or using technology for use in learning and human interaction to consider. Is it technology which:

- enables and enhances positive human interaction—coming as close to the complex levels of human face-to-face interaction as it can and in many and varied ways

- appreciates the moral, the aesthetic, and creative in human society and the higher order qualities of human beings
- recognizes, values, and utilizes the innate multisensory capability of human beings—their ability to process in parallel not just sequentially
- reduces or gamifies dull, routine tasks and focuses on exciting, challenging, complex understandings
- supports or is deployed in an environment of warm, human interaction
- supports openness and curiosity
- is tried and tested by potential users
- recognizes its own addictiveness and counteracts its own failings
- is robust, reliable, and trustworthy

POTENTIAL GENERIC FEATURES TO AVOID

The following features might be useful for people designing or using technology for use in learning and human interaction to avoid. Is it technology which:

- is designed without a deep understanding of how learning and human interaction happens and the emotional nature of learning
- is designed without extensive user input into the design
- is designed without large-scale real-world trials with both tutors and students
- is very functional and not aesthetically pleasing or intuitive or challenging
- controls or constrains human potential in thinking and action
- frustrates tutors or students and produces unhelpful negative feelings
- produces immoral effects or damages human interaction?

CREATING FUTURE SOCIETIES THROUGH HIGH LEVELS OF LEARNING AND EDUCATION

Visionary aspirations for humanity are required, which envisage and incorporate technologies but without the hyperbole driven by desire to make short-term profit. Critical appraisal is vital. The latest mobile, multisensory devices are increasingly human in some respects. They appreciate and facilitate the intuitive and aesthetic nature of human beings. They utilize tactile, visual, animated, and musical stimuli and allow for ease of global communication and sharing of unlimited information, and they can give intense pleasure and support learning. However, the pleasure they give also has the potential to become addictive and the longer-term effects must be considered.

Alcohol, drugs, and gambling, for example, can give short-term pleasure but have less beneficial long-term consequences for people, families, and communities. Companies often try to justify their profit at the expense of human beings' health and welfare. Technology has hidden potential to harm as well as bring pleasure. Designers, parents, carers, teachers, and leaders need to know when technology is helpful and when it can seduce the emotions and be harmful to human relationships. There is much research to be done in this regard. In the future, technology may carry a warning label, advising that the product could severely damage the ability to interact face-to-face. Designing technology to be used and not abused, with checks and balances and deployed for use in supportive, human-rich environments to enhance dialog and emotional connection could be an optimistic way forward.

REFERENCES

Anning, A., & Edwards, A. (1999). *Promoting children's learning from birth to five*. Buckingham: Open University Press.

Bowlby, J. (1951). *Child care and the growth of love*. Harmondsworth: Penguin.

Clark, D. (1996). *Schools as learning communities*. London: Cassell.

Cooper, B. (1997). Teaching Empathy. SPES, Plymouth University: 7, 24–32.

Cooper, B. (2003). Care—Making the affective leap: More than a concerned interest in a learner's cognitive abilities. *International Journal of Artificial Intelligence in Education*, 13(1), 3–9.

Cooper, B. (2006). The significance of emotion and empathy in learning with MC3. In *ICALT 2006, Kerkrade, Holland July 4th-7th*.

Cooper, B. (2011a). *Empathy in education: Engagement, values and achievement*. London: Continuum.

Cooper, B. (2011b). Valuing the human in the design and use of technology in education: An ethical approach to the digital age of learning. In P. Broadhead & A. Campbell (Eds.), *Working with young children and young people: Ethical debates and practices across disciplines and continents*. AG Oxford: Peter Lang.

Cooper, B., & Brna, P. (2002). Supporting high quality interaction and motivation in the classroom using ICT: The social and emotional learning and engagement in the NIMIS project. *Education, Communication and Information*, 2(2/3), 113–138.

Damasio, A. (1999). *The feeling of what happens: Body, emotion and the making of consciousness*. London: Vintage.

Damasio, A. (2003). *Looking for Spinoza: Joy, sorrow and the feeling brain*. London: Heinemann.

Docker- Drysdale, B. (1990). *The provision of primary experience*. London: Free Association Books.

Ephraim, G. (1986). *A brief introduction to augmented mothering*. Hertfordshire: Report for Leavesden Hospital.

Foucault, M. (1977). *Discipline and punish: The birth of the prison. Translated from the French by Alan Sheridan*. London: Allen Lane.

Freire, P. (1970). *Pedagogy of the oppressed*. London: Continuum.

Gibbs, G., & Simpson, C. (2004). Conditions under which assessment supports student learning. *Learning and Teaching in Higher Education*, 1, 3–31.

Gillard, H., Howcroft, D., Mitev, N., & Richardson, H. (2008). Missing women: Gender, ICTs and the shaping of the global economy. *Information technology for Development*, 14(4), 262–279.

Goffman, E. (1961). *Asylums*. London: Penguin.

Greer, G. (2010). *Inaugural Winifred Mercier public lecture*. Leeds Metropolitan University. 8 March, https://www.youtube.com/watch?v=SI7Le8rShHY [accessed 21/8/15].

Hargreaves, D. H. (1982). *The challenge for the comprehensive school, culture, curriculum and community*. London: Routledge and Kegan Paul.

Hay, D. (1997). Spiritual education and values. In *Education, spirituality and the whole child conference, Roehampton Institute, June 11th-13th, 1997*.

Hewett, D., & Nind, M. (1998). *Interaction in action, reflections on the use of intensive interaction*. London: David Fulton.

Illich, I. (1971). *Deschooling society*. London: Penguin Books.

Klein, J. (1987). *Our need for others and its roots in infancy*. London: Tavistock.

Konrath, S. H., O'Brien, E. H., & Hsing, C. (2010). Changes in dispositional empathy in American college students over time: A meta- analysis. *Personal Social, Psychological Review*, *15*, 180–198.

Macmurray, J. (1935). *Reason and emotion*. London: Faber and Faber.

Marx, K., & Engels, F. (1888). *Manifesto of the communist party*. Moscow: Originally Progress Publishers.

Noddings, N. (1986). *Caring—A feminine approach to ethics and moral education*. California, USA: University of California Press.

Noguera, P. (2007). Safety and caring in schools: Addressing the moral basis of school discipline policies. In *Annual conference of the association of moral education, New York University, November 15th-17th*.

Panksepp, J. (2008). The affective brain and core consciousness: How does neural activity generate emotional feelings. In M. Lewis, J. M. Haviland-Jones, & L. Feldman-Barrett (Eds.), *Handbook of emotions* (2nd ed., pp. 47–67). New York: Guildford Press.

Preston, S. D., & de Waal, F. B. M. (2002). Empathy: Its ultimate and proximate bases. *Behavioral and Brain Sciences*, *25*, 1–72.

Reay, D. (2000). A useful extension of Bourdieu's conceptual framework? Emotional capital as a way of understanding mothers' involvement in their children's education. *Sociological Review*, *48*(4), 568–586.

Rowe, N., Wilkin, A., & Wilson, R. (2012). *Mapping of seminal reports on good teaching* (NFER Research Programme: Developing the educational workforce). Slough: NFER.

Rudd, T. (2001). *The digital divide*. London: Becta, Crown.

Rudd, T. (2009). Rethinking the principles of personalisation and the role of digital technologies. In R. Krumsvik (Ed.), *Learning in the network society and the digitized school*. New York: Nova Science Publishers.

Sandel, M. (2009). Reith lecture: markets and morals. *BBC*. 26 August. BBC Radio 4.

Skinner, B. (1954). The science of learning and the art of teaching. *Harvard Educational Review*, *24*, 86–97.

US Dept. of Education (2007). *What works clearing house Intervention report: Reading Recovery*. Institute of Education Sciences: US Dept. of Education March 19th 2007. Available from http://ies.ed.gov/ Accessed 05.11.2013.

Vygotsky, L. S. (1978). *Mind in society*. London, Massachusetts: Harvard University Press.

Vygotsky. (1986). *Thought and language. Translation newly revised by Alex Kozulin*. Cambridge, MA: MIT Press.

Watson, B., & Ashton, E. (1995). *Education, assumptions and values*. London: David Fulton.

Winkley, D. (1996). Towards the human school—Principles and practice. In *Conference beyond market forces—Creating the Human School. West Hill College, Birmingham, February*.

INDEX

Note: Page numbers followed by *f* indicate figures and *t* indicate tables.

A

Affiliation-building, humor, 183–188
Anti-iPad commercial, 188–189, 191–192

B

Blackboard learning management systems
    (LMS), 46–49
Blackface images
    classroom construction of race, 206–207
    emotional turmoil, 210–212
    history, 199–200

C

Cinematography, emotions, 123–124
Cognitive theory of multimedia learning
    (CTML), 161–163
Computer-human interaction, 4–5
Computer-mediated discourse analysis
    (CMDA), 50–51
Connectivism and connectivity knowledge,
    5–6
Content management system (CMS),
    46–49
Coursera-type massive open online course
    (xMOOC)
    assertions, 38–39
    course period, 31
    data sources, 32
    effort and satisfaction, 35–36
    emotional engagement, 32–33
    forum participation, 33–34
    instructor relationship, 37–38
    participants, 31
    recommendations, 38–39
    regression analyses of, 36, 36*t*
    social engagement, 34–35
    social environment, 33
Critique, English classroom humor,
    188–192

D

Dinosaur paleobiology, Dino 101
    assertions, 38–39
    course period, 31
    data sources, 32
    effort and satisfaction, 35–36
    emotional engagement, 32–33
    forum participation, 33–34
    instructor relationship, 37–38
    participants, 31
    recommendations, 38–39
    regression analyses of, 36, 36*t*
    social engagement, 34–35
    social environment, 33

E

Edmodo interface, 141–142, 151
Ellipses, online learning environments,
    79–80
Emoticons
    advantages, 77–78
    indications, 76–77
    sad, 75
    smiley, 74–75
    wink and tongue signs, 75–76
Emotion expression, non-verbal cues
    alienation and negative effect, 72
    backchannel information, lack, 83
    community-building tool, 82–83
    constrained emotional expression, 72–73
    data source, 74
    emoticons, 74–78
    flaming phenomenon, 69–70

Cultural accumulation

Cultural accumulation
    conscious control, 258–259
    and education, 245
    and emotion, 245–246
    environmental manipulation, 259
    and technology, 246

Emotion expression, non-verbal cues
  (Continued)
  "Like" button, 80–82
    community-building tool, 82
    express support, 81
    friendly tone expression, 81–82
  negative signs, 71–72
  positive signs, 71–72
  recognizing cues, 73
  traditional view, 70–71
  unconventional punctuation
    ellipses, 79–80
    exclamation mark, 78–79
Emotions
  action program, 155
  cognitive sciences, 243
  constraints awareness, 249
  definition, 155–156
  embodiment, 256–257
  environmental manipulation, 259
  holistic interactions and the human
    system, 255–256
  intelligence of, 249
  and learning process
    anticipated emotions, 157–158
    digital immigrants, 158
    emotional states, 157
    empathy measure, 158–159
    groups of, 157*t*
    human instructor ability, 156
    intrinsic pathways and intrinsic
      emotions, 247–248
    memory and attention, 258–260
    reconceptualization of, 257–258
  long-term memory, 246–247
  network theory, 255
  neuronal pathways, 247–248
  psychological arousal, 155
  short-term memory, 246–247
  social emotions, 248
  spiritual traditions, 155
  systems view, 254–258
Empathy
  cash nexus effect, 273
  categories, 274
  features, 265
  fundamental empathy

  characteristics, 274–275
    technology support, 275–276
  future society creation, 286–287
  learning process
    intellectual awareness, 272
    intensive interaction, 268–270
    joint involvement episodes, 269
    joy and pleasure effects, 270
    positive environment, 270
    responsiveness, 267–268
  phone interaction conflicts, 267
  positive relationships, 267
  profound empathy
    act and take responsibility, 281
    appreciation of all relationships, 280
    benefits, 283–284
    breadth and depth, 280–281
    definition, 276–277
    developing positive emotions and
      interactions, 277, 279
    explaining understanding, 279–280
    moral aspects, 282–283
    observed in, 276–277
    richly adaptive and integrated concept,
      281–282
    technology support, 278–279
    understanding self, 279–280
  technology effects
    avoidable generic features, 286
    in constructive feedback, 271–272
    dynamic multimodal interaction,
      268–269
    experience, 266
    human interaction intervention,
      267–268
    intensive interaction, 268
    personalization of learning, 270–271
    problems of, 284
    required generic features, 285–286
    responsiveness, 267–268
    usage guidelines, 285
  video cases, 126–127, 131
  working environments, 272–273
Engagement
  behavioral and cognitive, 27–28
  components, 27
  definition, 27

dinosaur paleobiology, Dino 101
  assertions, 38–39
  course period, 31
  data sources, 32
  effort and satisfaction, 35–36
  emotional engagement, 32–33
  forum participation, 33–34
  instructor relationship, 37–38
  participants, 31
  recommendations, 38–39
  regression analyses of, 36, 36t
  social engagement, 34–35
  social environment, 33
  emotional component, 28
  instructor interaction, 30–31
  MOOCs, 29–30
  self-determination theory, 28–29
  social component, 28–29
Episodes and emotions, 122–123
Exclamation mark, OLE, 78–79

F
Finance 1.5 blended course
  academic performance
    effects, 17–18
    measure, 13
  challenges, 10
  lecture capturing system, 12
  lecture-lets, 11–12
  module design, 11–12
  passing rate, 10
  requirement, 9–10
  revision with SPOC, 10
  students' reactions to, 17t
  test anxiety
    effects, 18
    measure, 13

H
Human rights education (HRE) course
  emotive response, 232
  experts aspect, 231
  main tenets, 231
  sample coding, 231–232
  significance of, 232
Humor, English classroom
  adults fears, 190–191
  affiliation-building, 183–188

analytic methods, 182
anti-iPad commercial, 188–189, 191–192
change and development of, 185
classroom contexts, 177–178
communicative tool, 178
critique, 188–192
definition, 178
desirable emotions, 179
high school, 181–182
identifiable markers, 182
identified themes, 182–194
implications, 194–196
legitimize in schools, 195
letter conventions, 186–187
meaningful play, 196
multimodal texts, 180
pitfalls associated, 177
playful integration, 180
print-centric curriculum, 180
pronounced opportunities, 195–196
research questions, 181–182
social functions, 179
sociocultural theory, 178
unsettling
  bodies and space, 193–194
  official curriculum, 192–193
upper elementary school, 181
virtual "likes", 184
Huntley high blended program
  autonomy effects, 237
  built-in flextime, 236
  close student progress track, 237–238
  emotional connections to, 237
  mission statement of, 236
  social presence, 236–237

L
Learning errors and formative feedback
    (LEAFF) model
  academic performance, 93–94
  assignments and course, 102t
  feedback usage, 108–109
  feeling-scale ratings, 102–103, 104f
  interim-intervention instrument
    feeling scale, 114
    tally of learning errors, 114
  learning errors, 92

Learning errors and formative feedback
    (LEAFF) model *(Continued)*
    limitations of, 109
    mental models, 92–93
    participants, 94–95
    parts, 90–91
    pictographic representation, 91*f*
    post-intervention instrument, 100, 102*t*,
        115–116
    pre-intervention instrument
        demographic information, 99
        motivated strategies for learning
            questionnaire, 98
        patterns of adaptive learning scale, 99
        rating questionnaire, 111–114
        sample size, means, and standard
            deviations, 101*t*
        self-efficacy for self-regulated learning, 99
        student trust in faculty scale, 99
    quasi-experimental design
        demographic characteristics, 95–97, 96*t*
        dependent variables, 95
        instructional intervention, 95
        video-game development, 94–95, 97
    self-reported errors intervention,
        103–106, 108
    student preferences of, 90
    superior performance, 107–108
Letter conventions, humour, 186–187
Like button, OLE, 80–82
    community-building tool, 82
    express support, 81
    friendly tone expression, 81–82
Long-term memory (LTM), 246–247

M

Massive open online courses (MOOCs)
    academic emotions
        positive and negative, 7–8
        range of emotions, 7
        and success, 8
        test anxiety, 8
    academic performance
        effects, 17–18
        measure, 13
    advantages, 3
    analyses of data, 14–15

    cMOOCs *vs.* xMOOCs, 26–27
    connectivism and connectivity
        knowledge, 5–6
    course evaluation, 13–14
    data collection procedures, 14–15
    effectiveness, 5–6
    emergence, 26
    engagement
        behavioral and cognitive, 27–28
        components, 27
        definition, 27
        dinosaur paleobiology, Dino 101, 31
        emotional component, 28
        instructor interaction, 30–31
        MOOCs, 29–30
        self-determination theory, 28–29
        social component, 28–29
    enhanced students' learning, 18
    evaluations, 4
    finance 1.5 course
        challenges, 10
        lecture capturing system, 12
        lecture-lets, 11–12
        module design, 11–12
        passing rate, 10
        requirement, 9–10
        revision with SPOC, 10
        students' reactions to, 17*t*
    hybrid or blended learning, 6
    limitations and implications, 18–20
    necessity, 3
    negative binding study advice, 9–10
    participants, 12–13
    perceptions, 25
    problem-based learning, 9
    results
        effective passing rate, 16–17
        OLS regression, 15–16
        test anxiety, 15
    small private online class
        enrollment effect, 7
        multimedia involement, 6–7
    test anxiety
        effects, 18
        measure, 13
    vs. traditional learning, 4
    university and course setting, 9–10

video-based learning
   computer-human interaction, 4–5
   interactive video, 5
Vygotsky's theory, 26
Math discussions, OLE, 141–142, 151
   aggregate of terms, 143*t*
   coding method, 142*t*
   colors, shapes and arrows for, 143
   dangling conversations, 137–138
   edmodo interface, 141–142, 151
   environment effect, 135–154
   finding common terms, 141
   grouping students, 140
   identification analysis, 138–139
   learning environment, 140
   limitations, 150
   multiple intertwined threads, 146–149
   negative feelings, 138
   non-native speakers, 136
   non-traditional discussion patterns, 137
   operative terms usage, 144
   participants, 139
   percentage, math terms usage, 143*t*
   problem posting, 140
   procedures, 140–141
   substitution marker, 144, 146
   symbols used, 152
   systemic functional linguistics, 138–139
   tallied terms, 142
   teacher scaffold, 149–150
   team discussion, 140
   terms usage, 141–142, 141*t*
   textual math resources, 149–150

N

National Council of Teachers of English
   (NCTE), 203–204
Negative binding study advice (BSA), 9–10
Non-traditional discussion patterns, 137
North Carolina Virtual Public School
   (NCVPS), SPM
   applicability of, 233–234
   instructor involvement, 235
   quality teaching and learning, OLE, 233
   relevance perceptions, 234*f*
   teacher and student, positive relationships,
   234

O

Online discourse affects
   acceptance, 55–59
   accepting the lesson, 58–59
   achievement, 65–66
   agreement and questioning, 59–62
   analytical focus, 51–52
   arguments, 50
   assignment, 49–52
   communicative acts, 45
   computer-mediated discourse analysis,
     50–51
   course design, 46–49
   course goals, 48–49
   data analysis, 50–51
   educational systems evaluation, 43
   emotional responses, 50
   emotions, and awareness expressions,
     52–54
   enframe and reveal, 63
   increased critical thinking, 64
   instructors support, 47–48
   intersubjective acceptance, 56–58
   learning activity, 44–45
   learning platforms, 47
   limitations of, 65
   participants, 49
   postsecondary transfer problems, 44
   promote emancipatory discourse, 62–63
   public speech acts, 48–49
   social self growth, 65
   technology support, 50, 64
   transcendental phenomenology, 45–49
   transmedia experience, 63–64
   U.S. educational model, 43–44
Online learning and multimedia (OLaM)
   anger or frustration, 164
   anxiety, 164
   cognitive theory, 161–163
   coherence principle, 161–162
   computer enjoyment, 165
   CTML, 162–163, 162*f*
   emotional state and adoption, 163–164
   emotional states, 157
   emotion in the school setting, 165
   empathy measure, 158–159
   excitement, 164

Online learning and multimedia (OLaM)
    (Continued)
    happiness, 164
    human instructor ability, 156
    implications, 172–173
    meta-analysis, 159–160
    modality principle, 161–162
    motivation factor, 163–164
    multiple representation principle,
        161–162
    New York grade three study
        control and treatment group, 166
        MANOVA calculation, 169
        post-test data, 166–167
        pretest, 166
        qualitative analysis, 171
        semi-structured interviews, 167–168,
            168*t*
        software interaction, 168
        treatment period effects, 171
        validity assessment, 167
    positive effect, 172
    positive emotions, 164
    redundancy principle, 161–162
    rich experience, 158
    spatial contiguity principle, 161–162
    split attention principle, 161–162
    spoken words processing, 163
    statistical analyses, 159–160
    temporal contiguity principle, 161–162
    visual and verbal learning, 161, 161*f*
    written words processing, 163

P
Print-centric curriculum, humor, 180
Problem-based learning (PBL), 9
Problem solving efficiency, 253–254

R
Race, identities, and emotions
    blackface images
        classroom construction of race,
            206–207
        emotional turmoil, 210–212
        history, 199–200
    digital natives, 204–205
    dispossession legacies, 219
    embodied literacy, 204

    emotional as political, 205–206
    hypothetical choices, 220
    legacies of segregation, 201
    National Council of Teachers of English,
        203–204
    physical senses, 219
    political and social construction, 217–218
    qualitative case study, Shelly's classroom
        character analyses, 209–210
        class activity avoidance, 210–211
        conflicting emotions, 214–216
        emotional turmoil, 210–212
        engagement category, 208
        group sessions, 207–208
        group's excitement, 210
        instructor commitments, 209
        participant, 207–208
        safe and inclusive community built, 216
        social construction, 214
        social inequity, 212
        student attendance, 208
        student history, 209
        student resistance, 208
        students' perspectives, 217
        teacher's perspective, 212–214
        undiagnosed students, 209
    riots of, 200
    social recognition, 218–219
    sociocultural perspectives, 202–203
    teacher-led investigation, 219–220
    twenty-first century literacies, 203–204
    Washington's words, 201
    white privilege and blackface, 206

S
Schoology learning management systems
        (LMS), 46–49
School technology leadership (STL)
        program
    artifacts, 228
    coding data, 228
    data collection, 228
    five integrated elements, 230
    instructor interviews, 228–229
    leadership expertise, 229–230
    period and credits, 227–228
    social presence category, 228, 229*f*

Short-term memory (STM), 246–247
Small private online class (SPOC).
    See also Massive open online courses
        (MOOCs)
    enrollment effect, 7
    multimedia involement, 6–7
Social presence model (SPM)
    blended high school, 235–238
    community of inquiry, 226–227
    higher education, 227–230
    human rights education course, 231–232
    Huntley high blended program, 235–238
    influential literacy, 238–239
    origin, 226
    pictorial representation, 230f
    powerful emotional experience, 225–226
    reflections of, 238–239
    school technology leadership program,
        227–230
    significance of, 238–239
    virtual high school, NCVPS, 232–235
Sociocultural theory, humor, 178
Substitution marker, 144, 146
Systemic functional linguistics (SFL),
        138–139

T

Technology accumulation
    description, 249
    emotional subsystems, 260
    emotion and learning
        Greenfield differentiation, 252
        learning and memory processes, 251–252
    empathy
        avoidable generic features, 286
        in constructive feedback, 271–272
        dynamic multimodal interaction,
            268–269
        experience, 266
        human interaction intervention,
            267–268
        intensive interaction, 268
        personalization of learning, 270–271
        problems of, 284
        required generic features, 285–286
        responsiveness, 267–268
        usage guidelines, 285
    human advantage, 250–251
    survival basics
        declarative memory, 252
        education and teaching, 253
        environmental interaction, 253
        nondeclarative memory, 252
        problem solving, 253–254
The 2015 Project
    acceptance, 55–59
    accepting the lesson, 58–59
    affect, emotions, and awareness
        expressions, 52–54
    agreement and questioning, 59–62
    analytical focus, 51–52
    arguments, 50
    assignment, 49–52
    course design, 46–49
    course goals, 48–49
    data analysis, 50–51
    emotional responses, 50
    enframe and reveal, 63
    instructors support, 47–48
    intersubjective acceptance, 56–58
    learning platforms, 47
    participants, 49
    promote emancipatory discourse,
        62–63
    public speech acts, 48–49
    technology support, 50, 64
    transmedia experience, 63–64

V

Video-based learning. *See also* Massive open
        online courses (MOOCs)
    computer-human interaction, 4–5
    interactive video, 5
    MOOCs
        computer-human interaction, 4–5
        interactive video, 5
Videos and emotions in learning
    action tendency, 129
    appraisal component, 129
    characteristics, emotionally relevant,
        123–125
    cinematography, 123–124
    cognitive dimension, 119–120
    components of emotions, 121–122

Videos and emotions in learning *(Continued)*
  emotional
    potential, 123–127
    reactions, 120–121
  empathy, 126–127, 131
  episodes, 122–123
  instructional variety, 120
  learning processes, 128–129
  modeling methods
    appraisal approach, 125
    control-value theory, 125–126
  and moods, 121
  motoric component, 129
  narrative aspects, 124–125
  physicians and patient, 131
  physiological component, 129
  quality, 120
  recognizing emotions, 130
  showing emotions, 129
  understanding emotions, 130–131
Vygotsky's theory, 26

X

xMOOC. *See* Coursera-type massive open
  online course (xMOOC)

Y

Young children's computer inventory
  (YCCI), 165

Printed in the United States
By Bookmasters